MW01294518

WEYERHAEUSER ENVIRONMENTAL BOOKS

Paul S. Sutter, Editor

WEYERHAEUSER ENVIRONMENTAL BOOKS explore human relationships with natural environments in all their variety and complexity. They seek to cast new light on the ways that natural systems affect human communities, the ways that people affect the environments of which they are a part, and the ways that different cultural conceptions of nature profoundly shape our sense of the world around us. A complete list of the books in the series appears at the end of this book.

SEEDS OF CONTROL

Japan's Empire of Forestry in Colonial Korea

DAVID FEDMAN

UNIVERSITY OF WASHINGTON PRESS

Seattle

Seeds of Control is published with the assistance of a grant from the Weyerhaeuser Environmental Books Endowment, established by the Weyerhaeuser Company Foundation, members of the Weyerhaeuser family, and Janet and Jack Creighton.

Additional support was provided by the Association for Asian Studies First Book Subvention Program and the Humanities Center at the University of California, Irvine.

Composed in Minion Pro, typeface designed by Robert Slimbach
COVER ILLUSTRATION: A section of the Chōsen Rinya Bunpuzu (Korean Forestland Distribution Map), Chōsen Sōtokufu Nōshōkōbu, 1912. Courtesy of the National Archive of Japan, Digital Archive.
MAPS: Maps on pages xvi and 20 by Pease Press Cartography, www.peasepress.com

24   23   22   21   20   5   4   3   2   1

Printed and bound in the United States of America

UNIVERSITY OF WASHINGTON PRESS
uwapress.uw.edu

LIBRARY OF CONGRESS CATALOGING-IN-PUBLICATION DATA
Names: Fedman, David, author.
Title: Seeds of control : Japan's empire of forestry in colonial Korea / David Fedman.
Description: Seattle : University of Washington Press, [2020] | Series: Weyerhaeuser environmental books | Includes bibliographical references and index.
Identifiers: LCCN 2019045333 (print) | LCCN 2019045334 (ebook) | ISBN 9780295747453 (hardcover) | ISBN 9780295747477 (ebook)
Subjects: LCSH: Forests and forestry—Korea—History—20th century. | Forest policy—Korea—History—20th century. | Forest management—Korea—History—20th century. | Korea—History—Japanese occupation, 1910–1945.
Classification: LCC SD235.K6 F43 2020 (print) | LCC SD235.K6 (ebook) | DDC 634.909519—dc23
LC record available at https://lccn.loc.gov/2019045333
LC ebook record available at https://lccn.loc.gov/2019045334

The paper used in this publication is acid free and meets the minimum requirements of American National Standard for Information Sciences—Permanence of Paper for Printed Library Materials, ANSI Z39.48–1984.∞

For Lauren

CONTENTS

FOREWORD

Under Japan's Green Thumb

PAUL S. SUTTER

Sitting at the center of David Fedman's sophisticated new history of Japanese colonial rule in Korea, *Seeds of Control*, is a simple and surprising fact: among the most ubiquitous and far-reaching imperial activities undertaken by the Japanese in Korea was the planting of trees. Over several decades, from the imposition of protectorate status in 1905 until the eve of World War II, Japanese and Koreans together planted millions of saplings and seeds throughout the peninsula, covering Korea's denuded hills with a modern raiment of growth. In Korea, Fedman intimates, the Japanese Empire had a surprisingly green thumb.

Although afforestation may not be the first activity that comes to mind when one thinks of empire, environmental historians have long recognized that modern forestry regimes served colonial rule all over the world. But to scholars who have written the history of Japan's empire in Korea, Fedman's focus on forests represents an important departure. These scholars have emphasized the urban and industrial parts of the colonial story in Korea, and when they have ventured into the countryside, it has been primarily to examine Japanese control over arable lands and agricultural production. Until now, the forested periphery and the role that forest resources played in the urban-industrial story have not been central to histories of Japan's empire in Korea. And when historians have written about Korea's colonial forest history it has usually been through the lens of World War II, a period when the Japanese heavily exploited Korean timber to feed their war effort. This brief period of forest plunder, an episode with a powerful hold on Korean popular memory, has obscured the role of forests, forest management, and forest culture in the Japanese Empire. For most of the imperial period, Fedman insists, the conservation and restoration of Korean forests was the rule—in both senses of that term—and Korea's forested periphery sat at the very center of imperial ideology and practice.

What does it mean to recenter Korea's colonial history around Japan's empire of forestry? It certainly does not mean that we should celebrate Japanese power as environmentally benevolent. Japan's thumb may have been green, but it still pressed down on Korean subjects. Japanese forestry in Korea constituted a mode of environmental governance aimed at controlling natural resources for the sake of imperial power and capitalist profit, as forestry did in most colonial contexts. Japanese forestry was also a form of social control, as forest policies aimed to manage populations who lived within or near forests and relied upon the diversity of their resources. Even the rhetoric that the Japanese used to portray the supposed destructiveness of Korean peasant producers—a rhetoric of barren red hills and premodern stagnation—was similar to that used by imperial powers in other colonial settings to justify their forestry interventions. In all of these ways, *Seeds of Control* is an exciting new case study that reinforces the central lessons of a larger Eurocentric literature on imperial forestry. If that was all this book achieved, it would be worth the read. *Seeds of Control*, however, does much more.

One of Fedman's signal achievements is to tell a story not only of imperial power but also of the adaptations and adjustments that came with imperial ineffectiveness. As anyone who has tried planting trees on a large scale can tell you, success is usually partial and never assured. Seeds and saplings need water, nurturing soils, a salutary climate, protection from predation, and luck. Future trees may be latent in their seeds, but the environment determines their shape. So it was with the seeds of social control, which did not always germinate and grow in quite the ways that Japanese administrators wanted. Early Japanese attempts to transplant their vaunted forestry culture soon yielded to approaches that grafted that culture onto the root stock of Korea's land-use traditions and rural institutions. Rural Koreans themselves became essential to the project, and, in doing so, they used forestry as a locus of negotiation and resistance. Even the trees to be planted changed over time, as the Japanese recognized that their preferred species were not always well adapted to the Korean peninsula. The applied problems of imperial forestry were real and difficult. As a result, the Japanese engaged in a forestry of social and environmental accommodation, an approach that involved colonial collaboration between Japanese and Korean forestry scientists and citizens alike.

Fedman also argues that we need to see the Japanese empire of forestry as distinctive. Yes, European and American models influenced Japanese forestry practices, as Japanese and elite Korean officials bought into arguments that Euro-American forestry was a marker of modernity. But these models were not planted directly into Korean soils. Rather, they first traveled through Japan, acclimating to an island nation with its own forestry traditions, environmental ideologies, and imperial ambitions. They then came to Korea, which had a venerable history of local forest administration all its own. The Japanese operated with a mythos that their island nation was a lush green domain precisely because of a unique culture of sustainable forestry, and this sense of forestry exceptionalism served as justification for imposing their expertise on Koreans. Indeed, as Fedman convincingly argues, forestry was the realm in which the Japanese most easily convinced themselves of their imperial benevolence. They did this by inculcating their culture of "forest-love thought" among the Koreans. In colonial Korea, Japanese imperial forestry was not just a project of technical administration. It was also an attempt at cultural hegemony, and the extent to which Koreans adopted Japanese forest-love thought became a primary marker of their colonial assimilation. In bringing such a cultural approach to imperial forestry, Fedman demonstrates that Japan's well-studied national traditions of environmental thought have had their imperial analogues. In Korea, the seeds of control came wrapped in a distinctly Japanese cultural package.

World War II was a departure point for Japan's empire of forestry in Korea, a moment when tree planting ceased and rampant harvesting took over. This was indeed a period of forest plunder, Fedman admits, though it was a more complicated moment than many scholars have assumed. More importantly, and in an innovative move unusual among forest historians, Fedman shifts our gaze from Korea's forests to its domestic sphere, where the Japanese waged a "war on thermal inefficiency" that sought to reform Koreans' use of their distinctive *ondol* stoves. During the war, Japan's empire of forestry took a biopolitical turn as they tried to impose a "low-temperature lifestyle" on Koreans, whose alleged profligacy in heating their homes had long shaped Japanese perceptions of Korean inferiority. In its final gasp, Japan's empire of forestry became a campaign to regulate Korean bodies and households, an effort to control the most intimate of spaces.

Seeds of Control thus gives us a new chapter in the history of Japanese forestry, one that shows us the powerful continuities between the supposedly autarkic green archipelago of the Tokugawa period and the empire of forestry that emerged during the early twentieth century. More than that, though, it portrays a Japanese empire of forestry that was distinctive, culturally expansive, multifarious, and deeply compromised. It is perhaps not surprising, then, that Japan's empire of forestry has quietly lived on in postwar Korea's "greenification" campaigns. Although such campaigns were clothed in anti-imperial rhetoric and often operated with the expressed goals of both repairing the damage done by the Japanese during World War II and purging the Korean landscape of Japanese arboreal influence, they were also rooted in tree-planting practices and ideologies that originated in Japan's tree-planting empire. Without quite recognizing it, Fedman ingeniously concludes, North and South Koreans still live under Japan's green thumb.

ACKNOWLEDGMENTS

This book owes much to many people. My first words of thanks go to Jun Uchida, whose warm support, generous spirit, and incisive feedback have offered a model of mentorship to which I can only aspire. For her broad perspective and razor-sharp pen, I thank Kären Wigen, whose alpine enthusiasm is contagious. Yumi Moon challenged me with the big questions of Korean history, forcing me to always keep my gaze up from the weeds. Richard White, my fellow traveler in *ondol* studies, prompted me to follow the coal, opening up inquiries into energy that lay at the heart of this book. It was my great fortune to have Kerry Smith as a guide for my first forays into historical research, and this project would not have been possible without his encouragement.

Many friends and colleagues gave generously of their time to field questions, share sources, and read drafts. For this, I thank Todd Henry, Sakura Christmas, Victor Seow, Lisa Brady, Julia Adeney Thomas, Ian J. Miller, Micah Muscolino, Sayoko Sakakibara, Wenjiao Cai, Jonathan Arnold, Nick Heinz, Samuel Perry, Alex Bay, Quinn Javers, Jordan Sand, Cary Karacas, Kuang-chi Hung, Kirk Larsen, Tessa Braun, Tristan Grunow, Hirata Koji, Komeie Taisaku, Char Miller, Ben Geller, Sam Dolbee, Chris Hanscom, Yi U-yŏn, Takemoto Tarō, George Kallander, Joseph Seeley, Hajin Jun, and Albert Park. Special thanks go to Holly Stephens, John S. Lee, and Jung Lee, who cut right through my wooden thinking on key concepts. The influence of Aaron S. Moore is imprinted deeply in these pages and, though he was unable to see their final form, I can only hope that they help to build on the foundation he laid for the field. Despite the heroic efforts of so many to save me from myself, errors may remain, for which I take sole responsibility.

The sun-soaked campus of the University of California, Irvine, has proved an ideal environment for the growth of this project. For their encouragement and collaboration, I thank Mimi Long, Emily Baum, Jeff Wasserstrom, Serk-Bae Suh, Susan Klein, Amanda Swain, Bert Winther-Tamaki, Andrew Highsmith, Kyung Kim, Eleana Kim, Jerry Won Lee, and Chris Fan. I owe a special debt of gratitude to Anne Walthall and Kathy Ragsdale, who suffered through early drafts. For their assistance in translating materials and visualizing data, I thank Eun Yeong Seong and Chaeyoon Yoo.

The research and writing for this project would not have been possible without generous financial assistance from the National Endowment for the Humanities (FT-254269-17), the Japan Foundation, the Social Sciences Research Council, and the Northeast Asia Council of the Association for Asian Studies. This work was supported by the Core University Program for Korean Studies through the Ministry of Education of the Republic of the Korea and Korean Studies Promotion Service of the Academy of Korean Studies (AKS-2016-OLU-2250005). I am also grateful to here acknowledge generous subventions provided by the Association for Asian Studies and the Humanities Center at the University of California, Irvine.

This book is both leaner and bolder thanks to the editorial eye of Paul Sutter, whose investment and faith in the project offered a guiding light. At the University of Washington Press, I thank Andrew Berzanskis for his good cheer and thoughtful feedback, as well as Neecole Bostick for shepherding the manuscript through various production hurdles. Special thanks are also due to my anonymous peer reviewers, whose input is now reflected in the core arguments of the book. Portions of chapter 8 appeared in "Wartime Forestry and the 'Cold Temperature Lifestyle' in Late Colonial Korea," *Journal of Asian Studies* 77, no. 2 (2018).

My family has held up—in more ways than one—this project for many years. Alan Fedman, my first and most exacting editor, taught me the value and joy of studying the past. Beth Fedman introduced me to the wonders of the outdoors, even when they brought us face to face with Virginia's most menacing baby squirrels. Anna and Emily inspired me to make a career out of my oral report voice. Sam and Leah have been pillars of support. Maya has electrified our lives since the moment she arrived. Lily, mercifully, has introduced some much-needed calm as this project comes to close. Writing a book is fun; living with you two is joy. And then there is Lauren, who has never wavered in her support of my many questionable pursuits. With gratitude for all that she does, I dedicate this book to her.

NOTE ON NAMES
AND MEASURES

Following convention, Japanese and Korean names are provided with family name preceding personal name. Macrons have been omitted from commonly used place-names such as Tokyo or Seoul.

Conversions for the original Japanese units of measurements referenced in this study are as follows:

1 *chō* (町) = 0.9917 hectares = 2.451 acres; or 109.09 meters

1 *chōbu* (町步) = 0.9917 hectares = 2.451 acres

1 *jō* (丈) = 3.030 meters = 9.942 feet

1 *kan* (貫) = 3.7 kilograms = 8.267 pounds

1 *koku* (石) = 180.4 liters = 47.65 gallons

1 *ri* (里) = 3,927 meters = 4,295 yards

1 *shakujime* (尺〆) ≈ 12 cubic feet

1 *sun* (寸) = 0.030 meters = 0.099 feet

1 *tan* (段, 反) = 0.09917 hectares = 0.2451 acres

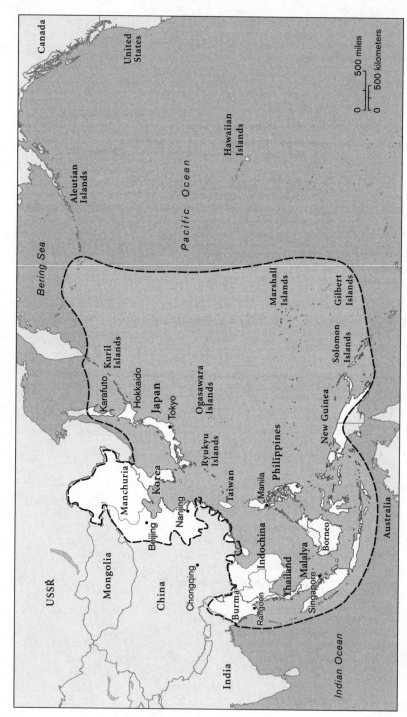

The Japanese Empire, ca. 1942

The provinces of Korea

SEEDS OF CONTROL

INTRODUCTION

THERE ARE FEW ALPINE ACTIVITIES AS HUMBLING AS HIKING IN South Korea. Any sense of athletic achievement that might come from a taxing ascent is quickly deflated by encounters with group after group of impeccably outfitted octogenarians. Those out to test their mettle in the mountains of Korea will indeed take little comfort in the discovery atop even the most demanding summits of bands of pensioners jollily sipping tea.

It was thus not entirely out of the ordinary when, in the summer of 2010, I happened upon a small group of elderly men hard at work on a hillside outside of Seoul. Initially, I assumed this was some sort of community-based trail maintenance project. But when I saw that they were uprooting what appeared to be perfectly healthy acacia trees, I realized that something else was afoot. My initial inquiry about their landscaping elicited only the vaguest of explanations. "We're cleaning up," one man replied. When, moments later, I began to inspect a pile of branches, another man indulged my curiosity. First planted by Japanese foresters during the period of colonial rule, he explained, acacia had run amok. These men had gathered to scrub the mountains of one of the material residues of colonial occupation.

Such cleanup efforts are not altogether uncommon.[1] As I would learn over the coming years, acacia's fragrant white flowers carry in some corners of Korean society, especially among the aged, painful connotations of colonial oppression. This sentiment stems in part from the nature of acacia itself.

3

Hardy and quick to grow, *robinia pseudoacacia* (more commonly known as the black locust tree) is a botanical colonizer with a long history as a tool of erosion control. To many Koreans, it is an invasive species in the truest sense—an ecological nuisance whose aggressive root systems have crowded native flora out of the soil.[2]

The Japanese did in fact introduce acacia extensively over the course of their four decades of colonial rule in Korea. Driven by utilitarian concerns about fuel scarcity and fears of cascading environmental disaster, colonial foresters placed acacia at the heart of their efforts to reform a landscape routinely (and hyperbolically) described as "a land of bald mountains and red earth."[3] Some of the acacia planted during the colonial period still exist in Korea today. In the Kwangnŭng Arboretum just outside of Seoul, for example, one can find an impressive stand—or, better yet, colony—of 133 acacia trees whose roots trace back more than one hundred years to a colonial-era reforestation project.[4]

But given that *robinia pseudoacacia* has an average life span of approximately sixty years, chances are the limbs I saw piling up in 2010 actually originated from a different forestry campaign: the greening of South Korea under Park Chung-hee. Carried out in conjunction with Park's New Village Movement (Saemaŭl Undong), an ambitious project of rural revitalization, reforestation proceeded over the 1960s and 1970s at a furious pace. So began acacia's second act. Eager to bolster erosion control and shore up village fuel supplies, officials in the Republic of Korea's (ROK) newly empowered Forest Service mobilized acacia and its aggressive root systems once more. With no small measure of irony, acacia assumed a prominent place in the South Korean campaign to rehabilitate the landscape from the damage wrought by decades of colonial occupation and war.

Acacia thus merits our attention not simply because it has become emblematic of Japan's terrestrial invasion of Korea but also because it gives material expression to important continuities in environmental governance. Its growth across the twentieth century testifies to a number of abiding aspirations of woodsmen in Korea: self-sufficient fuel supplies, sustainable timber yields, improved irrigation systems. Its pervasiveness likewise points to enduring arboreal anxieties: the perennial threat of floods, domestic fuel requirements, swidden agriculture. Acacia's flowers bloom in Korea as living monuments to the "forest dreams and forest nightmares," as Nancy Langston would have it, that have long animated conservation measures on the peninsula.[5] Understanding Korea's landscape as we see it today, in other words, requires that we examine the full sweep of state interventions in its forests. It requires, above all, that we move beyond facile binaries of colonial exploitation and native rehabilitation to consider how different ruling regimes with similar management goals have used forest regeneration as a platform for social control.

Given the red-hot intensity of anti-Japanese sentiment in Korean society, this is a tall order. Indeed, to suggest that the roots of the dense forests that today blanket much of South Korea are in any way tangled with colonial-era programs is to argue against the grain of long-calcified narratives of absolute exploitation. If stories of Japanese colonial rule are framed in stark black-and-white terms, those of its forest management are cast in green and brown. Whatever the gulf between North and South Korea in their historical interpretations of their colonial past, both societies adhere to strikingly similar accounts of unambiguous forest despoilment under Japanese occupation.

In North Korea, this outlook took hold almost immediately upon liberation from Japanese rule. As Kim Il-sŏng, the supreme leader and founding patriarch of the North Korean state, put it in 1947: "From ancient times our country has been widely known as a land embroidered in silk, a land with beautiful mountains and sparkling rivers. Its beauty, however, was long clouded over by Japanese Imperialist rule." Kim went on to implore his countrymen to "plant trees well and remove quickly the after effects of Japanese imperialist rule."[6] Such rhetoric has hardly abated. As part of his 2015 public appeal to "Cover the Mountains of the Country with Green Woods," Kim's grandson and the current head of state, Kim Chŏng-ŭn, bemoaned "the mountains and rivers of the country damaged by Japanese imperialist colonial rule" as he called upon his compatriots to launch "a war to ameliorate nature."[7]

A similar, if less bellicose, narrative prevails in South Korea. "Under Japanese colonization in the early twentieth century, forests were excessively overused and devastated," goes one account by the Korea Forest Service, noting how "the growing stock decreased significantly from 700 million cubic meters to 200 million cubic meters over the colonial period."[8] To be sure, not all South Korean scholars frame their research in categorical terms of forest ruination. A spate of recent studies has, for example, added considerable nuance to our understanding of colonial woodland-tenure reforms, revealing tensions long obscured by nationalist historiography.[9] Surging interest in the environmental history of preindustrial Korea has also touched off productive debates about the scope, drivers, and legacies of deforestation in the late Chosŏn era.[10] On balance, however, the notion that "Japan destroyed nearly three-quarters of Korea's forests in the 35 years of its colonial occupation" remains firmly entrenched.[11] Not surprisingly, when South Korean scholars *do* focus their attention on the reforestation of the peninsula, they typically avoid the colonial period altogether and instead lavish attention on the "forest miracle" under Park Chung-hee: what one group calls "the best orchestrated and publicly cohesive reforestation event in world history."[12] Wittingly or not, these accounts effectively compress the complexity of the colonial forestry project into a single phrase: forest plunder (K: *sallim sut'al*).

Guiding the arc of many Korean narratives is a powerful teleology: the fact that Japan's wartime mobilization of Korea from 1937 to 1945 devastated the peninsula's forests. To many Korean writers, *this* is the only story of colonial forestry worth telling. And who could blame them for fixing their attention on the depletion of forest stocks, the acute fuel shortages, or the ecological insecurity brought about by the war? Clear-cuts and sapped forests were, in the end, the material outcome of colonial rule, and it is only reasonable that the forces behind this wartime harvest would monopolize public as well as scholarly attention.

Yet, in the rush to take stock of the damage exacted by World War II, prevailing Korean narratives have given short shrift to the conservation program from which the wartime system evolved. As a result, many Korean accounts share a tendency to project back onto the whole of the colonial period a degree of coherence and forcefulness in forestry matters that was not always there. Before there was a command economy in forest products, there was a fledgling timber industry in the Yalu River basin, whose growing pains belie portraits of rapacious extraction. Underlying the draconian wartime promotion of a "low-temperature lifestyle" was a web of well-established civic forestry organizations, whose regulatory activities attest to the role of ordinary Koreans in implementing forest policy. By the time Korean subjects were forced during the war to bow daily in the direction of the imperial palace, they had already been subjected to decades of tree-planting rituals in celebration of the imperial line. Hardly the only story of colonial forestry, the wartime timber harvest was but the final chapter in a multidimensional effort to place forest conservation at the heart of everyday life.

What is obscured, not least, by the analytical pull of 1945 are the coercive practices inherent to reforestation itself. In telling stories only of hacking, sawing, and reaping, popular narratives overlook how sowing, stocking, and planting were also vectors of coercive force. The saw and the seed, after all, were two sides of the same imperialistic token. Like the "abacus and the sword," they were coequal instruments in Japan's economic and political penetration of Korea.[13] To acknowledge that the Japanese in Korea were energetic in their efforts to plant trees is not to diminish the intensity of colonial violence. It is rather to bring new depth to our understanding of the very nature of that violence. For while reforestation typically carries uniformly positive connotations of investment and renewal, the case of colonial Korea reveals a darker shade of green: a story of reclamation laced with hostility, displacement, and bodily suffering.

As the following pages make clear, the pursuit of green hills in Korea came at a significant cost to many. In reorganizing the boundaries of tenure rights, Japanese forestry bureaucrats cleaved farmers from materials essential to their livelihood and, come Korea's long and frigid winter, survival. By outsourcing the heavy lifting of reforestation, they bled off forestland to Japanese corporations, capitalists, and settlers. The brunt of implementation, moreover, was borne overwhelmingly by agrarian communities, whose labor, material inputs, and fees formed the lifeblood of reclamation. Although forest regeneration promised increased supplies in the future, it frequently ignored Koreans' short-term needs, leading to scarcity and strife in the present.

The greening of colonial Korea, in short, was a process rife with conflict and fraught with contradiction. A closer inspection of the mechanics of reforestation in Korea—the legal architecture, regulatory enforcement, and corporate involvement—indeed reveals a complicated story about the uneven consequences and power dynamics of colonial conservation. Unearthing that story requires that we bring the saw and the seed into the same analytical field. Only then can we fully understand how forest regeneration operated in Korea as a disciplinary framework for industrial capitalism and agrarian development—what historian Yi U-yŏn has aptly dubbed the "greenificationism" (J: *ryokkashugi*) of the colonial state.[14]

SEEDING LIKE A STATE

At its core, *Seeds of Control* argues that forestry in general and silviculture in particular functioned as a vital dimension of state power in colonial Korea. It shows that forest management left a deep impression on Korea and Koreans, etching into the social as well as physical landscape patterns of consumption, systems of regulation, and ideas of rationalization that outlived the Japanese Empire. Edict by edict, Japanese officials in the Bureau of Forestry tightened access and requisitioned resources, igniting in the process fierce resistance from agrarian society. Hamlet by hamlet, civic forestry institutions grew into ground-level organs of moral suasion and state surveillance, furthering the reach of foresters into the domestic sphere. All the while, discourses of sylvan enlightenment became fixtures of ideological campaigns aimed toward imperial indoctrination. The outbreak of war in 1937 only fortified these coercive mechanisms, as the colonial state leaned on its subjects to conserve every last joule of energy to wage total war. In short, forestry reforms in colonial Korea were intensive, wide-ranging, and increasingly intrusive.

I am far from the first to suggest that state forestry has historically been an exercise in community control. From E. P. Thompson to Ramachandra Guha, scholars working across regions and disciplines have used woodlands as a lens through which to examine the consolidation and limits of state power, as well as the resistance it inspired.[15] This is especially true of scholarship on the coevolution of colonialism and scientific forestry, which has done much to enrich our understanding of how officials saw forestry as a means to assert authority over the unruly margins of the state.[16] Pamela McElwee perhaps best captures this line of inquiry when she writes in her recent study of Vietnam that "forest policy . . . has rarely been about ecological management or conservation for nature's sake, but about seeing and managing people"—what she calls "environmental rule."[17]

The Government-General of Korea (Chōsen Sōtokufu, the official title of the colonial administration) ruled the forest environment with similar goals in mind. Like their British counterparts in India, Japanese forestry bureaucrats in Korea set out to reorganize patterns of fuel consumption and reorient modes of production around state-sanctioned market activities.[18] Like German foresters in Tanzania, they oversaw ambitious programs of population resettlement and social engineering.[19] Much as the French in Algeria condemned the "incendiary Arab," so did foresters in Korea launch a crusade against Korea's *hwajŏnmin*: "fire-field" cultivators whose purportedly primitive lifestyle became a convenient foil to Japan's enlightened stewardship.[20] In these and other ways, state interventions in Korea's woodlands touched the everyday lives and bodily experiences of residents across the peninsula—rural or urban, Japanese or Korean. As storehouses of resources, spaces of habitation, and archives of tradition, Korea's mountains and forests, which comprise over 70 percent of the peninsula's landmass, formed dynamic and highly contentious sites of colonial governance.

Yet forest politics remain in Korean studies a historiographical hinterland. In part, this can be explained by a pervasive urban bias in English-language scholarship on Japanese colonialism in Korea. Although recent work has done much to elucidate "the complex relations of colonialism, modernity, nationalism, and identity formation" in Korea, the interplay of these forces in the countryside, where more than 80 percent of Korean society worked the land, remains ill understood.[21] With a few notable exceptions, port towns, industrial belts, and cities—especially Seoul—remain the centers of analytical gravity.[22] One detects a similar bias toward arable landholdings. To the extent that historians have examined agrarian life in colonial Korea, they have focused overwhelmingly on questions surrounding land tenure, tenancy disputes, and the intensification of rice production. In consequence, our understanding of agrarian society stops sharply at the rice paddy's edge, leaving important questions about the connections between farmlands and the watersheds that surround them largely unexplored.

When we consider the developmental agenda of the colonial state in Korea, this interpretative gap appears all the more glaring. Few dispute that Japanese colonial rule had profound implications for the peninsula's built environment and physical infrastructure. References to the thickening railway system in colonial Korea, a development with profound symbolic and commercial implications, have become de rigueur in treatments of Japanese rule.[23] Historians have devoted equal volumes of ink to discussion of the heavy industrialization of the Korean peninsula: wartime investments in chemical plants, munitions factories, and energy infrastructures seldom seen in European "empires on the cheap."[24] Recent investigations into civil engineering have also shed light on the megaprojects of colonial modernization: hydroelectric dams, warm-water ports, and other monuments to Japan's "technological imaginary" in East Asia.[25]

Largely taken for granted, however, are the material inputs and implications of these undertakings. In most tellings, the constitutive components of these industrial transformations are seemingly summoned from thin air. Railway lines unfurl, factory engines fire up, and settler enclaves expand with only passing attention paid to the ties, fuels, and board sheets required by these projects. Behind each of these enterprises, however, stood an intricate chain of laborers, lumberjacks, beasts of burden, rangers, rafters, and merchants that delivered boards, fuel, and other forest commodities to market. This book brings these and other actors to the fore in order to call greater attention to the materiality of modernization: the fact that Korea's telegraph poles, crossbeams, furniture, charcoal, and paper products came from *somewhere*.

That place was the forest. But it was not Korea's forests per se. The resource flows and commodity chains created by Japan's imperial expansion meant that Hokkaido's timber sustained Korea's railways, Manchuria's coal powered Kyushu's factories, and Karafuto's pulp became Tokyo's newspapers. Working hand in glove with Japan's corporate colossi, colonial bureaucrats wired Korea and its forest resources into an industrial circuitry that crisscrossed colonial administrations and grew in tandem with Japan's steadily expanding sphere of interest. In effect, they integrated the Korean peninsula ever more tightly into the transpacific timber trade, linking its forests with markets and mills that stretched from British Columbia to Borneo. Any effort to understand the politics of forest management in Korea must therefore look beyond the peninsula itself. It must track the broader circulation of Korea's forests as they were transfigured into the ligneous commodities that vitalized Japan's continental expansion and, later, war.[26]

To do so, however, is to confront a fundamental but bewildering trait of any forest: its many uses. Both materially and functionally, Korea's forests were many things. As sources not just of timber but also pulp, turpentine, tannins, biofuel, fruit, fibers, and fertilizer, they were kaleidoscopic deposits of natural resources. As habitats, they provided shade for ginseng, moisture for mushrooms, and range for hunters. As spiritual sites, they were places of burial, reverence, and ritual. As spaces of subversion, they harbored smugglers, communist rebels, and vagrant farmers. If, as one forest historian has put it, "the various ways of using forest and wood have continually cut across one another," then the colonial forestry project in Korea is an illuminating case in point.[27]

It is little wonder, then, that Japanese efforts to ascribe new boundaries of forest ownership, intervene in local fuel markets, and police the woodlands were so contentious. At all levels of government, in each of the thirteen provinces, and in hamlets across the peninsula, efforts to reform customary forest-usage rights spawned conflict. In some cases this conflict took violent forms, as in the peasant protests over the levying of Forest Owners Association fees. In others, this contestation unfolded under the watchful eye of the public and the press, as in the timber tariff debate.

Much of this discord was far more mundane, occurring as it did in the policy memos and bulletins of the colonial state and its institutions. Buried beneath the boilerplate language and bureaucratic jargon of planning documents lay conflicting visions of productive forests and the governing frameworks behind them. What made sense at the national level was often impossible at the district level; what was a virtue to the Korean woodcutter was a vice to the Japanese merchant. Korea-based officials were not the only parties ensnared in these disputes. To trace the contours of debates over forestry policy is to appreciate the *interstitial* position of forestry bureaucrats—the fact that the goals of forest management were torn between the interests of Japanese settlers and Korean subjects, the metropolitan government in Tokyo and the frontier of Manchuria, local residents and transnational corporations.

At the heart of these conflicts lay tensions not merely between the multiple uses of wood and forest but also between the marketplace and the planning horizons of woodsmen. The problem, in the most basic sense, was one of time, and it was not peculiar to Japanese officials in Korea. "Foresters," in the words of Hugh Raup, "have always had trouble with time because the human mind produces changes in the uses of wood several times faster than trees can grow."[28] It follows that forest administrators in Korea often struggled to keep up with the vicissitudes of global supply and demand, the exigencies of industrialization, and the geopolitics of their time. Although they routinely drew up hundred-year management models with confidence and precision, they often watched helplessly as the value and utility of Korea's forests changed beneath their feet. Softwoods once eyed as cheap construction materials were later identified as sources of cellulose for the burgeoning synthetic fiber industry; charcoal once earmarked for domestic consumption was suddenly shipped off to the war front. Perhaps no single product better captures the volatility of resourcing the empire than the rail tie: a wooden material that, once assembled into lines, simultaneously opened up new markets, changed shipping costs, and collapsed the distance between timber reserves previously beyond reach.

Try as they might, in other words, bureaucrats could not simply dictate natural resource supplies or steer allocations. Using rotation schedules that forecast the needs of the colonial state twenty, fifty, and even one hundred years into the future, they could only hope to anticipate them. Forestry, in this respect, reveals a new face of the colonial bureaucracy. Far from the paragons of technocratic efficiency one often encounters in Korean portraits of a seemingly omnipotent colonial state, forestry bureaucrats in Korea were time and again forced to turn back to their drawing boards as they reckoned with forces beyond their control. When viewed through the lens of the Bureau of Forestry, the colonial state appears multifarious—less a monolithic entity than a collection of like-minded technocrats, less an almighty actor than a jumble of competing interests.

The pages that follow accordingly narrate a story as much of contingency and adaptation as of infringement and coercion. Owing in no small part to the enduring influence of James Scott's *Seeing Like a State*, scientific forestry has become the locus classicus of the "heroic simplification" of complex local conditions practiced by experts and engineers at the center.[29] Yet while much of Scott's critique of state hubris rings true in the case of colonial Korea, the history of twentieth-century forestry could never be so simple. Involving a host of nonstate actors (including corporations and civic bodies) and considerable discord among government agents, forestry reforms were not imposed from on high.

To the contrary, they were fashioned through regular exchange and periodic confrontation with different sectors of colonial society. Korean journalists and activists debated, lampooned, and publicized Japanese forestry policies. Japanese settlers and Korean landlords lobbied the Government-General to pursue land reforms, tariff schedules, and forestry regulations that best suited their economic interests. Rural women and children, the focal point of efforts to shape domestic fuel economies, consistently found their way around sumptuary codes. Through acts of resistance running the gamut from illicit fuel collection to violent uprisings, hamlets made it clear that the state could not simply commandeer Korea's forests or define their utility.

Japanese forest management, as a result, was marked by a number of policy pivots that attest to the limits of state authority and the constraints on its agents. These concessions should be understood less as markers of weakness than as strategies of environmental rule. As foresters would come to learn in Korea, a certain degree of flexibility in forest policy enabled them to bring more rural communities into the fold of their agenda. It furthered the reach of bureaucrats into agrarian households on the very edges of state authority—a grip that, once established, progressively tightened after 1937.

FROM GREEN ARCHIPELAGO TO EMPIRE OF FORESTRY

If a timberline view of Korean society affords new perspectives on the nature of state power and colonial violence, it also offers an opportunity to reconsider the history and legacy of Japan's "green archipelago." Since the publication in 1989 of Conrad Totman's seminal *The Green Archipelago*, scholars the world over have come to appreciate the centrality of wood and forest to Japan's preindustrial history. How is it, Totman asks, that despite its population pressures and vulnerable topography, Japan remains "a highly industrialized society living in a luxuriantly green realm"? As he sees it, the answer lies in the growth over centuries of a robust system of endogenous forest management.[30] By showing how different regimes responded to Japan's major "forest predations," Totman uncovers the roots of a rich tradition of regenerative forestry—one that emerged independent to that of Germany, long considered the cradle of sustainable forestry.

Globally minded environmental historians took note. Before long, early modern Japan had become something of a "cross-check for historians of the German and West European forest, indicating which conditions were essential to sustainable forestry and which were either marginal or replaceable."[31] Others were drawn to the story of the green archipelago as a case study in successful societal adaptation to ecological constraints. Whatever the case, Japan has since garnered considerable international recognition for its "precocity in forestry matters," as well as its pioneering tradition of sustainable environmental management.[32]

This book can be read in part as an extension of *The Green Archipelago* into the twentieth century. It examines how deep-rooted Japanese ideas about deforestation, statecraft, and silviculture interfaced with globally circulating theories of scientific forestry and natural resource conservation. It reveals how Meiji ideologues drew upon Japan's sylvan traditions to transform forestry into an instrument of emperor-centered nationalism. It likewise highlights how some of the vestiges of Tokugawa forestry shaped, and were shaped by, the administration of forests across Japan's imperial sphere.

But it also makes the case that the "luxuriantly green realm" described so vividly by Totman cannot be understood without looking beyond the boundaries of the Japanese islands. For the green archipelago was never hermetically sealed. It may have been true that Japan's island geography nurtured effective responses to deforestation, but it is also true that the forces of Japanese protocapitalism were steadily expanding their reach into the resource reserves of the archipelago's northern frontier. In this sense, in the words of Tessa Morris-Suzuki, "Totman's argument . . . might be turned on its head: Japan's forests could more easily be protected because, in the course of the seventeenth and eighteen centuries, Japanese merchants were extending their economic control over the land of Ainu, land from which they extracted fish fertilizer to replace green fertilizers formerly extracted from local forests."[33] In her recent study of whaling in early modern Japan, Jakobina Arch has suggested further that marine resource extraction not only supplemented agriculture on land but also impelled Japan's expansion across the Pacific, giving rise to what she (following William Tsutsui) calls Japan's "pelagic empire."[34]

At issue for both Arch and Morris-Suzuki is the very notion of sustainability in Japan's island context. Far from a closed system marked by equilibrium and stasis, they argue, the Japanese archipelago was dynamically enmeshed with the oceanic world around it. Arch in particular shows how blurring the analytical boundaries between land and sea allows for a richer understanding of natural resource management in preindustrial Japan. By painting a portrait of an archipelago less green than aquamarine, she reveals how new perspectives on Japan's environmental traditions emerge when we begin to map the fuller scope of its ecological imprint.

Something similar can be said of Japan and its forests in the twentieth century. When Totman set to work on *The Green Archipelago* in the 1980s, he did so against the backdrop of growing international opprobrium for Japan's role in clear-cutting Southeast Asian forests. Operating in the shadows of verdant mountains at home was a powerful Japanese timber industry abroad. With breathtaking efficiency, Japanese conglomerates (including Mitsui, Sumitomo, and Mitsubishi) positioned themselves as brokers of timber extraction.[35] Using loans, lines of credit, and subcontractors, they built what Anna Tsing has called "soft cooperation networks," commodity chains that, owing to their "odorless capital," offered little indication of Japan's actual involvement.[36] Less active in lumbering than lobbying, Japanese corporations worked quietly behind the scenes to mold favorable trade frameworks through which they funneled tropical timbers cheaply into Japan. The ensuing torrent of foreign lumber into postwar Japan—known shorthand to Japanese simply as *gaizai*, or "timber from the outside"—gave domestic stands space and time to grow. Whereas in 1965 *gaizai* accounted for only 13 percent of the timber consumed in Japan, by 1994 this figure had climbed to 75 percent.[37]

Totman, for his part, is careful not to leave his readers "with the implication that the rich forests of contemporary Japan can be attributed directly to pre-twentieth century polices." "Today's lushness," he explains, "is the immediate result of the decades of forest recovery—partly purposeful, partly attributable to the international market—that followed World War II."[38] Yet nowhere does Totman mention Japan's dependence on cheap timber from abroad or the central role of Japanese corporations in the degradation of Southeast Asian forests. Given his focus on early modern Japan, this omission is entirely reasonable. But his opening premise that "the people of Japan have done less to ravage their land and bring ruin upon it than have many other societies past and present" does beg the question, What impact have the people of Japan had on lands beyond the archipelago itself?[39]

If we take the twentieth century as our frame of reference, that impact is profound. Whether through the management of woodlands in its colonial empire before 1945 or industrial logging operations in Southeast Asia thereafter, Japan has had an outsized influence on forests across the Asia-Pacific. The expansion of Japan's woodland possessions did not stop at Hokkaido. Japanese timber companies continued their northern advance into the larch forests of Karafuto, while, to the south, they began to commercialize the camphor stands of Taiwan after its annexation in 1895. Korea and its forests came next, but hardly last. Manchuria, the Philippines, Indonesia: by 1942 Japanese proxies had assumed control over forests scattered across the Pacific Rim. So it was that an assorted lot of Japanese surveyors, scientists, administrators, military officers, and corporate contractors fanned out across the woodlands of Asia. Though bound only loosely by professional networks, research institutions, and market forces, these actors pursued corresponding reform agendas that indelibly shaped local forest politics for decades after liberation from Japanese rule. Together, they sowed the seeds for the growth of what I call Japan's empire of forestry in the Asia-Pacific.

This book uses the Korean peninsula as a lens through which to examine the green archipelago's transformation into an empire of forestry. Following the publication of Richard Grove's pathbreaking study of the colonial origins of environmentalism, scholars have grown increasingly sensitive to the relationship between colonial expansion and conservationist thought—what Grove christened "green imperialism."[40] Of particular salience to this scholarship has been the role of islands in stimulating new ideas about environmental change in the colonial periphery. As isolated fields of observation, islands threw into stark relief the environmental consequences of colonial rule, thereby nurturing a counter-discourse of environmental concern.

When viewed from Korea, Japan's empire of forestry offers an opportunity to consider the inverse: what happens when an island society long alive to the consequences of deforestation assumes control over nearby continental landscapes. New hues of green imperialism, that is to say, come to light when we move away from the Eurocentrism that has long defined scholarship on colonial conservation. "Green imperialism" remains the story of Western empires coming to terms with exotic (usually tropical) forests in distant (usually southerly) territories. Although this literature has greatly expanded the geographical boundaries of environmental history, it continues to, in the words of K. Sivaramakrishnan, "locate Europe as the metropolis and grant it an astonishing capacity to disrupt and colonize peripheral societies and ecologies."[41] It narrates an evolution of forestry practices in the colonial context that can, with few exceptions, be traced back to the French and Germanic forestry traditions.

This book shows that Japan's colonial forestry practices intersected but did not converge with those originating in Europe. To be sure, Japanese foresters went to great lengths to position themselves at the vanguard of enlightened stewardship and within the global currents of scientific best practices. In their fears and forewarnings of environmental collapse, their techno-scientific fervor, and their conviction that forests governed national destiny, Japanese forestry professionals were part of a transnational conservation movement that expanded markedly around the turn of the twentieth century. They were active agents in what Ian Tyrell has called the "nascent internationalism in conservation thought and practice."[42]

But while Japanese woodsmen enthusiastically translated foreign treatises, displayed their wares at international expos, and undertook study tours of the very timber company whose name appears in the imprint of this book, they did not blindly embrace Western forestry wholesale. To the contrary, as with so many other facets of Meiji industrialization, they tailored foreign techniques to the needs of the Japanese empire and its biome. In the process, they forged a composite set of forestry practices and conservationist discourses that evolved out of Japanese silvicultural traditions and cross-pollinated with globally circulating ideas about natural resource management.

Territorial expansion further differentiated Japanese colonial forestry practices. The biogeographical diversity of the Japanese empire demanded managerial adaptation. With the administration of ecosystems as disparate as the tropical forests of Taiwan and the Manchurian taiga came calls for *place-based* paradigms of forest management. Although Japanese forestry bureaucrats in Korea first fell back on familiar modes of governance, they came to appreciate the need to understand local conditions before cementing policy. Centuries of red pine monoculture, the combustion of fuels in radiant under-floor heating systems (known as *ondol*), and Confucian burial rites, among other things, had inscribed particular and regionalized patterns of forest use into Korea's soil. Recognizing this, forestry experts in Korea, as elsewhere, moved to survey local conditions, conduct ecological experiments, and undertake research into historical forestry customs. In these and other ways, Tokugawa forestry practices and European scientific principles changed in dynamic interaction with local traditions and material conditions encountered across the empire.

What united these different colonial forestry projects was not so much a particular approach to forest administration as an ideology of imperial stewardship. That Japan's centuries-old traditions of regenerative forestry were a source of legitimacy and strength as a colonial power in Asia was an article of faith among officials both in and outside the world of forestry. Colonial propagandists indeed went to great lengths to highlight Japan's supposedly timeless traditions of "forest love." They did so not only to boost Japan's conservationist credibility on the world stage but also to position Japan as the premier steward of Asia's forests, a sylvan pioneer that would protect these landscapes from axe-wielding Western imperialists. Forests and their stewardship were thus invested with added significance as they were woven into broader debates about climate, culture, and assimilation across Japan's empire. In Korea, as we will see, a general sense of "ambivalent sameness" toward Korean subjects gave rise to an unusually malleable rhetoric of forest conservation that tacked between claims to ethnic fraternity and racial supremacy. Abstract notions of sylvan enlightenment and ideals of forest reverence operated in Korea as plastic ideological devices used to herald harmony as well as demarcate difference, to invoke pan-Asian solidarity as well as celebrate Japanese purity.

Considered together, these facets of Japanese forestry allow us to track an alternative trajectory in the evolution of green imperialism, to provincialize Europe and its foresters. In charting the rise of "scientific forestry," historians relate what often feels like a metanarrative of convergence: a seemingly universal set of techniques and sensibilities, emanating from elite academies in Europe, that everywhere fashioned woodlands into legible grids, predictable stands, and sustainable yields. But forest management was never one thing. It has always been marked by its variation and shaped by singular intersections of politics, economics, and geography. To Peter Vandergeest and Nancy Lee Peluso, this variation gave rise to "empires of forestry" in another sense: distinctive "networks of knowledge, practice and institutions produced differently in different local contexts, and exchanged across sites through institutions facilitating this exchange."[43]

What form did these networks take in Korea? How did colonial forestry practices evolve when an imperial power absorbed forests that were geographically proximal, ecologically familiar, and situated at a crossroads of intra-imperial interests? How did the complex contours of race and ethnicity in Japan's empire—where officials sought to simultaneously signal their ethnic affinities and maintain racial hierarchies—impact the ideological register of colonial conservationism? More generally, how did colonial forest management take shape in the colder climates of northeast Asia, where forests offered different sorts of commodities and were integrated into timber markets that spanned the Pacific? To answer these questions, we must not only write empire into Japan's environmental history but also write Japan's empire into global environmental history.

SOURCES AND STRUCTURE

The architects of forest conservation in colonial Korea consumed more paper than they probably cared to admit. The archive of the former Bureau of Forestry in Korea overflows with reams of statistics, stacks of reports, and the myriad day-to-day documents that circulate throughout any bureaucratic enterprise. For the historian, this is both a blessing and a curse. On the one hand, it provides for an empirically rich analysis of the design and implementation of Japanese imperial forestry practices. On the other, the eye-numbing data tables and tedious policy proposals often obscure much of what makes forest history interesting: how forests touched the lives and shaped the thoughts of individuals.

A few words are therefore in order about the power dynamics embedded in the forester's archive. Prone to embellishment, distortion, and confirmation bias, the historical record generated by the Bureau of Forestry in colonial Korea tells a selective story. Relegated to the margins of this archive are the Korean families watching in anguish as their ancestral burial lands were leased out to Japanese settlers. Elided are the sensory and corporeal implications of wartime resource centralization and the fuel scarcity it engendered. Where possible, I have tried to address these gaps by turning to sources that offer alternative perspectives on forestry matters: police reports, popular literature, journalistic dispatches. But there is no work-around for the fact that those who shouldered most of the weight of colonial-era forestry reforms were only faintly committed to the historical record. This is especially true of the enduring communities of shifting cultivators, who, though vilified by Japanese foresters, remain for the most part faceless in the archive.

The nature of quantification further confounds the historian. At one level, colonial statistics on forestry matters are invaluable. They permit a fine-grained analysis of the material and ecological transformation of Korea's forests. They enable us to track the movement of myriad forest resources and monitor price fluctuations of forest commodities—issues of daily concern for residents of Korea. Any attempt to weigh in on the material register of forestry reforms—to assess what ecological good or ill came of Japanese rule—must rely on these sources. But these statistics were also products of official privilege and, quite often, instruments of propaganda. In defining what constituted a "fully stocked forest" or a "wasteland," forestry officials imposed their own ways of seeing and valuing nature. In compiling data on trees planted or hectares reclaimed, they broadcast the beneficence of their agenda without offering any sense of what actual benefit comes out of these numbers. Forestry statistics, as such, are far more vexing sources than their scientific polish might suggest. They demand serious scrutiny but also critical distance.

Seeds of Control proceeds in three parts. Part 1, "Roots," charts the emergence of new ways of using, governing, and revering woodlands in Japan and its colonies. It begins by outlining in chapter 1 what I call the "imperialization" of forestry in Meiji Japan: the transformation of forest management into a force of nationalism and a source of legitimacy as a colonial power. Drawing on the accounts of a wide range of travelers, settlers, and officials, chapter 2 tracks the growth of a new geographical imagination regarding Korea: a bifurcated view of the landscape as predominantly red, barren mountains in need of state intervention save for the green, primeval forests awaiting timber industrialists in the north.

Shifting its focus to the actual implementation of forestry policy, part 2, "Reforms," examines the consolidation of the Government-General's forestry agenda during the first three decades of Japanese colonial rule (1907–37). Chapter 3 takes up the contentious process of woodland-tenure reform: a series of enclosures and title transfers that laid the groundwork for all subsequent reforms. Through an analysis of the inner workings of the colonial government's flagship forestry research station, chapter 4 investigates the interpersonal and institutional politics of scientific collaboration in the colonial context. Taking the Yalu River basin as its focus, chapter 5 maps the growth of a regional timber industry on newly designated national forest-land (*kokuyūrin*), where a host of actors vied for access to Korea's northern treasure house of forest resources. Chapter 6 sets its sights on policies governing privately owned forestland (*minyūrin*), where foresters sought to compel farming communities to become energetic contributors to the project of civic forestry.

Part 3, "Campaigns," examines two different movements of social control that intensified during wartime (1937–45)—one targeting the spirit, the other the body. Chapter 7 surveys the ideological terrain of forest conservation in late colonial Korea, a time when "forest love" became a key marker in the spiritual assimilation of Korean subjects. Chapter 8 tracks the emergence of a command economy for forestry products, and the corporeal consequences thereof, as the peninsula's forests were mobilized to meet the material demands of Japan's "New Order" in Asia.

It is my hope that, collectively, these chapters might also prompt the reader to think beyond 1945 to consider the postcolonial transformation of Japan's empire of forestry. Smothered in foliage, South Korea today offers few indications of the colonial forestry enterprise that once was. Yet, as I suggest in the conclusion, Park Chung-hee's "forest miracle" did not emerge in a vacuum. Its developmental logic and regulatory frameworks grew out of the "greenificationism" of the Government-General, succeeding in ways that the colonial state had failed. In Southeast Asia, meanwhile, Japan's empire of forestry loomed—and looms—large. Although the technologies and patron politics of Japan's more recent forestry ventures in the region bear little resemblance to those described in the following pages, such distinctions would mean little to tenant farmers in Korea or shifting cultivators in Kalimantan, who toiled under the same ecological shadows cast by the rising sun in the Pacific.

PART I

ROOTS

ONE

IMPERIALIZING FORESTRY

OF ALL THE POTENTIAL THREATS TO JAPAN'S NATIONAL SECURITY AT the turn of the twentieth century, the "red pine army" was perhaps the least overtly menacing. Yet in the view of Honda Seiroku, a professor of forestry writing in the pages of *Tōyō gakugei zasshi*, Japan's first popular science magazine, the accelerating "red pine advance" posed a grave threat to the nation: "Having captured Shikoku, Kyushu, and the southern half of the archipelago, the red pines have already subdued the plains of Kantō. Now, they are aggressively advancing to the Ōshū region along the Eastern and Western coastlines of Hondō and the Rikū Kaidō. Moreover, beech forest, the original landlord of the region, was not able to withstand the attack of ruinous deforestation and wildfires, the vanguards of the coming red pine army."[1]

Seldom has forest succession been put more dramatically. Outlining what was soon to become known as his "red pine ruination theory" (*akamatsu bōkokuron*), Honda explained how human activities such as fire setting and fuel collection had stripped the forest floor of its nutrients. This in turn opened the gates for the red pine invaders, a pioneer species that was quick to set roots on open forest floor. Once established, Honda warned, the shade-intolerant *pinus densiflora* would monopolize access to light, water, and nutrients, leaving little space for the growth of other species and thereby raising the risk of timber blight.[2]

If Honda's outlook put forward a historical view of ecology, it was also an ecological view of history. In a manner reminiscent of George Perkins Marsh, whose *Man and Nature* (1864) was among the first texts to bring into focus the environmental consequences of untrammeled deforestation, Honda marshaled a wealth of historical evidence from the great civilizations of the past to underscore the gravity of forest depletion. Greece, Sicily, Babylon: the fall of these once great societies offered chilling reminders of how forest management determined, as he put it, the "rise and fall of nations."[3] For Honda, deforestation was but the prelude to an onslaught of environmental crises including erosion, drought, and floods. Unchecked deforestation, as such, spelled disaster—indeed potential ruin—for the nation. "The state of a nation's forests," he would later write, "is an expression of that country's destiny." This was not simply a matter of bureaucratic land management. To Honda, it raised the specter of the "attrition of national strength."[4]

Coinciding as it did with the wave of Japanese nationalism stimulated by Japan's victory in the Sino-Japanese War, this was a rousing message for readers in 1900. Honda soon found himself lecturing widely on the topic, which, despite resistance from the scientific community, garnered tremendous public interest.[5] More than any other Japanese forester of his day, Honda made a public case for the value and necessity of state-led forest management. His voice was only amplified as he rose through the ranks of academia to become one of Japan's most celebrated woodsmen as well as "the father of its parks," a title he earned as an advocate for green spaces in Japan and its colonies.[6]

Infused with technical jargon and European scientific theories, Honda's outlook would have been scarcely familiar to the generations of woodcutters, officials, and farmers who had managed for centuries the forests of preindustrial Japan. To be sure, the seventeenth-century rhetoric regarding the careful practice of erosion and flood control (*chisan chisui*) through tree planting propounded by Kumazawa Banzan and Uesugi Yōzan, among others, provided an ideological template for Meiji forestry officials. As early as the 1830s, moreover, scholars such as Satō Nobuhiro had begun to theorize, in the words of Federico Marcon, "a system of human dominion over nature that consisted of the state control of production and commercialization of agricultural products, an instrumentalist conception of knowledge, a notion of the material environment as a potential treasure holder of resources exploitable for human needs and the recruitment of scholars in economic activities."[7]

But whereas Tokugawa-era agricultural reformers advocated forest management as a means to increase tillage and forestall natural disasters, Honda and his generation promoted forestry as a linchpin of international commerce and military strength. When a seventeenth-century official in Akita Domain warned that "destitution in the mountains will result in destitution of the realm," his concern adhered to provincial boundaries.[8] When Honda warned of a looming red pine invasion, he appealed to national security in the face of Western imperialism. Especially novel was the manner in which Honda cast Japan's forests as pillars of its industrial strength. For Honda, Japan's breakneck modernization demanded a new set of methods that could not only harness the productive power of the archipelago's forests but also channel it into the developmental agenda of the Meiji state.

We begin, then, by charting the evolution of Japanese forestry practices across the Meiji era (1868–1912), a period marked by intensive state building and national reinvention. In particular, this chapter tracks the development of the Meiji state's forestry system in four interlocking registers: the centralization of authority, the sacralization of sylvan space, the professionalization of experts, and the expansion of territorial control. Considered together, these developments elucidate what I call the imperialization of forestry: the process whereby Japan's forests were freighted with new meaning as building blocks of capitalism, sites of emperor worship, and symbols of national prestige.

If the Meiji era witnessed "a state-led effort to alter how people saw the natural world," as Ian J. Miller has persuasively argued, Japan's forests were indispensable to redefining the relationship between nature and the nation.[9] At the same time that Meiji subjects encountered a carefully curated form of ecological modernity on the grounds of Tokyo's Ueno Zoo, they explored arboreta, tended to school forests, and participated in arbor days like never before. By the turn of the twentieth century, these and other activities had become fixtures of what more and more Japanese considered their national forest culture: a reverence of tree and forest supposedly imprinted into the Japanese character. From these invented sylvan traditions emerged a new quasi-official ideology of *airin shisō*, "forest-love thought." Built on what Julia Adeney Thomas calls the Meiji-era "conceit" of "Japan's permanent love of nature," forest-love thought equipped the state with a new vocabulary of sylvan nationalism used to assert national and imperial dominion over local forests.[10] More than that, against the backdrop of Japan's ascent as a colonial power, "forest love" became a centerpiece of its civilizing mission abroad. To understand how forestry operated in Korea as a source of ideo-logical as well as political authority, in short, we must first look at its evolu-tion in the mountains of the Meiji era, where Japan's empire of forestry set it roots.

CENTRALIZATION

Rapid industrialization followed closely on the heels of the 1868 Meiji Res-toration, the political revolution carried out in the name of the newly enthroned Meiji emperor. Convinced that the surest way to spare Japan from Western colonial subjugation was through rapid industrial growth, the Meiji leadership mobilized the material foundations of the archipelago to build, as one popular slogan of the day put it, "a rich country and strong army." More specifically, in the words of Itō Hirobumi, a leading statesman and later architect of the Japanese takeover of Korea, the Japanese government set out to "make good Japan's deficiencies by swiftly seizing upon the strengths of the western industrial arts; to construct within Japan all kinds of mechanical equipment on the western model, including shipbuilding, railways, telegraph, mines and buildings; and thus with one great leap to introduce to Japan the concepts of enlightenment."[11] The following decades witnessed considerable growth along these lines. Smoke-belching factory chimneys cut imposing figures across new industrial belts; railway lines branched out into new cor-ners of the archipelago; modern "materials of civilization"—iron, steel, ferroconcrete—gave rise to ever-more-imposing cityscapes.

Yet while this new materiality symbolized for many Japanese a rupture with their past, it was to no small degree underpinned by an age-old emblem of Japanese tradition: wood. Indeed, as Gregory Clancey reminds us, if one probes just beneath the surface of the material components of Meiji-era industrial modernity, Japan's dependency on wood is everywhere on display. Railways grew only as far as supplies of rail ties would allow. Coal mines were deathtraps without the pit props and mining timbers that stabilized shafts. Factories across the industrial spectrum required large quantities of charcoal and cordwood to keep engines turning and furnaces firing. Far from relegating Japan's wooden society to a bygone era, Japan's industrial takeoff only compounded its material dependencies on its woodlands.[12]

These swells in demand notwithstanding, the Meiji government was at first far more attentive to arable land than to forest. Owing to the fact that rice production was the foundation of the Tokugawa tax system—an issue of grave concern to the fiscally fragile Meiji state—officials initially prioritized the classification and redistribution of cultivable lowlands. This is not to suggest that Meiji officials were completely uninterested in sylvan matters. Eager to unlock new revenue streams through the creation of "imperial forests," Ōkubo Toshimichi, Kido Kōin, and other influential statesmen pressed for new titles to the "woodlands and wastelands" (*sanrin gen'ya*) that comprised roughly 80 percent of the landscape.

Woodland redistribution, however, was hamstrung from the start. In contrast to the relatively swift resolution of issues related to arable land tenure, the ascription of woodland ownership taxed the resources—and patience—of forestry officials for decades. Especially vexing was the need to distinguish between public (*kan*) and private (*min*) forests, which required hard-and-fast boundaries when in fact tenure rights were anything but clear-cut.[13] That many forests in the vicinity of villages were subject to *iriai* arrangements—centuries-old communal land-use customs that often spanned entire hamlets, mountains, and regions—only compounded the complexity. Any effort to unravel the skein of customary usage rights had to untangle multiple threads, creating friction not simply between the state and rural society but also between neighboring hamlets and households.

Early Meiji forestry was beset by another problem as well: toothless enforcement. Lines on a map do not a boundary make. Lacking the resources to police newly enclosed private and state forests, local officials could only watch in frustration as farming households continued to glean fuel and fertilizer from newly enclosed state woodlands. A string of edicts over the 1870s attempted to shore up woodland boundaries and respond to the material needs of farming communities through ad hoc licensing schemes, but irreparable damage to land-use arrangements was already done. In effect, the Meiji state's "assault on the commons," to borrow Margaret McKean's phrase, precipitated a policy collapse of the state's own design.[14] By pressing for the swift nationalization of the commons, government officials undermined the very elements of Tokugawa forestry that enabled it to function so well—the village autonomy, provincial variation, and compound authority that had historically diminished the need for a strong state forestry apparatus. The plasticity that had long allowed hamlets to tailor land-use patterns to local needs abruptly ran aground the governing impulses and fiscal priorities of the nation-state. With little incentive to comply with edicts from the center and with no small measure of antipathy injected into rural perceptions of the city-dwelling ruling class, farming households suddenly had less cause to think long term.

So it was that, as one Bureau of Forestry report later put it, "the political revolution in the beginning of the Meiji Era produced a disastrous effect upon the preservation of the forests": "The forests throughout the country were mercilessly cut down so that there appeared in all quarters of Japan hills and mountains deprived of trees. The consequence was that not only was the forests economy jeopardized but the economic order of the people at large was deranged, dealing heavy blows upon the productive industry of the people by giving rise to annual inundations which devastated many parts of the country."[15] Perhaps the forestry bureaucrat Takahashi Takuya best captured the frustrations of his colleagues when he described the immediate aftermath of the Meiji Restoration as a time marked by the "total erosion of the institutions of forest control and protection."[16]

For villagers, these shifts represented more than a policy failure; they were a betrayal of the very spirit of Tokugawa forestry: the notion that its benefits be shared equally between the government and the people. Farming households were not going to sit idly by as profit-hungry corporations and bureaucrats cordoned off local woodlands. Many took matters into their own hands. According to one official estimate, no fewer than two million trees were illicitly felled and five million lost to arson between 1878 and 1887.[17] Statistics of this sort were used in turn by Meiji foresters to assign blame for deforestation to upland communities when the reality was that new lumbering technologies and improving modes of transport were accelerating timber harvests across Japan. Whatever the cause, there is no question that the first two decades of the Meiji period witnessed considerable deforestation—a fact perhaps best evidenced by the appearance of "bald mountains" (hageyama) in some of the more densely populated regions of archipelago.[18]

With the deterioration of Japan's forests came the realization that the Meiji government needed to invest more robustly in the protection and oversight of its woodlands. To that end, Interior Ministry officials established in 1877 a Forestry Office in their Geography Bureau, which later became its own freestanding agency.[19] At the same time, a growing chorus of officials called for what many considered the centerpiece of state forestry: a comprehensive forestry law. Among the staunchest advocates for this legal overhaul were members of the Iwakura Mission, a diplomatic envoy and observation tour that traveled across the United States and Europe from 1871 to 1873. If the official chronicle of the mission authored by Kume Kunitake is any indication, trees and forests left a lasting impression on its participants. From the majestic redwoods of Yosemite to the white poplars lining the streets of Washington, D.C., trees of all types colored the envoy's perceptions of Western modernity. It was in continental Europe, however, where forestry matters sprang to the fore of Kume's account. As one might expect from a legal scholar and historian, Kume exhibits less interest in the physical geography of European forests than in the regulatory frameworks behind them: "Before the advance of industry in Europe, in an age when people did not know that iron could be used in place of timber, vast woodlands were cut down and forests decimated in Greece, Spain, France and Britain. It was in light of this that forestry systems were subsequently promoted so that nowadays, while liberal politics are increasingly practiced in Europe, in forestry laws alone the freedoms of former times are actually being curtailed." However "restrictive" these systems may have been, he concluded, their costs were clearly outweighed by the "long-term benefits brought to the people."[20] Insofar as this judgment reinforced the need for a strong central state, it neatly aligned with the broader political vision of the Meiji oligarchy.

Yet, for reasons both financial and political, a forest law was slow to materialize. It was not, in fact, until the 1880s that a broad coalition of interests, stirred to action by a series of catastrophic floods, finally rallied behind its promulgation. The result was the Forest Law (Shinrinhō) of 1897, the capstone of the Meiji state's effort to assert control over Japan's woodlands. Although the legal framework would see substantial modifications over the coming decade, it established, among other things, a criminal code for forestry and a complex web of land-use regulations. Arguably its most important provisions, however, were those governing Forest Owners Associations (Shinrin kumiai): local institutions of forest management that would, lawmakers hoped, operate as ground-level units of policy coordination and community surveillance.

Laws engendered record keeping. With increasing precision, hard data on timber yields, acreage, and stock accumulation filled the pages of the Bureau of Forestry's statistical reports. By 1910, there were ten major state forest reserves, each with its own branch office, as well as 211 minor forest divisions. A total area of 7,587,335 *chō* of state forest fell under the jurisdiction of a growing band of federal foresters: 10 forest managers, 22 commissioners, 35 technical advisers, 1,428 rangers.[21] After three decades of trials and tribulations, in other words, a truly national administrative framework for forest management had taken shape. Still wanting, however, was broad public support for the project of national forest conservation. The narrator of Shimazaki Tōson's popular historical novel *Before the Dawn* doubtless spoke for countless villagers when he asked of the enclosure of his native woodlands, "When it had caused so much suffering for such a long time, what reason could there have been for so rigorously controlling the Kiso forests?"[22]

SACRALIZATION

Chastened by the realities of governing remote upland communities from their offices in Tokyo, foresters had by the early 1880s begun to insist on the participation of the broader public in the cultivation of a new conservationist spirit alongside the forest itself. Such was precisely the charge placed before the Japan Forestry Association (Dai Nippon Sanrinkai), a civic institution established in January 1882 for the purpose of stimulating the "mutual support of the government and the people" in all matters related to forestry.[23] Comprised of a wide range of intellectuals and civil servants—from scientists to lawyers to educators—it rose to prominence as the premier institution for public outreach and the popularization of forestry research. What started as a group of 343 had by 1910 grown to more than 4,000 members, many of whom would become vigorous contributors to forestry work in Korea through the association's affiliate group on the peninsula.[24] Through lecture circuits, demonstrations, and youth group activities, this organization and its local chapters brought the agenda of metropolitan bureaucrats to the doorsteps of farming households.

Their efforts both reflected and promoted Meiji-era shifts in popular perceptions of the Japanese landscape. Given the cultural salience of forest, tree, and wood to Japanese society, it was only a matter of time before each was braided into the emperor-centered political ideologies of the Meiji state. At a time when some Japanese were growing wary of what seemed to be a slavish adherence to all things Western, Japan's forestry traditions presented a means to reconnect with the roots of pure Japaneseness. From the 1880s onward, that is to say, Meiji ideologues began to allude to a monolithic Japanese "forest culture"—supposedly timeless customs of forest reverence that transcended the regional, class, and social divisions of the nation. Blending theories of social Darwinism with the latest thinking in climate science, they turned to Japan's environmental setting for insight into their national character.

Few did so more evocatively than Shiga Shigetaka, "the John Ruskin of Japan," whose 1894 encomium to the Japanese landscape captured the attention of readers across the archipelago. Equal parts travel guide and scientific treatise, Shiga's *Theory of the Japanese Landscape* (Nihon fūkeiron) called on all Japanese to treasure the geographical diversity of the archipelago. To Shiga, himself a periodic contributor to the journal of the Japan Forestry Association, Japan's mountains and forests were more than latent backdrops to Japan's history; they were active agents that had molded the Japanese character over millennia. Stripped down to its core, he insisted, Japan's national fiber was much like that of the Japanese pine—weathered, resilient, upstanding. To understand what set Japan apart from the West and even the rest of Asia, he argued, one need look no further than the pine and the life-giving soil from which it grew: "The beautiful sceneries of mountains and abundant plants have long been nourishing the Japanese love of nature and will continue to do so in future." Shiga implored the Japanese public not only to actively enjoy their *terra patria* but also to work to ensure its protection: "To destroy such motivation for people would result in destroying humanitarian enlightenment."[25]

That Shiga would invoke "humanitarian enlightenment" as grounds for landscape protection hints at the growing influence in Japan of Western ideas about natural resource conservation. Indeed, for all his emphasis on the singularity of the Japanese landscape, Shiga relied heavily on European ideas about geology, botany, and even alpinism to convey the splendor of the Japanese islands. In this sense, his writings formed a bridge to not only European science but also notions of sylvan enlightenment: the conviction that forests were a visible metric of modernity, that the thickness of forest cover was an indicator of national progress. In this, Shiga kept close company with the members of the Iwakura Mission, who returned from their travels firm believers that a strong central forestry apparatus was a hallmark of great nation status. This was especially true for Itō Hirobumi, who traveled throughout Europe in 1882 alongside Nakamura Yaroku, a prominent forestry expert. For Itō, these experiences underscored the myriad virtues of forestry—tax revenue, industrial growth, military preparedness—that he would later champion in his position as the resident-general of Korea.[26]

Shiga's was but one of the earlier expressions of the environmental determinism that would come to undergird Japanese claims to racial and cultural superiority over their colonial subjects. Whatever its sensitivity to the geographical variation found in the archipelago, his was a project of cultural homogenization. In drawing attention to geographical structures that had ostensibly shaped Japanese society since time immemorial, he set out to distill Japanese identity down to its *kokusui*, its "national essence." Intentionally or not, Shiga and other like-minded writers equipped Meiji officials with powerful rhetorical devices used to bolster claims about the innate conservationist sensibilities of the nation. By coupling the conservation of the landscape to the conservation of Japaneseness, they gave the Bureau of Forestry a persuasive new argument for the centralized control of local landscapes.

Not all Japanese, however, embraced such characterizations of a unified forest culture. On the contrary, by the late 1880s, a countervailing project of sylvan localism was under way. Alarmed that Japan's rich mosaic of village forest traditions was being effaced by the centrifugal forces of sylvan nationalism, a small but vocal group of scientists and activists set out to preserve the intimate bond between farmer and forest, village and mountain. Front and center in this project was Yanagita Kunio, the folklorist who, over the course of numerous ethnographic surveys, produced detailed compendia of legendary, divine, and supernatural trees. More interested in the substance of individual trees than the abstraction of entire forests, Yanagita was naturally drawn to the relationship between local Shintō shrines and the groves that surrounded them—sacred forest parcels (*chinju no mori*) that, according to legend, offered spirits safe passage down to Earth. What emerges from his accounts is a prevailing sense of symbiosis and harmony—an interlocking social, spiritual, and ecological system finely attuned to the rituals of rural life.

Yanagita painted an idyllic portrait of village forestry in no small part as a critique of Meiji modernization. Together with the biologist Minakata Kumagusu, he sought to draw attention to what was truly at stake in the nationalization of woodlands: rending the social and spiritual fabric of agrarian society. Yet, Yanagita also partook in the invention of sylvan tradition. His romantic portrayals of a harmonious balance between village and forest helped to naturalize the idea that Shintōism was an age-old force of conservation. In turn, as state Shintō became a fixture of emperor worship, the Japanese state arrogated to itself and its imperial figurehead new conservationist credentials. In the process, the Meiji emperor was further elevated as the great forest warden of the realm. "Sacred forest, sacred nation": such was the logic of what Aike P. Rots calls the "making" of Japan's sacred forests.[27] Never mind that by the turn of the century the state's Shrine Merger Policies were then decimating the purportedly sacred forests surrounding Shintō shrines, Meiji officials increasingly invoked Shintōism and its associated rituals as the fount of a national environmental consciousness.

By the turn of the century, the scattered commentary on Japan's forest culture had coalesced into a new catchphrase of sylvan nationalism: *airin shisō*, "forest-love thought." Mixing universalizing rhetoric about national resource conservation with essentializing notions of Japan's timeless forest culture, *airin shisō* was a catch-all term for the habits of mind and body championed by foresters: rational use of the forest's bounty; an appreciation of the subliminal power of forest scenery; enjoyment of woodlands through hiking and other outdoor activities. It signified, among other things, thrift, duty, nature worship, and the recognition of the link between nature's protection and the nation's future.

In some cases, the language of *airin shisō* was imported from abroad. One treatise on forest-love thought took as its starting point Theodore Roosevelt's declaration that "a people without children would face a hopeless future; a country without trees is almost as helpless."[28] Yet, just pages later the author was plumbing the depths of the *Nihon shoki*, one of Japan's oldest written records, for evidence of its undying admiration of forests. *Airin shisō*, in short, was profoundly modern yet anchored in antiquity. It allowed Japanese officials to cloak the practical imperatives of forestry in the rhetoric of progress while simultaneously nurturing a distinctive sense of national pride based on enduring traditions.

Ceremonial tree plantings assumed an especially prominent place in the public celebration of forest-love thought. That the promotion of Arbor Day came at the behest of an American, despite Japan's own centuries-long traditions of regenerative forestry, further reveals the global inflections of the forest-love thought campaign. The initial catalyst for large-scale ceremonial tree plantings was the 1893 visit to Japan of the American minister Birdsey Grant Northrop. A leading proponent of Arbor Day in the United States, Northrop traveled to Japan to preach a message of reforestation, village improvement, and youth education—topics that he had championed during his time as an educator in his native Connecticut. As a Protestant minister, Northrop also fused the Holy Testament with the gospel of tree planting. He propounded a particular strand of Protestant environmentalism that married the conservationist ethos with a deep-seated faith in service to a higher power.[29]

Northrop's lectures in Japan caught the attention of Makino Nobuaki, then the vice minister of education. Just a year before Northrop's visit, Makino had opined that because forests are "naturally vital to the national economy," the public must strengthen what he called "the spirit of loving the forest."[30] Northrop's message appealed to Makino on many levels. Not only would Japan's own Arbor Day further fasten the bonds of local society, it would enable Japanese across class lines to express their love of nation by actively nurturing it, one sapling at a time.[31]

With these goals in mind, Makino began to lobby teachers' associations to set aside land for school forests. His appeal won support. In 1895, local and prefectural governments began to allocate woodlands to schools for just this purpose. Thereafter, school districts, with the backing of the Ministry of Education, began to implement a wide array of student-led tree-planting activities. As Takemoto Tarō has shown, these programs grew over the coming years into a central component of the state-led effort to shape Japanese—and, later, Korean—attitudes toward forest conservation from the bottom up.[32]

As symbols of Japan's national essence and spaces of imperial service, forests were imbued with new meaning over the course of the Meiji era. While the Forest Law was perhaps the clearest expression of the centralization of forestry, the promotion of forest-love thought and its attendant activities also reflected significant changes in the Japanese forest consciousness. Couched in terms of the national good and a love of country, the conservation and regeneration of forests became a civic duty. To plant trees was to improve local society, strengthen the state, and revere the emperor and his luxuriant realm.

PROFESSIONALIZATION

The seedbeds of the Nishigahara nursery proved fertile terrain for the growth of scientific forestry practices in Japan. Established in 1878 on a small plot of land on the outskirts of Tokyo, Nishigahara was initially envisioned by the Meiji government as a space for the experimental cultivation of foreign seeds and saplings. It was not long, however, before the space outgrew its original purpose. By the early 1880s it had become one of Japan's first forestry schools, where Japanese who had trained abroad began to graft the methods of European forest science and administration onto home-grown silvicultural practices.[33]

At the helm of this institution was Matsuno Hazama. Initially sent to Germany to study economics, Matsuno naturally gravitated toward the study of forestry, partly because both disciplines were closely linked in German higher learning. Upon completing his study at the Erbswalde Forestry Academy, then one of Europe's premier forestry schools, Matsuno returned to Japan, where the Home Ministry tapped him to establish the Nishigahara nursery. He found able partners in this mission in Nakamura Yaroku (a pioneering dendrologist who had earned a doctorate from the University of Munich) and Shiga Taizan (a renowned expert in physics and chemistry who had also studied in Germany). Together, these men—"the three elder statesmen of the forestry world in the early Meiji years"—became vital conduits for the diffusion of Germanic forestry in Japan.[34]

The institution at Nishigahara grew alongside its saplings. Following a merger in 1882 with the Komaba School of Agriculture, the Forestry School at Nishigahara was absorbed by Tokyo Imperial University, where it became Japan's flagship for forestry research. Although the appointment in 1887 of Heinrich Mayr, a respected German scholar of forest science, meant that Japanese students no longer had to travel abroad to gain exposure to European forestry methods, many continued to do so. Their primary destination was Eberswalde, where they studied under Robert Hartig, an expert in forest pathology. So central was Hartig to the training of Japanese students that, according to Fukushima Yasunori, a veritable "Hartig route" took shape—a path that led directly from the halls of the School of Forestry in Tokyo to Hartig's classrooms and back, in turn, to the offices of the Japanese government.[35]

Over time, however, Japanese students branched out to other knowledge centers in Europe. Takashima Hokkai, for one, matriculated from 1885 to 1888 at the National School of Water Resources and Forests in Nancy, France, departing just one year before the arrival of Gifford Pinchot, who would go on to establish the United States' own Forest Service.[36] The Meiji government dispatched still others to undertake study tours of forestry projects across the globe: from industrial logging outfits in Canada to riparian-improvement projects in the Netherlands. Japan's pursuit of knowledge about the tools and techniques of Western forestry, in other words, was wide-ranging. Although the influence of Germany on the professionalization of forestry in Japan should not be understated, it was but one of many points of reference. Much like their American counterparts, Japanese foresters set out to "adapt, rather than adopt" German and French practices, while turning to other countries for specific technologies and policy templates that aligned with their forest management priorities.[37]

In the case of erosion control methods, for example, Japanese foresters came to conclude that, given the unusually steep slopes found in both Austria and Japan, Austrian erosion control techniques were especially well suited for use in the archipelago. Working under the guidance of Amerigo Hoffman, an Austrian forestry engineer who spent an eight-year stint as an instructor at Tokyo Imperial University, Japanese officials launched pilot erosion control projects in Aichi Prefecture, where bald mountains stretched across the coast of the Seto Inland Sea.[38] On Hoffman's recommendation, they carved a complex system of dikes and terraced barriers into the hillsides. This was a heavily engineered intervention. It brought concrete and modern engineering methods into the toolkit of foresters and marked, as one Japanese participant would later recall, "a total transformation" of the erosion control methods of the past.[39]

One aspect of Japanese forestry, however, hardly changed: the day-to-day techniques of silviculture, the principal legacy of the "green archipel-ago." Europe may have offered engrossing intellectual rationales and policy frameworks for the managerial centralization of state forestry, but Japan had an advanced "silvicultural corpus" of its own—one tailored to its climate and sensitive to its botanical realities. Years of experimentation with seedlings imported from Europe and the United States left many forestry professionals convinced that many of their own regenerative forestry practices stood on their own merits. Why turn to French guidelines for coppicing when Japanese agricultural manuals had spelled out highly refined methods for centuries? Forestry practitioners also soon discovered that some voguish Germanic planting schemes—mixed-form regeneration (*Mischformen*) and selection cutting (*Plenterwald*), for example—already had Japanese analogues in the customary practices of *satoyama*: the integrated management of paddy fields and forestlands by agricultural communities. Although many scientists endorsed the use of select foreign species (such as acacia and American alcova) and filtered their plans through European theories on forest succession, morphology, and seed germination, Meiji-era planting practices often stayed true to their Tokugawa antecedents. Insofar as the preservation of Japanese planting practices offered a counterweight to the influence of more profit-oriented German methods, it also enabled Meiji ideologues to further play up Japan's uninterrupted traditions of forest love and care.

If any single discipline strove to integrate European scientific forestry concepts into Japanese management paradigms, it was the emerging field of *rinseigaku*: what Honda Seiroku's textbook on the subject described as an "academic approach to the relationships between forestry projects and the enterprise of the nation and its people."[40] In contrast to the emphasis placed on practical know-how by Tokugawa agronomists, *rinseigaku* was chiefly concerned with modeling, policymaking, and organizational efficiency. Students of *rinseigaku* were trained in the science of abstraction and resource commoditization: pricing and market demand, stand rotation schedules, scaling-up operations.

Of particular salience to the discipline was the "normal forest" (*Normalwald*) model, a German management principle whereby each stand is measured and placed into rotation stages that ensure its prolonged productivity. While nursery culture and rotation cutting had sustained the renewal of forests across Japan for centuries, *rinseigaku* systematized this process.[41] The task before the forester was not just the protection and cultivation of forestland but the construction of a long-term plan in which each woodlot and tree was reduced to a measurable whole and connected to the market economy. This outlook evinces a broader shift in Meiji-period thinking on the very meaning of the term resource (*shigen*): the disaggregation and objectification of "living" ideas about interconnected local life forms into discrete material resource pools.[42]

Japanese students traveled to Tokyo Imperial University from across the archipelago for immersion in this subject matter. Requiring as it did high competencies in math, science, and foreign languages, the barrier to admission to this program was high. Many of Japan's earliest students of forestry, as a result, came from elite samurai households. Matsuno, Shiga, and Nakamura all passed through domain academies before taking up forestry as a professional pursuit. Their career trajectories cannot be understood without accounting for the privilege afforded them by their social status. Nevertheless, as time wore on, these older, blue-blooded scholars were joined by the sons of middle-class merchants and farmers to comprise a diverse cohort of students hailing from regions across the archipelago. Officials in the Home Ministry, for their part, saw in this cohort the next generation of forestry bureaucrats. Indeed, much as the Yale School of Forestry was envisioned as an incubator for the forest rangers needed to flesh out the ranks of Gifford Pinchot's nascent US Forestry Service, so was Tokyo Imperial University seen as a launching pad for the careers of Japanese forest administrators.

No one embodied the ideal of the forestry scholar-bureaucrat more completely than Saitō Otosaku. Born in 1866 as the first son of a large farming family, Saitō grew up in the Sekikawa region of Niigata Prefecture, under the shadows of the western Japanese Alps. Like many other young men seeking to "rise in the world," as one Meiji-era maxim had it, he eventually made his way to Tokyo. In 1885, Saitō enrolled in the forestry school at Nishigahara, where he met Honda Seiroku, Kawase Zentarō, and other aspiring foresters who would become close friends and collaborators over the course of his career. Saitō's connection with colonial forestry began in 1895, when, upon his graduation from Tokyo Imperial University, he was dispatched to the front lines of the Sino-Japanese War to survey Korea's woodlands for military purposes. Saitō spent the next decade shuttling across the Japanese empire and its forestry institutions as an official for the Forestry Bureau of the Department of Agriculture and Commerce. By the turn of the century, he had earned a reputation as a versatile and dedicated forester—renown that he would bring with him to Korea, to which he moved in 1909 to take up a top post in Korea's newly established Bureau of Forestry.[43]

Like many of his peers, Saitō was also a devout Christian. Baptized at the age of twenty-five, he was a teetotaler and active member of his church. In keeping with the Puritan-style moralism of his pulpit, he considered austerity and diligence as inseparable from the daily work of forest conservation. He made no bones about his preference for hiring men of faith into the ranks of the forestry service and actively sought Christians to staff the Forest Management Bureau he eventually supervised in Korea. While not all forestry officials shared Saitō's religious zeal, something resembling a Protestant conservation ethic had gained traction in Japan.[44]

Saitō's narrow hiring preferences notwithstanding, avenues for entry into the forestry service were steadily expanding. While most of the top echelon of the Bureau of Forestry continued to bear the imprimatur of Tokyo Imperial University, the growing institutional infrastructure of forestry education began to channel more rank-and-file personnel—rangers, technicians, assistants—into the forestry bureaucracy. By 1910, there were as many as forty-seven different vocational or technical schools offering some form of training in forest management, usually tailored to the specific needs of each prefecture.[45]

Among the many young men to seize on the professional opportunities offered by these prefectural schools was Asakawa Takumi. Born in 1891 in the Kitakoma region of Yamanashi Prefecture, Asakawa's care was entrusted at an early age to his grandfather, who instilled in him a love of ceramics, poetry, and plant collecting. The latter passion prompted Asakawa to enroll in the Yamanashi School of Agriculture and Forestry at the age of sixteen—around the time he was baptized into the Methodist Church. After two years of instruction in the basic principles of forestry science, he took up work as a forest engineer in one of Japan's largest National Forest reserves in Akita Prefecture. When, in 1914, his brother Noritaka decided to move to Korea to teach in an elementary school, Asakawa followed. Once in Seoul, he was able to secure work in the first Forestry Experiment Station established by the colonial government.[46] There, he conducted a number of groundbreaking experiments in seed germination—efforts that would both accelerate reforestation efforts in Korea and launch his own lifelong investigation into Korean folk culture.

In a sense, Honda Seiroku, Saitō Otosaku, and Asakawa Takumi embodied the three tiers of the forestry bureaucracy. At the top of this system were charismatic, public-facing men of letters such as Honda: scholars and professors of forestry science who had earned doctorates from foreign institutions and cultivated a robust international network of scholarly exchange. Just below them were the seasoned bureaucrats, policy experts like Saitō who had cut their teeth administering forests across Japan's empire. For their plans to come to life, however, the system required technicians like Asakawa: low-ranking civil servants who could conduct research and implement policy. Collectively, these men designed, debated, and introduced a series of forestry reforms that markedly transformed Japan's landscape and, with it, the profession of forestry as a whole.

COLONIZATION

The professionalization of forestry in Meiji Japan took place against the backdrop of territorial expansion. Beginning with Hokkaido, Japanese officials took on the administration of timber landscapes as vast as they were unfamiliar. Japan's victories in the Sino- and Russo-Japanese Wars in 1895 and 1905, respectively, expanded the southern and northern limits of Japan's forest holdings to include the subtropical evergreen forests of Taiwan and the temperate coniferous forests of Karafuto. As a whole, these forest zones acquainted bureaucrats with an assortment of challenges inherent to establishing control over outlying woodlands. Just as importantly, they functioned as mirrors of ecological modernity, enabling the Japanese to define their own forest culture in contradistinction to the states of nature found in colonial hinterlands.

As a laboratory for forest science and a large-scale experiment in woodland-tenure reform, the expansive forests of Hokkaido were important sites for the development of colonial forestry practices. What distinguished Hokkaido in the eyes of Meiji foresters was not just its harsh winter climate; it was also the scarcity of woodland ownership claims. Although Ainu chiefdoms had complex customary arrangements regarding land use (and had for centuries relied on forests for fuel, forage, shelter, and rafts, among other things), forest exploitation was for the most part confined to areas immediately surrounding villages and fishmeal-fertilizer production sites. This is to say nothing of the fact that epidemic diseases such as smallpox had decimated Ainu communities, leading to a net population decline over the seventeenth and eighteenth centuries.[47] As a result, Ainu chiefdoms struggled to assert their customary rights to the island's woodland, which was routinely mischaracterized as untouched "primeval forest." The enclosure and redistribution of national or imperial forests was thus more or less freed from the competing claims that had beleaguered foresters on the densely populated islands to the south.

As officials would come to learn over the coming decades, the relative dearth of ownership claims on the island was both a boon and a burden. On the one hand, it enabled government-backed foresters to pursue a broad range of policies to develop, lease, or sell woodlands. On the other, it became patently clear that the commercial development of the island's sizeable forests would be impossible without the labor of Japanese settlers and the investment of Japanese corporations. That is to say, though enthusiasm for the ample forest resources of Hokkaido was high, the resources of the still embryonic forestry service were often inadequate to make use of them.

It was in Hokkaido, therefore, that foresters first confronted some of the more vexing puzzles of settler colonialism and industrial capitalism. How might foresters work in concert with corporations to develop forestry? What policies could be implemented to coax settlers and financiers into molding the landscape in a manner consistent with the state's designs? Questions such as these weighed heavily on the minds of the small cadre of forestry experts detailed to the Hokkaido Development Agency (Kaitakushi, hereafter HDA). Established in 1869, the HDA first set out to promote agricultural settlement in Hokkaido in order to fend off foreign claims and alleviate Malthusian concerns with overpopulation on the home islands. The development of forestry, as such, was secondary to immigration and agriculture, the twin imperatives of Hokkaido's early colonization.

At first, the harvesting of forests unfolded on a decidedly small scale. Carried out principally by farmers and migrants recruited from among former samurai (the lifeblood of Hokkaido's early colonization), timbering activities increased only slightly over the first decades of the Meiji period. The primary concern of many settlers was, in fact, clearing forestland they deemed "an impediment to development."[48] Even as demand for Hokkaido's timber products was growing in mainland Japan (as well as in more distant markets in China), industrial forestry operations were slow to start. In 1881, the total value of forestry products shipped out of Hokkaido was only ¥2,209—a trifling figure in relation to the estimated value of available timber stock.[49] The principal obstacle was infrastructure. With few roads and railways, it was difficult to both harvest Hokkaido's resources and attract corporations that would invigorate the lumber trade.

Frustrated with the sluggishness of industrial forestry operations on the island, HDA officials embarked in the 1890s on a new effort to entice capital. The passage of the 1897 Hokkaido Uncultivated Land Disposal Act marked a critical turning point in this regard. Among its key provisions was a land-leasing process that entitled parties to the eventual transfer of ownership rights, provided that they meet reclamation standards established by the state. In effect, the law was used to dole out of large tracts of Hokkaido's woodlands to Japanese corporations at cut-rate prices.[50]

And come they did. The arrival of corporate-backed prospectors in the late 1890s was just the first step toward the growth of large-scale private timber operations. Much to the delight of the HDA, small lumbering firms like the Kushiro Kōgyō Kaisha soon gave way to large corporations like the Ōji Paper Company. Lured by favorable laws, preferential treatment, and the boom in demand that accompanied the Russo-Japanese War, these corporations assumed control over substantial tracts of Hokkaido's forests. Of the many governing strategies fine-tuned in the forests of Hokkaido, this policy framework—the outsourcing of forestry operations to nonstate entities through an elaborate land-lease system—most directly shaped the architecture of forest management in Korea.

Alongside the growth of the timber industry in Hokkaido emerged a new set of forest management challenges in Taiwan, Japan's first formal colony. Abundant in resources and commercially underdeveloped by the Qing regime prior to Japan's takeover in 1895, Taiwan's predominantly subtropical evergreen forests provided forestry bureaucrats with an opportunity to demonstrate their skills in generating revenue and modernizing nature. In contrast to their counterparts in Hokkaido, however, Japanese foresters in Taiwan were determined to do so without the involvement of capitalists, whom they considered a corrupting influence.[51]

As would be the case time and again, the neat idealism of policy proposals confronted a messier reality on the ground. Early financial and administrative setbacks forced a temporary closure of the Forestry Bureau in Taiwan, leaving officials with little recourse but to set aside their concerns about profiteering and partner with Japanese corporations. Even then, many of the woodlands long prized by the colonial government defied profitable development. If the ruggedly mountainous terrain was not hindrance enough, survey parties had to carry out their work under the threat of attack by native mountain dwellers—"barbarians and savages," in the idiom of the time—whose contempt for colonial officials was well known. One of the more violent conflicts occurred in December 1897, when a survey party led by Saitō Otosaku was ambushed deep in the mountains—a confrontation that, following "pacification" efforts by Japanese gendarmerie, left twenty-three islanders dead.[52] These clashes left a deep impression on Saitō and his colleagues, who came to view uncharted forest regions in colonial territories as spaces of subversion. Less discernible threats also lurked in the forest: at home in the tropical climate, malaria posed a constant threat to the bodies of surveyors, officials, and laborers alike. Taiwan's forests, in short, proved far more recalcitrant to state control than many had anticipated.

The discovery of extensive stands of old-growth cypress at Ari Mountain (Alishan) in 1900 brought all of these issues to the fore. Hoping to seize the opportunity to exhibit their skills in woodland management, forestry officials again shunned the involvement of private capital and funneled considerable state resources into an ambitious commercial timbering venture. And disastrously so: as Kuang-chi Hung has shown, the Alishan forestry project soon became "the shame of Taiwan." After years of investment and the laborious installation of timber railways (modeled on those used in the northwestern United States), the project was declared bankrupt in 1915, leading some commentators to question the value of state-led forestry in the colonial context.[53]

If anything, these bruising episodes in Taiwan offered Japanese foresters a crash course in colonial politics. Although bureaucrats waxed enthusiastic about the commercial possibilities of Taiwan's natural endowments, they quickly learned that well-stocked stands and profitable ventures did not always go hand in glove. Industrial obstacles took many forms: infrastructural requirements, labor shortages, capital shortfalls. Facing stiff and sometimes violent resistance from indigenous residents, moreover, Japanese lumbermen had little choice but to turn to gift-giving rituals that aimed to build trust and open access—what Paul Barclay has called "wet diplomacy," given the frequent involvement of alcohol.[54] Other obstacles originated in the metropole. Although foresters agreed that Taiwan presented a trove of natural resources, issues surrounding how those materials should be developed and their profits distributed remained hotly disputed. Litigated publicly in the pages of Japan's rapidly expanding print media, these debates raised the political stakes of forestry, forcing officials to think more carefully not only about their relationship with nonstate actors but also about how to frame their work to the general public. Every so often, as in the case of Alishan, they riveted public attention to a question of burning concern at the time: For whose benefit and at what cost should the Meiji state commit its already limited resources to developmental projects in the colonies?

Echoes of this question reverberated northward as well, toward the resource-rich island of Sakhalin, the southern portion of which became Karafuto Prefecture after it was ceded to Japan in 1905 as a spoil of the Russo-Japanese War. Endowed with, by one account, "inexhaustible forests," Japan's "northern treasure house" grew from a small fishing outpost into the center of gravity for Japan's industrial logging operations.[55] Following a wave of surveys in 1906, many Hokkaido-based logging companies hastened to gain access to the island's timber reserves, touching off a race for felling concessions across the island.

In their initial stages, these timbering projects more or less mirrored those found elsewhere in Japan. But following the discovery by corporate-backed scientists that Karafuto's forests were ideally suited for paper-product manufacture, an industrial metamorphosis was soon under way. Naturally comprised of thick stands of white fir, spruce, and other softwoods coveted for pulp production, Karafuto became the primary resource reserve of the then burgeoning Western-style paper industry. What started as a run-of-the-mill lumbering enterprise thus became in the 1910s a proving ground for industrial innovation. Harnessing new techniques in chemical production and state-of-the-art technologies for wood-pulp processing (modeled partly on those pioneered in the United States and France), Karafuto-based manufacturers began to ramp up the production of pulp, rayon, and other synthetic fibers.[56]

Foremost among them was the Ōji Paper Company, which tightened its hold over Japan's northern forests and with them the paper and pulp industry writ large. Thanks in part to the breakthroughs in mechanical processing systems, Ōji emerged as a trailblazer of industrial forestry, whose operations and output were outdone perhaps only by the Weyerhaeuser Timber Company across the Pacific.[57] Ōji not only churned out large volumes of pulp but also began to manufacture rayon-based fabrics, innovating techniques for the mass-production of chemical components that fueled industrialization drives elsewhere in the empire. To accomplish all of this, Ōji and its industrial managers constructed a sophisticated supply chain that linked fir stands in Karafuto to pulp factories in Hokkaido to distributors in Tokyo and beyond. Ever-hungry for pulp and profits, beginning in the late 1910s, Ōji set its sights on the forest stocks of the Asian continent. Through strategic mergers and oligopolistic business tactics, Ōji steadily enlarged its market position, as its supply chains grew in tandem with the empire.[58]

In Karafuto and Ōji, then, we see the emergence of transnational forestry operations that became vital pipelines for the empire-wide circulation of natural resources. Once viewed as sources of timber, fertilizer, and fuel, Karafuto's forests became reserves of pulp and chemical components that corporations could harness with cutting-edge machinery and new processing procedures. Karafuto thus offered many foresters a hard look at the capriciousness of the market, the protean value of wood, and the ever-evolving relationship between technological innovation and forest management.

CONCLUSION

By the time Japan had established a protectorate over Korea in 1905, the forests under the control of the Japanese empire stretched over 3,500 kilometers—and over twenty-five degrees of latitude—from Taiwan to Karafuto. These forests were not simply ecologically diverse; each presented Japanese foresters with a unique set of policy challenges, climatic considerations, corporate allies, and political constraints. Whereas forestry bureaucrats had viewed capitalists as essential partners in Hokkaido, they begrudgingly tolerated them in Taiwan and gave them free rein in Karafuto. Whereas they set out to open up land in Hokkaido, they prioritized the stabilization of finances in Taiwan and the extraction of pulp in Karafuto. Foresters were not oblivious to this variation. To the contrary, the range of landscapes brought under their purview underscored for many the fact that forestry methods developed in Japan or studied abroad were not universally applicable. It was accordingly incumbent on officials in each region and in each bureau to customize policies to the ecological conditions, governing structures, and natural resource portfolios found in each territory.

A number of forces nonetheless bound these territories into a common management framework. One was the marketplace. Forest resources found throughout these new colonial territories were channeled via railways and shipping lanes into a regional timber trade that grew in lockstep with Japan's sphere of influence. It was not merely bureaucrats who shaped these resource flows. The forestry outfits of transnational corporations were also enmeshed in supply and production chains that redistributed materials to meet the growing demand for forest resources.

Further fastening these forestry projects together was the common language of professional forestry—the cameralist approach to forest management diffused through the premier academies of Europe and taught diligently in the growing institutions of forestry education in Japan. More and more, Japanese forestry professionals operated within intellectual networks that spanned the empire and even the globe. Many of their conversations happened in private, through letters, meetings, and conferences. But their successes and setbacks were also regularly discussed in the growing corpus of trade publications, research bulletins, and popular journals that took shape around the forestry enterprise. It was in the pages of these bulletins that foresters hashed out how to adjust their approaches to meet the demands of colonial landscapes, including those found in Korea. And it was in the institutions of forestry education that lasting interpersonal bonds were forged, comradely associations that shaped the composition of the colonial forestry bureaucracy and greased the palms of the timber industry across the empire.

Blending, among other things, German theories, American technologies, French laws, and Japanese planting practices, forestry in Meiji Japan was decidedly compound in nature. But at its core stood a set of axioms shared among forestry professionals. Modern forest management was to be calculative, rational, and planned—in a word, *scientific*. It was also to serve a greater cause. A handmaiden to agriculture and industry, forestry was closely linked to the developmental agenda and fiscal health of the Meiji state. The language of forestry was accordingly couched in terms of national progress—and its inverse, national decline. While it fell to the forester to devise plans that would maximize yields, forest management was only as good as the society within which it was practiced. Japan's woodlands, in this sense, became a new arena of national service, a space where virtuous subjects conserved on behalf of the emperor.

This rhetoric was only sharpened in Korea, where denuded red pine landscapes purportedly prevailed. To forestry professionals such as Honda Seiroku, the peninsula presented an object lesson in red pine ruination, a cautionary tale of the failure of centralized forestry. To Japanese settlers and colonial officials more generally, the peninsula's "bald mountains" became physical monuments to Koreans' allegedly malformed environmental ethics. "Nothing impresses on the traveller's mind the feeling of the desolateness of the country so deeply as the sight of Korean mountains," went one typically prejudiced Japanese account. Fortunately for Koreans, it continued, "the necessity of revivifying Korean forests was especially keenly felt by the tree-loving Japanese as they came over to this country."[59] In this and other ways, Japan used its status as a "forest-loving" nation to justify its colonial occupation of Korea. Despite the fact that Meiji forestry reforms gave rise to countless bald mountains of their own, colonial boosters in Korea wasted no time in burnishing Japan's credentials as a conservation leader in Asia—a forward-thinking "first-rank nation," whose enlightened experts and industrious settlers would clothe the peninsula's red soil in green.

TWO

KOREA, GREEN AND RED

BY ALL ACCOUNTS, THE BREAKDOWN OF EARLY MEIJI-ERA FOREST governance was a product of the tumult of the times. This stands in contrast to late Chosŏn Korea, where problems in forest management had compounded over decades. Indeed, to scan the Annals of the Chosŏn Dynasty, the annual chronicles painstakingly compiled by the Korean court, across the nineteenth century is to track a slow but steady crescendo of concern with the peninsula's woodlands. By the 1870s, just as the Meiji government was launching its assault on the commons, calls for reform could be heard coming from many corners of Korean society, from military commanders anxious about warship repairs to peasants alarmed by siltation.

So it was not entirely out of the ordinary when, in 1874, Yi Yu-wŏn, then chief state councilor to King Kojong, sought the monarch's ear to express his grave concerns with the accelerating pace of deforestation. "Felling trees with an axe has become worse until at last there is no tree in the mountains," he warned, "and the only reason is that the laws and ordinances have become loose." Kojong in turn offered anecdotal evidence in support of Yi's assessment: "Because pine trees used to grow so thickly in the surrounding mountains in the capital city, we were not able to see the ground before. But they are so bare now that we can count how many pines there are." Kojong went on to bemoan how "the cultivation of pine was not so difficult until recent times." As Yi saw it, the clearest path forward was to further clamp down on cutting pine, aggressively replant, and strictly prohibit farming within the confines of reserve forests.[1]

At the time of this exchange, Kojong presided over a sprawling institutional aggregation of forest administration, involving Buddhist monasteries, military garrisons, village guilds, and state functionaries. Hardly the conservationist vacuum alleged by Japanese officials, the Chosŏn period (1392–1910) witnessed the growth of a robust system of forest administration—indeed, one of the longest-running systems of state forestry in history. Through edicts such as the Great Code of National Governance (Gyongguk Daejon), the central state established a network of "reserve" (*pungsan*) and "restricted" (*kŭmsan*) forests and proscribed a variety of woodland uses. By the seventeenth century, the state had promulgated a set of "pine policies" meant to provide a sustainable timber supply, especially for naval construction and national defense—issues of grave concern following Hideyoshi's ruinous invasions at the close of the sixteenth century. At the local level, meanwhile, pine associations, temples, and other village institutions promoted forest conservation and negotiated communal usage rights.[2]

What held this system together above all else was the red pine (*pinus densiflora*), a highly serviceable conifer that came to prevail across the forested landscape of preindustrial Korea. Durable, quick to mature, and able to thrive across Korea's variegated climate, the red pine was coveted by generations of administrators. As a means to cordon resources and control labor, the management of red pine was central to the expansion of the Chosŏn state itself—so much so that John S. Lee has aptly dubbed it the "Kingdom of the Pines."[3] By the late Chosŏn period, the red pine occupied a prominent place in the environmental consciousness of Korean society, a fact to which the art, poetry, gazetteers, and literature of the time amply testify.

Hardy though it was, the red pine—and the forestry system that grew around it—could not withstand the turbulence of Korea's nineteenth century. Some of the stress was demographic. Korea's population boom beginning in the late seventeenth century placed intense pressures on Korea's already scarce forest resources.[4] Other problems were ecological. Centuries of pine monoculture had undermined biodiversity in some forests, leaving these areas vulnerable to timber blight.[5] Still other pressures were social. The expropriation of woodlands for burial sites by elite *yangban* scholar-officials—a practice deeply ingrained in Confucian social codes—exacerbated already mounting rural frustrations with the ruling class, prompting many rural communities to harvest local forests lest they be seized.[6]

Such strains were only exacerbated after 1876, when Korea formally entered the framework of Western international law by concluding with Japan the Treaty of Kanghwa. In addition to granting Japanese nationals in Korea many of the rights typical of the "unequal treaties" upon which it was modeled, the agreement authorized commercial activities in three sanctioned port towns: Pusan, Inch'ŏn, and Wŏnsan. Not to be outmaneuvered, other foreign powers pressed for treaties of their own. In quick succession, the United States, Qing China, Germany, the United Kingdom, France, and Russia signed treaties with the Chosŏn court, thereby triggering a flood of foreign travelers, merchants, and diplomats into Korea.

If the arrival of these newcomers ushered in a new era of multilateral imperialism, it also spurred unprecedented investigations into Korea's physical environment. With the surge in foreign travelers came a steady stream of commentary on the Korean landscape, especially its forests. Missionaries waxed poetic about pine stands as expressions of the Korean spirit, while merchants appraised the commercial opportunities of lumbering operations in the Far East. Orientalist scholar-adventurers offered fanciful portraits of the backwoods, while government-backed surveyors filed technical reports on forest stock. What emerged from this rich mosaic of reporting was, above all, a narrative of environmental decline—the story of a once verdant dominion that, apart from old-growth forests in the north, had deteriorated into "bald mountains and red earth."

In her important study of French colonialism in the Maghreb, Diana Davis has shown how French writers spun specious tales of North African desertification to advance their expansionist agenda. "In less than two decades," she writes, "there emerged a colonial environmental narrative that blamed the indigenous peoples, especially herders, for deforesting and degrading what was once the apparently fertile 'granary of Rome' in North Africa." Fashioned from an assemblage of revisionist historical interpretations, sensational travel accounts, and distorted visual representations, this declensionist narrative was used to "rationalize and motivate French colonization" across the region. It harkened back to a bountiful past in order to (wrongly, as Davis shows) lay blame for environmental decline squarely at the feet of nomadic pastoralists. The job before French colonial administrators was to restore a landscape that had "lapsed into decadence under the 'primitive' techniques of the 'lazy natives'"—to seize control of land and resources that had been plundered by the unenlightened.[7]

Strikingly similar stories emerged simultaneously about the Korean peninsula, but with two key differences. First, in contrast to the fixation of the French on the threat of nomadism, Japanese in Korea heaped scorn primarily onto the Chosŏn state. Although they harbored many of the same anxieties about shifting cultivation, fire setting, and vagrancy, Japanese writers attributed most of these issues primarily to failures in premodern statecraft and its Confucian foundations. Second, whereas Europeans in the Maghreb had to conjure up images of a once fertile landscape from faint traces in the historical record, the Japanese needed only to look north. There, straddling the Yalu River basin, stood dense primary forests: physical testament to what the peninsula's forestlands supposedly once were and, with proper management, could again become. Japanese narratives of environmental decline thus promoted a dualistic geographical imaginary that cast the northern uplands as a forest Eden and most everything south as blighted wastelands. Either way, these forestlands were deployed as evidence of Korea's stunted national development. Lush forests remained in the remote regions of the north, Japanese foresters asserted, only because the Chosŏn state had failed to commercialize them.

That Japanese authority in colonial Korea rested on fallacious theories of premodern stagnation is a well-established arena of historical scholarship.[8] From ethnographic data to archaeological artifacts, knowledge forms of all sorts have been subject to careful scrutiny from historians mindful of how the Japanese carefully curated Korea's past in order to promote their own political agenda.[9] Only seldom, however, have these investigations considered how theories of Korean stagnation were shaped by concurrent discourses on the peninsula's climate, ecology, and natural history. Despite the growing sensitivity of scholars to the scope of the colonial gaze in Korea, precious little has been written about how "imperial eyes" set their sights on Korea's imposing mountains and forests.[10]

It remains, in other words, to examine how stories about the land—Japanese, Korean, or otherwise—were mobilized in service of settler colonialism. More than simply propping up Japan's symbolic authority as environmental custodians, narratives of deforestation and environmental decline in Korea paved the way for the seizure of land and resources. What were badlands to Japanese observers were sources of fuel, spaces of cultivation, and sites of ancestor worship to Korean communities. Wittingly or not, foreigners' landscape interpretation consistently emptied Korea's uplands of any indication of social life, thereby softening the ground for their subsequent enclosure. Just as historians should carefully discriminate between the rhetoric of deforestation and the reality on the ground, so should they consider how discourses on the Korean environment shaped the mechanics of colonial occupation. Whether by courting Japanese settlement to Korea or convincing Koreans of the value of Japanese tutelage, stories about the land were tools of expropriation. They shaped the contours of public perception and, in turn, government policy, making them a natural point of departure for any assessment of environmental rule in colonial Korea.

MANICHAEAN MOUNTAINS

As the oldest treaty port and trading post of Korea, Pusan formed for most foreign merchants, missionaries, and migrants their first window onto the Korean landscape. While many different facets of life in the coastal city captured the attention of these travelers, few failed to note the extensive denudation of the mountains surrounding the area. One did not even have to set foot on Korean soil to gain a sense of this deforestation. "The traveller who coasts, as many of us have done, along the shores of this Peninsula and finds only desolate, rain scarred hill-sides," wrote the American missionary E. W. Koons, "will decide even before he has set foot on the land, that he can dismiss 'Forestry' from his note-book with the single entry, reminiscent of the well-known chapter on 'Snakes in Ireland,' 'There is no Forestry in Korea.'"[11]

Some saw in this barrenness a deliberate ploy of seclusion. "Tradition has it that the Korean in his desire to maintain his independence," observed the missionary and educator Horace Grant Underwood, "deemed that he could do it best by a determined exclusion of all outsiders, and, with the intention of making Korea appear desolate and unattractive, he purposely devastated the whole coast."[12] But most sojourners simply viewed the denuded coastline as evidence of the failure of the Korean people to make forestry a national priority. Never mind that the lumber trade in Korea had historically targeted the coastline due to ease of transport, these foreigners wasted no time in extrapolating from their first impression totalizing assessments of national decay. The American polymath-turned-diplomat Percival Lowell put it most pithily when he noted from the deck of his steamer how "One's first idea of Korea is as of the spirit of desolation made visible."[13]

This desolation was no less visible to Japanese observers. Among the first to relate the deforestation surrounding Pusan to Japanese readers was the geographer Masanaga Yazu, who encountered in the early 1890s "bald mountains as far as the eye can see"—the result, he wrote, of the "absence of a forest protection system and the overcutting of forests."[14] Yongdusan, the site of a centuries-old crown forest just outside Pusan, presented evidence to contrary. But for most travelers this strip of green only sharpened the contrast. In the words of the settler and journalist Shiozaki Seigetsu, it offered in its rows of "old and rich evergreen pines an exceedingly pleasant sight for eyes that have grown accustomed to the dreary landscape of the bald mountains of Korea."[15]

Assessments of the scenery beyond the treaty port were bleaker still. To traverse the railway connecting Pusan to Seoul was to pass through what the American theologian George Trumbull Ladd called "repetitious" terrain: "Each mile, while in itself interesting and possessed of a certain beauty due to the rich coloring of the denuded rock of the mountains and of the sand of the valleys, which are deprived of their natural green covering by the neglect to bar out the summer floods, was very like every other of the nearly three hundred miles between Fusan [sic] and Seoul. Here, as everywhere in Korea, there was an almost complete absence of any special interests, either natural or human, such as crowd the hills and valleys of Japan."[16] To Ladd, the most notable feature of the landscape was not so much brown denudation as the red subsoil, a distinctive coloration brought about by Korea's granitic composition and the abrasion that followed torrential rains. Countless other travelers would be captivated by Korea's red earth as they gazed through the pinhole frame presented by this railway, the principal artery of the nation's still-limited transportation infrastructure. Even Terauchi Masatake, the governor-general himself, was dismayed by the "chains of bald mountains" he saw streaking by the train window when he first traveled from Pusan to the capital to assume his duties in 1910. He went on to identify this resource squander as a "cause of Korea's withering."[17]

At best, such commentary was prone to embellishment. Couched in an absolutist vocabulary of degradation, descriptions of the Korean landscape inflated fears of nature's collapse at the same time that they obscured Koreans' own traditions of forest management. At worst, these accounts were laced with bigoted assumptions about the moral depravity of the Korean people. To allegations of sloth, squalor, and servility that historians have long highlighted as part and parcel of the civilizing discourse in Korea, one must add charges of imprudence and profligacy with natural resources. As one correspondent for an American timber trade magazine put it: "There is no one [in Korea] who thinks enough of future generations, or has even faith in his own generation ten years hence, sufficient to induce him to plant and care for trees, except the few native fruit trees. The motto is, 'After us the flood.' He knows not and cares not for the future."[18] Similar rhetoric infused Japanese ethnographies of Koreans, which cinched ever tighter the association between deforestation and the low "cultural level" (mindo) of Koreans. In this sense, emerging narratives of resource squander in Korea must be understood as products of the unmistakably jaundiced eye of foreign commentators, who spotlighted deforestation early and often to subordinate Korea in the hierarchy of nations.

But ample evidence also suggests that the profusion of commentary on Korea's "bald mountains and red earth" was hardly fantastical. Well before King Kojong and his advisers were lamenting the capital's pineless panorama, Koreans across regional, status, and occupational lines had sounded the alarm about deforestation. Since as early as the turn of the eighteenth century, for example, scholars such as Yi Chung-hwǎn had decried the damage wrought by "fire-field" farming—a practice linked directly to the acute population pressures in southern Korea. By the nineteenth century, agricultural manuals and farmers diaries had begun to register steadily rising prices for all manner of wooden products. So scarce was timber that by the mid-nineteenth century even coffins had grown prohibitively expensive—no small matter for a society deeply invested in ancestor worship. Even firewood, that most essential of forest commodities, became exorbitantly expensive, with prices quadrupling in some corners of southern Korea.[19] This is to say nothing of the diminishing presence of ginseng and tigers in Korea's forests, flora and fauna, treasured and feared, whose fade from the historical record serves as a telling proxy of thinning forest cover.[20]

In the face of such overwhelming evidence, few Korean scholars, even those of a strongly nationalist persuasion, actually dispute that the late Chosǒn period saw intensive deforestation. Rather, with some important exceptions, most forest historians simply look past the nineteenth century altogether in order to locate the early origins of a Korean tradition of environmentalism.[21] The nineteenth century, as such, remains something of a gray area in Korea's forest history, leaving some of the more interesting questions about political reform, social unrest, and environmental change unexplored.

Why was it that, to borrow the words of the celebrated philosopher Chŏng Yak-yong, "local magistrates remain helpless in the face of this [forest] deterioration"?[22] Part of the problem lay in the gap between bureaucratic mandates and local interests. Decreed by governors, supervised by magistrates, patrolled by garrisons, and carried out by peasants, forestry projects in Chosŏn Korea were multifaceted affairs. Adaptation to changing demographic and ecological conditions therefore depended on the convergence of a wide array of local interests. The state's overzealous protection of reserve forests made this rather difficult. Where in Japan provincial stakeholders from lords all the way down to laborers had a vested interest in cultivating forests, the Chosŏn government's pine policies often introduced an unwanted burden on those tasked with the maintenance of an unusable resource. Furthermore, with scant local oversight and widespread corruption, Korea's state-forestry apparatus was unable to swiftly respond once problems had emerged. When cracks in the system began to spider, the architects of these policies sometimes doubled down on what they knew— hence Yi Yu-wŏn's appeal for even stricter prohibitions and more pines, essentially more of the same.

None of this, of course, was of any material concern to newcomers to Korea in the closing years of the Yi dynasty. Beholding these landscapes from the comfortable distance of a ship deck, train car, or urban enclave, most simply saw what they wanted to see. Westerners, for their part, were predisposed to look for confirmation of what had come to be known in some academic circles as the "Oriental Decline thesis": the notion that once-powerful Asian states, China chief among them, had squandered their formerly plentiful natural resources, thus hastening their decline. To Progressive Era Americans, the Korean landscape offered something of an environmental parable: "Long ago these summits wore God's clothing and were rich in forests, the growth of ages," set forth the trader and preacher William Elliot Griffis, "but exactly like the wasteful Chinese of ancient, and Americans of modern date, the Koreans cut down their trees, neglecting to replant."[23]

To Japanese settlers (whose numbers had swelled from around 15,000 in 1900 to over 170,000 by 1910), Korea's bald mountains carried multiple meanings. For Nitobe Inazō, the agricultural expert and influential colonial theorist, these treeless hills signified nothing less than the desiccation of Korea's national spirit: "The mountains are bare, the forests devastated, exposing the rocks they once covered with verdure. The exhausted fields no longer make a generous response to the turning of the plowshare or the sickle of the reapers. Worst of all, the energy of the people is sapped to the utmost. Gone is all the spring of endeavor. There is no incentive to exertion. Men sit in their white robes, smoking their long pipes, dreaming of the past, heedless of the present, hopeless of the future."[24] Drawing on the geographical determinism of the times, Nitobe emphasized how the grim state of mountain and forest had actively corroded the national temperament.

Others began to question whether Korea's degraded alpine features actually qualified as mountains at all. "Perhaps you cannot state that Korea is without mountains," wrote Ide Shōichi, "but mountains truly resembling mountains are lacking."[25] The journalist and later Diet member Arakawa Gorō was less tentative with his language: "Looking out the train window to see in all directions treeless, bald mountains and washed out and destroyed fields would give anyone the impression that Korea is a land without mountains or rivers."[26] In Arakawa's view, it was Japan's obligation as a rising power in Asia to show the Korean people how to restore the grandeur of their homeland. "Should Japan," he continued, "use its powers to make Korea's mountains and rivers, its fields can be cultivated and prosperity will follow."[27] Herein lies a leitmotif in the writing of red Korea: that only with the leadership of Japanese settlers could forests and the cultivable land they surrounded be reclaimed.

Japan's growing international reputation as a lushly forested country only threw Korea's deforestation into sharper relief. "It is not generally known that Japanese forests have been managed longer than any of those in Europe," went one 1908 dispatch from Korea to the *National Geographic Magazine*: "They were controlled before the birth of Christ, and during the early Christian centuries forest planting on watersheds to prevent floods was enforced by frequent edicts, and the felling of trees was supervised by officers of the provinces. As a result, Japan alone among the nations began modern industrial progress with its forests not only unimpaired but improved after centuries of use." The author went on to set Japan's forests in opposition to those of Korea and, especially, China, where "hills have been largely stripped clean of vegetation and the soil is almost completely at the mercy of floods."[28] Indeed, to Western travelers as much as Japanese settlers, Korea became something of an ecological foil to the green archipelago. "The peninsula," wrote Homer Hulbert, with its "bare-tops, which appear everywhere," formed an "unwelcome contrast to the foliage-smothered hills of Japan."[29]

Nothing served to render this contrast in starker—or more public— terms than the poetry of the Korean crown prince Yi Ŭn, who, upon completing his high-profile 1907 tour of Japan, opened a commemorative poem with the following line: "The mountains of Japan are green, but the mountains of Korea are red." Had it been penned by anyone else, this phrase may well have fallen into obscurity. But because it was released on the heels of the prince's much-publicized tour, where he was paraded about as a symbol of Korea's submission to Japan, officials seized on the verse. Over the years to come it was trotted out as evidence of the Korean government's failure to curb deforestation. Needless to say, scarcely anyone ever paused to consider some crucial biogeographical differences between Japan and Korea: the fact that Korea's geological composition made its mountains far more erosion prone than those in Japan or that its significantly older, more weathered mountain slopes facilitated easy upland access. In spite of the fact that the peninsula's red soil was a product of geography as much as anything else, it was interpreted almost exclusively as an expression of the twisted environmental ethics of the Korean people.[30]

Of course, it was not colors alone that alerted the traveler to Korea's deforestation. The smell of the smoke hanging over Korea's large cities and the searing heat beneath the floor of Korean homes also drew attention to customs that, some alleged, had accelerated deforestation. "All day long," wrote the British adventurer Isabella Bird Bishop, "bulls laden with brushwood to a great height are entering the city, and at six o'clock this pine brush, preparing to do the cooking and warming for the population, fills every lane in Seoul with aromatic smoke, which hangs over it with remarkable punctuality."[31] In this way, observed an American diplomat, "the Korean populace, to the number of thousands of old men, women, and boys, with hundreds of bullocks and ponies, are engaged in exterminating the future forests in order to provide themselves with fuel, of which they will not be persuaded to make economical use, and which they cannot dispense with so long as their present tastes and contrivances for heating themselves and cooking their food are not changed."[32] Described here was the *ondol*: the cooking-stove-cum-heated-floor system conventional to Korean dwellings. By highlighting the quotidian routines of Koreans—from rural children collecting brushwood to urban housewives setting it alight—commentary of this sort suggested that Koreans of all backgrounds were the authors of their own ecological demise (fig. 2.1).

Even as bald mountains had become, as one former official recalled, a "famous feature of Korea" (Chōsen no meibutsu), they were not the only physical attribute of the peninsula that fired the mind of foreigners.[33] For those daring enough to travel beyond the confines of port towns and the

FIG. 2.1 A "dead-leaves vendor" en route to market. (Image courtesy of Special Collections and College Archives, Skillman Library, Lafayette College, and the East Asia Image Collection, image ip0468.)

capital city, red Korea often gave way to a strikingly lush landscape. "Forbidding are the bare hills and inhospitable seems the land from a ship's deck," noted William Elliot Griffis, who was then feverishly lobbying the American government to pursue commercial opportunities in Asia, "but once within, the rich valleys and fertile farms reverse grandly the picture." "Looking like a cave from the outside," he continued, "it is like Ali Baba's crypt of treasures when seen from within."[34] The thick forests straddling the Yalu River were particularly arresting. "The commercial possibilities of the region," wrote the British journalist Angus Hamilton, "which lies between the Ta-dong River and the water-shed of the Yalu, are in the earliest stages of development. Much might be predicted of the returns which these new fields would yield to intelligent exploitation. Its groves of pines and firs, and acres of woods, recall the time when Northern Korea was one vast forest."[35]

To foreign eyes, Korea's northern forests appeared endless. One British diplomat described them as "of almost unlimited extent, [with] pine trees rivaling those on the banks of the Amur and on the opposite coast of the Pacific."[36] Taki Kumejirō—who would in due course acquire large tracts of forestland in Korea through his eponymous fertilizer company—was shocked to see (again, through a train window) seemingly "inexhaustible" forest in the region.[37] As they penetrated farther inland, Japanese travelers began to speak of Korea's *daishinrin* (great forests)—a term typically reserved in Japan for the vast woodlands of Akita and Aomori Prefectures. As one Japanese *Handbook to the Colonies* later put it, "In Korea, any mountain truly resembling a mountain, mountains with trees atop them, the place that makes Korea a true mountain country, all are to be seen in the north."[38]

Perhaps no one captured both the promise and the peril of Korea's forest landscapes more evocatively than Isabella Bird Bishop, who offered the following overall evaluation:

> The denudation of the hills in the neighborhood of Seoul, the coasts, the treaty ports, and the main roads, is impressive, and helps to give a very unfavorable idea of the country. It is to the dead alone that the preservation of anything deserving the name of timber in much of southern Korea is owing. But in the mountains of the northern and eastern provinces, and specially among those which enclose the sources of the Tu-men, the Am-nok, the Tai-dong, and the Han, there are very considerable forests, on which up to this time the wood-cutter has made little apparent impression, though a good deal of timber is annually rafted down these rivers.[39]

This passage distills the Janus-faced portrait of Korea's landscape that would emerge over the coming decades: Korea as a land of parched bald mountains requiring swift state intervention yet with vast old-growth stands in the north awaiting the timber industrialist.

It was the latter that commanded the attention of foreign diplomats and their agents in the closing decades of the nineteenth century. The ample pine forests of northern Korea, after all, offered more than merely timber. They presented a geopolitical foothold in the hotly contested region of northern Korea, where Russian, Chinese, and Japanese strategic interests converged. Situated at the nexus of tsarist expansionism, Qing borderlands, and Japan's "cordon of interest," Korea's northerly forests formed the fault lines of the geostrategic rivalries then heating up in northeast Asia.

TIMBER WARS

As sources of railway ties, mine timbers, and telegraph poles, forests sat at the heart of "concession imperialism" in fin de siècle Korea: the jostle between foreign interests for contracts to undertake infrastructural projects and harvest natural resources. In the resource-rich Yalu River basin in particular, Chinese, Russian, and Japanese proxies vied for control of Korea's timber resources. This contest brought a wide range of actors deep into Korea's hinterlands for the first time: from engineers to soldiers, laborers to woodcutters. It also elicited strong protests from Korean communities, which naturally viewed these efforts as a first step toward the seizure of local resources. The turn of the twentieth century in Korea thus witnessed a contentious negotiation of timber rights—disputes that culminated in the outbreak of the Russo-Japanese War in 1904.

While international hostilities over felling rights first arose as early as 1884 on the well-wooded island of Ullŭng, it was not until a decade later, following Japan's victory in the Sino-Japanese War, that timber became a flash point in concession diplomacy.[40] An early step toward Korea's timber wars came in 1896, when King Kojong, then in hiding in the Russian Legation following the brazen murder by Japanese extremists of Queen Min, received Iulii Ivanovich Briner, a Russian merchant based in Vladivostok. Eager to tap into the timber reserves around the Yalu and Tumen River basins, Briner pushed for exclusive rights for a timber operation in the north. His timing was fortuitous. With a substantial faction of Korean officials growing wary of the staunchly pro-Japanese Kabo Reform Cabinet, a number of conservative advisers to the king had warmed to the idea of a Russian buffer against Japanese influence. Much to the dismay of Japanese diplomats, Briner was granted exclusive rights to fell timber on the Korean side of the Yalu and Tumen River basins, provided that the Korean government retain ownership of one-fourth of the company and reap one-fourth of its profits.[41]

Briner's business acumen, however, outstripped his resources. Unable to raise the capital needed to implement the terms of his agreement, he had little choice but to sell off his concession, which, after trading hands with speculators, fell under the control of the Russian Lumber Association. Despite a surge of employees into the region, months passed without anything resembling commercial timbering operations—a fact that aroused Japanese suspicions about Russia's true intentions. The epicenter of the enterprise was Yongamp'o, a site near the mouth of the Yalu that, while far from the actual sites of timber operations, was of great utility as an entrepôt. In effect, the Russian Lumber Association erected in Yongamp'o an enclave wherefrom it could project Russian control over the region and its resources. Although much of the labor was performed by Chinese contract workers, it was not unusual for work parties to include Russian soldiers in disguise, who steadily expanded the network of Russian camps, roads, and even telegraph poles in the region.

Coinciding as they did with an intensification of Japanese efforts to acquire the rights to construct the Seoul-Ŭiju railway, the trunk line connecting Korea to Manchuria, Russian activities along the Yalu unnerved Japanese diplomats and merchants alike. At issue for some high-ranking military officers was the very security of Japan itself. If Korea represented "a dagger pointed at the heart of Japan," as one Prussian military adviser once suggested to his Japanese counterparts, then the Yalu River basin was its hilt. To protect Japan was to control the peninsula from the Yalu down—a point perhaps most clearly expressed in Yamagata Aritomo's notion of Japan's "cordon of interest," the sphere of external geopolitical control he and other strategists viewed as essential to the protection of the home islands. The Yalu River basin, in short, was where Japan's national security had to be guaranteed.

Emboldened by the Anglo-Japanese alliance of 1902, Japanese officials in Seoul and Tokyo set out to contain Russian activities. One way they maneuvered to do so was by acquiring timber rights of their own. In April 1903, Abe Junsuke, a Seoul-based merchant, pooled capital with a consortium of Korean and Chinese merchants to incorporate the Nisshin Gisei Kōshi, a timber company that quickly acquired a concession granted to three Korean entrepreneurs just a month earlier. He did so with the backing of the Japanese Foreign Ministry, which saw in the venture a potential bulwark against Russian operations as well as a ground-level source of raw intelligence.[42]

While Abe was supposedly serving in his private capacity as a businessman, a close inspection of company records reveals strong personnel linkages with the Japanese military. Blurring the boundaries between commercial operations and covert intelligence gathering were men like Hino Tsutomu, who took up work at the company only after he had conducted detailed military surveys of northern Korea. For his part, the timber merchant Taketoshi Kumatarō also maintained close ties with the Japanese Imperial Army, leading in 1904 a survey expedition into the upper reaches of the Yalu.[43] One need only note the steady stream of diplomatic cables regarding Yalu River forestry that flew between Ŭiju, Seoul, and Tokyo to gain a sense of the strategic interests that had coalesced around this venture.[44]

Heavy summer rains in June 1903 swelled the Yalu and, with it, tensions in the region. As a result of the deluge, unmarked logs that had been stockpiled by various logging camps upstream were swept into the river's currents, scrambling the sawlogs cut by Russian, Japanese, and Chinese parties. Downstream, hostilities flared as Russians began to plant their national flag on the drifts of timber they claimed as their own. Convinced that their competitors were claiming more than their share, Japanese merchants followed suit.[45] In planting their flags on the timber, of course, they were laying claim to much more than the value of its wood. These confrontations only escalated over the coming months such that by late 1903 the foreign press was writing of a mounting "Yalu River Crisis." As one American correspondent in the region put it, "It is over the Yalu River where the war clouds have hung blackest."[46]

SILVA INCOGNITA

It was in the context of these flaring regional tensions that Japan's first systematic surveys of Korea's forests unfolded. Although Japanese officials had by the turn of the twentieth century acquired a reasonable understanding of the composition of Korea's forests in a few select regions (especially those surrounding the port towns to which settlers and traders were mostly confined), they lacked a comprehensive inventory of the peninsula's forest resources. Travelers' tales of boundless corridors of bald mountains, though vivid, were of little practical value to military strategists or prospective merchants. Reliable information regarding the composition and value of old-growth stands around the base of Mount Paektu was difficult to come by. Especially scarce was intelligence on the market conditions for fuel, timber, and building supplies—raw materials essential to the growth of settler communities.

For these and other reasons, in 1902 Japan's Ministry of Agriculture and Commerce commissioned the first ever silvical survey of Korea: a firsthand account, based on months of fieldwork by a professional forester, of the composition of woodland across the peninsula. Such, at least, was the mandate placed before Tanaka Kiyoji, a seasoned ranger who worked in both the Bureau of Forestry and the Ministry of Agriculture and Commerce. Tanaka was selected in part due to his considerable service as a surveyor in Japan's largest state forests—an experience that indelibly shaped his own views on Korea's forests and their history.

On arriving to Pusan in early May 1902 Tanaka was joined by Miyajima Takio, a career official in Japan's Bureau of Forestry. Together, the two men set out for Seoul. Equipped with only meager geographical intelligence and hobbled by Korea's limited infrastructure, the going was rough from the outset. Their slow progress, however, gave Tanaka ample opportunity to take in his new surroundings. Two particular belts of deforestation stood out in this first leg of his trip: those on the outskirts of Taegu and Ch'ungju, both sizeable cities where, according to Tanaka, rising demand for fuel had stripped hinterlands of their forest cover.[47] Of particular interest to Tanaka was the preponderance of second-growth red pine—a pioneer species that (thanks to Honda Seiroku) had gained notoriety as a harbinger of environmental mismanagement.

Tanaka and Miyajima parted ways in Seoul, with plans to rendezvous in Ŭiju after Tanaka had completed his survey of the northern provinces and Miyajima his excursion into the Chinese side of the Yalu. After hiring an interpreter, Tanaka cut an easterly path through the center of the peninsula toward Wŏnsan. Along the way he encountered impressive stands of Korean pine as well as compelling evidence of local conservation efforts, most notably those undertaken on the grounds of Buddhist temples. But he also espied another unsettling feature of Korea's uplands. While trekking through the mountainous outskirts of Hoeyang County in Kangwŏn, he happened upon large tracts of scorched earth: the signature stamp of Korea's migrant fire-field cultivators who burned, cut, and tilled their way up mountain slopes.[48]

Without any meaningful interaction with these farmers or firsthand observation of their land use, Tanaka cast aspersions on the practice of shifting cultivation. Like his counterparts in other colonial forestry offices, Tanaka's knee-jerk pyrophobia blinded him to a more complex reality of shifting cultivation: that, when compared to rice production, it was relatively sustainable, adaptive to climate and soil conditions, and favorable to biodiversity. Offering little more than a cursory assessment, Tanaka was one of the first to stoke anxieties that Korea's mountainous regions served as sanctuaries to those clinging to a primitive way of life. Added to this were fears of insurgency, especially following the formation of "Righteous Army" militias after 1905. With many Korean resistance fighters slipping into the mountains, forest space quickly took on an extra aura of hostility. If it seems puzzling that Japanese authorities would just a few years later move so assertively to control Korea's forests, passing a sweeping Forest Law well before annexation, this early association between swidden and subversion offers at least a partial explanation.

As Tanaka boarded a ship in Wŏnson a few days later that would deliver him northward along the coast to Sŏngjin, he had yet to see for himself the bountiful forestland rumored to take shape along the Yalu River. Such sights, however, would have to wait. Shortly after disembarking at Sŏngjin, Tanaka was thrown from a horse and broke his arm, forcing him to return to Wŏnson, where he recuperated for several weeks. His hopes of exploring the great forests of the north dashed, he reined in his ambition and traversed a more forgiving route to P'yŏngyang. But even as he made his way north, denuded mountain slopes and burnt-out fields remained widespread.[49] That deforestation was so pronounced even in the northern provinces of Korea— where population was sparser and cities fewer—tempered his expectations. Still, the ready availability of quality timber streaming into P'yŏngyang from the upper reaches of the Yalu inspired confidence that the more remote regions under Miyajima's purview remained well stocked.[50]

Tanaka quickly wrote up and submitted to his superiors a summary report of his findings. His treatment went well beyond a technical appraisal of the forest; it touched on Korean geology, hydrology, demography, urbanization, and many other forces shaping the past and present condition of forest vegetation in Korea. Above all else, it reads like a dossier on deforestation—the sources, scope, and broader ramifications of Korea's denudation. Tanaka took great pains to highlight the cascading ecological and economic effects of forest depletion. As he saw it, deforestation spelled misfortune not simply for uplands, but for waterways, wet rice paddies, fisheries, and hence commercial and agricultural ventures across Korea. To Tanaka, the erratic nature of Korea's watersheds was perhaps the most acute problem raised by deforestation, threatening both agricultural productivity and public health.

Tanaka did not hesitate to assign fault for deforestation to Chosŏn administrators, who, by his assessment, had failed to regulate fuel consumption and regenerate forests. But unlike most of his contemporaries, Tanaka did not write off Korea's own forestry system. To the contrary, he exhibited a keen curiosity in the preexisting institutions of forest management, of which he identified five types: commercial, military, household, official, and temple.[51] Tanaka drew a sharp distinction between official forests (those designated for state use) and private forests (those under the ownership of individuals). It was in this crude bifurcation of woodland-tenure rights that Tanaka's assessment erred most significantly. For Tanaka was essentially projecting onto the Korean landscape the conventions of Japan's own Meiji-era national forest administration. His conflation of private ownership with common-pool resources obscured the considerable diversity of customary use arrangements. Likewise, his rigid framing of official forests failed to recognize how the ruling class in Korea had carved out of reserve forests private landholdings for themselves. Like any surveyor, in other words, Tanaka viewed the landscape through the lens of his own experience and institutional inclinations.[52]

So, too, did Tanaka grossly overestimate the extent of deforestation. After reckoning that the peninsula contained approximately 15,000,000 *chōbu* of forestland, Tanaka concluded that roughly one-third of Korea's forests contained some form of forest cover, while the other two-thirds were comprised of denuded mountains.[53] He went on to observe that while bald mountains predominated the five provinces of Kyŏngsang, Chŏlla, Ch'ungch'ŏng, Kyŏnggi, and Hwanghae, extensive forests could be found in Kangwŏn, Hamgyŏng, and P'yŏng'an.[54] Still operating in a binary mode of interpretation—green or red—Tanaka's account more or less corroborated earlier accounts of a peninsula composed of worn-down highlands but for remote pockets of primary forest.

That Tanaka remained so sanguine about the potential of the timber industry in the north without having seen much of it attests to the speculative nature of his account. True to his background as a lumberman, Tanaka waxed enthusiastic about the potential for the growth of the industry and the positive benefits it would bring not only to Korea but also to Japan. He supported this position with a number of bullish conclusions: that great profits could be reaped from timbering ventures; that little capital would be required; and that there was a strong market for timber in northern China.[55]

Although Tanaka's report was meant principally for his higher-ups in Tokyo, it would soon become kindling used by colonial boosters and bureaucrats to ignite interest in Korea's timber industry. This is especially true after Japan's victory over the Russian Empire in 1905, when Japanese access to these forest stocks was all but assured. Tanaka essentially reimagined Korea's northern forests as state-operated timberlands cut in the mold of Japan's own national forests. More revealingly, he turned the rhetoric of deforestation on its head. By stressing the potential that future reforestation works held for agriculture and industry, Tanaka cast Korea's barrenness as a prospective asset—an opinion that in many ways prefigured the greenification project of the colonial state after annexation in 1910. Such was but one of a number of ways that Tanaka's survey foreshadowed the principal frames through which Japanese in Korea would approach the peninsula's forestlands for years to come. His sharp distinction between the northern borderlands and the rest of Korea and his fear of the rippling ramifications of deforestation would all be echoed, if not amplified, over the coming years as Japanese officials set out to reconfigure environmental governance in Korea.

CIVILIZATION AND SYLVAN ENLIGHTENMENT

If some of the judgments put forward in Tanaka's report came as a surprise to bureaucrats back in Tokyo, they were hardly news to Korean government functionaries in Seoul. From Sŏ Yu-gu to Chŏng Yak-chŏn, Korea's scholar-statesmen had for decades debated the causes and consequences of defor-estation. Chŏng Yak-chŏn, for his part, went so far as to issue in 1804 a "personal treatise" on forest administration, laying out a detailed and ambitious program of reform.[56] By the 1880s, however, little had changed—a fact not lost on a younger generation of reform-minded *yangban*. Neither blind to institutional malfunction nor deaf to foreign commentary on Korea's bald mountains, these young scholars set out to chart a new course for forest management. This process only accelerated after 1897, when Kojong embarked on an ambitious modernizing agenda under his new authority as the self-anointed Gwangmu emperor. Hence by the dawn of the twentieth century a small but growing group of Korean intellectuals were deep in thought about the relationship between forestry, national strength, and the threat of impe-rialism. Champions of Korea's pursuit of *munmyŏng kaehwa* (civilization and enlightenment) and often members of nationalist study groups such as the Korean Society for the Advancement of Learning (Taehan Hŭnghakhoe), these men took to the pages of proliferating Korean-language journals to put forward plans for a new era of state forestry.

In their sensitivity to the far-reaching consequences of deforestation and their views of forestry as a pillar of industrial modernity, Korean reformers closely echoed the rhetoric of Japanese forestry professionals before them. Yi Chong-il, a member of the Great Korea Association (Taehan Hyŏphoe), deemed Korea's forest resources a vital source of "national strength" and called upon all "men of industry," not just the landed elite, to usher in a new approach to scientific forest management. "Among all the agricultural matters before us," he opened one 1906 essay entitled "The Need for For-estry," "we should consider forestry a most pressing issue."[57] Citing the work of recent scholars, Yi went on to describe how the Korean pine had been marked as a "tree of national decay."[58] Although he questioned the grounds on which the Korean pine was disparaged, Yi implored his countrymen to place forestry knowledge front and center in the project of "self-strengthening." Despite the fact that Korea had become a protectorate of Japan a year prior, he saw in forest management a path toward national liberation.

Ok Tong-gyu struck a similar tone, underscoring for readers of *Sŏu*, the journal of the Friends of the West Academic Society, the foundational nature of the forest for Korea's national welfare and technological progress. According to Ok, Korea's sylvan woes could be attributed in part to the fact that while the "direct benefits of forestry" (e.g., railways, bridges, homes) were well known, its "indirect benefits" (e.g., a stable and salubrious climate) remained gravely underappreciated.[59] In contrast to "the enlightened countries of the world that have made forestry a cornerstone of industry," he asserted, Koreans "cannot even heed the teaching of the [ancient Chinese text] *Guanzi* to plant trees ten years hence in order to reap only a minor benefit." This set Korea starkly apart from what Ok labeled the "forestry countries" (*imŏpguk*) of the world, those whose robust forests had nurtured among its citizens "a courageous and moderate character" and an "independent spirit."[60]

One need not strain to here detect the influence of Honda Seiroku, whose essays on forestry and national destiny found wide readership in Korea. With newfound urgency, Koreans were pressing for a stand-alone forestry bureaucracy, a forestry academy, and state-sponsored study tours of overseas forestry institutions. The overriding concern, however, was with large-scale reforestation programs. Kim Chin-ch'o, for instance, called upon his countrymen to immerse themselves specifically in the academic study of afforestation (*cholimhak*)—what he considered the "key to ensuring the supply of vital timber products centuries into the future."[61] Other publications on forest regeneration were highly practical in nature, with one offering readers a step-by-step guide to reclaiming denuded areas with cedar—a long-standing Japanese practice that, the author noted, promised to enrich Korea.[62] Conspicuously absent in these accounts were references to Korea's own regenerative forestry practices, the cultivation of which dates back to the early Chosŏn period.[63] Spurning centuries-old Korean tree-planting customs, these scholars advocated for regenerative forestry techniques that were rooted firmly in Western or Japanese forest science and whose industrial-scale efficacy appeared well proven.

For some Koreans, it seems, Japanese stories about the Korean landscape had begun to supplant their own. Even though Yi, Ok, and Kim may have advanced somewhat different programs of forest modernization, they all more or less accepted the premise that deforestation was a source of Korea's national weakness. Gone were the paeans to Korea's national pine culture. In their place emerged appeals for new approaches grounded in the spirit of Western scientific inquiry. As an Asian power that had successfully immersed itself in European methods—a veritable "forest country," in Ok's formulation—Japan offered a clear bridge to scientific forestry. Japanese stories about the Korean landscape thus carried additional weight. The power of Japanese declensionist narratives lay not simply in how they shaped reform measures or influenced foreign attitudes but also in how they prompted some elite Koreans to buy into the logic of colonial tutelage. Even if they originated in the biased accounts of amateur observers, discourses on red Korea had by the turn of the twentieth century led some Koreans to conclude, first, that drastic measures were overdue and, second, that Japan held the keys to rapid rejuvenation.

The establishment of the Great Korean Forest Society (Taehan Sallim Hyŏphoe) in 1908 brought considerable institutional resources to bear on Koreans' pursuit of sylvan enlightenment. A civic group in some ways modeled on the Japan Forestry Association, the organization unified government officials, reform-minded intellectuals, and community leaders behind its mission to disseminate best practices in forest management.[64] Heading up its creation was the government minister Yi Yŏng-ha, who envisioned a grassroots organization through which Koreans could improve the material conditions of life in the peninsula. Revealingly, Yi openly lamented the fact that the first "impression of foreigners upon their arrival to Korea was one of degradation," and he used this point to drive home the need to swiftly move forward with afforestation.[65] To do so, he solicited the assistance of Japanese settler leaders like Matsushita Makio and the growing cadre of professional foresters staffing the recently established forestry office of the Residency General. Insofar as the Society worked to advance a set of goals that neatly aligned with the content of the Forest Law codified in 1908, it presented Japanese officials with a group of enthusiastic Korean partners who could help shepherd through these reforms at the local level.

If the Society set out to popularize the forestry cause in Korea, the School of Agriculture and Forestry (Nongnim Hakkyo), established in 1906, sought to train a new corps of Korean forestry professionals. This was not the first attempt by the Korean government to improve education in agriculture. As early as the 1890s, Chosŏn officials had established a model farm and agronomic research institute on the outskirts of Seoul. But the program initiated in 1906 marked the first major effort to train Koreans specifically in the tenets of scientific forest management. Created by the Korean Bureau of Agriculture and Commerce, the school recruited an initial class of twelve students with the goal of grooming technical specialists, especially those who could staff the nurseries needed for reforestation projects.

Instruction in the basic principles of forest management became considerably easier in 1909 with the publication of a Korean-language translation of a widely used Japanese forestry textbook. Entitled *The Latest in Forestry* (*Ch'oesin samnimhak*), its six chapters promised readers comprehensive practical guidance, including tutorials on surveying, thinning, and pest control. The textbook began, however, with a crash course in global forest history. In essence, it offered two contrasting narratives of forest history—one perilous, the other progressive. The cautionary tale came from the civilizations of Asia Minor, India, and China, where, according to the textbook, "the industry of forest cultivation and lumbering had once flourished," but officials had failed to "develop the regulations of forest management to compensate for consumption."[66] The result was deforestation and decline that was still reflected in their landscapes.

If, as Andre Schmid has argued, Korean nationalist thinkers in the closing years of the Chosŏn period pivoted away from China—what had long been for the Korean court the center of political and cultural gravity—severe deforestation in the "middle Kingdom" gave further impetus to a turn to the West and, especially, Japan. Channeling Western concerns about the "Confucian torpor" that had accelerated "Oriental decline" in China, some Koreans saw in China's forests yet another indication of "the changing winds of civilization."[67] According to *The Latest in Forestry*, the new model was to come, predictably enough, from France and Germany, countries that had early recognized the costs of deforestation and pioneered legal and managerial systems that made forest conservation an instrument of statecraft. The textbook cited statutes such as France's 1669 Colbert Ordinance as evidence of the forward-thinking values that paved the way to sustainable forestry and, by extension, national greatness.[68]

Such reasoning contributed to the perception in some elite corners of Korean society that forestry was not only a pressing matter of modernization but also a yardstick of national progress. "'Land of bald mountains, land of red earth'—this is usually how people who have been to Korea describe it in their travel accounts," observed the Korean essayist Chang

Hyŏk-chu decades into colonial rule. "These descriptions," he continued, "suggest its poverty and its degeneration. Seeing Korean farmers with long pipes in their mouths and working at a leisurely pace, they call the Koreans a lazy race."[69] Although only a handful of Korean writers would match Chang's pro-Japanese inclinations, few would have disputed the notion that bald mountains had acquired new symbolic resonance as icons to Korea's national decay.

We should be careful not to overstate the reach of these early environmental discourses. For most literate Koreans, their only real exposure to forestry matters came through Korean-language daily newspapers and a few select journals. This is especially true for urbanites, whose interest in forest policy began and ended with a single issue: fuel. For the roughly 80 percent of Korean society residing in the countryside, meanwhile, these early discussions of forestry reform hardly registered. This did not leave farmers entirely oblivious to the fact that shifts in forest management were close at hand. In some rural communities, the sudden appearance of caliper-wielding forest surveyors offered hints that major changes to woodland access were on the horizon. So began a nettlesome effort to fix the boundaries of forest ownership—a campaign of woodland-tenure reform in many ways premised on enduring narratives of native despoilment.

CONCLUSION

Many different narrative threads on the Korean landscape were woven into the thick tapestry of commentary put forward by foreign travelers, surveyors, and settlers in the decades straddling 1900. Undoubtedly, the most common image of Korea was one of debasement—a godforsaken land where lush forests had ceded to fire fields, where farmers raked up fuel with impunity, and where officials stood idly by. Insofar as it overstated the actual extent of deforestation and dismissed Koreans' own traditions of conservation, commentary of this sort was both hyperbolic and self-serving. It conflated rational responses to growing population pressures with the improvident nature of the Korean character. All too often, it also obscured the fact that foreign powers, including the Japanese, had a hand in Korea's late nineteenth-century deforestation, whether through commercial lumbering, compounding population pressures, or waging the Sino- and Russo-Japanese Wars.

The peninsula was also cast as a landscape rich in potential. In the south, this potential lay almost exclusively in Korea's arable lowlands: the fertile and abundant paddy fields that supposedly awaited Japanese settlers. In the north, this potential was materially manifest: the old-growth forests that clothed the slopes of Mount Paektu and mesmerized prospective industrialists. Korea's denuded landscape was also reimagined as something of a carte blanche for profitable forestry operations. Considered as a whole, these accounts put forward a portrait of a landscape begging for state intervention—a once heavily forested country in need of a strong bureaucracy. Although diverse in coverage and tone, writings on Korea's uplands all more or less affirmed that forests formed a vital arena of reform. Before there could be increases in agricultural yields, rationalized tax codes, or even steady supplies of potable water, there needed to be an overhaul to the state forestry system. Put another way, in these imaginings and scientific renderings of Korea's mountains and forests, all roads led back to the doorstep of the colonial state and its newly created Bureau of Forestry.

PART II

REFORMS

THREE

RIGHTING THE WOODLANDS

FROM CIVIL SERVANTS TO CARPETBAGGERS, JAPANESE FROM ALL walks of life made their way to Korea following the establishment of a Japanese protectorate in 1905. Among them was Dōke Atsuyuki, one of the first Japanese foresters to take up work in the Korean government. Hired in 1906 to serve as an expert adviser, Dōke initially reported directly to Song Pyŏng-jun, Ch'oe Sang-don, and other Korean officials in the Ministry of Agriculture, Commerce, and Industry. His marching orders began to change, however, with the signing of the 1907 Japan-Korea Treaty, an agreement that effectively ceded control over the internal affairs of the Korean government to the Japanese resident-general. With each passing month, Dōke assumed greater authority over the day-to-day operations of the recently established Bureau of Forestry (Sanrin Kyoku), the ranks of which were staffed almost exclusively with Japanese appointees.

Although Dōke and his colleagues were no strangers to disagreement, their first order of business was never in question: the "rationalization" of woodland-tenure rights. Indeed, to many among this first cohort of forestry bureaucrats, the sharpest tools at their disposal were not so much the axe, saw, and lathe as the deed, register, and map. Newcomers to an unfamiliar administrative landscape, they sought an unambiguous legal system of land tenure that would allow them to proceed with the title transfers, enclosures, and market controls instrumental to their broader agenda. As Ishida

Tsuneaki, a career forester and onetime professor at the Suwŏn School of Agriculture and Forestry, would later recall: "If you ask why [we started with the Forest Registration Survey], it's because we knew nothing. There were no registers in Korea. Moreover, there were no other types of diagrams, and no sketch maps. This survey was carried out because there was nothing to work with."[1] So it was that in 1910 a small group of surveyors set out to inscribe a comprehensive system of woodland-tenure rights upon what many Japanese officials considered a topsy-turvy jumble of customary arrangements. In addition to bringing clarity to "long-standing chaotic disputes related to forestland rights," officials intended for this survey to yield "documents foundational to forest management in Korea"—plats, titles, tax registers, and the like.[2]

It is not difficult to recognize the immediate utility of such documents to bureaucrats in Seoul. A sine qua non of scientific forestry, standardized property maps were vital to the workaday concerns of the Bureau of Forestry—policing access, adjudicating claims, harvesting resources. Land titles promised new streams of tax revenue that could be used to, among other things, underwrite reforestation projects. Precisely demarcating property boundaries also gave the state greater clarity over the status of national forests, resource reserves central to the Government-General's developmental plans.

Yet, if we look past these surface-level justifications for woodland-tenure reform, an additional objective also comes into view: land-use control. Simply put, the system of forest ownership devised by Japanese officials served to bind Korean communities to the Japanese framework of environmental rule. In delimiting what constituted legitimate claims to woodland, forestry officials sanctioned particular forms of labor, modes of consumption, and institutional configurations. By the same token, they used the strings attached to property rights to proscribe certain behaviors deemed inimical to their agenda: swidden, overharvesting, burning pine needles gleaned from the forest floor. Ascribing ownership, in other words, defined not just *who* owned the land but *how* it would be used. Behind interventions in domestic fuel economies, the promotion of civic forestry bodies, or the finances of transnational timber companies—behind, that is, all of the topics examined in subsequent chapters—lay this complex and changing system of tenure rights.

It thus comes as something of a surprise that, for all the depth of English-language scholarship on land reform in colonial Korea, the place of woodland in this process has eluded scrutiny. To date, historians have maintained an almost laser-like focus on the cadastral survey carried out by the Provisional

Land Survey Bureau from 1910 to 1918. This preoccupation is explained in part by the fact that the cadastral survey determined the fate of arable land, a treasured asset in Korea's rizicentric agrarian economy. Efforts to assess the extent of an agricultural land grab have accordingly pushed questions about the fate of the uplands that comprise the better part of the peninsula to the margins of scholarly inquiry. We know, thanks to Edwin Gragert, that the colonial-era cadastral survey facilitated the continued concentration of arable land ownership within the Yi dynasty aristocracy.[3] We know further, thanks to Carter Eckert, that these continuities in landholding patterns were decisive factors in the accumulation of capital among a nascent Korean industrial bourgeoisie, the "offspring of empire."[4] What remains to be asked is how these developments correlate to tenure rights over Korea's mountains and forests, which were determined by an entirely separate set of surveys.

The simple answer is that to a degree unseen with arable land, Korea's mountains and forests fell under Japanese title. With the help of an elaborate land-lease system described below, foresters began to farm out the work of reforestation to corporations and capitalists, most of them Japanese. First through a series of enclosures and then through a flurry of leases, the Bureau of Forestry reconfigured erstwhile "public mountains" into the sites of intensive silvicultural projects that traded investments of labor and capital for ownership rights. In the process, officials upended customary land-use arrangements, depriving countless small landowners and tenants of much-needed forest resources. This disruption to common-pool access may have aroused considerable conflict, but it also enabled officials to redefine the grounds of ownership on their own terms. Gradually at first but more swiftly after 1919, a land-lease system undeniably stacked in favor of Japanese investors began to make room for bite-sized Korean claims—small land concessions that, in the long run, afforded foresters more influence over the rhythms and routines of agrarian life.

Pressing though it was, woodland-tenure reform was slow in the making. Owing to early missteps as well as peasant pushback, efforts to finalize the maps of ownership dragged on far longer than anticipated. Japanese foresters, in fact, trod a meandering path through multiple governing strategies, legal instruments, and registration procedures as they struggled to balance the dueling imperatives of state-led development and grassroots conservationism. At the heart of this balancing act was a host of difficult questions about the pace, scale, and sequence of reform. To what extent, if at all, should the process recognize customary use arrangements? How could foresters lean on Japanese corporations to spearhead reforestation while also recognizing the most basic material needs of agrarian stakeholders? How, in other words, could they forge a reasonably inclusive woodland-tenure system while also advancing the interests of settlers, corporations, and the state itself? In their pursuit of answers to these questions, the colonial state forged a distinctive framework for "greenification" that would animate forest politics for decades to come.

THE CHOSŎN COMMONS

Of all the puzzles of forest administration in Korea, few vexed Japanese officials quite like the "unowned public mountains" bequeathed by the Chosŏn state: the expanses of mountain and forest that had for centuries been communally shared and collectively exploited without any formally delineated system of private ownership. As few Japanese commentators failed to point out, these commons lent themselves to shortsighted exploitation. "In Korea," went one standard account, "other than special forests, there were so-called 'unowned public mountains,' the private ownership of which was not permitted, leaving them subject to free exploitation. This is a severe failure of forest management, resulting in the degradation of nearly all of these public mountains."[5]

To Matsumoto Iori, a Japanese researcher who looked closely at the history of woodland tenure in Korea, this "extremely disorganized system" of land tenure was the root cause of "hundreds of years of disarray."[6] If, as Matsumoto suggested, the civility of a society was proportionate to the sophistication of its land-ownership system, then these public mountains had impeded Korea's national development.[7] Any self-interested party could freely enter such a forest to cut down trees or collect brush, but obligations to regenerate these resource pools remained ill defined. What Matsumoto described was, in essence, a tragedy of the late Chosŏn commons.[8]

With the clarity of hindsight, it is not difficult to see how Korea's growing population pushed some of these public mountains well past carrying capacities. Setting aside ongoing debates over the absolute population figures of Chosŏn society, we can say with some measure of confidence that the seventeenth century saw significant population growth, owing largely to the stability that followed the calamitous invasion of Korea by the Japanese warlord Toyotomi Hideyoshi (1592–1598). This growth slowed but did not stop over the next two centuries such that, by the time of Korea's annexation in

1910, the total population was approaching thirteen million.[9] Concentrated as it was around the rice belts of Korea's southern plains, this population boom spelled trouble for Korea's public mountains. For one thing, it accelerated the pace of urbanization and the centrifugal forces of forest-resource consumption. In the countryside, meanwhile, the size of per-capita landholdings was steadily diminishing. Although some peasants adapted through agricultural specialization and labor intensification, others had little choice but to seek out livelihoods deep in the mountains, primarily as shifting cultivators. All of this meant that demand for lumber, fuel, and fertilizer was waxing as its availability was waning, resulting in fierce competition over forest resources.

Tellingly, these population pressures hardly register in Japanese assessments of Korea's commons. Far more interested in disparaging the Korean monarchy than evaluating the rational choices of rural stakeholders, Japanese foresters simply maligned these depleted public mountains as the cancerous outgrowths of a forestry system designed to perpetuate elite privilege. In their lavish building practices, their tax-evasion schemes, and their dereliction of silvicultural duties, they alleged, the Korean monarchy had propped up a forestry system that was all but destined to fail.[10] Conversely, to the extent that Japanese forestry officials actually acknowledged a conservationist tradition in Chosŏn society, they located it in the agrarian customs of the countryside. It was in the meetings of village councils and the charters of mutual-aid societies—decidedly *not* within the organs of the state— where Japanese identified a supposedly latent Korean spirit of forest conservation. No doubt part of the appeal of these rural institutions to colonial officials lay in their resemblance to Japan's own traditions of *iriai*, the customary arrangements within and across hamlets that had historically facilitated collective forest management.

But *iriai* was an imperfect analogue. Indeed, in their propensity to filter Korea's commons through the familiar analytical prism of *iriai*, Japanese were slow to grasp Koreans' own distinctive forestry traditions. This is especially true of burial practices, which had for centuries shaped the contours of woodland use and protection on the peninsula. Ever-mindful of Confucian precepts to lay one's ancestors to rest in geomantically propitious sites on hillsides or in forests, Korean families had long interred the departed in swatches of woodland, where they created and meticulously maintained burial mounds. Family trees in the truest sense, these so-called "tomb forests" were the sites of protection regimes that sometimes spanned five or more generations. "There is no need to rehash how Korea's forests have since long ago been damaged by reckless felling," wrote the Korean agroforestry expert Yi Hang-jyun in one detailed survey of funerary rites. "However," he continued, "one cannot forget that, even in a place well known for its bald mountains and bare hills, there are also localized concentrations of thick, beautiful forest."[11] Wherever there was a burial mound, he explained, there had been prolonged and proactive forest stewardship. While some Japanese officials dismissed these forest patches as proof only of Koreans' continued devotion to outmoded Confucian ideas, others saw in customs of tomb maintenance the sprouts of grassroots conservationism.[12]

Although it would be years before Japanese officials would realize it, these burial practices had produced a trail of litigation invaluable to their agenda.[13] For as much as tomb forests had nurtured local protection, they also generated social conflict. Despite early injunctions by the Chosŏn state against the private ownership of woodlands, court officials made exceptions for royal family members (and, later, their own ranks) to cordon off land for burial sites. This quite naturally led to a spike in legal disputes over tenure rights as different parties, especially *yangban* families and their descent groups, sought to protect ancestral burial grounds against countering claims. Historians have accordingly dubbed the late Chosŏn period the "age of mountain lawsuits" (*sansong sidae*). Court records of the time indeed teem with references to clashes over burial mounds and the trees surrounding them—a documentary legacy that would resurface as Koreans of all backgrounds vied for recognition from the colonial government of their earlier claims to the land.[14]

If foresters were slow to appreciate the import of Korean burial practices, the opposite was true of pine associations, or *songgye*. Essentially self-governing mutual-aid organizations, pine associations had proliferated over the late Chosŏn period in response to the de facto privatization of woodland by the ruling class. Although scattered in coverage and inconsistent in their mandate, they often provided effective regulatory oversight of common-pool resources. Foremost among their duties was the enforcement of annual quotas for fuel collection and timber felling. To do so, *songgye* typically required members of each participating village to serve on a rotating basis as forest patrols. Anyone caught in violation of pine association bylaws—be they shaking needles from trees, lighting fires in the dry season, or conspiring with woodcutters—was subject to harsh penalties, usually involving some combination of lashings and fines. More broadly, *songgye* also functioned as collective labor pools that could be mobilized at a moment's notice in order to, say, put out a fire or pull up blighted trees. Although Japanese foresters were rightly concerned with the extent to which they prioritized the protection and regeneration of red pine (to the detriment of ecological resilience), policymakers were deeply impressed by their track record. They saw in *songgye* both the spirit and substance of *iriai*, and they wasted no time in strategizing how to co-opt them into their civic forestry agenda (the subject of chapter 6).[15]

Still, while Japanese woodsmen might debate the merits of *songgye* or marvel at tomb forests, hardly anyone disputed that a comprehensive overhaul to the system of woodland tenure was in order. The incidence of summer floods, as reliable as they were destructive, offered all the evidence foresters needed that major reforms were overdue. Tax officials, agronomists, and financiers also envisaged land-tenure reform as the first step toward a free-market capitalist system in which woodland and forest products could be bought and sold as commodities across the empire and beyond. Particularly emphatic were those calling for forestry reforms as a means to shore up district- and province-level tax collection. That Megata Tanetarō, a financial adviser charged with the revitalization of the Korean government's coffers, was among the first to request that forestry advisers be sent to Korea bespeaks the perception that forestry was closely entwined with financial improvement.[16] It was in the context of these larger dialogues about the revitalization of Korea's economy that Japanese debates over forest policy first took shape.

THE FOREST LAW

No sooner had the Korean government opened a policy section within the Bureau of Forestry in 1907 than Dōke Atsuyuki and Oka Eiji set to work to draft a new legal framework for woodland ownership. Their guiding principle was the realization of "one plot, one tenant," a maxim that had gained currency during Japan's own land reforms decades earlier. The fruit of their labor came with the passage in 1908 of the Forest Law (Shinrinhō), the legal rootstock of forestry in twentieth-century Korea. Besides enacting a forest penal code, the law conferred on Korea's Bureau of Agriculture, Commerce, and Industry sweeping authority to enclose as "reserve forest" any area requiring state protection. The law set forth a threefold criterion for the designation of reserve forests: historical preservation, the development of industrial projects, and military operations. Such broad parameters effectively empowered Japanese officials to close off whatever former public mountains and crown forests they pleased.

The Forest Law also made provisions for multiparty, or "shared yield," arrangements meant to lure nongovernment actors into the reclamation of Korea's forests. Modeled on the Japanese practice of *buwakebayashi*, a silvicultural scheme dating back to the Tokugawa period, this system enabled individuals, corporations, or partnerships to assume control over the management of national forestland through a profit-sharing agreement. Any party that entered into such an agreement was entitled to a predetermined share of income generated through the enterprise. Crucially, however, the state retained ownership of the land. This approach was to many Japanese officials a simple, time-tested way to shift part of the financial burden of forest reclamation to corporations capable of tackling large-scale projects. The first to seize this opportunity was the Pusan-based merchant Hazama Fusatarō, who in 1908 acquired the rights to undertake forestry work on Yŏngdo Island, just off the coast of Pusan, in partnership with ten investors, both Korean and Japanese.[17]

It was, however, Article 19 of the Forest Law that had the most far-reaching implications. In keeping with the four-part classification of forestland established in Article 1 (imperial, national, public, and private), this clause created a forestland-ownership registration process requiring all forestland owners to "submit within three years of the day of the passage of this law a land register, land area calculation, and sketch map to the Ministry of Agriculture, Commerce, and Industry."[18] All woods that were not registered within the allotted window, the law continued, "will automatically be designated national forest." The language was simple but the consequences profound: anyone who sought to assert a claim to private forestland—be it a smallholder, an aristocrat, or anyone in between—had to furnish documentation.

This was an exacting demand. Although the promulgation of the Forest Law was followed by a coordinated public relations campaign to inform Korean communities of its content, aims, and requirements, many households lacked the required documentation or were simply unaware of the specific land registration provision.[19] Others mistakenly assumed the process was part of a new land tax to be levied on forestland and thus avoided it altogether. Even among those Koreans who were fully aware of the registration requirements, only a small percentage had the financial wherewithal to survey their own land in order to meet the Government-General's standards of documentation. As one editorial in the *Korea Daily News* (Taehan maeil sinbo) pointed out, the survey could cost as much as ¥400 for large parcels of forestland—often four times as much as the value of what the land itself could produce.[20] For many farming households, surveying was simply out of the question.

The timing of this woodland-registration process is also significant, for it virtually ensured that the handling of claims to forest and arable land would proceed along two separate tracks, each with its own agencies and regulations. In their haste to fix the boundaries of woodland ownership, forestry officials foreclosed any possibility of coordination with the much larger and better-staffed cadastral land survey (1910–18). The irregularity between these twin tracks not only sowed confusion but also caused considerable friction in the countryside. Many landholders went to great trouble to gain title to paddy lands and dry fields through the cadastral survey only to watch disputes over the tenure rights of surrounding watersheds stretch out into the 1930s. To many Koreans, this aggressive initial posture toward woodland registration also reeked of duplicity. When a master narrative of Japanese forest exploitation began to take shape after 1945, scholars in both Koreas would point directly to this early gambit as evidence of a Japanese land grab.

The amount of land actually claimed by Koreans through this initial registration process was indeed small. All told, by the end of the three-year registration period only about 13 percent of Korea's forestland had been registered. "We expected Koreans to submit their land registers per the regulations [established in the Forest Law]," remembered the bureaucrat Gotō Hisaaki, "but because many commoners were accustomed to the longstanding system of unclaimed public mountains they seemed to perceive nothing of ownership rights. After two years had passed we had received only a small number of claims so our office ordered local officials to diligently inform [these communities] about ownership rights and, through the good graces of Korean experts, finally around the time of the annexation of Korea registers began to arrive in clusters."[21] The Bureau of Forestry's statistics more or less corroborate this account. From a meager 674 claims in 1909, the number of woodland registrants grew to roughly 100,000 in 1910 and thereafter surged to 520,000 by the 1911 deadline.[22]

Much to the dismay of Japanese forestry officials, however, the results were both geographically and demographically skewed. As one might expect, the lowest concentration of reported woodland ownership was in the ruggedly mountainous North Hamgyŏng. As eager as they were to nationalize former public mountains, forestry officials were wise to the risks of actively wresting these lands from aggrieved inhabitants, and in the restive northeast, it appeared, they had their work cut out for them. In North Kyŏngsang, meanwhile, they had the opposite problem: because dense settlement in the southeast had nurtured such a strong sense of tenure rights, the Bureau was now inundated with applications, many of them at odds with other claims. Most problematic of all was the fact that an inordinate number of those Koreans who did register forestland were absentee landlords, local elites, and their kin. With easy access to historical documentation verifying ownership claims and deep enough pockets to cover the cost of surveying, Korea's *yangban* class fared exceedingly well in the process.

By the end of the registration period, in other words, it had become clear that the process had failed to account for small-scale agriculturalists—the very parties who, in the view of policymakers, would make or break their broader plans for reforestation. If anything, it seemed that all the colonial state had achieved was to stir up the indignation of rural Koreans, who felt a wedge being driven between their communities and the forests to which they had long enjoyed access. As the Korean agronomist Hoon K. Lee would later recall, "To the many Koreans who failed to register their land [through the Forest Law] the Government is nothing but a hateful go-between who has deprived them of their property and given it to Japanese or Korean leaseholders."[23] At stake were more than material possessions. That many of the public mountains brought under state control were sites of spiritual significance—harboring everything from healing trees to burial mounds—only compounded the sense of heartless interference decried by many rural communities.

The rollout of the Forest Law, in short, threw into relief the limits of the state's reach. By late 1910 it was clear that warped woodland registration was more than just a public relations problem or legal snafu; it required a fundamental retooling of the process through which ownership boundaries would be drawn. The false start of the registration process came as a blow to many within the Bureau of Forestry, who were then eager to proceed with a host of large-scale reclamation projects. But these setbacks paled in comparison to the controversy surrounding the forests of Wando—what one official would remember as the great "failure story" of their tenure in Korea.[24]

THE WANDO AFFAIR

Few events thrust the world of forestry into the public eye quite like the Wando affair, a scandal over a timber concession on the thickly forested island off the coast of South Chŏlla. Once home to one of the Chosŏn state's largest reserve forests, Wando quickly caught the attention of Japanese fortune seekers. The origins of the controversy stretch back to 1906, when Katō Masao, a Japanese adviser to the Korean government, put forward a proposal to the cabinet to lease its forests to a Japanese merchant in Inch'ŏn. Almost immediately, his motion drew the ire of members of the populist Ilchinhoe (Advance in Unity Society), especially Song Pyŏng-jun, then the minister of agriculture and industry, who saw this as little more than a ploy to seize natural resources. The proposal was swiftly retracted and Katō forced to resign, but not before officials hastily surveyed the island and gave it a ¥1 million valuation.[25]

It was not until two years later, however, that the Wando affair began to unfurl. The catalyst this time was Etō Tsunesaku, a Tokyo-based businessman who, enticed by the siren song of boosters, sought to tap into new investment opportunities in Korea. In the fall of 1908 he traveled to Seoul, where he made the acquaintance of Oka Kishichirō, a top official in the Ministry of Agriculture, Commerce, and Industry. Later, at a meeting at the private residence of Dōke Atsuyuki, Etō learned of the fortunes that awaited in the forests of Wando, which officials, then eager to vivify the freshly inked Forest Law, assured him would be his to lease.[26]

With the completion of a follow-up forest assessment in December 1908, the lease application seemed on the brink of approval—until, that is, a journalist from the *Keijō shimbun* pulled the rug out from under the negotiations. As if the backroom dealings of these officials were not shady enough, the paper disclosed a glaring discrepancy in the appraisal of Wando's forests: woodlands that had just months earlier been given a ¥1 million valuation were being sold off for a paltry ¥150,000. It went further to level allegations of bribery. Other dailies followed with questions, speculations, and charges of their own. Overnight, a scandal was born.[27]

In the eyes of Dōke, who sat squarely at the center of the firestorm, the so-called "newspaper faction" turned a routine bureaucratic process into "a clamorous event."[28] But to the press and many members of the public, these disclosures unearthed evidence of insidious corruption. The *Taehan maeil sinbo*, the Korean paper most dogged in its coverage of the issue, blasted the "trickery" of the Japanese in their "theft" of Korea's forests.[29] Other periodicals questioned the moral integrity of forestry bureaucrats, especially Oka, who was pilloried in the press. Japanese settlers, for their part, soon joined the chorus of condemnation. Among the more strident voices came from Japanese business leaders in Mokp'o, who saw in Wando indications of how venal politicians were undercutting their own economic position on the peninsula. Not even Itō Hirobumi, the resident-general, could stay above the fray, as hearsay that lessees had greased the palms of cabinet members began to spread.

With criticism mounting, the Residency-General abruptly suspended the negotiations and launched an investigation into the matter. A thorough follow-up survey yielded an assessment of ¥300,000, a mere 30 percent of the initial figure. Officials chalked this variation up to the desperate measures taken by local residents to exploit resources before they were commandeered by the state.[30] All the while, scurrilous rumors about lavish banquets and personal vendettas fanned the flames of public anger. Eventually, journalists were also put in the line of fire.[31] Due in part to Ōmura Tomonjō's sensationalistic telegraph dispatches for the *Asahi shimbun*, which raised eyebrows back in Japan, reports began to spread that the Seoul-based journalist community had accepted bribes in return for burying the story of the pending agreement. Ōmura went so far as to suggest that Yi Yong-gu, a cabinet member and prominent member of the pro-Japanese Ilchinhoe, had bought off metropolitan officials during a visit to Tokyo, prompting the Ilchinhoe to publish a rebuttal.[32] Baseless though they were, these allegations set off a volley of recriminations between papers, especially the journalists from the *Taehan maeil ilbo* and the *Asahi shimbun*.

Although it would prove "difficult to discern in the final history of this affair any conclusive evidence of the commotion which it provoked at the outset," as one foreign correspondent put it, it nevertheless imprinted into the Korean public consciousness misgivings about the character of forestry officialdom.[33] It pitted different bureaucratic factions against one another—Oka (and the Ministry of Agriculture, Commerce, and Industry) split sharply with Kiuchi (and the cabinet). It arrayed different newspapers against one another—the Seoul-based *Taehan ilbo* crossed swords with the Tokyo-based *Asahi shimbun*. And at the most basic level, it matched Etō, who came to personify the greed of metropolitan capitalists, against local Korean residents. Few images better capture these fault lines (or the dramatized manner in which the press covered them) than figure 3.1, a political cartoon published in the magazine *Chōsen*.

For the Japanese parties involved, little actually came of the Wando affair, apart from some tarnished reputations and bruised egos. Insofar as it forced greater transparency upon the mechanics of woodland-tenure reform, it did continue to shape the work of the Bureau of Forestry. For Korean

FIG. 3.1 *The Wando Affair. From top left*: The *Taehan ilbo* newspaper faces off with the *Asahi shimbun*. Just below, the merchant Etō tramples over the rights of the residents of Wando. At the bottom, Oka and Kiuchi trade looks of suspicion. (From "Kantō mondai no shinsō," *Chōsen* 6 [1909]: 5.)

participants and observers, however, the Wando scandal had more lasting implications. As one of the first stories about the Japanese posture toward Korea's forests to reach readers nationwide, it raised suspicions about the true intentions of Japanese rule. *Was forest conservation just expropriation by another name?* Some version of this question would ring in the ears of Koreans for many years to come, and all the more so with the passage of the Forest Ordinance, the engine of the Government-General's reforestation campaign.

THE FOREST ORDINANCE

If the brief career of the Forest Law revealed anything, it was the poverty of information regarding woodland use at the village level. The line plot surveys and travel accounts of foresters such as Tanaka Kiyoji may have been helpful, but they were of little service to Seoul-based officials eager to understand local forest customs. With questions about burial rights, fuel economy, and documentation piling up, the Bureau of Forestry called for a new, truly comprehensive survey. And they knew just the person to oversee it: Saitō Otosaku, an experienced surveyor who, having researched charcoal production on the front lines of the Sino-Japanese War, was already familiar with the peninsula's forests. Saitō at first balked at the invitation, citing his duties in Hokkaido as an excuse. But letters urging him to cross to Korea kept coming, and in 1909 he relented, becoming a senior official in the Forest Policy office of the Ministry of Agriculture, Commerce, and Industry.

Saitō wasted no time in launching the Forest Registration Survey (Rinseki Chōsa). Errors and time constraints notwithstanding, this inventory yielded a far more granular portrait of forest quality and distribution than earlier efforts. Along with distinguishing more finely between state and private woodlands, it compiled information on a wide range of customary agreements and historical claims. Arguably its signal achievement, however, was the Korean Forestland Distribution Map (Chōsen Rinya Bunpuzu, a small portion of which adorns the cover of this book). Assembled by Saitō, the map delineates forest distribution across the peninsula and slots woodland into three types: stocked, sapling, and denuded forest. Two thousand copies of the map were eventually printed, which were distributed to government offices across Korea.

The survey also generated the first complete data set on forest ownership, calculations that would be repeatedly cited by forest administrators in the decades to come. In all, it determined that approximately 73 percent of the peninsula was forested—a proportion roughly equivalent to that of the Japanese archipelago. Of this, 47 percent was designated as private and 46 percent as national forest. The findings of this survey gave further substance to concerns that the Forest Law's registration process, which indexed only 13 percent of Korea's forests, was fatally flawed.

They also, however, buoyed the hopes of some administrators. Whereas previous estimates had it that as much as 80 percent of Korea's mountains was denuded, this survey determined that only around 25 percent was totally bare. "This is," wrote Saitō, "quite an encouragement with regard to forest conservation."[34] Such newfound optimism, of course, hardly registered in the stubbornly declensionist popular narratives of deforestation in Korea. Even though Saitō and his colleagues had come to a far more nuanced understanding of the composition of Korea's forestlands, the public eye remained firmly fixed on the peninsula's bald mountains.

Upon the survey's conclusion in August 1910, Saitō submitted to his superiors a summary report, *Opinion Regarding the Management of Korea's Forestlands*.[35] Much of the report was dedicated to a critique of the forest registration process, which Saitō viewed as a road only to future problems. But he also called into question the fate of the shared-yield approach to forestry development. Given the scale of deforestation, he reasoned, a system wherein ownership rights were transferred to woodland leaseholders upon successful reclamation—much as had been constructed in Hokkaido—might present a more expeditious means to reforest the denuded regions of the peninsula.[36] More than onetime profits, Saitō argued, it was the prospect of ownership that would stimulate and sustain future-minded conservation.[37]

His recommendation gained traction. By June 1911, a new legal instrument, cut in the mold sketched by Saitō, governed Korea's woodlands: the Forest Ordinance (Shinrinrei). Much of the ordinance retained the substance and spirit of the Forest Law. Its penal code, for example, did not radically depart from the system established in the previous law, while the Ministry of Agriculture, Commerce, and Industry retained its rights to cordon off reserve forests. But the inception of a system of forestland leasing for reforestation marked a significant policy shift. "If parties that have taken a lease on national forestland in the interest of afforestation succeed in the project," stated Article 7, "the Governor-General of Korea shall transfer the land to them."[38] Article 29 went further to establish that "any national forestland designated as protected in perpetuity prior to the enactment of this law is to be included in the land lease system outlined in Article 7." To facilitate these transactions, the Forestry Office commenced in 1911 yet another phase of mapping, the National Forest Distribution Survey, which sorted nationalized woodlands into two types: "reserved national forests" (those to remain under state control) and "nonreserved national forests" (those eligible for leaseholds).[39] The latter of these two was further subdivided into woodlands permitted for leases to third parties and those for leases to settle retroactive claims. This distinction was not trivial. For many Korean farmers, it determined whether or not they would be able to carve out a swatch of a former public mountain for themselves.

What emerged from the ordinance was a land-lease system that outsourced the heavy lifting of reforestation to anyone willing to plant their way to possession. Almost immediately, Saitō and other officials took to the pages of newspapers and trade publications to sing the gospel of reforestation in Korea. Not only was forestland being leased out at cut-rate prices, they proclaimed, but successful reclamation entitled the leaseholder to exclusive ownership rights of the land and any resources therein—timber, charcoal, fruit, fertilizer, or whatever else it might yield. They also took pains to highlight how the surplus of cheap labor and the comparatively light tax burden of woodland ownership in Korea cut costs appreciably. Apart from initial capital outlays, boosters maintained, all that was truly required of the investor was the protection of the land from fire, pests, and bandits.[40]

Statistics on these land-lease contracts speak eloquently to the immediate impact of this new approach. Whereas the shared-yield forestry system established under the earlier Forest Law gave rise to afforestation work on only about 4,300 *chō* of forestland, by 1912 this figure had grown to 12,533 *chō* and by 1914 to as much as 269,934 *chō*.[41] Thanks to the promotional efforts of officials back in Japan, conglomerates such as Nomura Forestry and Mitsui Holdings made haste to lease large tracts of forestland, as something resembling a "reforestation industry" began to take root on the peninsula. Especially tenacious in its pursuit of these leases was the Oriental Development Company (Tōyō Takushoku Kabushiki Kaisha, hereafter ODC), the quasi-governmental enterprise established in 1908 chiefly to facilitate Japanese settlement in Korea. Working through a forestry office created in 1911, the ODC leased 17,885 *chōbu* of woodlands, most of which was concentrated in Hwanghae and South Hamgyŏng.[42]

To scan a catalogue of the Government-General's largest woodland leases is to discover a veritable roll call of colonial Korea's captains of industry.

Many were well-connected settler leaders such as Kashii Gentarō (one of Pusan's "three men of wealth") or Taki Kumejirō (Korea's fertilizer tycoon). Their ranks also included some well-to-do Korean merchants and officials, including Pak Yŏng-hyo, the diplomat and later director of the Bank of Chōsen. Preponderant, too, were metropolitan-based financiers. Sumitomo Kichizaemon, then president of his family's conglomerate, acquired nearly 69,000 *chōbu* of woodland scattered across five provinces, while Imai Gosuke, the silk magnate and Diet member, leased over 13,000 *chōbu* concentrated in Hwanghae. If this land-lease system sowed the seeds of millions of trees, it also fertilized the growth of industrial capitalism in Korea.[43]

Corporations and industrialists were not alone in seizing these opportunities; a wide range of investors, institutions, and partnerships—both Japanese and Korean—tapped into these reforestation schemes. In fact, a vast majority of leases were much more modest in scope. As Kang and Ch'oe have shown, roughly 89 percent of 2,968 leases authorized between 1910 and 1916 were between 5 and 50 *chōbu*—a figure that suggests that, at least initially, the lease system was readily accessible to ordinary settlers, Korean farmers, and rural cooperatives.[44] Among them were men like Shiozaki Chōji, a settler based in Chongjin, who, together with four partners, leased in 1915 just over 124 *chōbu* of "nonreserved" forest in Puryŏng County, North Hamgyŏng. Over an eleven-year period Shiozaki and his associates planted more than 100,000 saplings on steep hillsides that had been previously overcut. Concerned with timber banditry and the perennial threat of fire, they also hired around-the-clock patrols. By 1926, Shiozaki had nurtured what was, by one account, "a beautiful forest" full of "high-quality stands."[45] A somewhat smaller lease was made to Yi Yong-uk, an entrepreneurial Korean landowner from Asan County, South Ch'ungch'ŏng, who acquired 106 *chō* of forestland in 1917. Planting more than 327,000 saplings of oak and black pine, Yi eventually transformed the area into "a dense, beautiful forest covering the entire mountain."[46] Such, at least, was the assessment of the Government-General, which never missed an opportunity to publicize—in Korea, Japan, and beyond—the achievements and exemplary figures of afforestation projects through a host of hortatory materials.

Needless to say, these publications were mute on the implications of these leases for Korea's ballooning population of tenant farmers and agricultural laborers. Having failed to register communally managed forests, countless farming households could only watch as the state enclosed, leased out, or sold off formerly unowned public mountains. "What the Japanese shall have completed [in] the process of grabbing these mountains," observed the political activist-turned-colonial-sympathizer Yun Ch'iho in 1921, "the Korean will one fine morning awake to the fact they have no more mountain to maltreat."[47] Many communities were consequently forced to purchase fuel, cordwood, and timber directly from Japanese leaseholders, often at steeply gouged rates. As Yuasa Katsuei relates in *Document of Flames*, a novella based on his upbringing as a settler in Korea, Japanese leaseholders were quick to "put wire fences around the mountains and build small shacks as police stations" such that "just to get firewood for their stoves in the winter, [Korean villagers] now had to go to faraway mountains."[48] Others begrudgingly entered into contracts with Japanese landlords that enabled them to secure a set quota of supplies in exchange for labor and patrol duty—agreements that created no small measure of antagonism across hamlets. Whatever the circumstances, the correlation between the increase in Japanese leaseholders and the growing resentment of Korean agrarian communities was becoming hard to ignore. The first decade of lease agreements may have broadened participation in tree planting, but it also exposed persistent structural inequities in land-tenure rights that, allowed to fester, could imperil sustainable forestry.

OLD GROUNDS, NEW CLAIMS

On March 1, 1919, just as the Bureau of Forestry was embarking on a supposedly final round of surveying to settle tenure rights, a paroxysm of popular unrest shook the foundations of Japanese rule. Inspired by Woodrow Wilson's notion of self-determination and emboldened by the calls for national liberation ringing out from Korean students in Tokyo, a group of Korean nationalist leaders gathered that morning in a small restaurant in Seoul, where they read aloud a Declaration of Independence. Although the document stopped short of alleging a land grab, it is not difficult to detect this sentiment between the lines. "From the outset the union of the two countries did not emanate from the wishes of the people," it proclaimed, "and its outcome has been oppressive coercion, discriminatory injustice, and fabrication of statistical data, thereby deepening the eternally irreconcilable chasm of ill will between the two nations."[49] In order to spread their message beyond Seoul, the activists also arranged for coordinated proclamations of the document in other city centers. And to great effect: what started as a small public display of defiance grew by the hour into a nationwide uprising, prompting spontaneous independence marches in hamlets, public squares, and schoolyards across the peninsula.[50]

The ensuing demonstrations came as a shock to officials at all levels of the colonial government, but they were perhaps less surprising to foresters. Years of work deep in the mountains had left forest rangers and surveyors finely attuned to the discontent simmering in different corners of rural Korea. As the face of colonial officialdom operating at the margins of state authority, employees of the Bureau of Forestry had become regular targets for the ire of disgruntled villagers. When compared, for instance, to the violent siege of forest surveyors on Pogil Island, off the coast of South Chŏlla, in 1913, the Wando affair seemed quaint.[51]

That said, even the most hardened forester could not have imagined the more than 1,500 demonstrations that sprang up that March, much less the coalition of students, farmers, intellectuals, and factory workers that took to the streets. This was the stuff of nightmares for colonial authorities. A bloody crackdown followed, resulting in the death of hundreds of Koreans and the imprisonment of thousands more. With international opprobrium growing and rural resentment still smoldering, the Japanese government had little choice but to moderate some of their policies. So began a shift to what became known as an era of "cultural rule," a turn toward a less nakedly repressive form of colonial governance. Restrictions on the Korean-language press were rolled back, more inclusive policies of capitalist development were introduced, and heavy-handed police tactics were reined in (only to be replaced by more subtle forms of coercion).

The March First Movement, as it would be known, spelled changes in the world of forestry as well. Of immediate consequence for foresters was the expansion after 1919 of Korean-language newspapers, especially the *Tonga ilbo*, whose journalists wasted no time in spotlighting the preferential treatment of Japanese timber companies and the harsh reality of the state's crackdown on shifting cultivation. Their feet held to the fire, forestry bureaucrats suddenly had to tread lightly in their dealings with Japanese corporations and their handling of itinerant mountain dwellers. This accountability lent new urgency to the problem of forest dispossession. Eager to soothe rural discontent, if not soften their public image, forest policymakers began to call for new measures to broaden the avenues through which claims to forestland could be filed.

Inroads had been made in this regard before 1919. As early as 1911, with the pivot to the Forest Ordinance, officials had attempted to rectify the biases inherent to their initial round of woodland registration. To do so, they built into the woodland lease system a set of provisions through which individuals, families, or communal organizations could retroactively assert their claims. This involved a two-step process. First, Korean "claimants," as they came to be known, had to prove, within parameters established by the state, a historical connection with a particular parcel of forest enclosed by the state. Those who met the state's burden of proof then had to demonstrate a "track record for silviculture" (*ikurin jisseki*) by bringing the quality of forest stock up to the state's standards. Should claimants be able to stock the lease to the point where natural regrowth (at least eight years old) or transplanted saplings (at least two years old) covered 30 percent or more of the plot, ownership rights would be transferred in perpetuity. All issues related to these claims would be settled through the Forestland Survey (Rinya Chōsa), a final step in the reconfiguration of woodland-tenure rights in Korea.

Gone were the unrealistic requirements for submitting land titles or costly maps. Instead, Koreans needed only to furnish evidence of a historical connection to a particular plot of forestland: family records, legal documents, or other materials that testified to a historical precedent of conservation. It was in this context that burial disputes from centuries earlier came back from the dead. For many Korean households, tomb forests were the clearest indication of conservationist precedent, making them key evidentiary exhibits in the claimant process. Particularly important to the letter of the law was the term kinyō (K: *kŭmyang*), a compound of the ideographs for "to prohibit" and "to nurture" that connoted both the regulation and regeneration of a given plot of forestland. Because it was so frequently invoked in connection with Chosŏn-era burial disputes, kinyō became in the colonial period a key linguistic touchstone in the adjudication of these retroactive claims. Such an approach alleviated, but by no means resolved, the problem of customary use: it provided a pathway for rural households to lay claim to small plots of land from the unowned public mountains to which they once had access.

By the 1920s, roughly 21 percent of Korea's national forests had been placed under the provisional management of claimants. Before any of these leaseholders could gain title to the land, however, they needed to demonstrate a capacity for stewardship, and it was here that the process was clearly stacked against them. In contrast to more solvent Japanese investors who could absorb the initial costs of reforestation (seeds, saplings, labor, and so forth), debt-ridden farmers often struggled under the weight of these financial requirements. The claimant process, as a result, had by the mid-1920s hit a ceiling. Although the number of claimants had increased markedly since 1911, the number of actual land transfers was not keeping pace.

This did not sit well with forestry bureaucrats, especially in the wake of the March First Movement. "In terms of both the stability of popular sentiment and forest policy, it is impolitic to leave [woodland] in its current state," went one official account, which underscored the need to "promptly sort out the administration of these [claimant] forests."[52] What was needed, in other words, was a pressure-relief valve for resource access in the countryside. By 1926, forestry officials had devised one: the Special Disposal of Claimant Forest Edict. Essentially a last-ditch effort to shore up village-level sufficiency in forest resources, this measure created a one-year window in which parties could apply for special dispensation for woodland title transfers. Between February 1, 1927 and January 31, 1928, the Bureau of Forestry received 114,053 bids for the potential transfer of 3,416,433 chōbu of woodland. After reviewing the applications, officials authorized the transfer of 2,773,256 chōbu of forest, denying only 14 percent of those who applied. The bulk of these plots—nearly 89 percent—were small parcels of 2–3 chōbu transferred to individual Koreans, with the remainder going to schools, temples, and municipalities.[53]

Although this measure brought a sense of finality to woodland-tenure reform, it remained to arbitrate the growing stack of petitions lodged by disgruntled parties—a process that dragged on for another decade. The nucleus of this juridical enterprise was the Forestland Survey Commission (Rinya Chōsa Iinkai), a panel of twenty-five arbiters drawn from the ranks of the colonial justice system. Those seeking an appeal were required to submit a written plaint to the commission within sixty days of the posting of the survey results.[54] Over the course of more than fifteen years of work, the commission reviewed a total of 111,377 disputes and retried only 462 cases.[55] Intriguingly, only a small percentage of these disputes actually involved the state. Far more common were conflicts between Korean parties, which often dredged up Chosŏn-era disputes over burial rites or tax evasion.[56]

Two particular issues mired the work of this commission. One was municipal redistricting. Because woodland-tenure reform had unfolded in tandem with the Government-General's push to consolidate Korean hamlets and villages into new administrative units called myŏn, the ambit of some former customary-use arrangements was rendered illegible. Even if households could produce the records required by the state, the contents of these documents sometimes had little to no purchase on the new maps of municipal governance. It thus fell to the commission to determine how, if at all, to honor claims that had been effaced by these administrative reforms.

Far more resources, however, were devoted to weighing the different forms of evidence brought before the commission. With the steady inflow of historical documentation—mutual-aid contracts, private correspondence, local magistrate reports, centuries-old maps—came a host of thorny questions about their authenticity and substance. Many cases in fact hinged on the interpretation of these timeworn records. Take, for example, the appeal filed by Kim Pyŏng-sik, a small landowner who in 1924 petitioned for title over woodlands in Gujŏng County, Kangwŏn, that, he maintained, had been protected by his ancestors for thirteen generations, dating back as far as 1531. To support his claim, Kim furnished fifteen centuries-old documents concerning local "mountain lawsuits" and seven related court documents. Although Kim argued that these met the state's standards for *kinyō*, the commission disagreed. According to their final judgment, apart from being difficult to authenticate, the records submitted by Kim did not sufficiently demonstrate sustained investment in the protection of the area in question. On this basis, his appeal was denied. Kim's was but one of countless stories of village politics and kinship networks that the commission resurrected and relitigated—a legal process that breathed new life into centuries-old conflicts over the commons.[57]

By the time the forest survey finally limped to its conclusion in 1934, the average forestland holding was 3.1 *chōbu*, an area that provided slightly over the 3 *chōbu* of forestland that, officials estimated, met the bare forest resource requirements of farming households. In the end, roughly 57 percent of Korea's woodland fell under private ownership—a marked expansion in woodland-tenure rights considering that just a decade or so earlier this figure was only 40 percent.[58] The Government-General routinely cited this trend as evidence of accommodation. In a turn of phrase that would be parroted over the years to come, officials touted these land-tenure provisions as a step toward bringing forestry policy into better alignment with "the sentiments of the people and the spirit of the age"—as proof, in other words, of the colonial government's benevolent management of Korea's forests.[59]

A closer look at the numbers, however, reveals a different story (fig. 3.2). Although in the final analysis Korean leaseholders vastly outnumbered their Japanese counterparts, the latter gained control over significantly larger areas of woodland per claim. As of 1934, 79,925 Korean individuals

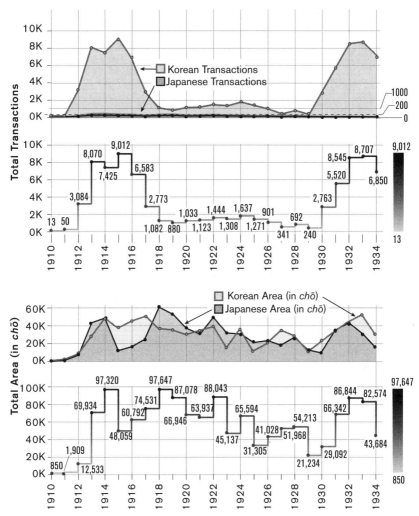

FIG. 3.2 Breakdown of annual afforestation leases. (Data from Chōsen Sōtokufu, ed., *Chōsen no ringyō* [1923, 1934, 1936], *Chōsen sanrinkaihō*, vol. 212; compiled in Hagino, *Chōsen, Manshū, Taiwan ringyō hattatsu shiron*, 63.)

had entered into lease agreements over an aggregate area of 720,001 *chō* of forestland. By contrast, only 2,448 Japanese had entered into these contracts by 1934, but their leases covered a total area of 642,118 *chō*. Put another way, Japanese comprised just 3 percent of those party to these leases, but they gained control of approximately 47 percent of the total forestland leased through this system.[60] Such was the subtle force of woodland-tenure reform—a long and tortured process that veiled the coercive mechanisms of expropriation and enclosure behind the optics of growth and renewal.

CONCLUSION

It is with good reason that many of the Korean historians who have studied colonial-era woodland redistribution policies have highlighted their discriminatory and even deceitful nature. Kwon Ok-yŏng perhaps set scholars down this path when he wrote in a pioneering article that insofar as the forestland survey became a vehicle for funneling land to Japanese leaseholders, it was an instrument of colonial violence.[61] In privileging Japanese capital, burdening farmers with unrealistic documentary standards, and drawing false equivalences with Japan's own forest management customs, the process was irrefutably fixed in favor of the colonial state and its partners. One need only track the steady succession of conflicts that punctuated the process—from local protests to national uprisings—to appreciate the strife it engendered.

But Japanese officials were not altogether indifferent to the needs of Korean farmers. How could they be, when so many farming households were left with little choice but to rake grass, strip bark, and collect branches within the confines of newly designated national forests? Wintertime spikes in illicit fuel collection attested to how agrarian stakeholders had been, quite literally, left in the cold by the colonial state's legal reforms. In response, bureaucrats at various stages retooled their approach to grant access, however minimally, to Korean agriculturists. Although they tried to dress the resulting claimant process in the language of goodwill, the impetus behind these retroactive transfers was much more utilitarian: the belief that those deprived of woodland access could unravel the progress of reforestation. Dispossession often resulted in displacement. A forest wrested from one community could mean fire-field farming somewhere else. To the extent that these small land concessions helped avert public attention from the huge tracts of forest falling under Japanese control, all the better. Regardless of the rationale, to forestry bureaucrats the clearest way forward was possession through plantation—that is, making reforestation the gateway to ownership.

Japanese officials in Korea were by no means unique in their commitment to reforestation. As the growing body of literature on "green imperialism" has shown, colonial states across time and space were attuned to the importance of forest regeneration, whether as a check against the spread of supposedly miasmatic diseases or as a means to provision sorely needed construction materials. Policy-wise, the reforestation measures launched in colonial Korea find a close historical parallel in French Algeria—a correlation explained in part by the fact that both colonies hosted two of the largest settler societies of the twentieth century. Both conservation programs rested on myths of native despoilment, relied heavily on metropolitan capital, and were animated by pervasive concerns with agropastoralism. If, moreover, "the Algerian case reveals some of the darker sides of environmentalism in a context of colonial domination," as Caroline Ford has suggested, it is of a piece with contemporaneous efforts on the Korean peninsula.[62]

But the particular set of legal mechanisms configured in Korea to regenerate forests also grew out of the distinctive conditions of the landscape and the administrative challenges it presented. What started as a seemingly straightforward effort to impose a comprehensive system of property rights on Korea's forests proved a decades-long negotiation of burial traditions, rural institutions, and the ecological bequest of preindustrial forestry. In the process, policymakers fine-tuned a land-tenure framework designed to permit a bare minimum level of access to Korean farmers and afford a maximum degree of control to foresters. In tying land ownership to forest reclamation, forestry officials saw a chance to tackle two problems at once: to accelerate reforestation while also bringing agrarian stakeholders more fully under their purview. A land-lease system that hung the prospect of private ownership on a host of centrally ratified criteria for conservation promised to do just that. It provided the Bureau of Forestry with new partners in reclamation at the same time that it paved the way for new channels through which to shape ground-level behaviors short of overt force. Whether by enforcing silvicultural standards in the lead-up to title transfers or requiring freshly minted owners to join civic forestry associations thereafter, the architects of forest policy pressed village and household forestry practices into alignment with their own agendas.

Those agendas, however, were often less than clear. It was one thing for bureaucrats to enact legal instruments and flesh out maps; it was another to know how to manage these forests, in all their variety, once ownership status had been settled. National policy, in short, meant little without a handle on local ecology, and in this respect foresters were at the mercy of scientists. With industrial-scale erosion control projects under way, questions about the peninsula's soil, climate, and drainage gained new immediacy. With fuel replacement campaigns dialing up, guidelines for charcoal production were more pressing than ever. To bring clarity to these and countless other matters, the Bureau of Forestry turned to a small but growing community of forest scientists in Korea. Together, this interdisciplinary team of researchers worked to empirically ground policy debates in the material realities of the Korean environment—a project that forged scientific innovations and intellectual communities that reached well beyond the peninsula itself.

FOUR

ENGINEERING GROWTH

IN 1919, A TEAM OF KOREA-BASED SCIENTISTS PUBLISHED THEIR findings on Specimen 1 (fig. 4.1), a small sprout with big implications. Reared as part of an investigation into its potential use in reforestation projects, the Korean larch seedling defied expectations. By nearly every metric—germination, growth, and survival rates—the specimen outperformed other larch varieties imported from Nagano and Karafuto. In retrospect, this seems a rather unremarkable result: as a native species, *of course* the Korean larch would be better conditioned to grow in Korean soil. But when the results of this experiment went public, they caused a stir.[1] Through empirical measurement and dispassionate analysis, the scientists behind the experiment dislodged what then seemed an unshakeable conviction of many foresters: that Korean species were, by their very nature, inferior to those native to Japan.[2]

This trial alone did not entirely disabuse Japanese foresters of their desire to transplant the woody vegetation of the archipelago onto peninsular soil. Even as subsequent experimentation came to similar conclusions about the viability of other Korean flora, many clung dearly to visions of Korean woodlands cast in the mold of Japan's own national forests. They did so not so much out of national pride as practical concerns with the acclimatization of Japanese bodies in the continental climate. Flooding, drought, infectious diseases: these and other challenges to settler colonialism, officials claimed,

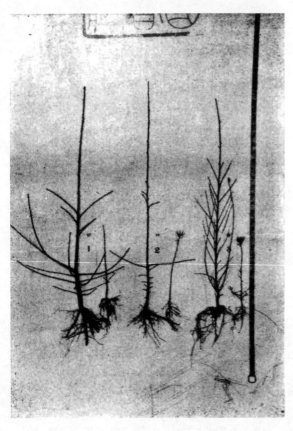

FIG. 4.1 Comparing the growth of three larch seedlings. (From Chōsen Sōtokufu, ed., *Jubyō yōsei shishin, Dai ichi-gō*; courtesy of the National Diet Library of Japan.)

could all be assuaged by transferring the best of Japanese and Euro-American flora onto the Asian continent.[3]

Such logic was hardly unique to Japanese imperialism. As Michael Osborne has shown, from Africa to Australasia "colonial settlers employed exotic species to renovate the biota of their adopted countries," making acclimatization nothing short of "the paradigmatic colonial science."[4] But whereas European settler colonialists for the most part relocated southward into sweltering tropical or subtropical climates, Japanese settlers were greeted just across the Tsushima Strait by a continental climate with punishing wintertime conditions. Due principally to the Siberian high-pressure system (known colloquially to Koreans as the "knife winds"), winters on the peninsula were both longer and colder than those back in Japan, save Hokkaido. Although life on the archipelago had prepared most Japanese settlers for Korea's summer monsoons, such was not the case with Korea's cold season. If Japanese were to "overcome Korean nature," as one settler leader put it, they needed forestry measures that would sustain fuel supplies and building materials vital to life and labor in the harsh continental clime.[5]

On the front lines of the effort to comprehend and thereby counteract the threats posed by Korea's climate was a growing cadre of Japanese forest scientists. A mixed band of biologists and botanists, eminent professors and aspiring graduate students, these researchers came to wield considerable influence over the silvicultural agenda of the colonial state. For no matter how well designed resource policies may have been, the management of Korea's woodlands rested to a large degree on the ability of the colonial state to respond to Korea's physical environment. The legal mechanisms devised to induce and monitor tree planting meant little if foresters did not know what they wanted to embed in the soil. For that they needed scientists, greenhouses, and laboratories, where Japanese and Western forestry practices could be calibrated to the biogeography of the peninsular context.

Such were the origins of colonial Korea's Forest Experiment Stations (Ringyō Shikenjo, hereafter FES), a network of research sites that placed Korea's forests firmly under the lab-coat authority of Japan's scientific establishment. What began as a four-man team of researchers looking at Specimen 1 grew over the 1920s into an elaborate apparatus of state-funded research branching into every subfield of forest science. This expansion and institutionalization of scientific inquiry both reflected and promoted Korea's integration into the Japanese empire of forestry. With close ties to international learned societies and metropolitan university departments, the FES became a major node in professional scientific networks that spanned Japan's sphere of sylvan control. Like its sister research stations in Taiwan and Karafuto, the FES in Korea facilitated place-specific research in an empire-wide framework. It afforded metropolitan-based researchers a new field of inquiry in which to collect specimen, test theories, and refine research methods, enabling breakthroughs in the colonies whose impact was sometimes felt across the empire.

If Korea's place as an incubator for new ideas about environmental management was quite typical of the colonial context, the extent to which its scientific resources were brought to bear on the state's reforestation agenda was not. Rarely have more scientists, more technicians, or more educators been so occupied with the applied problems of regenerative forestry than in colonial Korea. Although a diverse array of topics was explored at the FES, none garnered more attention than the mechanics of forestation. These issues were not merely scholastic. From the very outset of colonial rule, the laboratories and research facilities of colonial scientists doubled as seedling plantations and tree farms, where scientists put their research into practice to provision the state with the seeds and substances it needed to realize its plans. Forestry research thus operated in Korea with an immediacy scarcely seen in other colonies. Laboratory findings were scaled up and applied in the field such that these scientists actually had a material impact on the Korean landscape. Their research directly governed what was planted, where, and how—what might be called the state-imposed ecology of the colonial period.

Based solely on a reading of the research bulletins filed by the FES, it would appear as though this scientific enterprise was exclusive to highly pedigreed Japanese specialists. Yet, author lines and attributions tell only part of the story. When we look beyond research results to the collaborative processes behind them, the vital contributions of Korean scientists also come into view. Whether as lab hands or technicians, translators or field guides, Koreans played a major part in the colonial-era production of knowledge about the peninsula's forests. Their contributions were not nearly as ancillary as these job titles might suggest. They stood squarely at the center of some of the more consequential innovations in Korea precisely because they enabled the transculturation of local knowledge forms.

A critical consideration of the methods of forestry science thus elucidates a form of colonial collaboration seldom examined by historians of Korea: the uneasy alliance between Japanese and Korean scientists. However tempting it may be to view the work of forest scientists as value neutral, their research was not insulated from the ethnic discrimination, cultural tensions, and asymmetric power relations that colored everyday life in colonial society. It is not enough simply to acknowledge that Koreans were part of the scientific establishment; we must also, following Jung Lee, examine the "mutually transformative interaction" and "intimate yet remote" collaborations that set ideas into motion.[6] Only when we recognize the laboratory as not just a space of objective inquiry but also a microcosm of colonial society can we understand how science, technology, and imperial power intersected in Korea to inscribe a unique ecological signature in the soil.[7]

ISHIDOYA ET AL.

To trace the development of forestry science in colonial Korea one might begin in 1907 on a hillside in Ch'ongun-dong in the outskirts of Seoul. It was there that forestry officials, hoping to reclaim one of the more unsightly bald mountains looming over the capital, launched a trial erosion control project. To pilot the project they tapped Kobashi Shōji, a leading Japanese expert in erosion control. Working with a small team of assistants, Kobashi cut a series of terraced steps along the hillside, into which he planted a variety of trees whose efficacy in arresting soil was already well known: namely, black pine, red pine, and Japanese alder.[8]

Many of the seeds and seedlings used in this and other early trials were sourced directly from Japan. But sensing the need to provision future projects with the raw materials of regeneration, officials vigorously campaigned for the creation of domestic plant propagation systems. A considerable portion of the Bureau of Forestry's shoestring inaugural budget was allocated for just this purpose, breaking ground on nurseries in Seoul, P'yŏngyang, and Taegu. At each of these sites small teams of seed farmers labored to anticipate the material demands of the burgeoning reforestation industry.

But what to grow and how to grow it? These were the burning questions of forestry science in the first decade of colonial rule. To some senior forestry officials, the answer was obvious enough. Decades of field-testing and centuries of silviculture back in the archipelago had fostered a strong predilection for the use of certain species in reforestation works—larch, cypress, and cedar, among others. The geographical proximity between Japan and Korea also initially inspired (false) confidence that climatic differences would negligibly impact the growth performance of these species. Other Japanese foresters in Korea, especially those who had done their training abroad, enthusiastically endorsed the introduction of species preferred by their European counterparts, including American alcova, Douglas fir, and false acacia.[9]

Not all Japanese, however, thought it wise to proceed with costly and as-yet-unproven programs of biotic transfer. Indeed, a small but vocal faction of scientists harbored skepticism as to whether these trees would actually thrive in Korean soil. Differences in rainfall, soil mechanics, and seasonal temperatures were significant enough that the viability of select foreign flora was far from certain. The underwhelming growth performance of the nonnative trees planted in the pilot erosion control project at Ch'ongundong largely bore this out. What was needed were thorough investigations of the comparative utility of different tree species for forestry work on the peninsula. This, at least, was the position of Ishidoya Tsutomu, a graduate of the scientific agriculture program at Sapporo Agricultural College (the precursor to Hokkaido Imperial University), who moved to Korea in 1909, where he took up a post as one of the first scientists embedded in the Bureau of Forestry. Although scarcely familiar with Korea or its forests, Ishidoya, like many career-minded scientists, saw in colonial frontiers ample opportunities for professional as well as scientific advancement.

His lofty ambitions, however, were quickly deflated by the reality on the ground. Much to Ishidoya's disappointment, anemic budgets following annexation in 1910 downsized state-led forestry programs. Although the Forestry Section continued with its experimental reclamation projects in and around Seoul, other nurseries were mothballed. Not one to be deterred, Ishidoya decided to approach his superiors with a proposal of his own: that he pursue, with little more than nominal support from the Government-General, a systematic investigation of Korea's plant physiognomy.[10]

Ishidoya received the go-ahead from the Bureau of Forestry in 1911. But before he could proceed with his research, he needed to find the assistance vital to his labor-intensive plans. This was not as simple as it sounds. Qualified researchers (to say nothing of botanists versed in plant systematics) were few and far between in Korea at the time. Fortunately for Ishidoya, his search nearly coincided with the graduation of the first class of students trained in the incipient forestry program at Suwŏn Higher School for Agriculture and Forestry, an educational institution established in 1907 to "raise up trained men who will assist in effecting the progress and development of the agricultural and dendrological industry in Chosen [sic]."[11] Placed under the supervision of some of the Bureau of Forestry's most senior officials, students were immersed in basic sciences as well as forestry-specific skills.[12]

Although language requirements and entrance exams tilted the admissions process in favor of Japanese applicants, some Koreans also gained admission to the program. One of the first to do so was Chŏng T'ae-hyŏn, a native of Yong'in County, Kyŏnggi, who in 1905 broke with familial expectations to study the Confucian classics, as his *yangban* ancestors had done before him, to seek out schooling in Western science. Convinced that Koreans' poor faculties in rational sciences such as biology and physics had left it a "poor and powerless country," Chŏng set out to immerse himself in Western scientific disciplines rooted in "practical knowledge."[13] Even if embracing Japan's civilizing mission in Korea meant conceding the inferiority of his countrymen, he reasoned, it offered a direct line to Western scientific learning. Like many other young men at the time, he eventually made his way to Seoul, where he began to study the Japanese language. Just two years later, at the age of twenty-four, Chŏng was able to secure a government scholarship to enroll in the forestry course at Suwŏn.

Given that its forestry program was geared toward training technicians to staff the growing network of nurseries in Korea, Chŏng and his peers were put through a vocational program on the theories and techniques of seed propagation. The school was outfitted with its own greenhouse, bio-chamber, and model forest, where students put their theoretical training into practice. Much in the manner envisioned by its founders, upon graduation Chŏng took up work at a field office and nursery in Suwŏn. His stint as nurseryman, however, proved short lived. With Japan's annexation of Korea in 1910 came a restructuring of bureaucratic offices, leaving Chŏng with a pay cut and few other options—until, that is, he came into contact with Ishidoya.

Chŏng leapt at the invitation to work with Ishidoya, viewing it as an opportunity for advanced training rarely extended to Korean scientists. After joining the research project in 1913, the two men set to work building a rough-and-ready laboratory at Uiryŏngwŏn, just north of Seoul. In order to apply their findings outside of the controlled environments of greenhouses and grow rooms, they also sought and received permission to create a small experimental field site at Kwangnŭng, a forested area on the outskirts of Seoul that since 1468 had served as a gravesite for the royal family.[14] (Such were the origins of the National Arboretum of South Korea, a popular tourist destination and UNESCO-recognized biosphere.)

In 1914, Ishidoya and Chŏng were joined by Asakawa Takumi, who had just left a post in a forest reserve in Akita to follow his brother to Korea. Despite Asakawa's limited research experience (and rudimentary training in forestry science at the Yamanashi Prefectural School of Agriculture and Forestry), he proved himself an effective laboratory assistant and diligent field worker, making regular trips into rural areas to hunt for plant specimens.[15] Contributions were also made, albeit less directly, by Nakai Takenoshin, a doctoral student in botany, who, despite his armchair reliance on Korea-based collectors, made periodic research trips to Korea. Collaboratively, these men launched an ambitious and far-ranging research program that marked, as one Korean scientist would later put it, "the advent of experimental forestry research in Korea."[16]

One of their first major undertakings—and breakthroughs—was the experiment that opened this chapter: the comparative investigation of the growth properties of different varieties of larch. The bulk of their subsequent experimentation continued in this vein. Seeds and cuttings were collected (or imported), carefully grown in controlled laboratory settings (or experimentally in the field), and meticulously analyzed for insight into their germination traits and optimal growing conditions. As their data set grew, so did the case against the introduction of many trees favored by foresters back in Japan—Japanese cypress, Japanese cedar, and American catalpa, among others.[17] These efforts culminated in the 1919 publication of their *Guide to Seedling Development* (Jubyō yōsei shishin), a data-rich compendium of their findings. In spite of its technical language, the *Guide* became something of a field manual for nurserymen in Korea, offering practical guidelines on cultivation techniques, conditions, and desired outcomes. Revealingly, Ishidoya is credited in its preface as the lead researcher and Asakawa identified as an assistant, while no credit whatsoever is given to Chŏng—an omission all too familiar to Korean scientists at the time.[18]

If their collaboration raised questions about the universalism of Western science, it also inspired further inquiry into the mechanics of reforestation. Determining that certain plants thrived in carefully controlled laboratory conditions was not in itself all that helpful. For their work to translate into meaningful practice, it was imperative that scientists also attend to the methods through which different trees were actually planted in the field to achieve different outcomes. Doing so required that they pay heed not just to scientific principles but also to the practical constraints and everyday realities of forestry: cost, time, labor, available expertise, and so forth.

The experimental forest at Kwangnŭng witnessed much trial and error in this regard, but none proved more productive than Asakawa Takumi's investigations into the "exposed burial storage method" (*roten maizōhō*) for the propagation of Korean pine seeds. In essence, Asakawa fine-tuned a process of provisional seed transfer, whereby pine seeds were mixed with a loamy soil concoction, deposited in a roughly foot-deep hole, covered with an additional layer of leaves and soil, and left to germinate. Simple, cheap, and effective, the exposed burial storage method offered a highly practicable approach to seed propagation that could be easily implemented in the field, even by the most novice of laborers. By returning the process to nature, in other words, Asakawa freed silviculturists from the everyday burdens of seed farming.

On the face of it, his breakthrough appears a triumph of hard-nosed scientific inquiry. Through careful observation and data analysis, Asakawa seized on promising growth patterns and, step by step, refined his methodology. It would be a mistake, however, to attribute his success entirely to the scientific method. For though Asakawa adhered strictly to professional standards regarding laboratory procedure and replicable empirical evidence, the true source of his ingenuity resided in his sustained social engagements with Korean farmers.

Far from being cloistered in his laboratory, Asakawa took every opportunity to immerse himself in the Korean way of life. Unlike most Japanese settlers, he threw himself into the study of the Korean language. His fascination with Korean folk culture often led him into the countryside, where, in addition to seeking out plant specimens, he made an effort to interact with farming communities. According to one of his contemporaries, it was through just this sort of outreach that Asakawa was initially tipped off by farmers to the potential germination of Korean pine seeds through outdoor burial.[19] This suspension of judgment animated what Takasaki Sōji, Asakawa's biographer, has called his "philosophy of afforestation" (zōrin no tetsugaku): a frame of mind that viewed Korea's bald mountains not as wastelands begging for rejuvenation but as biocultural systems calling for exploration. To Asakawa, the job of the forester was not simply to methodically plaster these mountains with green; it was to understand how these biomes were intermeshed with the human settlements around them. Rejecting the utilitarianism of many of his colleagues, Asakawa worked to broaden arenas of scientific inquiry so as to better understand the links between forest and hamlet, nature and culture.

In this, he was not alone. Ishidoya, for his part, was determined to incorporate Korean knowledge systems into his research agenda. What good were ecological interventions, he reasoned, without any sense of how local communities used, valued, or ascribed meaning to forest and tree? One of the ways he went about answering this question was through an ethnographic survey of Korea's "great, old, and famous trees." Inspired in part by Honda Seiroku's own 1913 digest on Japan's "old and famous trees," Ishidoya spent three years compiling, with the support of Asakawa, detailed information on the size, ownership status, age, and location of roughly 3,200 different charismatic trees across the peninsula.[20]

They identified several different categories of preternatural or otherwise extraordinary Korean trees: spirit trees believed to harbor deities, prayer trees thought to govern the fate of local communities, and village trees that were focal points of ritual. As varied as the types of trees were the sources of their powers. Often, their genesis was attributed to a particular king, wizard, or mystic. It was not uncommon for trees of this sort to become the subject of spiritual observances: healing rites, fertility ceremonies, prayers for protection from natural disasters, and so forth. Also common was the practice of counting germinated tree buds during auspicious periods of the year to forecast, say, the number of floods or the yield of crops. Many trees were thought to hold healing powers, thus inspiring elaborate rituals surrounding births, deaths, and illness. Conversely, others were believed to bring misfortune or death to anyone who molested them. Whatever their power, these trees offered ample evidence of an alternative value system operating in Korea's forests. To Ishidoya and Asakawa, they stood as testaments to less visible forms of communal conservation—customs of woodland worship and protection that could not be easily dismissed. These trees drove home how the longevity of Korea's forests was not solely the product of physiognomy or climate; it was also the outcome of ritual practice and village life.

That both men would embark on such a research project testifies to the incredible range of research undertaken by foresters in Korea. Intentionally or not, these scientists muddled disciplinary boundaries, venturing as they did into the fields of history, geography, ethnobotany, architecture, and even religious studies. Neither Ishidoya nor Asakawa were formally trained as ethnographers or folklorists, but that did not stop them from conducting investigations of the spiritual landscape of rural life. Along the way, both men fused global ideas about botany, metropolitan standards for scientific inquiry, and local expertise into hybrid knowledge forms that pushed their research in new and fruitful directions.

None of this, of course, would have been possible without Chŏng, whose fingerprints can be detected on nearly every piece of research produced by his supervisors. More than merely a lab hand, Chŏng was an interpreter of vernacular landscapes. When not escorting his colleagues into the field, he was tracking down rare Korean books—publications that opened the eyes of Ishidoya to the value of Korean herbalism. When not working with rural communities to locate plant samples, he was translating Korean-language botanical terminology. That Chŏng was paid on par with Asakawa—a practice seldom seen in most colonial scientific institutions—offers some indication of his value to their research program.[21] As remarkable as Ishidoya and Asakawa were for their investments in Korean culture, they were to no small degree dependent on Chŏng to render that culture legible. Thus, although Chŏng was initially drawn to forestry science precisely because of its foundation in Western practices, his intellectual labor gradually led him back, even if reluctantly, to Korean knowledge forms.

If not for Ishidoya's initial laissez-faire arrangement with the colonial state, much of this collaboration would have been impossible. Having arrived early to the task of investigating growth in Korea, these men enjoyed broad latitude to research what and how they pleased. Theirs was a collaboration largely unencumbered by institutional oversight. It is somewhat ironic, then, that their initial success in demonstrating the value of localized studies ultimately undermined the very nature of that collaboration. As the Government-General moved to institutionalize forest science, this research program was progressively regimented and systematized. These changes were enough to push out Ishidoya, who in 1925 made his way to Manchuria, where he continued his study of Asian botanical and medicinal traditions. Reluctant to give up an official research position seldom granted to Koreans, Chŏng stayed put, at least until his contract was terminated in 1933. One can only wonder as to Asakawa's future in the FES. Stricken in 1931 with a severe bout of pneumonia—one of the afflictions his climate-stabilizing plants were supposed to mitigate—Asakawa's life was cut short. As befits a man who devoted much of his career to Korea's mountain culture, Asakawa elected to bury his bones not in his native soil in Yamanashi but in a Korean-style burial mound on a hillside just outside of Seoul.[22]

THE PROPAGATION MACHINE

In 1922, the research agenda set by Ishidoya et al. received a shot in the arm. Concerned that some of Korea's most pressing environmental problems remained poorly understood, forestry officials lobbied lawmakers back in Japan to underwrite the construction of a Forest Experiment Station, what was to become a flagship research institute and a central hub in the expanding network of nurseries in Korea.[23] That their investment followed in the wake of a series of catastrophic floods—with one 1920 deluge destroying roughly seven thousand homes and claiming more than one thousand lives—is no coincidence.[24] Beyond serving as a center of knowledge production, officials saw this facility as a brain trust for research into riparian improvement and flood control.

They chose for its location Ch'ŏngnyangni, just a stone's throw from the experimental forest at Kwangnŭng. There, piece by piece, a state-of-the-art research complex took shape. Biologists used bio-chambers for seed propagation; climatologists employed a host of powerful meteorological instruments; material scientists worked with expensive wood fiber-testing machines. The crown jewel of the facility was the field office erected in the model forest at Kwangnŭng, from which researchers oversaw experimentation in a greatly expanded swath of forest spanning five different counties.

As the facility grew, so did its staff. By the mid-1920s, a workforce of seventeen researchers and assistants were placed on its payrolls, which grew to eighty-six by the mid-1930s. The departure of Ishidoya in 1925 handed control over the FES research agenda to Tozawa Matajirō (its first director) and Ueki Homiki (who concurrently held a position as a teaching professor at the Suwŏn Forestry Program). Working in coordination with more than a dozen researchers and technicians, Ueki oversaw the FES's afforestation research program, which remained its foremost scientific concern.[25]

The research activities pursued at the FES defy easy description. They can, however, broadly be gathered into what one official chronicle called its "four great functions": (1) forestry experiments; (2) seedling appraisal; (3) the distribution of afforestation materials; and (4) lectures and workshops on forestry topics.[26] Unsurprisingly, most of its resources were devoted to further research into the theories and methods of forest restoration. Like Ishidoya et al. before them, researchers tested seed growth and resilience by controlling for light exposure, soil compaction, temperature, moisture, and a host of other variables. In greenhouses, they investigated the effects of manure mixtures on survival rates. In laboratories, they crossbred seeds to select for desirable moisture-retention traits. On hillsides, they calculated root depth, fruit production, and stomatal resistance.[27]

One of the more pressing questions placed before FES scientists concerned the use of seeds versus seedlings. Should denuded forests be regenerated through planting nursery-grown seedlings (thought to be heartier) or directly seeding the soil (known to be cheaper)? This was far from an academic question. Their conclusions held direct implications for the implementation of the state's forestry plans, especially as related to cost and labor. Following Asakawa, FES scientists began to advocate for the direct seeding of different plants. "Since direct seeding is more simple and economical than planting and since the later growth of the seedlings is assumed better than the planted stocks," concluded the FES scientist Hayashi Yasuharu, "it is at present highly desirable as a means of reforestation."[28] Like other FES employees, Hayashi wrote as much for forest administrators as for his fellow professional scientists. Although his work delved into the technical growth dynamics of different woody plants, practical policy considerations were never far from the surface of his reports.

So concerned were some FES scientists with questions of practical implementation that they created a patchwork of imitative forest zones designed to mirror the actual conditions of rural Korea on the grounds at Kwangnŭng. Three particular types of sites absorbed their attention. One was erosion control zones (*sabōchi*): erosion- and flood-prone areas in need of rapid reforestation. By re-creating the conditions faced by project managers and engineers tasked with erosion control, scientists set out to maximize the relevancy of their research to the day-to-day work of the Bureau of Forestry. And so, just as massive erosion control operations were breaking ground in the mountains of southern Korea, FES researchers launched trial balloons to assess, among other things, methods to prevent sand drift, the use of silt fences, and the design of retaining walls.[29] Given the gargantuan scale of these projects— often involving many hundreds of laborers and millions of seeds—cost reduction was at the forefront of their agenda. In this regard, Asakawa's continued experimentation in outdoor seed germination proved vital, reducing in some cases the cost of these projects by as much as 50 percent.[30]

The protection of woodlands from pests and diseases formed a second arena of focused field site experimentation. Whether through breeding blight-resistant plants or studying fungal infections, FES tree doctors devoted considerable resources to diagnosing and treating forest pathologies. Of the many different threats to Korea's woodland health, few gnawed at FES scientists quite like the *matsukemushi* (*Dendrolimus spectabilis*), a pine moth whose larvae had for centuries bored into and feasted on Korean pine. In the view of Kamiya Kazuo, an FES scientist who pioneered research into disease vectors in Korea's woodlands, early detection was of paramount importance. More concerned with practice than theory building, Kamiya devised a set of guidelines, defensive schemes, and quarantine procedures that enabled farming communities to fight the disease without needlessly felling healthy stands.[31]

A third type of experimental site took the form of so-called "agriculture-use forests" (*nōyōrin*): parcels of forest grown and maintained by farming communities to enhance agricultural productivity and stabilize fuel demands. Together with their counterparts at the Agricultural Experiment Station at Suwŏn, FES scientists investigated livestock grazing patterns, the viability of fruit- and nut-bearing trees, and green fertilizer production.[32] They took particular interest in fuel collection and combustion patterns.[33] After building a model *ondol* using traditional Korean techniques on the grounds of the FES, one group of researchers proceeded to assess the thermodynamic properties of eight different types of tree branches, sixteen types of fallen leaves, and ten agricultural products.[34] These calculations were used in turn to formulate policies of caloric regulation that brought the Korean home and its hearth under the surveillance of the colonial state.

The results of these experiments were not only published in scientific journals or presented at empire-wide conferences; they were also often put to work straightaway in FES-run nurseries. Years of investigation into charcoal production had left FES scientists enamored with sawtooth oak as a fuel source in Korea. FES nurserymen accordingly dialed up its propagation in order to stock so-called "fuel forests" (*shintanrin*): communally managed parcels of forest meant to shore up village fuel supplies. Laboratory experiments on pulp production and chemical manufacture similarly informed decisions about postcut artificial regeneration in industrial forestry operations in northern Korea. In this and other ways, the FES came to hold considerable sway over the particular ecological interventions pursued by the state.

By the 1930s, FES-affiliated nurseries and experimental forests had been established in every province of Korea, from Nyŏngbyŏn County in the north to Wando County in the south. Decentralizing experimentation and propagation operations enabled scientists to better align the supply of seeds and saplings with the particular climate and soil conditions of each region. These nurseries in turn became the sites from which civic forestry organization and agricultural associations purchased raw materials, making FES sites important touch points in local oversight. In keeping with the pedagogical function of the FES, scientists often gave lectures and performed on-site demonstrations, where they worked directly with local communities to advise on best practices. These demonstrations brought the scientific authority of the laboratory to the countryside, underscoring for many Koreans how Japan's forestry reforms were backed by the latest techniques and technologies born of modern science.

The FES, in other words, amounted to more than a collection of labs, instruments, and researchers. A far-reaching network of seedbeds and nurseries, it was one giant system of plant propagation. It was also an important institutional anchor for the scientific networks that bridged Japan's empire of forestry. As a publishing house, the FES produced regular issues of its own research bulletin, disseminating research to interlocutors across the empire. As a convention center for international scientific conferences, it plugged Korea's scientific community into professional scientific networks that spanned the globe. The FES became, in short, a beacon of imperial Japan's scientific prowess and a showcase window through which to display the depth of the colonial state's investment in Korean soil.

GIRDLING GROWTH: THE CASE OF HYŎN SIN-KYU

Offering a good wage, board, and access to a suite of powerful research tools, the FES was a coveted assignment for forest scientists. In the view of Kaburagi Tokuji, however, its true appeal lay in the autonomy it afforded its staff. Recalled the onetime FES director: "The Experiment Station in Korea was different than that in mainland Japan. As an independent office of the Government-General operating outside the mandate of the [Japan-based] Bureau of Agriculture and Forestry, it was not restricted to technical experimentation or research requested by the forest management office. Rather, research directly or indirectly related to forest management in all of Korea's provinces was funded and managed on the basis of our own viewpoints."[35] FES scientists, in sum, enjoyed a fair degree more freedom to pursue research questions that would have been passed over in metropolitan institutions beholden to bureaucratic directives.

For a veteran scientist such as Kaburagi this may have very well been the case, but such liberties were not extended equally. To appreciate the deeply entrenched hurdles facing Korean researchers one need only track the colonial career of Hyŏn Sin-kyu, a brilliant forestry student and FES researcher who would become after 1945 "the doyen of Korean forestry science."[36] As a child, Hyŏn offered few hints of a green thumb. Born in 1912 in Anju, South P'yŏng'an, he aspired from a young age to follow his father's footsteps to become a scholar of literature. His family's worsening financial state, however, scotched his literary dreams, forcing him instead to consider more practical career paths. As a well-known gateway to a stable government job, the Suwŏn College of Agriculture and Forestry offered access to just one such path. So, despite having only the faintest interest in agricultural issues, Hyŏn decided to apply. What he lacked in enthusiasm he made up for in intellectual acuity. On account of strong test scores Hyŏn gained admission in 1930, entering as one of twelve Korean students (of a class of sixty-five).[37]

Hyŏn's initiation into the politics of colonial science came immediately upon his arrival to Suwŏn, which was then a strikingly segregated learning environment. Recalled Kang Pyŏng-ju, one of his classmates: "At the college everybody was supposed to live in a dormitory—the West Dorm for the Japanese students and the East Dorm for Koreans. Each dorm was self-governing. . . . So either intentionally or unintentionally, each side did not associate with the other. We studied together in class and did laboratory experiments together, but we seldom compared notes or talked to each other. Usually we just nodded to acknowledge the other's presence. This is the kind of symbiotic relationship we had with the Japanese students."[38] Further poisoning the atmosphere was the fact that Koreans faced persistent discrimination in the classroom. Allegations of mistreatment, ethnic favoritism, and systemic neglect were rampant, prompting Korean students to stage regular walkouts and organize protests into the 1930s. Among their demands were the recruitment of additional Korean faculty and reforms to the entrance exam so as to level the playing the field.[39]

For Hyŏn, there was no escaping the fact that he was a second-class pupil at Suwŏn. But he also found buoys of support among Suwŏn's faculty. This is especially true of Ueki Homiki, whose mentorship Hyŏn would later warmly recall. Under his guidance, Hyŏn received a wide-ranging forestry education, studying French, American, and Japanese theories and methods. In 1933, thanks in part to strings pulled by Ueki, Hyŏn entered the master's program at Kyushu Imperial University, the first-ever Korean to enroll in its forestry school. There, he undertook a highly specialized training in plant physiology and seed germination, arenas of inquiry that were neatly aligned with the research portfolio of the FES back in Korea. Degree in hand, Hyŏn returned to Korea in 1936 to apply for an entry-level research position at the FES, which he was granted on a probationary basis. This was no minor achievement. With a growing pool of highly qualified Japanese scientists applying for work at the FES—a product as much of the worsening job market in Japan as the research institute's reputation—Korean applicants were seldom considered for anything other than clerical positions or contract labor.

Hyŏn was initially quite encouraged by the professional milieu he found at the FES. Even if it had an "air of bureaucratism," he remembered, the FES was unparalleled in its research lifestyle.[40] A good portion of Hyŏn's labor went into supporting the day-to-day work of his supervisor, Fukunaga Kosuke, then head of an afforestation laboratory. But he was also permitted to continue the research he had started as a graduate student in Kyushu. This modicum of independence was possible only because of Hyŏn's advanced degree, a marker of legitimacy conferred on very few Koreans at that point. Not even Chŏng T'ae-hyŏn, pioneer that he was, was given full license to pursue his own research at the FES.

Hyŏn's favorable outlook was fleeting. With Fukunaga's reassignment to Manchuria after the outbreak of war in 1937, Hyŏn was suddenly placed under a new research supervisor, Tomana Kōtarō, who did not share his predecessor's permissive attitude. This personnel change coincided with a broader shift in the mandate of the FES: the mobilization of science to, quite literally, fuel Japan's war in China. Seemingly overnight, Hyŏn was forced to set aside years of his own research to assist with humdrum laboratory work increasingly geared toward the exigencies of resource extraction. Adding insult to injury was the fact that, due to the colonial government's name-change policies—a wartime push to intensify the assimilation of Korean subjects by compelling them to take Japanese names—Hyŏn was forced to adopt and publish under a new name, Kayama Nobuo. For these reasons, Hyŏn decided to leave the FES in 1943 to return to Kyushu Imperial University. Only by earning a doctorate in forestry science, he reasoned, could any Korean surmount this institutional discrimination.[41] Whether or not Hyŏn was correct, his frustrations betray the persistent prejudicial attitudes that pervaded professional scientific bodies throughout colonial Korea, if not the empire.

In a broader sense, Hyŏn's career also reflects the bureaucratization of forestry science. Whereas a generation earlier Chŏng conducted his research in the intimate context of a four-man research team (shaped by the personal bonds and intellectual whims of his superiors), Hyŏn operated within a clinical scientific institution, with rigid hierarchies and firm divisions of labor. That Hyŏn advanced as far as he did within the FES was in many respects extraordinary. Only a select group of Koreans were able to gain admission to graduate programs in the hard sciences back in Japan, let alone find stable careers within the premier scientific institutions of the colonial state.

The next-best option for many aspiring Korean forest scientists was to find work as a primary school instructor in natural history. To the extent that these independent Korean scholars were able to pursue their own research agendas, they did so through the Korean Natural History Research Group (Chosŏn Pangmul Yŏn'guhoe). Founded in 1933, this research group quickly emerged as the premier intellectual space for exclusively Korean scientific collaboration. Snubbed by the scientific establishment, its members banded together to pursue research questions that only Koreans could:

classifications of vernacular plant names, analysis of Chosŏn-era botanical treatises, and so on. What essentially emerged from these projects was an alternative track of scientific inquiry: regionalized studies of Korea's ethnobotany. In focusing their efforts around regional ecology, these scientists saw an opportunity to not only advance botanical knowledge but also probe research question largely overlooked by (and beyond the capacities of) Japanese scientists. This "grand political move," in the words of Jung Lee, allowed amateur Korean scientists to pursue a new and unquestionably constructive scientific research program free from the strictures and prejudices of colonial institutions.[42] By cataloguing Korean plants in their own terms, these scientists carved out a professional niche for themselves while also leveling subtle critiques of Japanese scientific practice.

This compartmentalization of knowledge forms marked a far cry from the collaborative practices of Ishidoya et al. By the late 1930s, it seems, the ideological intensification that accompanied Japan's "holy war" in China had precipitated a turn away from interactive knowledge production. Koreans were left to probe their own local botanical traditions within the narrow bounds permitted by the state while Japanese scientists threw themselves into the research needs of wartime forestry. Early efforts to embed forestry science in the social context of Korean life were thus foreclosed by a project of wartime assimilation that sought to efface that social landscape altogether. If this fragmentation of knowledge production was to the detriment of scientific innovation in late colonial Korea, it was a gift to Korean scientists after 1945. It enabled Koreans to point to their own uninterrupted traditions of forestry research at the same time that it allowed Korean scientists who had worked in colonial institutions to highlight their marginalized place within that system.

CONCLUSION

That territorial expansion encouraged new ideas about environmental change is by now a truism of empire. Richard Grove no doubt primed this field of inquiry when he observed that the colonial enterprise "helped to create a context that was conducive to rigorous analytical thinking about the actual processes of ecological change as well as thinking about the potential for new forms of land control."[43] Historians of forestry have long since shown how the colonial context shaped the training and toolkit of foresters, whose experiences in colonies from India to Indonesia left a deep impression on the profession writ large. In so doing, scholars have arrived at yet another widely held principle: that colonial science facilitated the *hybridization* of knowledge forms. More than simply imposing Western epistemologies on foreign lands, natural scientists pursued a research agenda that is best understood as an interaction between and interpenetration of local and global knowledge forms.

Both axioms apply to forestry science as it was practiced in colonial Korea. Scientifically speaking, it can safely be said that in imperial Japan, too, the colonial tail wagged the metropolitan dog. Innovations such as Asakawa's exposed burial method shaped seed propagation practices back in mainland Japan. Together with Ishidoya, he likewise challenged Japanese scientists, in both word and deed, to think more rigorously about the universal application of European scientific practice. One can only speculate as to the reach and reception of their critique, but research on local forest ecology only proliferated thereafter, as forest scientists were dispatched into increasingly distant landscapes brought under Japanese control. Behind these investigations—and the conversations they provoked—stood a thickening cobweb of scholarly and scientific exchange. The geographical proximity and strong institutional bonds between Japan's colonial knowledge centers nurtured a tight-knit network of forestry scientists, through which ideas, findings, and even material specimens circulated fluidly.

To a limited degree, Koreans had access to this network. Both Chŏng and Hyŏn were able to matriculate at Suwŏn and found gainful employment in state-run laboratories. But roadblocks were many and career advancement opportunities few. To their repeated frustration, the ethnic discrimination they initially experienced in the classroom spilled over into the laboratory itself. Any sense of camaraderie that might have energized their collaborative work was always tempered by the stigma of their Koreanness. Eager to take part in knowledge creation but never empowered enough to do so fully on their own terms, they spent much of their colonial-era careers on a tightrope, pulled between their intellectual inclinations and the power structures of the scientific profession. Fortunately for both men, their careers outlived the Japanese empire, with Chŏng emerging after 1945 as an eminent teacher and Hyŏn as a prolific researcher and reforestation adviser to Park Chung-hee.

If Chŏng and Hyŏn were at the mercy of Japanese scientists at the FES, so were colonial forestry bureaucrats much higher up the chain of command. As the principal engineers behind the mechanics of silviculture, FES scientists had a direct impact on the conservation goals set by the state and the ecological interventions pursued to achieve them. This influence was not just a product of the weight of empirical evidence generated in FES laboratories or the reputation of its scientists. It was also a direct result of the fact that FES research facilities often doubled as propagation sites, churning out a significant portion of the raw materials used in the field.

This is not to suggest that every seed sown or seedling reared at the FES was for the lasting benefit of Korea's forests. Despite spirited propagandistic efforts on the part of the colonial government to frame this scientific enterprise as a driver of progress, its legacy was mixed. A good number of the species introduced fared poorly. Intensive erosion control efforts sometimes did little to actually stanch summer flooding, while research into the industrial uses of Korea's woody plants actually accelerated forest exploitation elsewhere on the peninsula. Thus, while the state did much to ballyhoo statistics on seedlings grown or yen invested in research, Korean landowners, farmers, and woodcutters often saw things quite differently.

Capturing their perspective requires new scales of analysis. At one level, it demands that we shift our attention northward to map the growth of the regional timber industry in the Yalu River basin. Whatever the gains in forest accumulation, the aggregate growing stock on the peninsula actually decreased due to lumbering operations in these rich old-growth forests.[44] For every seed sown there were board feet of timber extracted by timber companies in the north. At another, it requires that we examine the implications of state forestry for village politics and agrarian life. Reforestation, after all, was about more than planting trees. It became a mechanism for reorganizing local society, shaping domestic life, and diffusing Japanese ideas about imperial stewardship. The next two chapters accordingly take up these scales—the industrial region and the agrarian village—to offer a more finely textured account of the changes wrought by colonial-era forestry reforms.

FIVE

THE TIMBER UNDERTAKING

DESCRIBED VARIOUSLY AS A "LIMITLESS TREASURE HOUSE,"[1] "THE Kingdom of the forest,"[2] and "a partial solution at least of the problem of the world's future timber supply,"[3] the Yalu River basin occupied a distinctive place in the imagination of Japanese, Koreans, and Westerners alike. To Koreans, these were the forests of Mount Paektu, the birthplace of Tan'gun, the legendary progenitor of the Korean bloodline, who had for centuries enjoyed pride of place in mythology and folklore. Stretching across the three northernmost provinces of the peninsula, they also demarcated what Koreans themselves had considered a rugged frontier and cultural backwater, where smugglers operated with impunity and bandits ran amok. If, as Sun Joo Kim has argued, the northernmost provinces of Korea shared a "historical fate as a spatial object of political discrimination in the late Chosŏn period," prevailing perceptions of the region's forests as primordial wilderness helped stoke these sentiments.[4]

However, with the onset of Japan's colonial occupation, some of the supposed defects of the region morphed into its virtues. Once blemished by its proximity to a supposedly barbarous Manchurian frontier, the Yalu River basin was valued after annexation as a stepping-stone for expansion onto the continent. Inaccessible alpine terrain that had previously inspired administrative dread was now celebrated as a sanctuary to old-growth forest.[5] In Japanese eyes, this was the last preserve of green Korea, a forest Eden that represented the richness that once was. It was only natural that, after decades of speculation about Korea's northern bounty, Japanese prospectors would rush into the region after 1910, forerunners to a flood of corporate investment. Within a decade, the dense conifer forests of the upland north had become the locus of a rapidly expanding lumbering enterprise, transforming the Yalu River basin into a hub of the regional timber trade (map 5.1).

Many institutions grew around this enterprise, but none exercised greater authority than the Forest Management Bureau (J: Eirinshō; K: Yŏnglimch'ang; hereafter FMB), a freestanding office created by the Government-General to directly oversee the management of Korea's national forests. With stations scattered across the northern provinces and a branch office in Seoul, the FMB presided over a sprawling system of field offices, logging sites, and roadways. Stretching from Hyesan near the headwaters of the Yalu to Sinŭiju at the river's mouth, these stations formed intensive sites of exploitation and vital nodes in the circulation of material goods across Korea and beyond. It is rather fitting, then, that the colonial government elected to call these outposts "Timber Undertaking Stations" in their annual progress reports for Western readers—"where proper exploitation with adequate capital should yield a considerable revenue to the Treasury."[6]

That the growth of this timbering enterprise prefigured the broader industrial transformation of northern Korea is a remarkable and largely

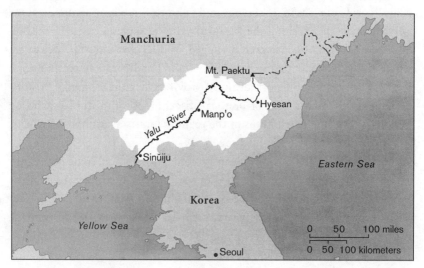

MAP 5.1 The Yalu River drainage basin

overlooked feature of colonial-era forest management. Radiating out from each of its field stations was an ever-growing web of logging roads, rails, and shipping routes that became the infrastructural skeleton of the region's commercial development. Before there were munitions factories churning out war material, before there were plants manufacturing chemical components, before there were hydroelectric dams powering these facilities, there were Timber Undertaking Stations, whose work crews, technicians, and rangers etched into the landscape new patterns of employment and modes of mobility that guided the commercial growth of the region. In its delivery of timber to market, that is to say, Korea's timber trade primed the pump for the "northern development" agenda of the 1930s, when the Yalu River basin was targeted for heavy industrialization and, later, material mobilization for war.

Yet the region's forests were not the Forest Management Bureau's alone for the taking. A powerful syndicate of Manchurian interests was also alive to the region's commercial potential. To chart the growth of this regional industry is thus to probe the politics of the timber trade at a touchpoint of empire. At once the physical demarcation of the political division between Manchuria and Korea and a fluid riparian borderland, the Yalu and its forests formed both connective and contested tissue in the creation of what some envisaged as a "Yalu River economic bloc" (*Ōryokkō no keizaiken*).[7] It was along the banks of the Yalu—and especially in the "sister cities" of Sinŭiju and Andong—that colonial interests most deeply crosscut.

These cross-border tensions, like the Yalu itself, chilled and thawed over time, but they did little to stifle the ambitions of industrial planners. Indeed, the Yalu River basin became after 1931 the focal point of a new, distinctively imperial approach to regional planning: "comprehensive development" (J: *sōgō kaihatsu*). Intoxicated with notions of an ultramodern industrial utopia on the continent, Japanese technocrats and engineers began to integrate plants, ports, hydroelectric dams, urban complexes, and infrastructure into a master plan for regional development. Here, "Scientific Japan" would embark on a project of "building Asia for Asians," a demonstration of rational planning, engineering prowess, and colonial power all wrapped into one.[8]

Standing shoulder to shoulder with these technocrats were FMB officials, who, as custodians of the region's vast forestland, held the keys to surrounding resources and infrastructure. As abstract visions turned into material realities— as blueprints turned into work plans—industrial planners turned to their colleagues in the FMB to secure land, marshal labor, and reconfigure timber production around the exigencies of heavy industrialization. Bureaucrats and engineers may have, as Aaron S. Moore notes, "formed their conceptions on technology by getting their hands dirty on the ground," but they also relied on woodsmen to do much of this dirty work for them.[9]

The northern timber undertaking was thus distinguished not only geophysically by the region's steep topography and severe winter climate but also managerially by the logic of comprehensive development. Out of Korea's northern interior uplands emerged a more soldierly approach to forest management: systems of labor discipline, population resettlement, and regulatory enforcement that required considerable force on the part of foresters. These systems demand our attention not only because they facilitated the buildup of plants, railways, and dams in the region but also because they anticipated some of the more militarized approaches to forestry practiced under Park Chung-hee. Although the division of the peninsula after 1945 would bequeath this industrial legacy to North Korea, notions of comprehensive development lived on in the Republic of Korea, where foresters worked in lockstep with economic planners to launch South Korea's industrial takeoff.

TIMBER TO MARKET

In 1917, the Yalu River timber industry received a boost from an unlikely source: a folk ballad entitled the "Yalu River Song" (Ōryokkō bushi). Much to the surprise of the region's industrialists, the languid tune grew in popularity not just in Korea but also back in Japan, where it did much to raise the profile of the peninsula's northern riverscape. Crooned from the perspective of raftsmen floating timber down the serpentine river, the lyrics vividly capture its changing course:

> The Yalu River dividing Korea and China
> The flowing dinghies are all well and good, *yoisho!*
> Trapped by snow and ice, *yakkora*
> Unable once more to reach Andong by tomorrow

> The Yalu River dividing Korea and China
> The best improvised steel bridge in all of the East, *yoisho!*
> Open the crossroads, *yakkora*, the sails large and small
> The to and fro of milling junkyard ships

After introducing listeners to the dynamic movement of the river, the lyrics next turn to its transcendental source:

> Mount Paektu, the highest point in Korea
> The permafrost may melt, *yoisho*
> But what is in my heart, *yakkora*, does not
> I dream of you every night, *choichoi*

Lumber barons similarly dreamed of Mount Paektu, but for a different, less exalted reason: the old growth that climbed up its slopes. As the source of both the Yalu and Tumen Rivers, this stratovolcano also enabled the conveyance of timber to market, making it the geophysical fountainhead of the timber undertaking.

With Mount Paektu as their polestar, logging crews first made inroads in the region in the 1910s, proceeding only as fast as forest inventories would allow. Unfettered access to the region's national forests enabled the FMB to hit the ground running, but private companies needed to do their due diligence before making any investments. What they found did not disappoint. One estimate put the total accumulation of the timber in the basin at 851,860,000 *shakujime*[10]—a supply that would last, by another reckoning, for as long as 268 years.[11] It was not just the volume that excited prospectors. As a mixed sub-boreal and cool-temperate forest zone, the region presented a choice blend of softwoods (e.g., fir, spruce, larch, and pine) and hardwoods (e.g., walnut, birch, elm, and oak) of great utility to building plans and infrastructural projects.[12] Especially coveted were the region's old-growth stands of Japanese larch, which were, by one account, so extensive that "it is possible for one to ride on horseback for several consecutive days and see scarcely another tree but Larch."[13]

Before any of these trees could become commodities, however, they needed to make their way downstream, and that was no easy feat. The boom of the axe and the grind of the saw announced the start of each season, which commenced in the fall, once soils had hardened enough to facilitate the sledding of logs. On the front lines of these operations were small teams of lumberjacks, who felled, delimbed, and bucked the timber, transforming standing trees into uniform logs (fig. 5.1). Larger work crews then hauled these logs to a nearby logging road or water source, often with the help of an ox-driven sled or a *shura*, a chute-like conveyance system long used by Japanese woodcutters to move cumbersome sawlogs downslope.[14]

FIG. 5.1 A lumberjack at work in the northern uplands. (From Nakama, ed., *Nihon chiri fūzoku taikei*, vol., 16, 357.)

This was backbreaking, bone-chilling labor, suitable for only the hardiest of souls. Cramped mountain huts, frigid temperatures, thick brush, pittance wages: such tribulations, noted the seasoned Korean lumberjack Yi Sung-jun, were everyday realities of the industry. Much of this drudgery was delegated to Chinese bodies. Indeed, as was the case with industrial timber outfits across much of modern world, the division of logging labor cut sharply along ethnic lines. Japanese foremen were especially eager to recruit so-called "Shandong coolies," wage laborers from the nearby Chinese province considered especially well constituted for the rigors of lumbering.[15] The rest of the labor force was drawn primarily from surrounding Korean farming communities, where winter lulls in farmwork freed up farmhands and pack animals, both. In the eyes of those supervising these efforts, the recruitment of Korean farmers had an added virtue: it diminished the likelihood that these individuals, come spring, would burn their way through valuable stands of old-growth forest to clear land for agriculture.[16]

The highly anticipated spring melt ushered in the next stage of the timber undertaking: the float downstream. For Japanese raftsmen, the first run of the season was typically preceded by a ritual ceremony, held on the grounds of FMB field stations, that sought divine assurance of safe passage down the river. Those intimately familiar with the Yalu were quick to direct their prayers to the "water gods" (*mizukami*) presiding over the rapid shoots at Radanpo, a particularly perilous stretch of whitewater in Samsu County.[17] The river spirits thus appeased, work crews assembled stockpiled logs into rafts, usually about one hundred feet long and twenty feet wide, that could withstand the long journey downriver (fig. 5.2).

Once properly outfitted, the raftsmen of the Yalu—of "Yalu River Song" fame—began their snaking path downriver. Although rafting was initially contracted out to Japanese lumberjacks from the famous logging regions of Kiso and Yoshino, Koreans became a major contingent of these crews over time. There was also, it seems, no small measure of antagonism between Japanese and Chinese rafters—ranging from shouting matches to kidnappings— as competing crews vied for access to the river's most navigable currents.[18]

FIG. 5.2 Rafters enjoying a placid stretch of their run down the Yalu. (Image by Harold Hardy-Smith; courtesy of the Pictori Media Archive, Korea Institute, Australia National University.)

Often sealed in by the famously steep banks of the upper Yalu, these teams negotiated a variety of hazards including islets, shallow waters, and the occasional logjam in order to guide their woody payloads as far as 700 kilometers downstream. En route, they passed a string of FMB field stations that lined the banks of the river at places like Chunggang, Manp'o, and Wiwŏn.

Upon their arrival to the mouth of the Yalu, log drives navigated a maze of sluices into one of the many lumberyards that lined the widening banks of the river near its confluence with the Yellow Sea. The fate of sawlogs from this point on depended on market conditions, which were, as one forestry official noted, wrapped in "mutually entangled relations" with global supply and demand.[19] In some cases, raw logs were sorted, graded, and stockpiled, pending procurements by retailers or middlemen. In others, they were cut into dimensional lumber, the standardized widths and depths purchased in bulk by builders, engineers, and architects. Statistics on the movement of timber products in and out of Sinŭiju reveal a portrait of a volatile marketplace shaped by futures trading, shipping costs, and global market swings. During the 1920s, the most common destination was the "demand center" of the colonial capital, where many lumber firms and industrial combines were headquartered.[20] But for reasons elaborated below, Sinŭiju's timber market orientation shifted decisively northward after 1931, as the Yalu basin became a timber depot for Japan's expansion into northeastern China (fig. 5.3).

Whatever the vicissitudes of the market, the trend of production was relentlessly *up*. This is perhaps most clearly reflected in the annual output of the FMB, which, as gatekeeper of Korea's timber treasure chest, enjoyed ready access to the region's most sought-after stands. While in 1907, its first year of operations, the FMB processed only 20,000 *shakujime* of lumber, this figure had by 1925 grown to 644,372 *shakujime* with more than one million additional *shakujime* of unprocessed timber felled.[21] Much of this timber was funneled via railway directly into state-led developmental projects across the peninsula. The FMB churned out three particular materials indispensable to the Government-General's building plans: utility poles for the growing electrical grid, construction materials for a host of engineering and urban improvement projects, and sleepers for the rapidly expanding railway system. The latter product formed an especially pressing priority for the FMB, which struggled to keep up with Railway Bureau's seemingly insatiable appetite for rail ties. Given that the operational life span of most ties was only five years, demand was driven as much by upkeep as expansion.[22]

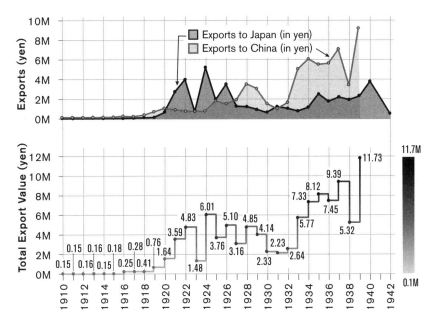

FIG. 5.3 Annual exports of lumber, boards, and rail ties. (Data from Chōsen Sōtokufu, ed., *Tōkei nenpō* [each year]; compiled in Pae, "Ilcheha Chosŏn ŭi mokchae sukŭp chŏngch'aek e kwanhan yŏn'gu," 28.)

The arrival of these materials to markets, depots, or building sites did not bring an end to the work of lumbering. Apart from regenerating forests in areas cleared of timber, it remained to ensure that these stocks were spared the bandit's axe, the farmer's torch, and the moth's larvae. Each field station thus devoted considerable resources to policing the region and safeguarding its resources. In this, the FMB was part of an alliance of security officials, customs agents, and corporate employees working to enforce ownership boundaries, combat smuggling, and subdue the guerilla insurgency that took refuge in the region. No matter how robust, this coalition did little to change the fact that, on average, each FMB field office was responsible for the oversight of 277,000 *chōbu* of woodlands, a full 70,000 *chōbu* more than better-staffed stations back in Japan.[23] With impossibly vast tracts of forest placed under the watchful eye of just a few forest rangers, the FMB had to get resourceful. When, for example, airplanes became more readily available in the 1930s, woodsmen took to the skies to scout for fires, monitor migration patterns, and survey remote forest stock.[24]

Though thinly spread, these foresters propped up management schemes that introduced new methods of social control to a ruggedly defiant hinterland. From their expanding network of field stations they worked with security officials to tighten border security and rein in vagrancy. Through year-round hiring schemes, they shaped the seasonal migration patterns and labor of Korean farmers, Chinese laborers, and Japanese contractors. Using rope, oxen, road, rail, and rapid, they blazed infrastructural trails that enabled the movement not just of timber but also coal, gold, and a host of other materials. By dint of the region's topography and climate, the effects of this timbering enterprise were felt unevenly across both space and time. There was, however, one place in the north where the work of lumbering never stopped: Sinŭiju, a timber boomtown whose fate was inextricably linked—in good times and bad—to the resource that put it on the map.

TIMBER CAPITAL

If the Yalu River and its tributaries formed the arteries of the timber industry, the port towns of Andong and Sinŭiju were the opposing ventricles of its heart. It was there that the FMB and the lion's share of timber companies established the factories, processing plants, and lumberyards that rendered trees into the "building materials, warship construction materials, electricity poles, bridge construction materials, railway ties, matches, and small paper products" that made their way to markets across the empire.[25] Timber was the lifeblood of Sinŭiju, so much so that it was quickly dubbed the "timber capital" of Korea.[26]

Before the capital was the railway. Built in 1906, the Keijō-Sinŭiju line provided the raison d'être of the city: it shifted the center of industrial gravity on the Korean banks of the Yalu from Ŭiju downstream to Sinŭiju—*new* Ŭiju. This new railway held weighty implications for timber firms. Where lumber once had to be laboriously loaded onto ships in Ŭiju or Andong, it could now be entrained on railcars bound for urban markets across Korea. And with the completion in 1911 of the "Iron Bridge"—a rail- and road-bridge connecting Sinŭiju with its "sister city" across the river—Korea and its forests were linked directly to Manchurian markets and resource reserves. Sinŭiju was, by one assessment, "a city of international importance regarding China," critical to "politics, national defense, and military preparedness" alike.[27] It was not long before both cities were paired in maps, timber industry booster publications, and travel guides, as a new and vibrant commercial center began to take shape.

Yet, whatever their industrial or infrastructural linkages, both towns were proxies for distinct colonial authorities. Indeed, key differences in governing structures, market orientations, and industry regulations gave rise to singular sets of forestry policies that were recurrently at loggerheads with one another. Although Japanese industrialists in Andong contended with the entrenched interests of Chinese timber merchants, they found no such competition in Sinŭiju. And whereas the Kwantung Army wielded increasing authority over forestry operations in Andong, oversight was left largely to private capital and the FMB in Sinŭiju.[28]

The latter group in particular played an outsized role in shaping the timber trade on the Korean side of the Yalu. Wielding authority over nearly every aspect of forestry policy—from pricing to access to shipping—the FMB did its utmost to create conditions that were friendly to Japanese capital and competitive in the regional marketplace. Equal parts sawmill and corporate clubhouse, the FMB headquarters in Sinŭiju was the nerve center of the Korean timber industry. The influence of this office stemmed as much from its consistent surplus of raw material as its authority to set prices or negotiate leaseholds. In an industry characterized by high risk and low margins, disruption to supply chains could prove devastating. Fortunately for timber capitalists, the FMB routinely downed far more logs than its sawyers could process. This enabled FMB officials to set aside a good portion of its annual harvest for direct procurement by local parties, providing firms in need with a material buffer and the Government-General with a steady source of income. These material dependencies made it all the more important that private companies remain in the good graces of the FMB—a fact that gave its employees considerable leverage in pressuring local actors to play by their rules.

Such arrangements left smaller lumber dealers at a decided disadvantage. This is especially true for Korean businessmen, who not only harbored "mistrust" toward the FMB but sometimes felt actively bullied regarding its terms of sale.[29] A particular source of irritation for Korean retailers was the FMB's proration of timber prices: sales schemes that enabled larger (that is, Japanese) corporations to make bulk purchases at heavily discounted rates. That the lumber trade was stacked in favor of Japanese capital is perhaps best evidenced by the fact that of thirty-seven timber firms established in Korea by 1921, only two were Korean-owned.[30] Despite efforts by the Government-General after 1919 to nurture a more inclusive business climate (and thereby win the support of Korea's industrial bourgeoisie), the barriers to entry remained prohibitively steep in the timber world.

Any such commercial tensions, however, were papered over at the twenty-first annual convention of the National Timber Industry Federation, held in the Yalu River basin in August 1919. Bringing together two hundred industry representatives, administrators, and experts, the convention was meant to "introduce the border and its forests" to participants from across the empire.[31] Those in attendance shuffled back and forth across the Yalu, as they toured forests in Jilin and inspected milling machinery in Sinŭiju. Policy-minded attendees also had the opportunity to take part in forums convened in both Andong and Sinŭiju, where industry leaders sat down to hash out proposals that would steer the continental timber trade toward an even brighter future: better port access, cheaper freight, and the standardization of timber inspection practices. In what amounted to a coming-out party for the Yalu River timber industry, the convention concluded with a lavish garden party held behind the FMB's headquarters—a space that would grease the wheels of industry for years to come.[32]

Its international visibility raised by promotional efforts such as this one, Sinŭiju became the base for a host of timber ventures, large and small. One of the first corporations to set up shop in the region would quickly become the biggest: the Ōji Paper Company, whose paper mill grew over the 1920s into one of the most voracious consumers of forest material in the region. Offering "ample forest resources, the ability to float timber and move products on the Yalu River, and cheap labor," Sinŭiju was a natural base for the corporation's expansion into the continent.[33] Furthermore, as the first major pulp producer to make headway in the region, Ōji was more or less free of competition for the particular stocks sought for pulp production—namely, Yezo spruce (*Picea jezoensis*) and Sakhalin fir (*Abies sachalinensis*).

By the 1930s, however, Ōji's once prime real estate on the banks of the Yalu had become crowded with lumberyards, not to mention the heaps of sawdust, slabs, and other waste products of the industry. As of 1938, Sinŭiju was home to thirty-one different sawmills, seating wood processing squarely at the "throne of industry" in the city.[34] Yet a number of other commercial enterprises also gravitated to the timber capital. Particularly quick to set its roots was the mining industry, which concentrated principally on the extraction of gold, iron, coal, and graphite—the "Four Great Minerals of Korea."[35] Insofar as the transport of timber to market opened up a new extractive infrastructure in the region, it was to the immediate benefit of the mining industry. On the heels of timber moved a variety of minerals that markedly expanded the material (and pollutive) footprint of regional commerce.

Steering the growth of Sinŭiju's industrial profile was a small but influential community of Japanese settlers. Among them were entrepreneurs like Nakagome Seiichi (a onetime FMB employee who became "a magnate of the timber world")[36] and Masaki Seijirō (a "timber strongman" known for his connections with business interests on the other side of Yalu).[37] The true embodiment of the timber capital, however, was Tada Eikichi, the unofficial "governor of the border." This title, it seems, was well deserved, for Tada worked to quite literally link business interests across the border through his involvement in the construction of the Iron Bridge. Like many others, Tada was initially drawn to the region through happenstance and opportunity. Unlike most, however, he chose to stay in Sinŭiju, where he tried his hand at a variety of ventures including rice trading, automobile sales, and lumbering.[38]

Tada's greatest service to the timber industry came in his capacity as adviser to the Sinŭiju Chamber of Commerce. Founded in 1918, this assembly brought together hundreds of Japanese and Korean businessmen to promote the interests and wares of local businesses. From the Japanese timber broker Takagi Nobutō to the Korean sawmill operator Song Sil-chŏl, lumbermen dominated the composition of its board and executive committees.[39] The particular interests of timber capitalists accordingly drove its proceedings, the records of which often read like an industry wish list. Whether by negotiating freight fees or courting investment, the Chamber of Commerce and its members advocated tirelessly—and sometimes, as we will see, fruitlessly—for the primacy of the timber trade in the region's industrial portfolio.[40]

As Sinŭiju grew, so did the ambitions of its business leaders and timber tycoons. By the late 1920s, many Chamber of Commerce members were beating the drum for the construction of "Greater Sinŭiju" (Dai-Shingishū): an expanded area of commerce that stretched from the city down the coastline to Tasado, where the Yalu's estuary could support shipping activities year-round. Keen as always to cut down shipping costs and facilitate transport to new markets, the region's lumber firms, led by Ōji Paper, partially financed the construction of a roughly forty-kilometer railway line connecting Sinŭiju with the port. Promising the shipment of as much as one million tons of freight per year, the construction of this warm-water port garnered broad support from mercantile associations on both sides of the Yalu as well as those back in the archipelago.[41]

Projects like the Tasado port and railway heralded to some observers the fruition of the "Yalu River economic bloc": a scheme of economic integration between Manchuria and Korea that stood at the foreground of the industrial imaginary of the empire. Yet, common ground proved as difficult to navigate as the rapids at Radanpo. Beneath the veneer of solidarity were clashing visions of forest governance and industrial policy in the region—a bitter truth laid bare by the timber tariff dispute. As a test case for regional cooperation, a knotty policy puzzle for lawmakers in Tokyo, and an existential crisis for Sinŭiju, this trade spat made plain the challenges inherent to brokering politics and profits in an expanding imperial sphere.

POLITICAL LOGJAMS

It is a testament to the interconnectivity of the global timber market that the effects of scarcity brought about by World War I held profound implications for the Yalu River basin and its lumber barons. Fueled in part by the realization that national security could not be guaranteed without forests—the enduring lesson of World War I for European foresters—fears of an impending timber famine grew such that "after 1920," in the words of geographer Michael Williams, "forests everywhere in the world were coming under scrutiny and being assessed. What happened in one part of the world had repercussions in another part."[42]

The repercussions of World War I for the forests of Japan and its empire were many and various. For one, market analysts in Japan began to foretell a "great alteration in the global timber marketplace," as export centers shifted from Europe toward the United States, Canada, and northeast Asia— the burgeoning Pacific Rim timber trade.[43] More immediately, the prevailing sense of anxiety about Japan's domestic supply of timber prompted Japanese officials to rethink its long-standing tariffs on foreign timber. In 1920, trade officials pressed forward with tariff reforms that reduced or removed import duties on pine, cedar, and fir. Seemingly overnight, Japan was awash in North American timber, nearly all of it from the Pacific Northwest. Though lower in quality, this imported lumber was cheap, abundant, and sufficient for a host of industrial applications.[44]

To understand what this meant for the Yalu timber trade one must go back to the passage of the Korean Tariff Ordinance in 1912 and the Adjoining Nations Tariff Ordinance the following year. Aiming to weld Korea's patchwork of treaties into a unified customs law, the former standardized preexisting timber tariff rates while the latter reduced by one-third the duties levied on all articles traded by rail between Manchuria and Korea. There was, however, a rub: the rates set out in the Tariff Ordinance came with an expiration date, August 28, 1920. Anticipating this, trade officers in Japan moved to more fully integrate Korea into empire-wide tariff regimes. To that end, the Japanese Diet passed in 1920 four separate laws intended to assimilate Korea's customs duties with Japan and its colonial dependencies.

This adjustment could not have come at a less opportune moment for Korea's timber capitalists. While by 1920 the timber industry had unquestionably matured, productive capacities were still only blossoming. Indeed, for all the talk of achieving "self-sufficiency" (*jikyū jizoku*) in the domestic production of timber, Korea-based timber companies fell well short of meeting the rising domestic demand. Petitions lodged by the Sinŭiju Chamber of Commerce for some degree of timber trade protection—as had been granted for a variety of other goods, including salt, tobacco, and carbon fuel—were denied by the colonial government on these very grounds. In the eyes of forestry officials, this was merely a stopgap arrangement meant to facilitate the flow of much-needed timber products into Korea from nearby Manchuria. Quite reasonably, they figured that Korea's domestic timber industry would continue to grow to the point where these tariffs could be phased out.

Thus, just when North American timber was beginning to flow into Japan, Manchurian timber inundated the Korean marketplace (fig. 5.4). Imports of construction materials from Manchuria increased by 277 percent in a single year and rose a staggering 455 percent by 1922.[45] This did not augur well for businessmen in Sinŭiju, many of whom had just set up shop in the region only to see the market potential of their investment plummet. Some factories in Sinŭiju were forced to shutter their doors at the very time that Andong-based merchants just across the river were seeing surging profits. This included Ōji Paper's brand new paper mill, which was forced to suspend its operations for a full two years.

The grumblings of the Sinŭiju's lumbermen were soon drowned out, however, by urgent appeals for timber supplies in the wake of the September 1, 1923, Great Kantō Earthquake. Rocking the Greater Tokyo

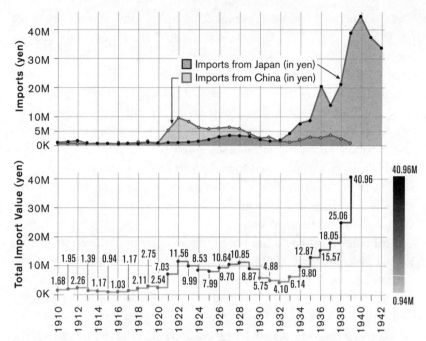

FIG. 5.4 Annual imports of timber, boards, and rail ties. (Data from Chōsen Sōtokufu, ed., *Tōkei nenpō*; compiled in Pae, "Ilcheha Chosŏn ŭi mokchae sukŭp chŏngch'aek e kwanhan yŏn'gu," 29.)

metropolitan area just as residents were lighting stoves for lunch preparation, the temblor ignited a firestorm that ripped through the city's wooden built environment. What for Tokyoites was a historic calamity was for Sinŭiju's timber dealers a stroke of good fortune. At once, Japanese officials in the Special Emergency Timber Relief Office began buying up lumber from northern Korea to supplement supplies brought in from Hokkaido, Akita, and Aomori Prefectures as well as the United States.[46] By 1924, as a result, well over 80 percent of Korea's timber exports were bound for Japan.

These emergency procurements provided a welcome salve to the Korean timber industry's ailments, but they did little to address what many business leaders in Sinŭiju saw as trade policies skewed plainly toward the interests of Manchuria. Whether out of ignorance or venality, metropolitan lawmakers, they claimed, had straightjacketed the Korean timber industry. This was not a mere matter of profit margins. In the eyes of the Sinŭiju Chamber of

Commerce, the so-called "timber tariff problem" (*mokuzai kanzei mondai*) "governed the destiny of the timber capital."[47] In 1927, this economic angst gave rise to a political action committee: the Alliance for the Repeal of the Special Tariff on Timber in Korea. Drawing its members primarily from the ranks of the Korean Forestry Association, the Korean Industrial Commission, and the Sinŭiju Chamber of Commerce, the group began to press the case for the annulment of the Special Tariff Edict. When more traditional political pressure tactics bore little fruit, its leaders decided to take their case directly to the Imperial Diet, sending a delegation to Tokyo in 1926. There, they turned to the metropolitan "Korea Lobby" to persuade lawmakers to fold Korean tariff revisions into already pending motions for domestic timber tariff reforms.

This politicking jolted Andong's own timber interests into counteraction. Fearing that timber tariff reforms would put a damper on their own commercial prospects, Manchuria's timber merchants huddled with high-ranking officials in the Kwantung Bureau and the Southern Manchurian Railway Company to hatch an opposition movement. In February 1927, leaders of this bloc issued a tract on the matter, directed as much at policymakers in Tokyo as lumbermen across the Yalu. In no uncertain terms, they cast the repeal as a reckless and needless reform that could undermine both "continental policies and peninsular governance."[48] Therein lay the nub of their argument: that any major change ran the risk of jeopardizing Japan's foothold in Manchuria, an all-important geopolitical buffer and resource reserve. Caving to Korea's timber interests, they protested, was as short-sighted as it was misguided. Industrial growing pains across the Yalu were a small price to pay for unfettered access to Manchuria's riches.

The conflict came to a head on February 26, 1927, when Korean and Manchurian proxies "crossed swords" over a Diet measure on the repeal.[49] Those seeking swift resolution were in for disappointment. Committee members quickly realized that this was a complicated issue, raising thorny questions about military operations, colonial self-governance, and natural resource management. Among the more common refrains of the proceedings was a general wariness of undercutting "continental policies." Echoing Ministry of Foreign Affairs officials, lower house member Mutō Kinkichi, for instance, noted that any change to the status quo might unsettle not just the three thousand timber merchants in Andong but also Japan's foothold in the "gateway of Manchuria."[50] Even Foreign Minister Shidehara Kijūrō weighed in on the matter, calling for circumspection in light of the delicate diplomatic situation on the continent. By session's end, it was readily apparent that strategic concerns over the administration of Manchuria were to supersede abstract projections about the commercial potential of Korea. Calling for more research, the Diet tabled the measure.

By the time lawmakers revisited the issue in 1929, however, the climate of opinion had changed. Where the 1927 Diet session had focused chiefly on the politics of continental expansion, the 1929 debate zeroed in on the question of how to shore up Japan's domestic timber supply, which was then subject to capricious shifts and ballooning prices. Parties to the 1929 Diet debate were therefore concerned less with accommodating special interests on the continent than with streamlining the empire-wide flow of timber products. Korea provided a partial solution to this problem: as processing capacities expanded with each passing year, Korea's timber industry promised to drive down costs and offset trade imbalances.

The findings of the Special Committee on Tariff Revision—a panel established by the 1927 session to undertake further research into the measure—tilted opinion clearly in favor of repealing the Special Edict. After months of research, the committee arrived at something of a compromise: Should the Diet agree to phase in the tariff over a period of three years, damage to Andong's timber industry would be minimized.[51] Incremental annual increases would grant timber firms on both sides of the Yalu time to adapt to their new commercial circumstances. This recommendation held. Just one month later, on March 30, 1929, the special edict was repealed as part of a larger package of tariff reforms.

Yet, owing to some clever foot-dragging on the part of the Kwantung Army and Southern Manchurian Railway Company, little actually changed. Only in 1931 did the trade winds begin to blow in a different direction. This came as a result not of commercial policy but of military adventurism: the Mukden Incident, a provocation orchestrated by officers in the Kwangtung Army then eager to expand Japan's military presence in Manchuria. To do so, they engineered a small explosion near a railway track in Mukden—a pretext used to trigger a full-on invasion of China by the Japanese Imperial Army. Months of conflict had by 1932 given way to the making of Manchukuo, a satellite state on the continent. A frenzy of construction was soon under way north of the Yalu, as urban planners and settler leaders set to work in building what propagandists soon likened to "a new heaven on earth."[52]

Even as unprecedented volumes of Korean timber thereafter flowed into Manchuria, many of Sinŭiju's sawmills still teetered on the brink of closure. The source of their tribulations was an unexpected shift in FMB policy: orders from on high that its procurement office begin to earmark much of the timber harvested at its field stations for shipment directly to Manchukuo. Their privileged access to the Government-General's stockpile suddenly no more, many Sinŭiju-based timber firms found themselves helplessly wanting for raw materials. Fewer logs to process meant fewer factory jobs. Unemployment rates began to climb. Most unnerving to authorities in Sinŭiju was the marked uptick of Red Labor union activity, which put Chinese and Korean wage laborers in direct confrontation with mill operators and police.[53]

Neither tariff reforms nor a regional construction boom, it seemed, were enough to assuage the "great distress of the timber world."[54] The arrival in 1933 of 20,000 *koku* of timber imported from Karafuto by the Mitsui Corporation was for many local lumbermen emblematic of the persistent commercial disparities that had for decades suffocated the industry.[55] Little did they know that by then the exigencies of continental expansion were stacked irreversibly against them. As many began to herald a "Yalu River Era of Development," Japanese officials envisioned northern Korea anew as a linchpin of the emerging Yen bloc and a focal point for comprehensive development on the continent.

NORTHERN DEVELOPMENT

Few colonial officials had grander plans for the Yalu River basin—or higher hopes for its timberlands—than Ugaki Kazushige. On returning to his post as governor-general in 1931, the erstwhile minister of war threw the weight of his office behind an ambitious agenda for industrial growth in Korea, the Northern Development Plan. A fifteen-year roadmap for *nōkō heishin* (the parallel development of industry and agriculture), the plan called for road improvements, railway construction, and myriad plant-construction projects in the eight northernmost districts of the region—that is, the borderlands abutting the Yalu River. Forestry, unsurprisingly, occupied a central place in this comprehensive industrial scheme, which put a tripartite directive before the FMB: increased output, improved protection, and a crackdown on swidden agriculture.[56]

The last of these tasks was the most trying. Dismayed by the initial reports of surveyors, Japanese foresters in Korea moved early and vigorously to curb the practice of shifting cultivation. Both the Forest Law (1908) and Forest Ordinance (1911) established measures to punish anyone caught setting alight or otherwise clearing national woodlands for agriculture. In 1916, a conference of provincial administrators went further to decree a strict topographical threshold for agriculture: thereafter, any party found tilling land on slopes of a gradient of thirty degrees or steeper was subject to fines and other penalties. These early efforts were the opening salvoes of a campaign against swidden cultivation practices that agronomists had come to describe as "a social disease," threatening forest health, crop yields, and civic values alike.[57]

Progress was elusive. In a major blow to the FMB, the population of shifting cultivators only increased over the 1920s. Driving this growth was a northern migration of Korean tenant farmers who, displaced by land reforms and financial insecurity, had little recourse but to try to eke out a living in the region's remote mountain interiors. Early efforts to expel these farmers from national forestland revealed that many simply had nowhere else to go. Thousands of Korean migrant cultivators evasively struck off to Manchuria, while countless others temporarily returned to their home-towns only to head back to the mountains just weeks later. Needless to say, forest rangers struggled to keep track of the movement of these transient communities, much less prosecute their legal transgressions.

Simply put, Korea's northern uplands were not a blank slate upon which the Japanese could impose comprehensive plans. They were rather, as one forestry official lamented, the domain of the "lumpen proletariat of the mountains," an alpine demimonde populated by Korea's outcastes of empire.[58] Left unchecked, officials feared, these mountain dwellers would be easily coaxed into the ranks of bandits, smugglers, and communist guerilla fighters (fig. 5.5). The latter group became a particular menace to the FMB, as insurgent raids—led by none other than Kim Il-sŏng—grew in scope and frequency after 1931. More than simply an agronomic issue, rectifying the so-called "fire-field problem" (*kaden mondai*) was framed in terms of law, order, and national security. If plans for northern development were to come to fruition, foresters needed to shore up their control over restive upland spaces—a project that started with the region's farmers.[59]

Not all Japanese thought ill of these mountain dwellers, however. Odauchi Michitoshi, for one, a geographer who spent many months observing

FIG. 5.5 The living quarters of shifting cultivators in the upland north. (From Nakama, *Nihon chiri fūzoku taikei*, vol. 17, 334.)

these communities in the Kaema Plateau, saw in their practices of fire-fallow cultivation and crop rotation a sophisticated agricultural regimen. Although their agrarian strategies were "primitive" in some respects, he argued, no small number of hamlets engaged in swidden cultivation had achieved considerable social stability and economic vitality. To Odauchi, as to others, simple caricatures of torch-wielding primitives—the bogeymen of deforestation—obscured sensible agricultural adaptations required by the distinct soil conditions and climatic fluctuations that characterized the north. Of particular interest was Odauchi's conclusion that there were, in actuality, two distinct types of swidden communities: those that had practiced an advanced form of shifting cultivation in the region for generations; and a newer, poorer type of nomadic cultivator who burned their way through the region's forests out of sheer desperation. It was the latter group, he maintained, that required the full weight of foresters' resources and attention.[60]

The measures taken by FMB employees in Kapsan County on June 17, 1929 were most certainly *not* what he had in mind. Overzealous in their interpretation of orders to ward off shifting cultivators setting fires within the jurisdiction of the Hyesanjin field station, a posse of rangers and local police officers decided to carry out a raid on a settlement near the village of

Taep'yŏng. A gratuitous exercise of force ensued. Taking a cue from the farmers themselves, the raid party torched the cluster of shacks and farm structures, many of them only recently built by area residents displaced by summer floods. By nightfall, a total of eighty-three households—and all the worldly possessions within them—had been reduced to ashes, leaving hundreds of individuals homeless and a community in shock.

If not for the work of Korean journalists, this assault might have been written off as a police action gone awry. But thanks to the tireless on-site reporting of the *Tonga ilbo*, the incident was thrust into the national spotlight, drawing ignominy upon the FMB and its employees. Faced with swelling public sympathy for the farmers, forestry bureaucrats in Seoul had little choice but to unequivocally condemn the raid and enter into negotiations over compensation for damages. Korean political activists demanded more than payouts. They called on the Government-General to approach shifting cultivation as a grave "problem of humanitarianism," a crisis that required a hard look at the socioeconomic forces that drove these communities into the mountains in the first place.[61] Korean commentary took particular exception at the dehumanizing Japanese rhetoric that likened these mountain dwellers to, among other things, criminals, lepers, and pine caterpillars—in a word, a plague on the land.[62]

Journalists and editors at the *Tonga ilbo* in particular saw in this affair a call to action. After elevating the plight of these mountain dwellers to the national stage, they set out to give these communities a face and a voice. To that end, their regional correspondents conducted a long series of travel surveys deep into the mountains, where they tried to shed light on the forces of displacement: sudden crop failures, chronic indebtedness, crushing tax obligations.[63] In keeping with the paper's role as a mouthpiece for cultural nationalism, this vein of reporting also often positioned these cultivators within broader debates on Korea's national heritage and history. "Although in a state of starvation," declared one nameless farmer, "we know that we are the people of this nation and that this area is Korean national land. . . . It is natural for the people to cultivate fire fields on their national land as they have done in the past."[64]

Natural or not, by the time of the rollout of the Northern Development Plan in 1932, the tenor of the debate on shifting cultivation had appreciably softened. Alert to the strategic limitations of expulsion and under newfound scrutiny from the broader public, foresters decided to channel their resources into sedentization. By anchoring shifting cultivators to the land through intensive agriculture, they hoped to shake these communities of their incendiary inclinations. What was needed, in other words, was a bold program of homesteading—precisely the task assigned to the Kyoto Imperial University agronomist Hashimoto Denzaemon, who spearheaded the Government-General's subsequent efforts to fix these communities to the land.[65]

At the heart of Hashimoto's approach was the promotion of intensification techniques that would supplant what he and others called the "predatory agricultural practices" of these households. As urgent as it was obvious to Hashimoto was the village-level production of manure, mulch, and compost, sustainable supplies of which were indispensable to achieving higher crop yields. A second reform proceeded from the first: animal husbandry, which would not only expand commercial opportunities but also yield compostable manure for crop farming. That this initiative dovetailed with ongoing efforts to promote sheep farming in the north—a push to diversify agricultural production in Korea following problems in the rice market—only broadened the appeal of Hashimoto's proposal.

By the early 1930s, an elaborate experiment in upland resettlement was afoot. At the same time that corporations and provincial governments were buying out and relocating landowners to clear land for dam sites, FMB officials began to round up and relocate shifting cultivators. Using both the promise of free land and the threat of force, they concentrated entire hamlets into so-called "agricultural guidance zones": collective settlements (of around five hundred households) where officials could model upland agricultural practices and monitor the habits of residents. Each guidance zone was subdivided into distinct agricultural cooperatives, in which roughly seventy households would share resources, patrol landholdings, and practice self-governance.[66] By 1940, as many as 430,000 individual cultivators had received "settlement land" free of charge. As a result of these and other measures, government officials were quick to note, the average annual income of "mountain farming" households—a new label applied to *settled* upland cultivators—gradually grew from ¥252 in 1933 to ¥848 in 1941.[67]

Accompanying these settlement schemes was a push to tighten the screws of legal enforcement and prosecution. Sedentization spurred criminalization. On top of creating a set of specially designated "forest-protection zones," the FMB hired more than two hundred additional forest rangers to crack down on shifting cultivation and timber theft. They were joined in this effort by a growing number of privately funded "self-defense forces" (*jietai*): armed security outfits hired by timber companies to protect their assets and work crews.[68] Regulatory teeth were further sharpened by a series of legal reforms that raised the penalty for illicit fire-starting from a fine of up to ¥200 to imprisonment for as long as three years. One need only inspect statistics on forest crimes to appreciate the ensuing crackdown: whereas the colonial state prosecuted a total of 5,143 infractions of the Forest Ordinance in 1930, this figure rose to 12,152 in 1937.[69] This increase attests not only to the newfound vigilance of the state but also to the utter desperation of rural communities hit hard by the economic downturn of the 1930s, a "time of crisis" marked by tenancy disputes, organized protest, and diasporic friction.

Involving mass relocation, communal surveillance, and expert guidance, the response of the FMB to the "fire-field problem" was social engineering on a grand scale. Despite their limited resources, the forest wardens of the north labored mightily to assert control over the migration patterns, cultivation methods, and economic activities of shifting cultivators. Their efforts left virtually no aspect of daily life untouched: from dietary intake to fuel collection to home construction. Such, at least, was the case within the confines of guidance zones. Judging by the Government-General's own statistics, the impact of these measures remained patchy at best. As of 1942, the last year for which reliable statistics are available, there were as many as eighty thousand individuals still practicing shifting cultivation. If the persistence of these communities was an indication of the enduring destitution of tenant farmers, it was also a testament to the ruggedness and fluidity of the northern terrain. Whether on account of political convictions or financial necessity, many chose to melt into the northern highlands or, come winter, slip north across the frozen Yalu.

COMPREHENSIVE CHANGE

It is no coincidence that the Japanese response to the fire-field problem intensified over the 1930s, just as northern development was taking off. The crusade against swidden agriculture in many ways grew directly out of Japanese blueprints for the region's industrialization. Foresters did not relocate thousands of families solely in the name of fire prevention; they did so to clear land for buildings, roads, and dams. They did not concentrate households into guidance zones (at no small cost to the colonial government) just so that they could lead a bucolic existence; they wasted no time in mobilizing these very villages as labor pools that would bring their industrial plans to life. Fixes to the problem of shifting cultivation, in other words, offered a pretext for broader programs of labor mobilization and resource control. Tapping into deep wells of anxiety over fire setting and insurgency, forestry officials granted themselves what were essentially emergency powers used to lay the foundation for the colonial state's comprehensive industrial plans.

These plans dealt a mixed hand to the Yalu River basin's timber interests. In the short term, northern development meant a surge in government and corporate investment in the region's extractive infrastructure. To the 560 kilometers of logging roads and skid-ways constructed in the first twenty years of colonial rule were added 916 kilometers of timber transport lines in just eight years from 1933 to 1940.[70] Private capital also enjoyed a multitude of positive externalities that came with the colonial state's newfound interest in boosting timber production—fire watching, aerial surveying, and erosion control benefited all who did business in the region.

Yet, the buildup of plants, factories, and railways in the region also began to scramble the supply circuits of long-standing logging operations. The extension of new railways (such as the easterly line connecting Kilju with Hyesan) allowed lumbering operations to bypass Sinŭiju entirely, thereby compounding the timber capital's material shortfalls. A more consequential spatial realignment came with the completion in 1939 of the Chian Yalu River Border Railway Bridge—a new passageway over the Yalu at Manp'o that raised the prospect of an "economic revolution" in the eyes of some Sinŭiju-based businessmen.[71] Strategically placed farther upriver and able to handle much larger volumes of freight, this bridge wired northern Korea and its factories into commodity chains extending deeper into northern China.

Enticed by cheaper shipping rates and the promise of energy subsidies, a growing number of corporate giants hitched their wagons to the Northern Development Plan. Ōji Paper's North Korea Paper and Chemical Manufacture Plant (in Kilju), Mitsubishi Mining Company's Iron Refinery (in Ch'ŏngjin), the Onoda Cement Company's three new factories (in Komusan, Samch'ŏk, and on the Yalu): these and other industrial sites were trumpeted not just as vanguards of a new era of development but as material expressions of the colonial government's new watchword of *naisen ittai*—"Japan and Korea as one body." None of these projects, however, would have proceeded without the backing of the FMB, which stood behind a subtle but significant shift in the nature of forest governance: the arrangement of woodland leases outside of the afforestation loan system. As officials had hoped, corporations jumped at the opportunity to gain leaseholds over woodlands without having to enter into agreements regarding forest regeneration. Whereas in 1930 woodland leases without afforestation provisions accounted for just 34 of 2,797 transactions, by 1936 they comprised 655 of 716 transactions.[72]

Most of these contracts were issued in furtherance of energy development. Take, for example, the Chōsen Nitrogenous Fertilizer Company's flagship plant in Hŭngnam. A massive chemical production facility financed by Noguchi Jun, the "king of Korean industry," the plant was constructed in the hope of cornering the market for ammonium sulfides, phosphates, and other chemical components. Its operations would have ground to a halt, however, without the eighteen different woodland leases that enabled Noguchi's family-owned conglomerate to construct hydroelectric turbines along the upper Jangjin River. Although totaling only 831 *chōbu* in area, this patchwork of leases effectively permitted the company to build and then maintain the electrical power grid and transportation networks crucial to the economic viability of the project.[73] In this respect, the FMB functioned as an industrial landlord of sorts, using its broad discretionary powers to dole out strategically located parcels of national woodland to key corporate partners.

In hydropower, the timber capital found its greatest foe. Indeed, of all the changes carried out under the banner of northern development, none dealt a graver blow to the regional timber trade than the push to dam the Yalu, the "economic lifeline of Sinŭiju."[74] In 1937, following nearly a decade of research into the river's hydroelectric potential, the Yalu River Hydropower Company broke ground on the construction of the Sup'ung Dam, then one of the world's largest hydropower projects. The response of timber companies to this project ranged from skepticism to indignation. At minimum, they sought nonobstruction guarantees and compensation for damage to their businesses. In the earliest stages of construction, Yalu Hydropower made assurances that their engineers would accommodate the timber industry by constructing special channels to facilitate the flow of timber. But their pledges outstripped the capabilities of their engineers. It was immediately evident that the dam hampered the transportation of timber downstream. In 1940, just a year after its completion, the amount of timber collected at Sinŭiju fell by a staggering 95 percent. Led once again by Tada Eikichi, timber industry representatives took their frustrations to the Government-General, which tried to broker a deal between Sinŭiju's timber industry and Yalu Hydropower. After a series of contentious mediations, Yalu Hydropower agreed to improve its system of sluice gates and allocate special resources to improve timber transport, but to little effect.[75]

Sinŭiju would never be the same. Choked off from raw materials, timber companies began to migrate their operations upstream to Manp'o. A geographical reorientation of the timber industry was quickly under way. Timber companies now floated sawlogs to Manp'o, whereupon they were shipped by rail either north into Manchuria or south on the new Manp'o rail line through Kanggye, Chŏnch'ŏn, and Hŭich'ŏn—the new timber towns of Korea.[76] In the meantime, Sinŭiju accelerated its transition from a timber town to a more diversified industrial hub, taking advantage of the power generated by its dams and making the most of its prime access to shipping routes. This was perhaps the inevitable outcome for a regional industry that had long seen its place in the market subordinated to the broader geopolitical imperatives of continental expansion.

CONCLUSION

By all outward appearances, the Yalu River timber industry of the 1910s was poised to thrive. All the ingredients were present for profitable growth. Expanses of rich forest sustained steady supplies of quality timber, while the good favor of the FMB facilitated ready access. The Yalu itself allowed for rapid conveyance of timber to market, while a growing transportation infrastructure plugged the region's products into empire-wide commodity chains. Yet, harvesting the region's evergreens left many timber firms ever in the red. Handicapped by volatile market conditions, unfavorable trade laws, and oligopolistic business tactics, many companies were forced to downsize their operations or sell off their assets entirely. This is not to suggest that all corporations suffered equally. Larger conglomerates like Ōji Paper often did quite well for themselves in region, due largely to their deep capital pools and government connections.

The timber undertaking, in short, was not always as clear-cut as industry boosters made it out to be. While investors and operators celebrated the Yalu timber industry as a high-octane motor of economic growth, it perennially came into conflict with other developmental aims and aspirations. Caught in the crosswinds of Diet politics in Japan and military expansion in Manchuria, Sinŭiju's timber industrialists could only marvel at the protean value of the region's resources. If these frictions induced growing pains for private corporations in the region, they barely blunted the saws of the FMB, which harvested timber at a furious pace. No less than 80 percent of timber processed in the peninsula over the 1930s was harvested from national forests located in the northern provinces.[77] It is indeed for good reason that the FMB has become synonymous with what Korean scholars now call the colonial-era "northern primeval forest plunder."[78]

What these statistics largely fail to convey, however, is the fluid geography of forest exploitation. Lumbering operations were only as good as the modes of mobility that surrounded them. The timber undertaking accordingly gave impetus to an expansive infrastructure that allowed firms to penetrate deep into previously inaccessible mountain areas. Where there were logging camps, field stations, and sawmills, there were new rails, roads, and tramways transforming trees into timber, nature into capital. In this way, the timber undertaking anticipated the broader industrial metamorphosis of the region. Wittingly or not—and sometimes to their detriment down the line—lumber firms blazed industrial trails that expedited the commercial diversification and resource exploitation that gained momentum over the 1930s.

The timber undertaking did not extract resources haphazardly, moving from one clear-cut to the next. Rather, it painstakingly imprinted onto the northern interior highlands, often at great expense to the colonial state, systems of resource transport, processing, and supervision scarcely seen elsewhere on the peninsula. To be sure, issues of vagrancy and labor discipline transcended regional and jurisdictional divides. But only in the northern provinces did foresters track and relocate thousands of households in the name of industrial development. Nowhere else did they work closely with engineers to erect and maintain hydroelectric turbines and alpine roadways. Nowhere else did logging crews exchange fire with communist bandits. The FMB, as such, should be understood not just as an office tasked with resource extraction but also as an active agent in industrial planning and border security. It brought forth a more forceful approach to upland control that evolved in response to the administrative anxieties of colonial officials and the comprehensive visions of the empire's technocratic class.

Considered as a whole, the Yalu River timber industry reveals the materiality of colonial modernization in all its complexity. From raftsmen on the Yalu to sawyers in Sinŭiju, from Diet members in Tokyo to engineers in Seoul, many different parties steered the flow of Korea's forest resources within and beyond the peninsula. By tracing the delivery of timber to market, we arrive at a richer understanding of the myriad forces shaping environmental governance in colonial Korea—transnational timber corporations, trans-imperial trade disputes, seasonal change. But while this macroregional approach brings the contours of industrial forestry into sharper focus, it offers little insight into the lived experience of forest management schemes as they unfolded at the village level. For that we must turn our attention to forest politics within the confines of privately owned woodlands, where an equally robust set of reforms held sway over local politics, agrarian finance, and, increasingly, the domestic sphere.

SIX

CIVIC FORESTRY

FOR ALL THEIR TALK OF FORESTRY AS AN INVESTMENT IN KOREA'S future, Japanese woodsmen exhibited a keen interest in the forests of Korea's past. Shioda Masahiro, for instance, combed the *Annals of the Chosŏn Dynasty*, the 1,893-volume dynastic chronicle, for any insight it offered into the forestry policies of previous centuries.[1] Yielding a weighty compilation of local forest histories, Tokumitsu Nobuyuki, a Forest Experiment Station (FES) researcher, conducted exhaustive documentary and physical surveys regarding Korea's *rinsō* (K: *imsu*): parcels of protected forests whose history often dated back to ancient times.[2] Although these and other studies did little to alter Japanese perceptions of the Chosŏn era as a parable of forest mismanagement, they did on occasion inspire optimism that the Korean peasantry was primed for conservation.

This was especially true of Japanese views on *songgye*, the pine associations that had for centuries overseen the protection and regeneration of pine trees in villages across Korea. To be sure, research into these communal organizations sharpened the focus on a number of practices that were, at least in the eyes of Japanese administrators, as deeply flawed as they were ingrained: red pine monoculture, cutting over culling, and the lax regulation of the commons.[3] But they also presented evidence of collective conservationist inclinations. As one longtime forestry bureaucrat put it, "In Korea's past, pine associations, afforestation associations, and the like were formed, whereby forest landowners banded together to jointly protect the forest and plant trees, a beautiful custom of neighborly cooperation that achieved substantial results."[4] If these associations hinted at the latent potential for stewardship in rural communities, they also reaffirmed for these officials the absolute primacy of *state-led* forestry. *Songgye* had failed to curb deforestation on a national scale, they argued, precisely because of their parochialism. Their legacy was atomized pockets of protected pine forest scattered about the peninsula. For village forestry to flourish, the state now needed to step in to coordinate these local institutions.

This left forestry policymakers with two seemingly contradictory imperatives. On the one hand, they needed to shore up the rights of private woodland owners through the Forestland Survey. On the other, they needed to bind individual woodland owners into collective regulatory bodies. How, then, to honor individual tenure rights while also encouraging communal forestry efforts? To many, the obvious answer was the creation of Forest Owners Associations (J: Shinrin Kumiai; K: Sallim Chohap), Japanese-style institutions that merged the resources and labor of local stakeholders to carry out the work of forestry at the village level. Forestry officials held high hopes that Forest Owners Associations would function in exactly the ways that the *songgye* had not—closely supervised by the state, comprehensive in coverage, and institutionally standardized.

Forest Owners Associations, in other words, were quickly designated the optimal instruments for the project of civic forestry: the state-led effort to mold hamlets into self-sufficient sites of agricultural production, households into woodland watchdogs, and individuals into keepers of the emperor's realm. Forest Owners Associations were hardly the only collective forestry institutions born of these objectives. Charcoal production associations, erosion control associations, and forest-love mutual-aid societies, among others, all proliferated during the colonial period. At the center of it all was the Korean Forestry Association (Chōsen Sanrinkai, hereafter KFA), an umbrella organization that orchestrated an impressive array of forestry activities throughout the peninsula.

Underlying each of these arrangements was a desire on the part of the colonial government to compel rather than coerce forest management. Whereas Forest Management Bureau employees were relatively unconstrained in their management of the national forestlands discussed in chapter 5, the oversight of privately owned forestlands (*minyūrin*) required a softer touch. It necessitated a union of what, in the context of urban Japan,

Sheldon Garon has called "moral suasion" with what, in the context of rural Korea, Gi-Wook Shin and Do-Hyun Han have called "colonial corporatism": the creation of "new, semiofficial, semivoluntary, intermediary associations for colonial control and mobilization."[5] Seeking to shape the routines of agrarian life, officials turned to semi-official institutions to promote behaviors conducive to prolonged forest conservation: industriousness, frugality, civic-mindedness, and so on.

To the extent that colonial forestry measures touched the daily life of Korean farmers, semi-official organizations were the points of contact. Only rarely did agriculturalists interact directly with forestry officialdom, the forestland survey being the major exception. Rather, their experience of forest governance was mediated at every turn by rural institutions—many state-controlled, some loosely regulated, and others operating beyond the limits of its authority. If, following Holly Stephens, historians of Korea are to "make visible the hand of the state in the rural economy," they might start with these semi-official organizations, which formed vital ligaments between the colonial state and agrarian society, allowing flexion in either direction.[6]

When examined from the standpoint of these rural institutions, we can also see forestry more clearly for what it was to a vast majority of Koreans: an adjunct to agriculture. The forest may have furnished a number of materials critical to everyday existence, but it did not absorb the thoughts or finances of Korea's cultivators like cotton, silk, or rice. The latter foodstuff in particular insinuated itself into nearly every major forestry decision, be it a policy directive proposed by bureaucrats or a business investment by a village council. Irrigation improvement, erosion control, and tree planting all found broad support in rural society less out of future-minded concern with forest health than immediate interest in rice yields and, by extension, farm incomes. What happened upstream had direct implications for agricultural productivity down the line, and this raised the stakes of forest management—all the more so given that much of Korea's rice was bound for markets in Japan, where it was used to offset domestic scarcity.

And yet, historiographically, the view of the forest from the farm remains sketchy at best.[7] Despite the fact that the *nō* (agro) and the *rin* (forest) were consolidated into a single bureaucratic office (the Nōrin Kyoku) in colonial Korea in 1932, scholarly predilections have left these analytical spheres strikingly partitioned. This is regrettable, not least because it conveys the false impression that forestry was somehow divorced from the quotidian grind of farm life. Forestry, it stands to reason, is performed in the forest. Yet, if the activities of civic forestry associations are any indication, it was also per-formed in the home, the school, the town square, and, especially, the kitchen. Not merely the domain of the lumberjack or ranger, the forest was the responsibility of every housewife preparing food, every child collecting brush, every yeoman planning finances. To a large degree, *these* were the tar-gets of civic forestry outreach. The KFA and other local institutions made it their job to ensure that farming families saw the forest in a pot of hot soup or a toasty *ondol* floor on a winter's night. Colonial rhetoric about the connec-tions between "the forest and human life" was not empty. At the same time that officials called on Koreans to conserve forests for the sake of the empire, they turned to civic forestry associations to bring domestic fuel consumption under their thumb.

They were met in this endeavor with resistance of all kinds. Although forestry bureaucrats painted Forest Owners Associations as "operating thoroughly in accordance with the will of the people," the dogged protests of many Korean communities often suggested otherwise.[8] Where there were civic forestry projects, there were disgruntled farmers who pursued wide-ranging "repertoires of resistance" against the state's incursions in private property and private lives: poaching, civil disobedience, and even armed resistance. Well over 80 percent of woodland owners in Korea, after all, owned parcels of woodland less than five *chōbu* in area—plots hardly size-able enough to turn any sort of profit. A far cry from landed gentry or petty capitalists, these were dirt-poor farmers simply trying to eke out a living off the land. Firmly embedded within what Yun Hae-dong has aptly called a "colonial gray zone" (K: *hoesaek chidae*), they variously worked alongside, around, and against the state to maximize their own access rights and advance their familial and communal interests.[9]

The county of Tanch'ŏn is a case in point. If "historically, the state, the peasantry, and other external interests have acted out their tensions in the natural theater of the forest," as Nancy Lee Peluso has put it, then this restive region provides a dramatic mise-en-scène.[10] Saddled with membership dues well beyond their means, Tanch'ŏn's farmers pushed back, drawing in 1930 a line in the sand over an institution they found oppressive in both function and form. The colonial state met this uprising, first, with brutal force, mobi-lizing its strong military apparatus to restore order to the region. But it did not pursue further confrontation with rural society. Rather, in light of this and related setbacks, forestry officials abandoned their signature civic forestry project, electing instead to revive traditional Korean forestry institutions.

The maelstrom of economic depression left them little other choice. By the early 1930s, civic forestry advocates were staring down an agricultural crisis. Confronted with tanking rice prices and deepening rural unrest, they tried over the 1930s to make the best of whatever local allies and resources they had, be they sympathetic elites or centuries-old institutions. They set out, in short, to reshape pine associations and other Korean customs from the inside out. Operating under a new banner of "rural revitalization," agro-forestry experts kicked off a series of programs designed not only to insulate farmers from a global economic panic but also to stake out a broader role for the state in the agricultural economy. In this way, civic forestry activities paved the way for wartime forestry. Semi-official associations forged in the name of social harmony and self-sufficiency became after 1937 channels for resource centralization and caloric control.

COORDINATING CONSERVATION: THE KOREAN FORESTRY ASSOCIATION

If the project of civic forestry had a brain trust, it was the men gathered at the Chōsen Hotel on February 17, 1920. A mix of senior bureaucrats and business leaders, this group had, in one configuration or another, left its mark on every major forestry reform launched in Korea. Uniting the group were more than mutual concerns over production costs, tariff schedules, and financial regulations. They also all shared a membership with the Japan Forestry Association, by then a well-oiled instrument of civic forestry back in Japan. It was long overdue, they decided, that a sister organization be launched in Korea, where the growing number of woodland owners demanded greater coordination between state policy and agrarian society.[11]

Out of this meeting emerged the founding committee of the KFA, which over the months to follow worked to gain the consent of the Government-General, raise funds, and recruit its first cohort of members. On June 11, 1921, the KFA held its inaugural meeting in the Keijō Civic Auditorium. "If speeches were trees," logged Yun Ch'iho in his diary following the event, "there was enough of them to have reforested all the bare hills of Korea."[12] Along with prepared remarks from the Government-General's top brass, the three hundred attendees took in congratulatory statements from prominent journalists, military officers, and provincial governors. By meeting's end, the primary aims of the KFA were abundantly clear: to "develop forestry and advance forestland reclamation"; to "share opinions regarding forestry"; and to "exchange views with officials."[13]

In its early years, the KFA was a decidedly elite organization, drawing both its membership and funding through the revolving door of industry and bureaucracy. Minobe Shunkichi, the KFA's first president, was ideally positioned to bring these communities together. As a senior official in the Bureau of Agriculture and Industry who also sat on the board of the Bank of Chōsen, the central bank of the Government-General, Minobe knew better than most how to court the corporate sector. He found an able Korean partner in Han Sang-nyŏng, a KFA board member who, through his leadership roles in the Keijō Chamber of Commerce and Hansŏng Bank, worked to bring Korean businessmen and landlords on board. It was no accident that the KFA's board of directors was mixed almost evenly with Japanese and Korean members. Inaugurated amid the shift to cultural rule, the KFA had clear marching orders to foster an inclusive spirit of cooperation between Japanese and Korean industrial elites.

Promoted through journal advertisements, newspaper articles, and the interpersonal network of the forestry world, membership of both "Korea's influential [forestry] officials and lay people" steadily rose.[14] A surge in KFA membership took place after 1924, when it opened its provincial branches. From then on, the KFA took on more rank-and-file members: rural entrepreneurs, craftsmen, village leaders, and the like. Typical of these branch members was Kim Yŏng-mu, a resident of Sunch'ang County, South Chŏlla, who joined the KFA in 1924. By turns a judicial official, educator, provincial assembly member, and businessman, Kim was in many ways an ideal intermediary in the eyes of the KFA. A graduate of Meiji University in Tokyo, where he earned a law degree, Kim was a fluent Japanese speaker and vocal advocate of Japanese scientific and technological prowess. His senior positions in the South Chŏlla Agricultural Association also gave him a prominent platform from which to promote a variety of agrarian reforms, many of them closely aligned with the interests of the KFA.[15]

Further fleshing out the ranks of the KFA's provincial branches were Japanese settlers such as Nakano Sōzaburō, a native of Yamaguchi Prefecture who moved to Korea in 1911. After acquiring land in Kimje County, North Chŏlla, Nakano incorporated Nakashiba Industries, a firm specializing in the manufacture and sale of agricultural implements. As a well-connected agricultural entrepreneur, Nakano offered insight into a wide array of topics of interest to the KFA: rural finance, tenancy conditions, labor require-ments. No less valuable were the connections that Nakano provided to the other rural institutions in which he participated, including the Korean Agricultural Association, the Korean Livestock Association, and the Kimje Irrigation Association.[16]

Kim and Nakano were the true targets of the KFA's outreach—rural men of influence, both Korean and Japanese, who could help close the gap between official policies and ground-level realities. In this sense, they merit comparison with the "brokers of empire" profiled by Jun Uchida: the Japa-nese settler leaders "who not only oversaw their communities but actively mediated the colonial management of Korea as its grassroots movers and shakers."[17] Although carrying far less clout than most of the urban-dwelling business leaders who drive Uchida's account, the likes of Nakano and Kim were key mediators in the colonial management of the agricultural econ-omy. From their positions within rural institutions, they variously advanced, fine-tuned, and rebuffed directives from the center. "Both agents and pawns of colonial power," to borrow Uchida's phrase, these agrarian brokers actively negotiated the breadth and depth of agroforestry reforms.[18]

As a broad-tent organization, the KFA offered a vital forum for just this sort of negotiation. Reform plans drawn up by colonial bureaucrats were often floated in the context of national KFA meetings and taken back to each region for input. Men like Kim and Nakano were invaluable sounding boards, enabling forestry officials to better anticipate local pushback and regional differentiation. Less interested in expertise than access, the KFA eagerly recruited businessmen, landowners, and village elders—anyone, that is, who could put a softer face on forestry officialdom. As much as any-thing else, they saw in these rural intermediaries points of entry into a wide array of complementary rural institutions. Holly Stephens has shown through careful readings of farmers' diaries how cultivators across class lines were often active in multiple agricultural institutions at once. In the course of a single season, a farmer might turn to a cotton spinning *kye* to diversify production, join a financial cooperative to gain access to capital, and enter a life insurance *kye* to dilute risk.[19] In the eyes of civic forestry advocates, these semi-official organizations presented toeholds with which the KFA might maneuver itself into agrarian affairs. By the end of the 1920s, the question had clearly shifted from whether to how the KFA might use these institu-tions to shape fuel economies, compel tree planting, and enforce property boundaries.

Forestry professionals did not harbor any illusions that tenant farmers or small cultivators would join the KFA. Membership dues alone were enough to preclude the participation of the vast majority of Korean farmers. Instead, the KFA leadership prevailed on its members to make inroads with other semi-official associations in their locales, using their positions of authority to coordinate forestry activities within and across preexisting institutions. To do so, the KFA turned to what would become a staple activity: agroforestry demonstrations. In partnership with FES scientists and provincial officials, the KFA orchestrated a wide array of exhibitions of best forestry practices—erosion-control seminars, pest-prevention workshops, coppicing tutorials. More than one-off performances of scientific authority, KFA representatives worked carefully with local leaders to ensure that their recommendations had some degree of staying power.

Consider, for example, the fuel improvement drive launched by the KFA in the late 1920s. For most participants, workshops on charcoal production were only the beginning. Fuel substitution methods introduced in the context of expert demonstrations were quickly put to work in stocking local "fuel forests" with energy efficient woods. Sales schemes and subsidies offered by the KFA channeled a variety of new technologies and seeds into the countryside. Wherever possible, the KFA also worked to set up Charcoal Production Associations (Seitan kumiai), village units responsible for collectively processing charcoal. In addition to systematizing charcoal production, these associations routinized quality inspection, ensuring that charcoal was bought and sold in state-sanctioned markets.[20]

A decade in, the KFA was operating much in the way envisioned by its founding committee. Through its provincial branch offices it had built ties with an expanding web of semi-governmental associations. For every charcoal workshop, there were tutorials on fertilizer production, roundtables on irrigation improvement, and inspections of erosion control projects. With nearly 4,300 members, the KFA had emerged as Korea's premier civic forestry institution, an esteemed body that granted access to the latest research, subsidized equipment, sales schemes, and government connections.

Yet, the KFA remained a voluntary organization. To most tenant cultivators, its programs and proceedings remained distant affairs. This concerned forestry bureaucrats, and all the more so in light of the fact that, by the late 1920s, the boundaries of private ownership were markedly expanding as the forest survey progressed. What left them nervous was not so much the growing number of private landowners as their socioeconomic background.

Here we should recall that most of the woodland titles transferred in the mid-1920s went to lower-class farmers—small cultivators whose silvicultural savvy was especially suspect in the eyes of the state. All the more reason, then, to create a new sort of regulatory entity: Forest Owners Associations, smaller units of communal governance that would leave no parcel of private forest beyond state oversight.

INDIVIDUAL RIGHTS, COLLECTIVE REGULATION

Many of the Japanese forestry professionals dispatched to Korea brought with them an abiding faith in the efficacy of Forest Owners Associations. For while they often went to great lengths to distinguish the scope and sources of Korea's denudation, they saw in the peninsula's past a policy vacuum not unlike that of the early Meiji period: a lapse in local forest governance that could be rectified with new and improved village institutions. Forest Owners Associations were one such institution. First promoted in the 1890s to reinvigorate the management of communal forests after the early-Meiji forest upheaval, Forest Owners Associations took on many of the responsibilities traditionally accorded to *iriai* and other customary arrangements. In Korea, policymakers hoped that they would do much the same for the private forests carved out of former "unowned public mountains."

The formation of Forest Owners Associations thus became the back end of woodland-tenure reform: a maneuver to retain a degree of control over private woodlands once title had been finalized. In contrast to the more compartmentalized functions of Korea's forestry *kye*, each Forest Owners Association was to be a full-service entity responsible for every aspect of local forest management: planting, cutting, finance, labor recruitment, fuel regulation, and more. An ulterior motive also impelled their creation: stabilizing and, where possible, expanding provincial finances. Indeed, while Japanese officials steeped the promotion of these institutions in the rhetoric of social cohesion, they simultaneously salivated at the prospect of the revenue their fees would generate for local governments.

Due to regional differences, changes to land-ownership procedures, and the early emphasis on irrigation and agriculture, the formation of Forest Owners Associations remained piecemeal throughout the 1910s. In some cases, Forest Owners Associations simply subsumed the organizational architecture of already existing pine associations and pine protection associations. In others, they grew organically out of the collective efforts taken by farmers to combine capital and other resources in order to cover the cost of surveying and woodland registration.[21] Whatever their origin, these associations were only loosely related to one another. Of carefully coordinated, institutionally uniform, legally codified forestry institutions there were few signs.

In light of this, civic forestry advocates began in the 1920s to demand some measure of institutional standardization. Forest Owners Associations had worked so well back in Japan, they pointed out, precisely because their mandate was spelled out in the Forest Law. In Korea, no such law existed, allowing a host of thorny questions to grow amidst the thicket of incongruous bylaws. Most of this disarray was rooted in confusion over the *scale* of these institutions. If Forest Owners Associations were to be standardized, at what unit of administrative governance should they be chartered—the hamlet (*ri*), the township (*myŏn*), or the county (*gun*)? Insofar as the *myŏn* formed the Korean equivalent to the *mura* (village)—the standard scale of forestry associations in mainland Japan—it was considered, at least initially, the most natural ambit of these institutions.

Yet, the *myŏn* was in many respects an artificial creation. A product of administrative reforms meant to streamline Korea's bureaucratic architecture, the *myŏn* consolidated different hamlets and villages into new district subdivisions. This redistricting stimulated a great deal of societal strife. As Kim Kwang-ok has shown, kinship ties and marriage networks that had historically facilitated village politics were suddenly strained, while different social status groups were uncomfortably amalgamated into "new administrative villages" (K: *sindongni*).[22] Consequently, communities and social groups that had long lain outside one another's orbit were forced into the same local governing bodies and property arrangements. Questions regarding the hierarchy of leadership and woodland access routinely roiled village councils, making Forest Owners Associations a tough sell.[23]

In response, forestry bureaucrats stepped up their efforts to define the legal status of Forest Owners Associations, as had just been done with Agricultural Associations. In 1927, the Government-General passed a temporary fix: the Forest Owners Associations Financial Assistance Regulations. Essentially a financial incentive package, this budget measure offered substantial subsidies to Forest Owners Associations, provided that they charter at the level of the county (*gun*). Among other things, the Financial Assistance Regulations underwrote part of the annual salary of technical specialists embedded within county-level Forest Owners Associations.[24] By 1933, there were as many as 1,900 full-time employees of Forest Owners Associations, who promoted planting methods, advised on all forestry-related matters, and negotiated with other associations as well as the state itself.[25]

What was to foresters a welcome overhaul to village forestry was to Korean farmers an uninvited intrusion into village life. Having already bent over backward to meet the onerous requirements of the Forestland Survey, many cultivators chafed at the idea that the state would not only continue to intervene in the management of their property but also demand payment to do so. With good reason, Korean woodland owners came to view these organizations as local arms of state power: regulatory entities that stood between them and their rightfully owned resources. The KFA would come and go—a workshop here, a planting ceremony there—but Forest Owners Associations were permanent fixtures of village life. High-minded ideals of civic duty and village harmony used by the state to promote Forest Owners Associations rang hollow to farming households buried in debt or struggling to meet their daily caloric requirements. Many communities instinctively ignored injunctions to join, leaving some Forest Owners Associations financially anemic, uneven in coverage, and often ill-equipped to tackle countywide problems.

How, then, to boost membership? The most obvious approach was to turn to local notables (yuji) and township leaders (myŏnjang), whom many officials viewed as the keys to unlocking communal support. Where tone-deaf appeals to voluntarily join these associations made little headway, forestry officials began to lean on local elites and landowners to pick up the pace of village recruitment. They often did so through the KFA, which had already identified a roster of sympathetic agrarian intermediaries. Before long, KFA members such as Kim Yŏng-mu were spearheading the formation of Forest Owners Associations in their own communities, working through different rural institutions to advertise its benefits, allay fears, and turn up the heat on hold-outs.

Judging by the numbers, these recruitment tactics were effective. By the late 1920s, 211 out of 220 counties in Korea had established a Forest Owners Association, with a total of 1,700,000 members and as much as 9,370,000 chōbu of forestland placed under their oversight. Just as impressive was the sum total of the annual membership fees collected, for example, in 1929: ¥1,227,550. A good portion of this revenue was used to fund the operations of these associations: the afforestation projects, raw materials, and processing costs that formed the very core of their mandate. To the delight of provincial bookkeepers, much of the remaining funds were steered into municipal administrative offices.[26]

In provinces such as Kyŏnggi and North Kyŏngsang, participation rates among forestland owners were as high as 99 percent. Drawn in by the promise of new economic opportunities, many farmers cast aside their reservations and joined these associations. But in remote, poorer areas, entire villages resisted, owing largely to their inability to incur the costs of membership fees. While annual dues could be as little as four sen, the average fee imposed on an association member was about fifteen sen per *chōbu*—a sum far beyond the wherewithal of many farming households.[27] These fees were often compounded by a variety of other circumstantial costs including stumpage-inspection fees, permission-processing fees, and the procurement of saplings and other tools. So, too, did they come with a substantial opportunity cost: members were expected to carry out communal forestry projects at the expense of their own farmwork.

Korean forestland owners did not take the imposition of these costs sitting down. Especially in the early 1930s, as provincial officials began to twist the arms of individual forest landowners to join county-level associations, Forest Owners Associations became the source of considerable rural unrest. Mostly, this amounted to written protest, demonstrations, or what James Scott calls everyday forms of peasant resistance—"foot dragging, dissimulation, desertion, false compliance, pilfering, feigned ignorance, slander, arson, sabotage, and so on."[28] But every so often this resistance metastasized into violent expressions of rural discontent. To understand how this latter form of opposition took shape one need only turn to Tanch'ŏn County, where farmers, intellectuals, journalists, youth groups, and village leaders set into motion a series of protests that dealt a decisive blow to the promotion of Forest Owners Associations nationwide.

THE UNQUIET WOODS OF TANCH'ŎN

The Tanch'ŏn uprising was borne of a climate of tumultuous change in rural Korea. While for some landlords the surging economic productivity of the 1920s spelled newfound prosperity, the commercialization of agriculture also gave rise to what Gi-Wook Shin has described as a process of "social differentiation of the Korean rural classes, into big landlords and some managerial farmers on the one hand and small tenants and wage laborers on the other."[29] Whatever sense of community had traditionally bound these groups together wore increasingly thin. The resulting rural strife is clearly evidenced in the upswing of tenancy disputes, of which there were more than 140,000 incidents between 1920 and 1939.[30] This acrimony also found expression in coordinated opposition movements against obligatory participation in rural institutions. In 1927, hundreds of peasants in Yangyang County, Kangwŏn, organized weeks of marches and demonstrations to protest the creation of an Agricultural Association. A similar struggle took place the following year in Hwanghae over the labor requirements of an Irrigation Association.[31]

Enlivening these peasant movements was a host of new alliances forged among different agrarian constituencies. Youth groups, tenant farmers associations, missionary-backed Farmer's Institutes, and other social bodies grew apace with—and sometimes in response to—state-sponsored institutions.[32] Despite the efforts of the Government-General to stamp out formal Communist Party activity in Korea, these groups often drew inspiration from communist rhetoric on class conflict, colonial subjugation, and peasant liberation. Many parts of rural Korea witnessed an efflorescence of socialist thought, as organizations such as the Singanhoe built coalitions between intellectuals, farmers, youth, and other groups. Preaching a heady admixture of universal socialism and ethnic nationalism, these organizations advocated a form of class conflict and independence activism closely aligned with the Comintern's December Theses of 1928: "Only by bringing the peasants under the influence, only by appealing to them by means of intelligible and popular slogans and demands, will the working class and its vanguard be able to accomplish a victorious revolution in Korea."[33]

Nowhere were these forces more conspicuously operative than in Tanch'ŏn, a heavily forested county in the northeastern corner of South Hamgyŏng. Just a short distance from the southern slopes of Mount Paektu, where lumberjacks routinely skirmished with guerrilla fighters—who, according to one police report, "had to move like monkeys through the woodmen's paths in the dense forest"—the area was then a hotbed of communist activity.[34] The formation in 1925 in Tanch'ŏn of a Youth League (Tanch'ŏn Ch'ŏngnyŏn Tongmaeng), a local affiliate of the New Rising Youth Association (Shinhung Ch'ŏngnyŏnhoe), brought newfound organizational discipline to protest in the region.[35] Comprised principally of "young local leaders, usually modestly educated, whose main occupation was agriculture," local groups such as this one tapped into a deep vein of rural frustration to recruit farmers into the socialist cause.[36]

Peasants themselves also began to organize. In 1926, farmers in the area formed the Tanch'ŏn Peasants League (Tanch'ŏn Nongmin Tongmaeng), which quickly joined hands with the Tanch'ŏn Youth League. In an effort to broaden their base of regional support, both organizations held recruitment drives throughout the county such that, by 1930, the Tanch'ŏn Peasants League and the Youth League had grown to roughly 1,200 and 1,600 members, respectively.[37] Jointly, they tackled the myriad social concerns of farming communities in the region: corvée labor requirements, compulsory sericulture sale schemes, and the mistreatment of shifting cultivators, to name but the most pressing issues.

Such an alliance naturally left Japanese officials on edge. With concerns about a local insurgency mounting, provincial authorities began to crack down on their activities by dissolving rallies, searching the homes of organizers, and aggressively interrogating participants.[38] It was against this background that the promotion of Forest Owners Associations in Tanch'ŏn became a lightning rod for agrarian discontent. Although provincial officials had gestured toward establishing such an association early in the 1920s, it was not until the summer of 1928 that they began to strong-arm its creation. In 1928, following a provincial decree mandating the creation of county-level Forest Owners Associations, administrators, KFA members, and other local allies embarked on an enlistment campaign. For months, they traveled from hamlet to hamlet, where they met with local elites and village councils to cajole forestland owners to come on board.[39]

Resistance to this campaign was as immediate as it was intense. Especially in the townships of Ijung and Pokkwi, farmers strenuously objected to Forest Owners Association membership. Their hostility stemmed in part from exasperation over the Private Forest Protection Regulations, a series of edicts that put into effect strict quotas for the collection of fuel sources in the area. The crux of their opposition, however, was financial. With most farming households already shouldering the burden of Agricultural Association fees, the membership dues required by a Forest Owners Association were simply untenable. Given that as of 1931 there was a total of 140,833 *chōbu* of privately owned forestland in Tanch'ŏn County split between 14,934 individuals, the average area of a privately owned woodplot was roughly nine *chōbu*. All else being equal, according to Yi Chun-sik, this would have required each Forest Owners Association member to pay out approximately 74 *sen* in annual membership fees—far more than most farming households, then suffering from sharply declining prices in rice, had to spare.[40]

As the weight of this financial encumbrance sank in, many landowners turned to the Youth and Peasants Leagues to rouse opposition. Local police answered by clamping down even further on Youth League activities, going so far as to shut down its first public forum on the topic of Forest Owners Associations. Provincial officials, meanwhile, used threats of detention to browbeat village leaders to join the Tanch'ŏn County Forest Owners Association, which was formally inaugurated on May 1, 1930. While local officials promptly touted the organization as a vital organ for the promotion of forest-love thought and prevention against forest fires, membership rates in Tanch'ŏn were among the lowest in the province. The holdouts were primarily from the same three townships in the county: Ijung, Pokkwi, and Hada—all strongholds of the Youth and Peasants Leagues.

Resentment simmered in the region for weeks. On July 17, 1930, however, it reached its boiling point in the hamlet of Ryŏngdae. At the center of the commotion was Yang Sŏng-hwan, a forest inspector whose aggressive tactics had earned him the ire of the local community. That the catalyzing force behind the violence was not a Japanese ranger but a deputized Korean villager reflects the complex contours of forest use regulation on the ground. Although the exact chain of events remains unclear, the altercation came to a head when Yang paid a visit to the home of Hŏ Tal-kyu, a villager he suspected of filching cordwood. There, an exchange of words with Hŏ's wife turned into a physical assault, prompting a mob of angry locals to track down and assail Yang just hours later. The conflict further escalated the following day when Gotō Soichi (an assistant administrator of the Tanch'ŏn Forest Owners Association) and one Mr. Pak (its executive secretary) traveled to Ryŏngdae to issue a court summons for villagers accused of illegally felling trees. Defiantly, a group of approximately two hundred farmers marched to the Hada Township Office, where they demanded a legal justification for Gotō's actions. After trading insults with officials, the crowd stormed the office and battered Gotō. As night fell, police forces moved in to round up those responsible for the disturbance.[41]

Any semblance of order was not to last. As word of the conflict swirled around the county, political activists sprang into action. Contrary to contemporary Japanese characterizations of the ensuing conflict as an episode of spasmodic violence, the opposition movement that took shape revealed a sophisticated social infrastructure of political mobilization. Rallying support were seasoned youth leaders including Yi Tae-un, Yi Yong-hwan, and Kim Sung-mo, who called on locals to assemble the morning of July 20 to protest the wrongful incarceration of their peasant brethren. Following a series of stirring speeches, hundreds of farmers marched on the Tanch'ŏn County Office to hold yet another demonstration, which soon spilled over to the nearby Tanch'ŏn Police Office.

As the assembly grew and tempers flared, the protest took a violent turn. When efforts to repulse the throng of protesters failed, Japanese security forces opened fire on the crowd. By the time the smoke had cleared, sixteen Koreans were dead and another fourteen injured.[42] Panicked, provincial officials called in a surge of gendarmes under the auspices of the Peace Preservation Law—a statute routinely invoked to suppress political opposition movements and round up the "malcontent Koreans" (*futei Senjin*) behind them. More than four hundred individuals, most of them young men in their twenties, were arrested in the subsequent "pacification campaign."[43]

In his now classic study of the "unquiet woods" of the Indian Himalayas, Ramachandra Guha has shown how the forestry practices of the British Raj "struck at the very root of traditional social and economic organization," prompting hill societies to push back "against the tentacles of the commercial economy and the centralizing state."[44] It is tempting, based on outward appearances, to equate these resistance activities with those in Tanch'ŏn. Focused as they were on the restoration of customary rights, the rallying cries of peasants in both places were certainly in harmony. These resonances hint at a broader convergence in the literature on scientific forestry that portrays the closing of the commons as a seemingly uniform process across continents, if not centuries. Yet, similar grievances did not necessarily translate to an identical "social idiom of protest."[45] Rather, as Guha shows, peasant resistance activities grow out of the historical experience of individual villages and the particular socioecological context in which they were embedded.

In Tanch'ŏn, Korean farmers were stirred to action by more than merely resentment over forest policy. One need only canvass the crowd gathered before the district office on July 20 to gain a sense of the myriad issues at stake: farmers asserting their claims to lawfully owned resources; youth leaders voicing their right to assembly; intellectuals advocating for the proletariat. Far from binary conflicts between colonial oppressors and peasant resistors, these disputes were shaped by a variety of actors with multiple, sometimes overlapping agendas. In this sense, the Tanch'ŏn Forest Owners Association conflict affords a broader view of the evolving relationship between forest and village politics. It allows us to appreciate how forestry disputes were informed by farmers' engagements with socialism, nationalism, and agrarianism.

For Japanese forestry officials, the sobering events in Tanch'ŏn confirmed what many had already suspected: that the political costs of Forest Owners Associations outweighed their administrative benefits. Whatever potential they might have held for coordinating forest improvement or generating revenue, they were only sharpening divides in rural society at precisely the time that the colonial state was trumpeting its rhetoric of "harmony between Japan and Korea" (*Nissen yūwa*). Hence, by the early 1930s a critical mass of forestry experts were beginning to push for an overhaul to the guidelines for the management of privately owned woodlands, if not the abandonment of Forest Owners Associations altogether.

RURAL REVITALIZATION

Life only spiraled further downward in the 1930s for the many Korean tenant farmers unable to escape the vortex of global economic depression. The gravest blow came in the form of precipitous drops in the price of rice, a cash crop that accounted for well over half of farm incomes. In some areas, rice prices fell by as much as 60 percent compared to just a decade earlier, plunging many smallholders into debt, bankruptcy, and despair. The silk industry, another important source of earnings for rural households, similarly went bust. Even landlords, long buoyed by preferential treatment from the colonial state, fell on hard times, further rending the social fabric of rural society. While many farm households had grown accustomed to "spring hunger" (K: *chungunggi*), food scarcity was for many no longer a seasonal affair—a harsh reality that would only grow more acute with the onset of war. A rural exodus was soon in progress, as many agriculturists sought out wage labor in the burgeoning industrial sector or set out to Manchuria in search of a new beginning.

Hoping to forestall the flight of farmers, stabilize agricultural conditions, and diversify the agricultural economy, the Government-General launched in 1932 an ambitious agenda of agrarian improvement: the Rural Revitalization Campaign. In addition to hitting production targets for agricultural commodities and tackling the problem of rural debt, this farm-relief campaign aspired to fortify the communal bonds of rural life. Marrying practical farming improvements with lofty rhetoric on spiritual purity and social harmony, agroforestry officials set out to uplift the countryside by bringing discipline and frugality to every aspect of farm-work. If rural revitalization had a watchword, it was "self-subsistence" in the material underpinnings of rural life—fertilizer, seeds, and, of course, fuel.

To forestry officials in Seoul, the Rural Revitalization Campaign offered something of a reboot for the oversight of private woodlands. The fierce resistance sparked by Forest Owners Associations in communities such as Tanch'ŏn was only one of a number of problems dogging the management of private forestland. Of equal concern was the fact that, in spite of all of their efforts and investment, the quality of forest stock in private forests in some regions had not materially improved by the early 1930s. Twenty years into Japan's colonial administration the accumulation of timber stock per *chōbu* had actually begun to *decrease* in some private forests—evidence that in many areas extraction continued to outstrip reforestation.[46]

For these and other reasons, in 1933 Japanese officials drew the curtains on Forest Owners Associations. Their dissolution posed a number of problems, and none more pressing than the fate of municipal finances. If Forest Owners Association fees had provided sorely needed revenue to local governments, what should replace them? The answer, though straightforward, was a delicate proposition: raising a forest tax. Despite the vehement protests of Korean landowners, Japanese settlers, and corporations, the Government-General pressed ahead with the tax. When compared to the burden of previous fees, officials claimed, the proposed forest tax would form a "just system"—sensitive to the financial constraints of farming households, progressively structured, and rooted in "social policy."[47]

The appeal of this tax system to forestry bureaucrats lay in part in the flexibility it afforded to the project of civic forestry. By shifting revenue flows directly to provincial coffers, it spared local officials the trouble of having to squeeze communities of membership dues. Instead, following the recommendation of agrarian reformers, forestry officials began to grant broad latitude to individual hamlets to reinstitute time-honored folkways: from *hyangyak* (village contracts) to a variety of forestry-related *kye*. Such was a defining feature of the colonial corporatist strategy pursued by the Government-General over the 1930s: the push to, in the words of Shin and Han, "mobilize Korean tradition as a cultural resource to make the Rural Revitalization Campaign effective."[48] Although officials hungered for compulsory, interlocking forestry associations, they were willing to tolerate multiformity so long as it moved them closer toward realizing the goals of rural revitalization.

Lest there be any confusion over what those goals were, officials unveiled in January 1933 a new set of agroforestry precepts, the Outline of Private Forestland Guidelines. Devised with the "cultural level" of Korean farming communities in mind (the pejorative of choice for forestry bureaucrats), these guidelines offered practical guidance in three particular arenas of private forest management.[49] The first, predictably enough, was the encouragement of afforestation. Although the *Guidelines* recycled much of the tired rhetoric about the virtues of green hills, it marked a departure from previous practice in one crucial way. It urged farming communities to prioritize natural regeneration (*tennen zōrin*) over capital-intensive and technically complicated artificial regeneration (*jinkō zōrin*). In a bid to simultaneously reduce the cost of reforestation projects and simplify their long-term management, officials instructed communities to do away with the painstaking work of transplantation and focus instead on the protection of natural regenerative processes.

Another central tenet of these guidelines was prudence in tree felling. In the view of Kakeba Sadakichi, a longtime policy expert, administrators' nearly myopic focus on silviculture had inadvertently sidetracked oversight in what he considered an equally important management principle: selective cutting. It was exigent, Kakeba argued, that local advisers offer clearer instruction in the mechanics of thinning, coppicing, and, to borrow the parlance of the woodsman, "stand structure."[50] To this end, officials disseminated a wide range of publications on the best practices of tree felling. One such text was an instructional pamphlet entitled *The Key to Afforestation* (Shokurin no hiketsu), published in both Japanese and Korean in May 1933. Opening with the familiar rhetoric of the venerable Chinese sage Mencius— "If axes are allowed in the mountains and forests only in the appropriate seasons, there will be more timber than can be used"—the pamphlet proceeded to break down, in the simplest language possible, the fundamentals of tree harvesting. The use of ancient Chinese precepts on forestry was in fact a common strategy pursued by forestry bureaucrats, who thought Koreans might digest Confucian rhetoric more readily. Using the catchphrase "nurture the small and fell the big," it implored farmers to retire their sickles: "What has devastated Korea's mountains and forests is not the saw or the axe. It is the sickle, which is used to gather small plants for fuel."[51]

The third key tenet of revitalization forestry was closely connected to the second: the improvement of ground cover. For some farming households, the only forests in their immediate vicinity were depleted stands of red pine.

This required family members to periodically travel great distances—by one estimate as far as three *ri* (roughly seven miles)—to collect green manure, fuel, and other materials for use back on the farm.[52] In the view of agronomists, these land-use patterns worked to the detriment of both productivity and forest health. Every hour spent searching for fuel was an hour lost from farmwork or other forms of productive labor. Korea's fuel problems did not stop at access. No less unsettling were the raking techniques used by agriculturists to gather brush from the forest floor—a customary practice that, according to FES scientists, deprived the understory of nutrient-rich detritus and hastened siltation. Rural revitalization provided officials with a new opportunity to confront these issues head on. In particular, it galvanized efforts to create so-called "agricultural-use forests": forest parcels that were maintained in close proximity to hamlets so as to streamline the production of "the three materials of agricultural life"—fuel, fertilizer, and fodder.[53]

In setting their sights on fuel collection, by-employments, and market activities, forestry officials took aim at the farmhouse as much as the field. In theory, recommendations on fuel substitution were meant to stabilize domestic fuel supplies and minimize waste. In practice, these same recommendations constrained the culinary practices of women, the fuel-collection habits of children, and the leisure spaces of the home. Everything from the mushrooms foraged from the forest to the bedding used in winter was brought under the scrutiny of foresters and, in turn, civic forestry associations. Working through newly created Charcoal Production Associations, officials set out to reorient the fuel marketplace away from firewood and brush toward charcoal and other alternative fuel sources. In partnership with industrial groups (*siksangye*), they restructured debt and steered new lines of credit to forestry projects. Women in particular became a focal point of these efforts, as foresters sought to, first, channel their surplus labor into new economic spheres and, second, groom them as the guardians of domestic fuel economy.

The sheer volume and variety of forestry projects catalyzed by rural revitalization programs confounds generalization, but the case of Yongsang, a township in Naju County, South Chŏlla, is broadly representative of these trends. For residents of the primarily rice-producing region, a major expansion in village forestry efforts accompanied the growth of a Forest-Love Association (*aelimgye*) created in 1931. One of the first steps taken by its members was to elect a salaried "mountain inspector": a villager whose primary occupation was to monitor fuel collection and combustion practices.

In a manner entirely consistent with the Government-General's new *Guidelines*, this particular Forest-Love Association strictly forbade the collection of fallen pine needles from the forest floor. In order to offset demand for this long-favored fuel source, members pooled their resources to purchase a rice huller, which in 1934 produced 7,500 *kan* of rice husks for fuel—or about 10 percent of the village's annual fuel requirements. They also carried out a local *ondol* improvement campaign, using provincial subsidies to install 172 *ondol* mouth covers in eighty-six different homes.[54]

One cannot begin to understand the shift to wartime forestry without tracking the evolving role and growing reach of just this sort of semi-official association. Charcoal Production Associations formed early in the 1930s to reshape the marketplace for fuel quickly became after 1937 key instruments of energy discipline. Pine associations revived in the name of sylvan beautification transformed into units of resource centralization and rationing. Simply put, the proliferation of these civic forestry bodies in the 1930s heralded the broader role that the colonial state would take in managing the rural economy. The Government-General may have traded away its favored forestry institution in 1933, but it hardly relinquished its influence over agrarian life. To the contrary, in the stabilization of a rural agricultural economy under crisis, agroforestry bureaucrats found new grounds for social control.

CONCLUSION

By the early 1930s, state-sponsored erosion control projects, civic forestry ventures, and other planting schemes had in some corners of Korea grown into eye-catching swatches of second-growth forest. Where earlier Japanese settlers were once awestruck by the abraded soil they witnessed through the train window, some railway passengers now took note of "the growth of pine forest in nearly every mountain across the horizon" they saw streaking by.[55] Westerners' travel writings on Korea register a similar shift in perception. Kermit Roosevelt, the son of US President Theodore Roosevelt (a champion of state forestry in his own right), was positively captivated by the growth he witnessed during a tiger hunting expedition to Korea: "The country through which we drove was bleak and barren, but many of the hillsides showed proofs of a very tangible benefit the Koreans are reaping from Japanese administration, in the excellent work being done in reforestation. The long-denuded hills have been scientifically replanted, and the result is already being felt by the Korean, who is now allowed to cut the lower branches for fire-wood."[56] Such statements were often accompanied by photographic series such as figure 6.1, a four-part snapshot of the progress of an erosion control project in Koryŏng County, North Kyŏngsang. By the 1920s, an entire genre of before-and-after landscape photography had begun to circulate across the empire and beyond—visual evidence of how, as one piece of propaganda put it, Korea's "bare red mountains are now clothed in green."[57]

Accounts such as Roosevelt's were no doubt music to ears of men like Saitō Otosaku, who wanted nothing more than for their conservationist efforts to garner international praise. But foreign commentary of this sort was remarkably superficial, often using a single patch of incipient forest or a carefully curated study tour to make blanket claims about the entirety of Korea. It offered little insight into the longevity of reforestation projects,

FIG. 6.1 (*top right*) The original site of erosion. (*top left*) The site after initial construction. (*bottom right*) The site after two years of growth. (*bottom left*) The site after six years of growth. (From Keishō-Hokudō, ed., *Sabō o kataru* [Keishō-Hokudō: n.p., 1938]; courtesy of the National Diet Library of Japan.)

their overall utility, or how they offset forest exploitation elsewhere in Korea. More interested in what these fledgling forests said about Japanese colonizers than what they meant for the Korean colonized, foreign observers seldom gazed beyond the window dressing of colonial propaganda to consider the broader consequences of forestry reforms for agrarian society.

It is precisely for this reason that the account of the German geographer Hermann Lautensach is so valuable. Although he, too, proved sympathetic to colonial bureaucrats (who facilitated his expedition at every stage), no foreign observer got a closer look at the ground-level repercussions of colonial forestry in Korea than Lautensach, who over eight months in 1933 traveled some 1,500 kilometers by rail, boat, car, and foot to survey its terrain. As a trained academic versed in German principles of scientific forestry, Lautensach was amply qualified to weigh in on sylvan matters, which infuse his meticulous study on Korea's physical geography.[58]

What Lautensach found in Korea in 1933 was a sophisticated forestry system that remained out of touch with peasant life. Although he stopped well short of assigning blame, his account exposed a number of unresolved problems related to fuel economy, rural finance, and woodland access. "For the time being Korea's forested areas are entitled to the name 'forest' only inasmuch as they are under the control of a forestry office. Tall stands of timber that are rationally used and managed are found only to a very modest extent thus far," he observed. "At present they form only a link in the chain beginning with the unused virgin forests with a decaying surplus of wood and ending with the barren areas recklessly exploited to the last tick on granitic yellow soils."[59]

In short, Lautensach's fine-grained assessment of the state of forestry in colonial Korea cut to the bone of a cold, hard truth: that even the most well-laid plans could not patch over the structural inequities built into the state's greenification framework. For every timber corporation that was energetically planting trees in newly leased woodlands, there were dozens of surrounding hamlets that were suffering in the name of reforestation. For every model forest steward methodically stocking their property, there were scores of displaced tenant farmers left with no choice but to clear land on steep mountain slopes. Any step toward rectifying such discriminatory policies (such as the retroactive claimant process) was inevitably followed by another setback (such as the crash in the rice market) that only further destabilized the livelihood of these communities. Many farmers jumped through hoop after hoop to acquire Lilliputian plots of forest only to be forced to sell them at cut-rate prices to Japanese landlords when farm incomes cratered.

By the mid-1930s, forestry officials had grown wise to these realities. Seeing a natural opportunity in the Rural Revitalization Campaign, they began to pursue a host of strategies that better squared their agenda with the multiple patterns of forest use that took place at the embedded scales of the farm, hamlet, county, and province. The command center of this effort was the KFA, which after 1932 set out to make "agricultural-use forestry" a central plank of rural revitalization.

More and more, the KFA and other civic forestry associations also began to serve as vehicles for cultural assimilation. Concurrent with the turn in the 1930s toward the lofty rhetoric of "Japan and Korea as one body" was a redoubled effort to align the conservationist mentality in Korea with that found in Japan. Many KFA members feared that "forest love" remained an abstract principle rather than a credo suffusing everyday behavior. The outbreak of the Second Sino-Japanese War in 1937 only heightened their concern. As natural resource conservation shifted from an enlightened idea to a strategic exigency, the KFA embarked on a series of more ideologically oriented campaigns meant to promote resource austerity and imperial sacrifice. To the practical demonstrations, workshops, and roundtables that had become staples of the KFA were added a host of programs geared toward "sylvan patriotism."[60] Suddenly a new system of wartime forest management was thrust upon residents of Korea—a mobilization of both soil and spirit that ushered in a new and turbulent phase of forest management.

PART III

CAMPAIGNS

SEVEN

FOREST-LOVE THOUGHT

FOR THOSE TUNED IN TO THE KEIJŌ CENTRAL BROADCAST ON APRIL 2, 1936, the "moving tales of afforestation" (*shokurin bidan*) came in quick succession. As part of the lead-in to Korea's twenty-sixth annual ceremonial planting, Yajima Sugizō, then chief of the Bureau of Agriculture and Forestry, took to the airwaves to share with listeners the great achievements and colorful personalities of Korea's conservation movement. He began with a well-known story from Japan: that of Kinbara Meizen, an entrepreneur from Shizuoka Prefecture, who, upon seeing the damage wrought by the flooding of the Tenryū River, moved mountains to reclaim his native soil. Using his own resources, Kinbara embarked on a decades-long reforestation project that later became a large tract of imperial forestland, earning the praise of the emperor himself.[1]

Kinbara's efforts were extraordinary. But they were not without comparison, for, as Yajima noted, Korea had produced "small Kinbaras" in each region—what he called the "afforestation pioneers of Korea" (*shokurin senkakusha*).[2] Yajima offered by way of example the story of Kim Ch'ang-su, headman of the township of Pyŏngkok (Hamyang County, South Kyŏngsang). Alarmed by the state of the mountains surrounding his hamlet, Kim planted thousands of oak trees and founded a local Forest Protection Association. In Yajima's telling, as time passed the community gained steadier access to fertilizer and fuel, allowing residents to boost agricultural productivity and mitigate flood risk. Although Kim's passing in 1921 meant that he could barely see his plans to fruition, the subsequent leadership of his son ensured that the surrounding woodlands grew to maturity. To commemorate their vision and leadership, villagers erected a monument in the thickening forest to honor both father and son.

Ever the loyal bureaucrat, Yajima did not skip a beat in attributing the success of the Kims to the guidance of the colonial state itself. By "arousing awareness" in Korea of the means and merits of forest reclamation, he asserted, the state had groomed a cadre of afforestation pioneers to lead the way. Yajima took great heart in the fact that "one can now hear various moving tales of afforestation for each region [of Korea]."[3] Although the details were different, the story was essentially the same: a local leader, called to action by the state of environmental decline, organizing a collective response for the betterment of forests, hamlets, and, ultimately, the empire.

What united all of these cases was the ostensible realization of *airin shisō*—forest-love thought, the ideological cornerstone of forestry in colonial Korea. To its proponents, forest-love thought offered both self-improvement and spiritual salvation: "A pristine mountain environment," proclaimed Yajima, "brings great comfort to the individual and a verdant mountain area exerts great power to purify the spirit."[4] But in their advocacy of forest-love activities officials also envisioned a societal transformation. "The protection of the forest," wrote Kada Naoji, then chairman of the Korean Chamber of Commerce and Industry, "is the responsibility of the entirety of society."[5] Revealingly, Kada took as a model for this unified effort Italy's Blackshirts, the paramilitary wing of the National Fascist Party. Following the example set by Benito Mussolini himself, the group had brought Italian society together "in an all-out effort to plant trees and prevent forest fires." In a gesture toward the clouds of totalitarianism gathering on the horizon, Kada implored woodsmen in Korea to do the same. Regardless of the strides made in regeneration, much work remained in "the socialization of forest-love activities"—turning forest conservation into a truly mass movement.

By the time Kada put this challenge before the Korean Forestry Association (KFA) in 1931, the basic tenets of forest-love thought were familiar to Korean subjects, if not painfully so. Registering land, policing profligacy, paying dues, and so many other activities described in previous chapters were all carried out in the name of forest love. Over time, abstract ideas of forest reverence had also crystallized into concrete events and programs. Ceremonial plantings begot national arbor days, which in turn became entire weeks of greenification activities (*ryokka undō*). Festivals, radio hours, and exhibitions of forest love all found extensive (if disproportionately urban) audiences in Korea. Classrooms, an incubator for steward-subjects in the eyes of the colonial state, went to great lengths to make the principles of forest love a learning objective.

The changing geopolitical winds of the 1930s, however, blew in a new and supercharged phase in the promotion of forest-love thought. Faced with deteriorating market conditions and growing international isolation following Japan's invasion of Manchuria, the colonial state in Korea began to tighten its control of natural resources. Resource autarky became a mantra of the times. Forest-love thought provided just the sort of ideological lubricant needed to facilitate the establishment of a command economy for natural resources. It placed all residents of Korea within a disciplinary framework of self-sacrifice and state-sanctioned consumption that set the stage for wartime forestry. As fuel sources and forest products grew scarcer, exhortations to "love thy forest" grew all the more vociferous.

The intensification of forest-love thought control in Korea calls attention to a colonial career of Japanese nature-love myths scarcely considered by environmental historians of Japan. For generations now, scholars have taken aim at the straw man that just won't blow away: the hoary notion that Japanese society has nurtured over centuries an unusually deep and harmonious relationship with its environment. A rich body of scholarship has elucidated the historical construction of these ideas and their origins in the growth of the modern nation-state.[6] Little, however, has been written about how these same ideas were put to work in the assimilation of colonial subjects. We have already seen how discourses of red Korea were framed in contradistinction to a national Japanese forest culture, one whose environmental traditions supposedly stretched back to deep antiquity. This chapter picks up these discursive threads to examine the place of forests in the assimilation of Korean subjects—a project that introduced Japan's invented sylvan traditions into the ideological bloodstream of the empire.

By the 1930s, stocking forests, conserving fuel, and revering nature were all widely recognized as vehicles for, and barometers of, the Japanization of Koreans. Decades of sermonizing by forestry bureaucrats had drilled into Koreans the idea that each seed sown and joule of energy conserved brought them one step closer to the "nature-loving" Yamato spirit. Of course, such logic was shot through with contradiction. Grand proclamations about the shared burdens of Japanese and Koreans behind the conservationist cause were sharply at odds with inequitable land-use policies. Moralistic appeals to protect the forests for generations to come were drowned out by the accelerating horsepower of state-owned saws. These tensions are suggestive of a hitherto overlooked ecological dimension to what Oguma Eiji has called the "ambivalent sameness" inherent to Japanese assimilation discourse and practice.[7] Just as Japanese wavered between invoking their ethnohistorical affinity with the Korean people on the one hand and upholding their own racial supremacy on the other, so did they reluctantly appeal to a shared forest heritage. At the same time that they gestured toward a broader pan-Asian environmental tradition, they upheld their place at its pinnacle. Purity of forest-love thought was fixed to the purity of one's ethnic stock, and, rosy rhetoric to the contrary, Koreans were never fully embraced as coequal partners in conservation. No matter how many trees they planted, they would always be "little Kinbaras"—silviculturists budding in the shadows of their older Japanese siblings.

Recognizing these rhetorical inconsistencies allows us to better appreciate the plasticity of forest-love ideology. At once a state of mind, a set of behaviors, and a spiritual plane, *airin shisō* was a many-sided rhetorical device. In a single breath, its champions could appeal to factory workers in Wŏnsan, housewives in Daegu, and merchants in Inch'ŏn. It could be used to invoke a sense of nostalgia for one's native place or to remind imperial subjects of their role within the Greater East Asia Co-prosperity Sphere.

Given its many valences, it was only natural that forest love found expression in many different domains of everyday life. Japanese officials came quickly to the conclusion that its espousal required more than essays, speeches, and words on a page. It required, first and foremost, calls to action—days of imperial service that put the practice of forest love on spectacular display. But they also brought the full weight of their public relations infrastructure to bear on daily decision making. Art, photography, poetry, prose, film, and music were all put to work in an attempt to inundate the Korean sensorium with a relentless stream of encouragement and admonition. In their attempt to sway the consciousness of Koreans, forestry officials and their KFA counterparts went to great lengths to ensure that forest love was a lived experience, manifest in the signs that colored public spaces and the radio broadcasts that echoed through homes. A closer look at its promotion thus reveals more than a little-known component of assimilation politics in colonial Korea. It also provides a more focused campaign through which to examine how ideology actually worked on the ground, how forest-love crusaders tried to make conservation the stuff of daily life.

A RITE OF SPRING

For many among the crowd of onlookers gathered at Tongdaemun in Seoul, the imperial procession of May 5, 1910 was a familiar scene. Dressed in formal robes and flanked by a large retinue of flag-bearing attendants, Emperor Sunjong bore a strong resemblance to earlier monarchs who had participated in similar processions down the thoroughfare. So it must have come as something of a surprise when the Korean emperor picked up a hoe and began to dig a hole. With the assistance of Japanese advisers, he then placed into the earth a Japanese umbrella pine, the first of the literally hundreds of millions of trees to be ceremonially planted during the colonial period.[8]

The brainchild of the Japanese officials who shadowed the emperor throughout the proceedings, this sylvan pageantry sought to, according to one retrospective, "instill a love of tree planting by conveying the ideals of the top down to the bottom."[9] In particular, it was choreographed to impress upon Korean spectators another popular slogan of the forest-love thought campaign: *shokuju airin*, "plant trees, love the forest." That Koreans were supposedly lacking in *regenerative* instincts was of foremost concern to Japanese forestry advisers to the Korean government. Although they could point to a long list of policies implemented during the Chosŏn period regulating access to forests and identify a host of customs of tree worship, these advisers strained to amass evidence of large-scale grassroots reforestation programs—that is, those operating outside of state-imposed requirements on pine plantation. (Had these advisers looked a bit harder, they might have learned that Sunjong's spectacle was not quite as novel as it seemed, considering that Korean monarchs had for centuries presided over ceremonies of agricultural cultivation on royal palace grounds.)[10]

What they could find in spades, however, were indications of tree-related superstitions—what Saitō Otosaku identified as the source of "the weak sense of tree planting and forest love among the Korean people."[11] Koreans, he claimed, did not plant trees out of fear that they harbored evil spirits or might disturb geomantic energies. Never mind that folklorists such as Yanagita Kunio were then valorizing Japan's own forest mythology or that researchers such as Asakawa were offering favorable assessments of

Koreans' forestry folkways, Japanese officials flagged these customs as actively hostile to their agenda.

To the veteran forester Dōke Atsuyuki, Koreans' inclinations toward occultism made it all the more important that the greening of bald mountains be waged on two fronts simultaneously. Just as there were both "physical and metaphysical forms of assimilation," he argued, so were there material and spiritual components to forests. However, due to chronic overcutting that had left "mountains without trees and rivers without water," he wrote, "beautiful scenery in Korea is rare."[12] The result was a vicious cycle: Koreans had little awe for their landscape, which led in turn to further degradation of its terrain. Some but by no means all Koreans shared in this outlook. Yi Kwang-su, for one, a pioneer of modern Korean literature, minced no words about the dreary state of Korea's alpine scenery:

> How miserable a sight
> How could a mountain be so pathetic
> That pitiable appearance
> That shape so bare from base to peak
> Who has done this?
> Whoever until now was keeper of the mountain
> Your blood will flow as you too are made bare[13]

Although Japanese and Koreans did not necessarily see eye to eye on who or what was to be blamed for these "pitiable" peaks, the task before them was clear: to break the cycle of sylvan dread by carpeting these hillsides with trees. As second-growth forests matured, so would Koreans' conservationist sensibilities, or so the logic went.

For forestry bureaucrats eager to see results, mass plantings presented an obvious platform for just this sort of expedited change of scenery. Few, in fact, were more enthusiastic about the transformative power of stately plantings than Saitō, who saw in Japan's appropriation of American-style Arbor Day activities a blueprint for Korea's own brand of silvicultural spectacle. Saitō offered his roadmap for the institutionalization of ceremonial plantings at a meeting of provincial governors in January 1911. Among his chief recommendations were that these events take place in prominent locations (such as parks and roadways) easily observed by passersby; that local experts cooperate with provincial authorities to advise on the particular trees and techniques used in each site; and that officials provide food and drink (barring alcohol) to drum up enthusiasm for the undertaking. Saitō went further to suggest that these plantings be held each year on April 3: a date that coincided not only with the arrival of spring but also the anniversary of the death of Emperor Jimmu, the mythical first ruler of Japan.[14] By tying these plantings to the imperial calendar, forestry officials turned them into performances of imperial fealty. They were to mark an occasion for all residents of Korea to actively serve the imperial cause by materially improving the emperor's realm and the resources therein.

On April 3, 1911, Saitō's vision became a reality. The festivities began early in the morning with a ceremony in the rear garden of the governor-general's residence, where a mix of politicians, bureaucrats, and schoolchildren, positioned before a gaggle of press, planted some three hundred trees. By day's end, similar ceremonies in provincial capitals and mountain hamlets had brought about the planting of more than 4,650,000 trees—an achievement trumpeted by nearly every major news outlet in both Japan and Korea. Heartened by the success of what he would later call "ceremonial plantings praised by the world," Saitō worked to streamline the logistics of this annual event.[15] Thereafter, ceremonial plantings became a fixture of the spring calendar and a centerpiece of the Government-General's greenification programs.

With each passing year, they also grew more ambitious in scope. Pruning bushes, installing birdfeeders, reinforcing property boundaries, and various other activities were woven into the day's proceedings as officials sought to channel civic energy into village and neighborhood improvement writ large. Logistics that were initially orchestrated by county-level officials were increasingly off-loaded onto village institutions and youth groups. In many areas, ceremonial plantings were expanded to include practical demonstrations and festivals of forest culture. Each planting similarly occasioned countless speeches that recycled the well-worn tropes of sylvan enlightenment: the links between forestry and industry ("one can discern the strength of the nation based on the color of its mountains");[16] the spiritual virtues of reclamation ("a clean mountain, a pure heart");[17] and the indispensability of forests to modern life ("the timber furnished from the forest is the foundation of human life").[18]

It was no accident that, of the hundreds of thousands to participate each spring, media coverage of these plantings was preoccupied with the involvement of top-ranking officials. In what were carefully staged publicity stunts, representatives of the colonial government—be they governors-general, provincial assemblymen, or cabinet ministers—labored side by side with ordinary Koreans. Images such as figure 7.1, a photograph of former governor-general Saitō Makoto getting his hands (and, presumably, suit) dirty, were used to bolster the claim that forestry was a truly cooperative project, involving the highest levels of government as much as homemakers and school-children. Japanese settlers were also expected to turn out for these planting events, if only to demonstrate their arboreal ardor. Foresters called on Japanese communities to participate less out of concern with their conservationist ethic than with their unfamiliarity with Korea's climate and soil. Even as colonial officials expressed their apprehension about the character and influence of lower-class Japanese migrants to Korea, hardly ever did they call into question their bona fides as forest caretakers. For the "forest-loving" Japanese people, ceremonial plantings served merely as tutorials in planting in the peninsular context.

FIG. 7.1 Former governor-general Saitō Makoto breaking ground during the ceremonial planting festivities of 1934. (From *Chōsen sanrinkaihō*, vol. 120 [1935].)

Needless to say, ritual plantings were not restricted to April 3. Sylvan pageantry also accompanied the inauguration of new buildings, parks, and other public sites, as well as the commencement of state-sponsored projects. When, for instance, project managers in Chŏngsŏn County, Kangwŏn, broke ground on a massive erosion control project, they brought in a Shintō priest to perform a ritual so as to "pray to the gods of mountain reclamation" (fig. 7.2).[19] And when, in 1935, colonial officials set out to commemorate the tenth anniversary of the enshrinement atop Namsan of Chōsen Jingū, the premier site of Shintō worship in Korea, they planted hundreds of trees from various regions of the peninsula in an arboretum established just adjacent to the shrine. These trees were meant to simultaneously "exalt divine virtues" and "draw all eyes to the greening of the peninsula."[20]

As both events suggest, ceremonial plantings also grew more conspicuously militaristic. Especially in the late 1930s, when the exigencies of war energized the "imperialization" (J: *kōminka*; K: *hwangminhwa*) of everyday life in Korea, officials cloaked these rituals in the rhetoric of service and sacrifice. After 1937, tree plantings were routinely accompanied by mass recitations of *Fundamentals of Our National Polity* (Kokutai no hongi), a political manifesto steeped in the language of totalitarianism. "Harmony as in

FIG. 7.2 A Shintō ceremony honoring the gods of forest reclamation. (From Keishō-Hokudō, ed., *Sabō o kataru* [Keishō-Hokudō: n.p., 1938]; courtesy of the National Diet Library of Japan.)

our nation," went one passage, "is a great harmony of individuals who, by giving play to their individual differences and through difficulties, toil, and labor, converge as one." In the collective labor of silviculture, forestry officials identified a path toward this convergence. Just as tree plantings were to bind Koreans and Japanese of all walks of life into the project of bioreclamation, so were they to unite the entire empire behind the protection of the emperor's domain.

If such was the abstract goal, its fullest realization came in 1940, a year that marked 2,600 years since Emperor Jimmu supposedly ascended to the imperial throne. Ranging from precisely timed mass rituals to tourism campaigns, celebrations of Japan's "unbroken imperial line" took many forms.[21] Coordination between the Japan, Korea, and Taiwan Forestry Associations ensured that forest conservation activities would be among them. Rather than mandate specific events, this empire-wide network of conservation leaders encouraged local communities to undertake any number of suggested activities, including "regenerative plantings, special tree-planting ceremonies, distributing saplings, establishing parks, opening forest paths, founding forest institutes, and creating forestry halls." These projects were framed as much in terms of the empire's future as its time-honored past. They were to yield resources that would only "grow with the passage of time, carrying on the meaning of the memorial in perpetuity."[22] They were carried out, in other words, to ensure that the empire saw another 2,600 years.

The sum total of trees born of Korea's thirty-four ceremonial plantings is almost unfathomably large: 596 million. Not surprisingly, statistics on seeds, saplings, and trees planted through these ceremonies were broadcast by the colonial state as evidence of its benevolent rule.[23] Such precise figures, however, belie the fact that many of the saplings planted did not survive or offered little benefit to those who planted them. This did not stop Japanese officials from trumpeting these plantings as unprecedented milestones in Korea's long forest history.

To Ueki Homiki, the scientist, bureaucrat, and educator, these forest-love activities set Korea on a trajectory toward national strength and, ultimately, parity with the great forest nations of the world. In the rows of women and children tending to the hillsides, Ueki saw the outlines of imperial Japan's own Civilian Conservation Corps, the popular New Deal program that put the unemployed to work in land reclamation projects across the United States. Yet Ueki also took pains to clarify that this mass movement was not an act of blind imitation of the West. He heralded Korea as a "green country of Asia," one born of Asiatic traditions of reforestation. As evidence of the latter claim, Ueki turned to a verse from China's oldest collection of poetry, *The Book of Odes*, which conveyed what he considered the ethos of East Asian conservationism:

> On the branches of the oaks,
> How abundant are the leaves!
> To be rejoiced in are the princes,
> Guardians of the regions of the son of Heaven.[24]

Depending on the context, then, Korea shared in Japan's deep history of conservation. Despite decades of disparaging China's forestry practices, Japanese woodsmen did not hesitate to nod to the Sinosphere as the source of a shared regional tradition of environmental thought. Forest-love ideology may have radiated out from the imperial center, but it could also be used to build solidarity with Japan's neighbors and colonial subjects.

It is significantly more difficult to gauge what Koreans made of these planting spectacles. A good number of businessmen, landlords, technicians, and government officials were regular participants and even patrons of these events. Hong Chong-hwa, a member of the KFA's North Kyŏngsang branch, spoke for many Korean forestry professionals when he called the ceremonial plantings "an extremely effective mechanism for the diffusion of forest-love thought" and pushed for an expansion of these activities into a full week of forest-love proceedings.[25] But given that the various costs of these plantings—in time, energy, and materials—were often passed on to participating villages, it is not surprising that most Koreans steered clear of these events. The wildly fluctuating figures on participation certainly raise questions about the overall engagement and follow-through of those involved.[26] The combustion of some of the trees planted during these events also suggests that not all Koreans embraced the spirit of the undertaking. No sooner had civic associations planted rows of trees in parks and public spaces as part of urban beautification projects than some city dwellers began to hack down these very trees for fuel.[27]

Policymakers and event planners were neither oblivious to the limitations of these spectacles nor indifferent to their sometimes superficial impact. Most alarming was the fact that participants in these activities were skewed overwhelmingly toward the elite stratum of colonial society. Scarce among the neat rows of participants traversing hillsides with seedlings in hand were Korea's tenant farmers, factory workers, or the working-class poor. Officials were also concerned with the forestry practices exercised the other 364 days of the year. If forests were truly indispensable to modern life, then forest-love thought needed to be a daily observance and a household affair. It needed to seep into the minutiae of ordinary consciousness. For this to happen, suggested Nakashima Kan, civic forestry bodies needed to create new ways to "diffuse forest-love thought through the senses."[28]

STIMULATING CONSERVATION

As an intellectual movement, the forest-love thought campaign rested on two primary pillars of academic authority. One was the climatic determinism popularized by scholars ranging from the colonial theorist Nitobe Inazō to the philosopher Watsuji Tetsurō. By the 1930s, notions of "climate and culture" (*fudō*), as Watsuji would have it, had come to undergird essentialist claims to a uniquely Japanese and even Asian environmental tradition.[29] The other was a field of study known as forest aesthetics (*shinrin bigaku*), then a flourishing discipline back in Japan. Originating in the ideas of the German scholar Heinrich von Salisch, forest aesthetics inquired into the relationship between forest scenery, individual perception, and collective values. As concerned with the qualities of a single tree as with panoramic scenery, forest aestheticians aimed to create as welcoming and awe-inspiring a forestscape as possible. They called, in practice, for the tender maintenance of woods so as to harness the emotive power of forests.

According to Maruyama Jōzō, one of many Korea-based foresters to write on forest aesthetics, four principal factors determined the beauty of forests (*shinrin no bisei*): (1) spatial relations; (2) the passage of time; (3) uniformity; and (4) their gestalt qualities.[30] Braiding together the ideas of John Ruskin (the environmental aesthete), William Gilpin (coiner of the term *picturesque*), and William Wordsworth (the Romantic poet), Maruyama laid out an almost transcendental philosophy of the forest. In his view, the economical management of forests, while critical, had obscured their sentimental force. For a lasting transformation of forest values to proceed, Maruyama maintained, officials needed to approach forest management "from the standpoint of forest aesthetics." Only then could they connect with the Korean spirit on a deeper plane.[31]

Like many of his contemporaries, Maruyama feared that, despite gains in clarifying the practical benefits derived from the forest, the forest-love-thought campaign had failed to fully stimulate the sensory faculties of Koreans. Urbanites were too removed from nature, factory workers too confined to their workshops, and farmers too absorbed in their harvests to take time to smell the roses, as it were. This is where the KFA was to step in. With members scattered across the peninsula, branch offices in each province, and a sophisticated media infrastructure at its disposal, the KFA was particularly well positioned to prod the senses of Koreans into daily communion with forest nature. Its members became the chief movers and shakers of a multifaceted, multisensory public relations effort to, as one KFA roundtable put it, "promote closer relations and interactions with trees."[32]

Their efforts were channeled into a variety of creative arenas. Seeking to harness what some officials identified as Koreans' innate love of music, the KFA commissioned and circulated a wide array of forestry-related songs. They did so in part through the KFA bulletin, which devoted considerable print space to sheet music, poems, songs, and ballads. Adding sonic depth to this lyrical canon was the radio, a technology that enabled forestry officials to beat the eardrums of residents of Korea with reminders to celebrate and protect the forest. Typically, forest love found expression over the air in the form of public-service announcements, transmitted in both Japanese and Korean. Interspersed with regularly scheduled programs were appeals to conserve fuel, refrain from fire setting, or participate in forestry projects. Heading into each April, however, forest love was given a dedicated block of airtime, involving some mix of songs, skits, and speeches. Whatever the content, officials found in the radio an instrument through which to broadcast a sylvan soundscape to some 277,000 radios licensed (as of 1942) for use in homes, schools, restaurants, and meeting halls across Korea.[33]

For the more visually inclined, the KFA solicited and distributed forestry-themed posters, signs, and artwork. In May 1928, for instance, the KFA sponsored a forest-fire prevention poster contest and displayed as many as eleven thousand copies of the winning submissions in public spaces across the peninsula.[34] It similarly organized forest-love slogan competitions, an undertaking that quite naturally lent itself to artistic expression. Reminding readers that reforestation requires "the full cooperation of the government and the people," one such poster depicted a bucolic scene of farmers making their way to a ceremonial planting event (fig. 7.3). More than empty exercises, by the 1930s forest-love signage could be found in schoolyards, along roadways, and plastered about town squares all over Korea. One of the more imposing sights to emerge out of this visual

FIG. 7.3 A "forest-love poster" disseminated by the KFA. (From *Chōsen sanrinkaihō*, vol. 120 [1935].)

campaign were *airin* mountain gates: two towering spires—one bearing the ideograph for love (*ai*), the other forest (*rin*)—placed at mountain trailheads to remind travelers to proceed reverently along the path ahead. Not one to overlook opportunities presented by new media, the KFA also began to host forestry film festivals, at which they would screen such titles as *Forestry along the Upper Yalu*, *The Sylvan Beauty of Mount Kŭmgang*, and *The Japan Alps of the Summer*.

Few spaces were more saturated with this audiovisual content than the classroom—a veritable pulpit for the gospel of forest conservation. What better down payment on future forest resources, figured many in the KFA, than to imprint a love of planting in still impressionable youth? Forest-love evangelists accordingly applied considerable pressure on educational institutions at every level to integrate some form of forestry subject matter into classroom curricula. Their efforts bore fruit. By 1936, Japanese-language (*kokugo*) readers used in primary schools contained entries on "pine moths,"

"Mount Fuji," "forestry in Korea," and "paper production," while science textbooks included units on the red pine, the *ondol*, and fuel.[35] In the minds of educators and foresters alike, rearing trees while rearing children comprised an "ingenious plan to kill two birds with one stone": to achieve "spiritual refinement" alongside "forest improvement."[36]

In the main, forest-love pedagogy sought to groom the next generation of village leaders and experts—those who would head up civic forestry associations. Educators were aided considerably in this pursuit by special measures taken by the Government-General to create "school forests": modest plots of woodland placed directly under the oversight of classrooms. Impressed with the success of similar arrangements back in Japan, Korea-based officials began to set aside land for any institution that could demonstrate a capacity and enthusiasm for forestry education. By 1924, as many as 1,179 schools in Korea administered their own forest, in which educators worked to cultivate "ideas of forest protection" and introduce the work of silviculture to youth.[37]

Alongside the push to outfit schools with their own instructional forests was a campaign to integrate trees and forests into the spatial matrix of Korea's cities. To city planners, urban forestry was about more than manicuring a scenic backdrop to the built environment. It was a matter of purification, vitality, and public health. Through their seasonal transformations and circulation of oxygen, woody plants, by one assessment, "brought a freshness to the city" that shook its residents from their *ondol* lifestyle.[38] Trees were regularly likened to the "lungs of the city," offering myriad benefits for public health and hygiene. As officials moved to transform parts of the capital into "showcase thoroughfares," they turned to trees as a means to structure, beautify, and even vivify urban space.[39]

City planners, in other words, came to view green parks and tree-lined streets as hallmarks of urban modernity. Such was certainly the case in metropolitan Japan, where municipal officials and foresters had worked hand in hand to establish green spaces in the capital and other major cities.[40] At the forefront of this movement was none other than Honda Seiroku, who by the 1910s had emerged as a leading proponent of urban forestry in Japan. Although Honda is best known as the visionary behind Hibiya Park in Tokyo, he also left his mark on the parkscapes of urban Korea. He did so at the behest of the Government-General, which in 1916 commissioned Honda to draw up a plan for the construction of a park in the center of Seoul. The result was his 1917 blueprint for Namsan Park, a recreation area that wrapped an arboretum, observatory, orchard, botanical garden, and hiking trails all into one expansive green space. Honda's vision for a leafy-green capital stretched beyond the confines of the park itself. He enjoined residents of Seoul to plant trees in public sites across the city and provided local officials with detailed instructions on how to do so.[41]

Of the many trees endorsed by Honda, few were embraced as enthusiastically by urbanites as the cherry blossom, arguably the most eye-catching symbol of Japan's empire of forestry. Often planted at the initiative of settler communities, cherry blossoms took root in highly visible public spaces across Korea—parks, plazas, town squares, and so forth. Public interest in cherry blossom trees was piqued as much by the festivities surrounding their flowering as the trees themselves. Owing in part to the participation of members of the Korean royal family in springtime viewing parties, cherry blossom observation steadily grew in Korea into a popular national pastime.

Nowhere was more gravitational in this regard than the Ch'anggyŏng Botanical Garden, an erstwhile royal palace that the colonial government renovated into a sprawling outdoor amusement park, including gardens, museums, a conservatory, and Korea's first zoo. In 1909, "in response to the unanimous suggestion of those who came from Japan to create a garden in the Japanese format," park managers transplanted three hundred cherry trees on its grounds.[42] By the 1930s, this figure had grown to roughly two thousand trees, which enjoyed (over a six-day period in, say, 1929) the spectatorship of nearly 165,000 visitors to the park (fig. 7.4).

The Korean novelist Kim Yu-jŏng offers a hint in his 1936 short story "Cherry Blossoms at Night" (Yaaeng) that for some Koreans this experience had an olfactory dimension. "You don't know how to appreciate flowers!" snapped one café waitress at another during a discussion of the gardens at Ch'anggyŏng: "Looking at the flower is not enough. One needs to smell it. . . . You know nothing. This is probably because you have not acquired culture. The true value of a flower can only be appreciated by smelling it."[43] Setting aside the satire that runs through much of Kim's oeuvre, we can glean from this exchange that for some Koreans the act of flower appreciation signaled cultural refinement. Communing with trees and flowers had, in certain circles, become a marker not only of sylvan enlightenment but also of a more cosmopolitan sensibility.

Japanese officials certainly took heart in the idea that more city folk were electing to spend their free time outdoors rather than on their *ondol* floors. Even as moral reformers expressed misgivings about the raucous revelry at Ch'anggyŏng, they came to associate the flowering of these trees with a

FIG. 7.4 Families picnicking under the cherry blossoms at the Ch'anggyŏng Botanical Garden. (Courtesy of Special Collections and College Archives, Skillman Library, Lafayette College, and the East Asia Image Collection; image ip1736.)

springtime awakening, a stirring of the national body following the long winter hibernation. In this sense, parks and green spaces represented more than places of rest and relaxation. According to Yajima Sugizō, they also served as spaces in which to "purify the spirit, promote health, and preserve the vigor of the people."[44] What Yajima intimated were the brewing forces of alpinism in Korea: the largely metropolitan movement to escape from the stresses of urban life in the growing system of parks, mountain trails, and climbing routes that promised physical, if not spiritual, rejuvenation. As in Japan, the rhetoric of forest conservation was laced with references to mountaineering, a decidedly modern (and, at first, masculine) activity that would deliver Koreans deeper and higher into the hills. Spurred by the growing ecotourism industry, the establishment of mountaineering clubs, and a rapidly expanding national transportation infrastructure, Korean city-dwellers took to Korea's mountain trails, alpenstock in hand, as never before.[45]

If Ch'anggyŏng Garden was Korea's botanical repository, Mount Kŭmgang and its environs was its alpine playground. Famed as much for its craggy, weathered spires as its scenic hot spring resorts, the "Diamond Mountains" steadily grew over the course of the 1920s into Korea's premier ecotourist destination. Thanks in large part to a robust promotional campaign by the Railway Bureau, tourists from across the empire—and even Europe and the United States—streamed into the park, where they visited centuries-old Buddhist temples, beheld pristine waterfalls, and traversed mountain passes.[46] If the following verse, penned by a Korean student after a trip to the park, is any indication, the terrain left a lasting impression:

> A noted mountain of the world with twelve thousand peaks
> While you are most reputed for the scenic beauty and solemnity
> We are so desolated in the same country
> I am so ashamed to you I cannot hold my head before you
>> Mt. Kumgang!
> We promise you to be just as brilliant and shining as you with
>> struggle[47]

As notable as the content of the poem is its author: Park Chung-hee, then a third-year student at the Taegu Normal School. When, three decades later, Park would rise to power as the president of the Republic of Korea—and assume leadership over a massive reforestation program of his own—this composition would gain new currency as proof of his conservationist bona fides.

Whether through a picnic or a brisk hike, a mountain ditty or forest film, forest-love observance took many forms. Such an assault on the senses was precisely per the design of forestry bureaucrats and their KFA proxies, who strove to make the principles of forest conservation an inescapable component of everyday cognition. Binding each of these ideological registers together was the proposition that forests and forestry were instrumental to everyday existence. Indeed, although *airin shisō* was a key linguistic touchstone for forestry officials, their idealized visions of productive woodlands rested on a different refrain of the colonial period: *sanrin to jinsei*, "forests and human life." At nearly every turn, forestry officials called attention to the inextricable linkages between modern civilizations and the forests that nourished them. It was thus entirely predictable that the KFA selected "forests and human life" as the guiding motif of the 1935 Korean Forest Culture Exhibition, what in many ways marked the apotheosis of conservationist spectacle during the colonial period. As a carefully curated exhibition of Korea's forest culture that doubled as a marketing ploy, it throws into sharp focus the relationship between the conservation and consumption of Korea's forest bounty.

FOREST LOVE ON DISPLAY

The Korean Forest Culture Exhibition (Chōsen Sanrin Bunka Tenrankai) of 1935 was not the first colonial showcase of Korean forestry, but it was easily the most elaborate. Envisioned by the KFA as the marquee affair of Korea's twenty-fifth annual ceremonial planting, it endeavored to celebrate Korea's forest culture by illuminating the indissoluble bond between the forest and daily life. The organizers also had a more practical goal in mind: to promote the growing variety of consumer goods sourced from Korea's forests. To that end, they solicited product samples from a wide range of companies, cooperatives, and craftsmen. Roped in by the promise of on-site orders and discounted shipping rates, more than 170 different sellers contributed 478 forestry different products for display—from charcoal briquettes to railway ties to custom furniture.[48]

The Mitsukoshi Department Store in downtown Seoul was an ideal venue for this exhibition. As a "retail palace" located in the heart of the capital's busiest shopping district, it offered both an easily accessible public location and an already consumer-oriented space in which to market forest merchandise.[49] In the weeks leading up to the event, organizers placed advertisements in newspapers and magazines, posted fliers, and even convened a press conference in the Chōsen Hotel. To attract foot traffic, they also arranged flowering tree branch displays in Mitsukoshi's show windows and adorned its promenade with cherry blossoms. As event coordinators would later recall, once the exhibition opened its doors on the morning of April 1, 1935, these ornate arrangements elicited a "surging interest" in the exhibition.[50]

The real sights were to be seen in the fourth-floor hall and fifth-floor gallery of the department store. To get there, however, one first had to journey through the "forest tunnel": a stairwell and walkway elaborately lined with cedar, fir, and spruce branches and bedecked with cherry blossom flowers and white birch leaves. By reassembling Korea's mountain scenery into an interactive space, the organizers tried their best to simulate a walk in the woods. More practically, the forest tunnel was used to usher participants past a series of display cases and sales tables that condensed Korea's sylvan commodities and traditions into a single space. To walk through the tunnel was thus to be transported across the woodlands of the entire peninsula, in all its "local color," as one organizer put it.[51]

The tunnel also offered transport across a single life span. Indeed, as part of their effort to shed light on the linkages between forests and everyday existence, the curators of the exhibition divided the displays into different stages of human life. The first phase ("birth") featured a mother tending to her baby in a wooden cradle, surrounded by a range of ligneous products including bottles and toys. The next phase ("childhood") focused on the carefree joys of climbing a tree and exploring nature. This was followed by a scene of young girls ("youth"), sporting the latest in alpine fashion, on a picturesque hike through the woods (fig. 7.5). The adulthood phase ("the prime of life") trained its gaze on the interior furnishings of a modern home, while the display for old age ("the elderly") exhibited a number of forestry products (such as newspapers and canes) enjoyed by retirees. The conceit of this display was essentially to give material expression to an aphorism often quoted by timber-industry boosters: "From the washbasin used at birth to the casket at death, all are thanks to wood."[52]

As much as these displays conveyed a seemingly universal consumer culture, they also highlighted Korea's unique regional handicrafts. One could

FIG. 7.5 A display featuring two smartly dressed hikers on a walk through the woods. (From Chōsen Sōtokufu Nōrinkoyku, ed., *Chōsen sanrin bunka tenrankai shi*, 23.)

hardly ignore the local delicacies on offer: the bamboo umbrellas of North Chŏlla; the walnuts of North Ch'ungch'ŏng; the furniture of Kyŏnggi. The inclusion of Manchurian timber, Osaka plywood, and forestry products from elsewhere in the empire also reminded visitors of their place within the burgeoning "yen bloc": a zone of economic autarky that situated Korea and its forest commodities within the currents of broader natural resource flows.

Noteworthy, too, are the gendered representations of domesticity. At each stage of life a woman is seen surrounded by the material trappings of the modern home. Staging of this sort strongly suggests that, while all ticket-paying customers were welcome, exhibition organizers consciously tailored the displays to the sensibilities of urban-dwelling women. Given the widespread commentary on housewives as practitioners of "domestic household scientific management" and forces of "dutiful consumption," it should come as little surprise that organizers would appeal to their particular tastes and desires.[53]

If anything, the Korean Forest Culture Exhibition was a call to consume conscientiously, to open your pocketbooks only to forest products endorsed by the KFA. One clear takeaway from the showroom floor was the idea that loving the forest meant supporting the businesses that responsibly transformed Korea's natural resources into marketable wares. Every yen spent on properly sourced furniture or energy-efficient coal briquettes was, by this logic, an investment in forest conservation. At a more subconscious level, the showroom floor functioned as an index of material dependency. In the rich cornucopia of goods for sale, consumers received a stark reminder of all that could be lost if careless consumption went unchecked.

The fourth-floor display also offered something of a history lesson. Although the subject matter would have been familiar enough to any grade-school pupil, the method of transmission was entirely novel: a slice of a 688-year-old hemlock harvested on Ullŭng Island. A monument to Korea's own forest history, this tree and its growth rings offered a colossal reminder of the fact that forests had transcended the ebbs and flows of politics and spanned generations—that, when protected, trees could become records of the deep past. To illustrate this point, event planners created a dendrochronology of Japanese and world history, showing how, for instance, at age five the hemlock grew through the birth of the Japanese regent-warrior Hōjō Tokimune; how at age 242 the tree grew through Columbus's discovery of the Americas; and how at age 688 it grew through the hostilities of the Russo-Japanese War (fig. 7.6). That this wooden chronicle made little room

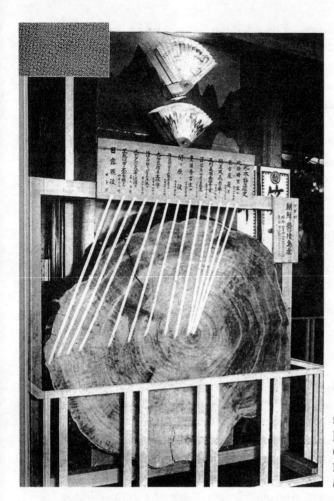

FIG. 7.6 A dendrochronology of Japanese and world history. (From Chōsen Sōtokufu Nōrinkoyku, ed., *Chōsen sanrin bunka tenrankai shi*, 20.)

for Korea's own history is as true a testament as any to how colonizers projected their own narratives onto the landscapes of the colonized.

Such arboreal curiosities were hardly to be found on the fifth floor, however, which shifted the focus to advancements in forestry science and technology. Here, visitors delved into the technological wonders behind the manufacture of veneer, tannin, cellophane, Ōji Paper pulp, and a variety of other chemical components. As part of an exhibit on "forestry and national defense," for example, one corner of the fifth floor contained an array of military hardware (such as airplane propellers and frames) deemed vital to national security. Another flaunted accelerating Forest Management Bureau lumbering operations along the Yalu River basin, which, thanks to the

Northern Development Plan, were then aiding in the region's heavy indus-trialization. For its part, the Forestry Experiment Station also contributed an elaborate diorama of cutting-edge runoff prevention methods, which strikingly visualized changes in forest cover in a number of regions targeted for reforestation. Eventually, visitors made their way to the outdoor space set up on the roof of the building, where they could enjoy a break room (built with Sinŭiju timber) and see for themselves a new and improved *ondol* (burning lignite coal, rice husks, and other substitute fuels).[54]

Event coordinators pulled out all the stops to ensure that the exhibition received significant and sustained media attention. The attendance on the opening day of Governor-General Ugaki Kazushige, who was shadowed through the exhibition by journalists and photographers, certainly lent grandeur to the event. The press took particular interest in Ugaki's face-to-face with Fujiwara Ginjirō (president of Ōji Paper), whom many considered to be the most powerful corporate operative in the forestry world.[55] The organizers were pleased overall with the general attendance figures: accord-ing to official estimates, the exhibition drew no fewer than seven thousand and as many as fifteen thousand visitors per day, with a total of about sixty-three thousand visitors over the course of the week.[56]

Although these numbers offer little sense of the socioeconomic back-ground of those in attendance, one can safely assume they were predomi-nantly middle- and upper-class Japanese and Koreans—that is, individuals with the time and income to shop at one of Korea's major department stores. In this sense, the Forest Culture Exhibition was distorted in favor of bour-geoisie pursuits and predilections. Apart from idealized representations of farm life and the material contributions of rural craftspeople, the large majority of Koreans who worked the land were scarcely reflected in these displays. This omission was befitting of an ideological campaign that from the outset painted roseate portraits of societal harmony with nature—one often at odds with the rigors and realities of agrarian life.

CONCLUSION

Whether or not foresters succeeded in their effort to arrest the senses of resi-dents of Korea, there is no question that the forest-love thought campaign gave rise to a far-reaching public relations machinery concerned with natu-ral resource conservation. Bureaucrats took to the airwaves while village leaders convened workshops. Pupils competed in poster contests one week and tended to their school's forest the next. Sanitation Associations manicured parks in Korea's cities as Forest-Love Associations guarded stands deep in the mountains. These more workaday activities, moreover, were often punctuated by grandiose celebrations, especially those carried out in conjunction with the ceremonial plantings of April 3. Running the gamut from the mundane to the spectacular—and targeting *all* of the senses—these activities left their mark on many different facets of everyday existence. Although it is difficult to draw conclusions about the extent to which the promotion of forest love actually shaped the daily decisions of colonial subjects, the sheer breadth of this campaign nevertheless underscores how invested the colonial state was in Japanizing Koreans' forest culture.

Ironically, however, back in Japan something of a Koreanization of forestry was also taking place. By the early 1930s, that is, Korea's greenification framework had become a regularly referenced case study for Japan-based foresters who were then strategizing how best to replenish forest stocks in the face of economic turmoil and rural hardship. Of particular interest were the mass planting activities orchestrated by the Government-General. Although Japan was no stranger to tree-planting rituals, it was not until 1928, with the commencement of the Enthronement Memorial Afforestation Campaign, that the full sweep of Japanese society took part in carefully coordinated nationwide acts of reforestation. In 1934, the Japan Forestry Association went further to inaugurate the national observance of Forest-Love Day (Airinbi), a festival dedicated to the improvement of the archipelago's forests. Involving many of the same programs, abiding by similar operational guidelines, and recycling the rhetoric on agrarian improvement, Japan's own Shōwa-era conservationist activities owed much to the early exigencies of reforestation in Korea. In this sense, Japan's Forest-Love Day should be understood in part as a reflection of how Korea's greenification framework reached back to the metropole—of how metropolitan foresters turned to Korea for insight into how to effectively mobilize civic society behind national projects of woodland regeneration.[57]

The architects of Korea's greenification were well aware of the empire-wide appeal of their template for mass reforestation. According to Okazaki Tetsurō, while tree-planting events back in Japan were "not insignificant," they did not begin to approach the degree of coordination or material impact found in Korea, where "planting activities across the land have continued for twenty-five years with the deep involvement of officials and the people." It had progressed, by his assessment, to a level "without comparison elsewhere."[58] Saitō Otosaku, the mastermind of these plantings, went so far as to crown Korea's forest-love activities the "*yokozuna* of the empire," that is, the best in their class.[59]

Rather tellingly, Japanese forestry officials stopped short of conceding any sort of ascension in Korea's place within the forest hierarchy of the empire. Koreans' conservationist credentials remained fully subordinated to those of their Japanese rulers. Regardless of how earnestly they pruned tree branches or how avidly they explored mountain parks, Koreans' exercise of forest-love thought was never quite enough to free them of racially tinged charges of sloth, superstition, and self-absorption. As with so many other aspects of Japanese assimilation policy, colonial-era discourses on the relationship between race, climate, and forest conservation were teeming with contradiction.

What impressed Japan-based foresters about Korea, then, was not so much the depth of forest-love thought as it was the breadth of the policy framework erected by the colonial government to achieve grassroots reforestation. Already two decades into what some had begun to call the Government-General's "greenification-first principle" (*ryokka daiichi-shugi*), colonial foresters had constructed mechanisms of public engagement that were closely aligned with the emerging imperatives of forestry back in the metropole—rural improvement, labor mobilization, statist control. Japanese leaders, in other words, were growing increasingly interested in using forestry as a means for greater social discipline. They saw in Korea's greenification framework opportunities for surveillance, synchronization, and social cohesion—in a word, imperial indoctrination.

Driving the convergence of conservation policy on both sides of the Tsushima Strait was the ideological intensification that accompanied the shift to total war. Following the opening salvos in 1937 of the Second Sino-Japanese War, romanticized conceptions of forest-love thought gave way to a growing list of draconian directives governing forest consumption in the face of material scarcity. In Korea, the rhetoric of forestry was quickly laced with the language of sacrifice and duty. Confronted with the demands of industrial warfare, the priorities of forest management and the mechanics of regulation rather abruptly transformed. So began a new chapter in environmental governance and a marked uptick in the extractive activities of the colonial state.

EIGHT

A STIFF WIND BLOWS

LIKE SOME OF THE SECOND-GROWTH FORESTS PLANTED EARLY INTO colonial rule, the Government-General's forestry apparatus had filled out considerably by the mid-1930s. From the rootstock of the 1908 Forest Law had grown a host of regulatory bodies, enforcement agencies, and public partnerships that oversaw the day-to-day work of forest management. Equally striking was the enlargement of the colonial forestry agency itself: what started as a small outfit of senior advisers had by 1938 swelled to 4,949 employees, overseeing scores of nurseries, sawmills, research centers, mountain outposts, and provincial offices.[1] Never a crowd to pass up an opportunity for self-congratulations, forestry officials appraised these developments as nothing less than a volte-face in the administration of Korea's forests. As one characteristically embellished retrospective from 1934 put it, under Japan's tutelage Korea had morphed from a denuded landscape "without forestry or forest management" to the site of a grand state forestry enterprise—rooted in law, supervised by experts, and operating in accordance with a "one-hundred-year plan."[2]

Whatever that plan had in store for Korea, however, was not to come to pass. For just as colonial forestry officials in Korea were beginning to feel settled in their commission, a new and urgent mandate was thrust upon them. Inciting this shift was neither the crack of an axe nor the roar of a flood but the boom of artillery fire. Indeed, with the sudden exchange of fire between Japanese and Chinese garrisons on July 7, 1937 at the Marco Polo Bridge, just north of Beijing, came a sea change in the administration of Korea's forests. Japanese ground forces surged into northern China, triggering the declaration of the Second Sino-Japanese War and a rising war fever back in Japan. Rather suddenly, Korea became an "advance military supply base" (*zenshin heitan kichi*) for the war in China. It fell to forestry bureaucrats and Forest Experiment Station (FES) scientists to figure out how to mobilize the peninsula and its forests for war on the continent.

So began a process of forest resource centralization that radically altered the industrial composition and energy distribution networks of the peninsula. In response to soaring demand for war material, the Government-General ramped up the production of timber, charcoal, and a host of chemical components. To facilitate this push, lawmakers in Tokyo and Seoul called for an extension of the Law for Control of Major Industries from the metropole to Korea, thereby tightening the colonial state's grip on key war industries. A slate of laws thereafter restructured Korea's heavy industrial base so as to meet the requirements of its so-called "national defense economy." By 1938, a full-fledged National Spiritual Mobilization Movement was also under way, as the colonial state dialed up its ideological efforts to enlist Korean subjects into the war effort.

If these transformations marked the advent of Korea's wartime system, they also heralded the beginning of what many scholars have come to call the colonial state's wartime "forest plunder."[3] As reservoirs of fuel, lumber, sleepers, chemicals, and other raw materials—what were increasingly gathered under the label "national defense resources"—the Government-General pressed Korea's forests into military service. The Japanese Imperial Navy recruited red and black pine as boatbuilding materials. The Imperial Army Air Service called up birch, maple, and walnut as propellers and frames. New market restrictions went up as old-growth came down. In short order, forestry bureaucrats transformed the timber industry into a state enterprise, changed land-use guidelines into sumptuary laws, and placed resource austerity at the heart of forest love.

To understand what all this meant for Korea's forests—or the lives of those who lived in their midst—one must first recognize that, as Micah Muscolino has written, "militaries have metabolisms." Energy courses through every aspect of warfare. Wars are powered by and fought over oil, coal, and other types of fuel. Militaries travel great distances, consume vast quantities of food, and produce just as much waste. For these and other reasons, argues Muscolino, it is imperative that environmental histories of warfare attend to the "the energetics of militarized landscapes": that is, how the exigencies of war reconfigure the energy flows that sustain both military operations and civilian life.[4] In the case of colonial Korea, where "Commander Frost [Fuyu Shōgun] had everyone shivering," as one settler recalled, it is not hyperbole to say that even slight shifts in energy distribution held profound physiological implications for civilian life.[5] Considering that winter temperatures routinely dropped—and, in the northern provinces, remained—well below zero degrees Fahrenheit, shortfalls in fuel could spell discomfort, sickness, or, in rare cases, even hypothermic death.

Although scholars of colonial Korea have done much to elucidate the effects of the war, rural unrest, and economic autarky on food security and caloric intake, they have largely taken for granted the fuel that kept bellies full and bodies warm. To forestry officials, however, domestic fuel consumption was all-important; the path to military victory led over the hills, through the woods, and directly to the *ondol* stove. With one edict after the next, the wartime state tightened the fetters of fuel regulations, leaving households with difficult daily choices about how to access the materials necessary for subsistence, if not survival. In this way, the logic of total war incorporated Korean bodies into the cold calculus of natural resource management—a form of biopolitics that has to date eluded scrutiny.

Viewing the colonial state from the perspective of the household firebox offers insight into more than the market dynamics and material dimensions of war; it also enables us to broaden conceptualizations of colonial and wartime violence. In contrast to the more spectacular displays of oppression that figure so prominently in nationalist histories, these privations and the state-imposed thermal regulations behind them hint at the operation in colonial Korea of something akin to what Rob Nixon has called "slow violence": "incremental and accretive" forms of suffering that occur largely out of sight and over prolonged temporal frames, whose "attritional lethality" injures both people and their surrounding ecosystems.[6] Of particular salience to the case of late colonial Korea is Nixon's notion of "displacement without moving": how state-imposed landscapes can prompt the "loss of land and the resources beneath," leaving "communities stranded in a place stripped of the very characteristics that made it inhabitable."[7] That colonialism and war prompted the physical displacement of Koreans—to factories in the north, to frontiers in Manchuria, to coal mines in Japan—is a well-established fact. But the onset of the war and the subsequent tightening of resource allocations gave rise to a different form of displacement. To make sense of daily life within the landscapes of Korea's own "dark valley," then, we must not only map the emergence of a command economy for forest products but also consider the bodily implications of caloric control.[8]

THE WARTIME HARVEST

Provisioning the wartime state with timber, charcoal, pulp, and other forest products was a tall order. With battlefronts expanding in China, timber trade relations deteriorating with the United States, and the industrial applications of wood fibers broadening, demand for Korean forest resources had never been higher. Bureaucrats in Korea accordingly took measures to control prices, commandeer transport routes, and, where possible, expand productive capacities. They did so in part by authorizing in 1939 new felling operations within Korea's extensive network of Forest Management Bureau (FMB) stations, effectively accelerating the "timber undertaking" in northern Korea. Higher production quotas gave rise to shorter stand rotations. According to Ch'oe In-hwa, when compared to the stand-rotation models established for national forestland in the period from 1913 to 1918, the standard volume of felling had by 1940–41 accelerated by as much as 150 percent and even 500 percent in certain areas.[9]

Oiling the wheels of wartime forestry operations was a rapid expansion of the network of logging roads and timber railways used to transport remote forest stocks—precisely the objective of the Northern Development Plan. With Korea's freight suddenly packed to the brim with war material destined for northern China, the creation of alternative transportation pathways was more exigent than ever. In 1939, work crews laid an additional 100 kilometers of track, bringing the total web-work of logging transport routes to 518 kilometers comprised of sixty-three lines.[10] Statistics on aggregate timber production speak clearly to the expanding scope of felling operations (fig. 8.1). Whereas in 1932 approximately 3,500,000 *shakujime* of timber was harvested from national forestlands, this figure had by 1939 increased twofold to 7,780,000 *shakujime*.[11]

Headsaws, lathes, and edgers were especially busy in the northern provinces. To be sure, wartime demand intensified timber extraction across the peninsula, leading to new industrial forestry operations in places like Kangwŏn, Mount Chiri, and even Cheju Island. But forestry planners remained unflinching in their resolve to reap the old-growth conifer forests

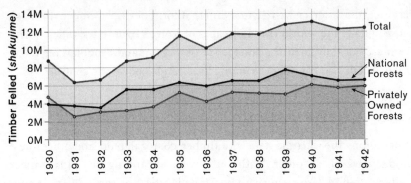

FIG. 8.1 Breakdown of timber felled by ownership category, 1930–1942. (Data from Chōsen Sōtokufu, *Rinya tōkei*; compiled in Hagino, *Chōsen, Manshū, Taiwan ringyō hattatsu shiron*, 141.)

of the Yalu and Tumen River basins such that, by one estimate, 80 percent of the timber extracted from national forestlands after 1935 came from the northern provinces.[12] Higher yields in the north were hardly a boon to Korea's timber industry. Hobbled by the damming of the Yalu and chronic labor shortages, many private lumbering operations fell on hard times. In Sinŭiju, factories of all sizes found themselves desperately wanting for raw materials. As a consequence, many of Korea's sawmills and workshops had little choice but to merge into larger cooperatives—a trend that the Government-General would later exploit by repurposing these milling consortiums into de facto regulatory entities of the state.

A similar integration took shape within Korea's afforestation industry: the private nurseries, experts, and corporations that sought to profit from the state's silvicultural ambitions. Early into the war forestry officials remained steadfast in their commitment to reforestation. Invoking the lessons of World War I—a conflict that threw into sharp relief the causes and consequences of national timber famine—foresters called for robust regeneration efforts alongside increased production drives. They did so in concert with agricultural experts, who underscored the importance of healthy forests to military preparedness. If Korea was to feed soldiers and subjects across the empire, as war planners envisioned, then the state should take care not to overharvest its forests.

These considerations prompted policymakers in Seoul to push for a greater concentration of capital in state-prioritized reforestation projects. Such was precisely the raison d'être of the Korean Forestry Development

Company (Chōsen Ringyō Kaihatsu Kabushiki Kaisha, hereafter KFDC), a parastatal "afforestation entity" responsible for restocking national forestlands. To that end, the Government-General leased the KFDC 220,000 *chōbu* of woodlands (concentrated in North Kyŏngsang and Kangwŏn) and subsidized the cost of afforestation by as much as one-third over the first fifteen years of its operations. This was no paltry promise. By their own estimates, these subsidies could cost the Government-General as much as ¥16 million over twenty years.[13] Their plan was essentially to lure the investment of outside capital by ensuring the solvency of the company as it got off the ground.

Just as bureaucrats had hoped, Korea's largest corporations gobbled up its initial public offering. Straightaway, 77 percent of its shares were purchased by just seven corporations: the Oriental Development Company (22 percent), Ōji Paper (20), Mitsui (10), Mitsubishi (10), the Japan Nitrogenous Fertilizer Company (5), Sumitomo (5), and the Dai-ichi Mutual Life Insurance Company (5).[14] The appointment of Yajima Sugizō—who just a year prior had been chief of the Bureau of Agriculture and Forestry—as president more or less ensured that the company would operate in close alignment with the will of the bureaucracy. Following its charter in 1937, the KFDC promptly established a branch office in Kangwŏn, as well as 125 different patrol outposts designed to protect the afforestation projects it oversaw.[15]

Some executives and employees had other plans in mind. With stumpage rising steeply, the growing profitability of the timber within their leasehold was becoming difficult to ignore. Cracks in the corporation's afforestation mandate began to grow. Just two years into its operations, the KFDC started to harvest timber and process charcoal from the very woodlands it was supposed to stock and protect, reaping in 1940 a net profit of ¥155,000.[16] By 1941, of the approximately 300,000 *chōbu* of land leased to the KFDC for afforestation work, only about 46,000 *chōbu* had been restocked—just 15 percent of the total area of its leasehold.[17] In this sense, the KFDC may be seen as yet another vehicle through which the architects of forest policy used the pretext of reforestation to siphon forest resources into the hands of Japanese corporate entities.

It was not just national forestlands that saw intensified exploitation; industrial planners also targeted privately owned woodlands—those belonging to counties, temples, cooperatives, or individuals—for extraction. Civic forestry institutions were crucial to this undertaking. Semi-official organizations initially established in the name of "rural revitalization" became after 1937 the vanguard of wartime resource mobilization. The rapid intake of timber resources from privately operated woodlands is perhaps best reflected in the aggregate value of timber product transactions. While in 1936 about ¥118,060,000 worth of timber products was sold, by 1941 this figure had increased almost threefold to ¥344,260,000.[18]

Behind these market transactions grew an ever-evolving regulatory framework designed to tighten the state's grip on key forest resources. At first, these measures took the form of temporary price controls targeting forestry products bought and sold in Korea's four main timber markets: Seoul, Sinŭiju, Kimch'aek, and Hoeryŏng. In 1940, however, the Government-General issued the first of a series of edicts designed to bring new regulatory oversight to the timber industry as a whole. Thenceforth, the Bureau of Agriculture and Forestry required all merchants, brokers, and millers involved in the trade of timber or charcoal to gain permission to lease or sell any resources. Additional regulations were put in place at the provincial level, where district forestry offices enforced a series of harvesting guidelines meant to improve stand structure. In effect, these requirements saddled Korean merchants, brokers, and farmers with additional operating costs, forcing many to sell off their timber to state entities at cut-rate prices or to dispose of their land altogether.

Every so often, these market interventions also went awry. As Ch'oe Pyŏng-t'aek has shown with the colonial capital, for instance, price controls set shortly after the outbreak of war in order to stabilize supplies of charcoal had the unintended consequence of flooding the market with firewood.[19] Initially, as a result, the Government-General actually induced exactly the *opposite* market adjustment officials had desired: supplies of charcoal diminished as Koreans bought up and burned firewood, thereby undercutting fuel replacement drives. The Government-General responded by placing strict limitations on firewood distribution. Although effective in driving up the production of charcoal, these stiff measures aroused the protests of merchants and consumers alike, setting the stage for a prolonged struggle over the domestication of heat under wartime conditions.

WEAPONIZING WOODLANDS

True to Korea's status as an "advance military supply base" for the Kwantung Army, large volumes of its forest resources were channeled directly into military operations. The better part of the wartime harvest took the form of traditional products such as rail ties, construction materials, and mine timbers that were vital to the maintenance and expansion of military supply lines. As the conflict deepened, however, forestry bureaucrats also worked to steer resources into the production of more specialized military products. Airplane frames, shipbuilding materials, plastics, and munitions were all manufactured in whole or in part with Korean forests. "Timber," proclaimed one 1943 editorial, "is a weapon for the decisive battle"—a battle, it went on to explain, of assembly-line production.[20]

Of increasing utility and strategic importance was the production of synthetic fibers and biopolymers: wood-pulp derivatives in high demand as replacement for fabrics and tire cord. As quickly as production would allow, rayon was tied into the fabrication of semi-synthetic fibers, cellophane was incorporated into packaging processes, and cellulose acetate fiber became a standard ingredient in the mass-production of textiles. Demand for these and other pulp-based products was met in part by scaling up the operations of the Ōji Paper–backed North Korea Paper and Chemical Manufacture Company, which from its flagship factory in Kilju churned out impressive volumes of chemical components.[21]

Fueling all of these industrial undertakings was a more basic commodity: charcoal. Even with significant advancements in the generation of hydro-power in Korea, many factories remained dependent on charcoal to sustain a diverse array of more specialized industrial processes: from the forging of pig iron to the oxidation of sulfide. Charcoal was used alongside fossil fuels to keep industrial engines humming and smelting furnaces fired around the clock. It is little wonder, then, that the colonial state moved as quickly as it did to control charcoal prices and stimulate production. At stake was more than home-heating or cooking fuel. To industrial planners, charcoal was vital to the growth of heavy industry itself—and all the more so as much of Korea's high-quality anthracite was exported to Japan.[22]

Increasing the domestic output of forest resources and efficiently inte-grating these materials into supply lines abroad were two very different things, and this was not lost on war planners. The movement of any given forest product depended principally on two interrelated factors: the geogra-phy of existing production chains and the available modes of transport. Working through supply chains that had grown in tandem with the "Korea-Manchuria Economic Bloc," bureaucrats, merchants, and FMB officials guided growing volumes of lumber, sleepers, and engineering timbers into northern China, where they were delivered directly to their sites of utilization.[23]

By 1939, the total value of timber shipped to Manchuria had nearly doubled from prewar levels, with lumber and board sheets worth almost ¥9 million crossing the Yalu.[24]

Korean corporations engaged in manufacturing were also becoming heavily dependent on timber and charcoal imports from the Japanese archipelago to offset shortfalls in domestic supply. Between 1937 and 1942, average timber imports from Japan amounted to approximately ¥32 million per year, while average annual exports from Korea to Japan in that same period were only around ¥2 million.[25] These wartime trade currents suggest a far more complex portrait of wartime forest resource consumption than conventional narratives often convey. Insofar as the Government-General scaled up its harvest of Korean timber to support the war effort in Manchuria, we can say that the state stripped Korea of much of its forest stock, particularly that in the north of the peninsula. But only small volumes of Korea's forest resources were actually exported for use back in Japan, despite the growing scarcity in fuel and timber in the archipelago. Far more impressive were the volumes of timber shipped from Japan to Korea. In this sense, the peninsula and its factories formed something of a timber sink for the empire. While Korea's northern national forests supplied raw materials for industrialization at home and battlefronts abroad, the rising demand of private enterprise was met only by importing significant quantities of timber from the archipelago.

For industrial planners tasked with the bewildering logistics of resource provisioning, one thing was clear: Japan needed to build more ships, and fast. With military vessels engaged in combat operations across the Pacific and the merchant marine spread thin, the need for cargo ships had never been greater. In 1942, as a result, the Japanese government launched a boatbuilding drive meant to boost the tonnage of motorized vessels and so-called "Emergency Standard Ships"—stripped-down workhorse watercraft that would enhance haulage capacities. These ships did not easily materialize; each required large quantities of high-quality lumber, among other woody components. The search for suitable boatbuilding materials led project suppliers rather quickly to the Korean peninsula. By April 1943, a "Wooden Vessel Construction Encouragement Campaign" had commenced, which ambitiously set out to raise domestic boat production in Korea by 30 percent.[26] In a twist of irony that only history can muster, some of the very coastal forests that had been assembled in the sixteenth century into the "turtle ships" that countered Hideyoshi's naval armada were targeted once more to provision a war on behalf of their erstwhile invaders.[27]

Alongside concern with shipping lanes grew a foreboding anxiety over the air lanes of the empire. With the Japanese military engaged in aerial bombing operations against Chinese cities (and European skies thick with smoke from incendiary raids), the Japanese public was well aware of both the promise and the perils of industrial war in the age of air power. Indeed, as defense officials were only too aware, neither the colonies nor the homeland lay beyond the sights of American bombardiers, whose range expanded markedly once the United States Army Air Force Twentieth Bomber Command had set up shop in Chengdu, China.

The implications of aerial warfare for forestry were twofold. First, it prompted a peninsula-wide search for trees and other materials instrumental to airplane manufacture. Aviation authorities urged woodland owners to spare large, old-growth hardwoods (especially maple and walnut)—trees whose circumference and tensile strength made them ideally suited for the assembly of airplane frames and propellers. Second, it raised the stakes of fire suppression. As Stephen Pyne reminds us, World War II witnessed the weaponization of fire on an industrial scale. Added to the usual agents of forest fire (lightning, slash-and-burn agriculture, human negligence) was the menace of incendiary bombs.[28] Forest-fire protection duly became a major component of civil defense. In Korea, many civic forestry associations began to form their own fire-watching and -fighting brigades. The Japanese military also put fire on the offensive, deploying thousands of intercontinental fire balloons across the Pacific in a creative, if desperate, attempt to ignite wildfires in the western United States.[29]

Yet the greatest threat to the resiliency of Korea's forests seemed to come from within the peninsula itself. Only a few years into the war, forest scientists had already begun to express concerns that Korea's forests were approaching an ecological threshold beyond which relatively minor disturbances could spell drastic changes in overall productivity. The strains placed on the peninsula's woodlands only seemed to magnify as one resource problem begot another. With nitrogen prioritized for munitions production, fertilizer grew scarce, resulting in greater soil degradation and erosion. With gasoline earmarked for military use after 1941, many vehicles were crudely jury-rigged with inefficient wood-burning engines. All the while, many Korean communities had set about the production of pine resin, root tar, and turpentine—"arboreal alchemy" that reflects the desperate need, felt across the empire, to sap the forests of any sustenance they could offer.[30] Turpentine production jumped from nearly nothing in 1936 to almost 500,000 *kan* in

1942. To the detriment of oak stands, cork and tannin production similarly soared.[31]

Where the extraction of wood-derived products proved difficult, the Bureau of Agriculture and Forestry worked to develop woodlands into sources of foodstuffs. In partnership with the Korean Forestry Association, agroforestry officials coordinated a series of workshops meant to train local communities in maximizing the nourishment gleaned from forests. Arboriculturists were particularly enthusiastic about raising fruit-bearing trees, especially the apple and persimmon varietals known to thrive on the peninsula. Wartime forest management plans also took care to preserve wild herbs, mountain vegetables, and mushrooms—alternative food sources that increasingly made their way into dietary guidelines and foraging baskets of rural households.

Such measures, however, fell well short of alleviating the malnourishment that was pervasive in rural Korea. Forest rangers were no strangers to one of the more common responses to famine: swidden. In defiance of wartime injunctions on fire prevention, tens of thousands of households continued to engage in shifting cultivation for whatever soy, millet, or barley it might yield. But the closing years of the war also brought rangers face to face with a new and disturbing sign of the times: barkless trees. One 1942 report filed by the Public Prosecutor's Office in Hamhŭng, for example, related widespread destruction of protected pine forests due to the last-ditch efforts of farmers to strip their bark for food. "A considerable number of village people," the author noted, "have swollen bodies since they feed only on wild roots and tree-bark." Another researcher discovered forty-three different types of roots and bark consumed by farmers around the Taegu area.[32]

Perhaps the clearest indication of the shift to what might be called "total war forestry" was the fact that beginning in 1942 afforestation activities were severely curtailed. With supplies of seeds, saplings, and labor dwindling, colonial officials had little recourse but to resort to natural regenerative approaches and call upon Korean landowners to plant trees of their own volition. Although the spotty nature of data collection makes it difficult to assess deforestation after 1942, it is reasonable to conclude that forest stocks continued to diminish as the war wore on. The degree of depletion might be clearer to historians if not for empire-wide shortfalls in paper, the scarcity of which is in itself a testament to the intense demands placed on woodlands across Japan's "new order" in the Asia-Pacific.

If boosting timber production was the primary concern of bureaucrats in Seoul and Tokyo, regimenting fuel consumption was the wartime mandate of provincial officials. The war on thermal inefficiency proceeded on two fronts: one about encouragement, the other restraint. Provincial authorities tightened controls on the collection of fuel by increasing forest patrols, fortifying the forest penal codes, and monitoring local burning practices. When efforts early into the war to stimulate charcoal production unintentionally spurred an uptick in woodcutting and firewood sales, these regulatory mechanisms became all the more restrictive. Best practices for fuel conservation once merely suggested in forestry guidelines were codified into sumptuary legal ordinances that targeted individual and household fuel-consumption patterns. In August 1940, for instance, the Government-General promulgated a set of Charcoal Distribution Regulations that mandated the formation of district-wide Charcoal Distribution Associations. This was followed in 1942 by the passage of the Korean Timber Control Edict (Chōsen Mokuzai Tōseirei), a far-reaching decree that further empowered village-level institutions to supervise fuel allocations. With this, colonial Korea's rationing of forest products was effectively brought onto total war footing.

The nucleus of this operation was the newly established Korean Timber Corporation (Chōsen Mokuzai Kabushiki Kaisha), which began to merge the patchwork of sawmills, vendors, and retailers into a tight-knit network of timber apportionment. It did so primarily by taking over the reins of the operations of timber and charcoal production associations, then vital nodes in the circulation of "national defense resources." From 1943 onward, each of the thousands of woodcutters and millers operating in Korea were required to sell their merchandise directly to the provincial offices of the Korean Timber Corporation at carefully controlled prices. What remained of this timber after military and government procurements was then distributed back to local consumers via timber production associations.[33]

The flip side of resource centralization was fuel substitution. One way or another, households were going to find a way to make up for the fuel sources requisitioned by the state. It was the responsibility of district forestry officials and village leaders to ensure that they did so in ways that were conducive to forest health and in line with state-sanctioned market activities. Three particular energy sources inexorably rose to the forefront of this substitution agenda: rice husks, culm, and charcoal. Of these, charcoal was unquestionably the substitute fuel of choice. Building on headway made during the Rural Revitalization Campaign, civic forestry associations invested their resources in the cultivation of tree species known to efficiently yield charcoal. According to one official estimate, by 1938 fully 30 percent of privately owned forests had been functionally converted into some form of "fuel forest."[34] On account of these efforts, the production of charcoal rose sharply from about 38,240,000 *kan* in 1940 to 76,135,000 *kan* in 1944. Conversely, the production of firewood dropped from around 1,500,000 *kan* in 1936 to 1,000,000 *kan* in 1942—a welcome trend in the eyes of the state.[35]

Concurrent with the push for fuel substitution was a renewed effort to remedy the thermal inefficiencies of the *ondol* stove. In urban Korea, officials and businessmen enthusiastically promoted the installation of reformed *ondol* models (*kōseishiki ondoru*) in the homes of those with the wherewithal to implement improvements or build new structures. Some urban kitchens also saw the installation of "forest-love cook stoves": a kitchen appliance invented by Kim Pang-hun (and endorsed by the KFA) to economize the energy requirements of food preparation.[36] In rural Korea, focus narrowed after 1937 on the gaping, uncovered mouth (*agungi*) of the *ondol*—a design flaw that many saw as easily rectified through simple retrofits. Provincial governments accordingly began to issue subsidies for *ondol* mouth improvement, which often amounted to the installation of a tin-plated or cement door. Some rural communities went so far as to appoint local *ondol* inspectors to ensure that *ondol* lids remained in place and to thwart illegal fuel collection.[37] Given that a major part of the thousands of forest code infractions prosecuted by the wartime state arose from the *ondol*, these inspectors clearly had their work cut out for them.[38]

If such efforts speak to the growing reach of the wartime state into the domestic sphere, they also hint at how natural resource conservation was freighted with new meaning against the backdrop of imperial indoctrination. Indeed, much as officials came to view the Korean home as a microcosm of the Shintōization of the Korean spirit, as Todd Henry has shown, they marked domestic fuel conservation efforts as an expression of imperial fealty.[39] Household rates of caloric consumption were increasingly interpreted as indexes of spiritual assimilation. Appealing to familial as well as communal obligations, forestry advocates called on Koreans to exercise thermal discipline however possible. After imbibing for decades the notion that "forests determine national destiny," imperial subjects were finely attuned to how any wasteful behavior—an uncovered stove here, an overly hot bath there—could be perceived as undermining what was increasingly described as Japan's "holy war." Fukushima Eisaku, vice president of the Korean Chamber of Commerce and Industry, captured this outlook when he opined that conserving just "one lump of charcoal or one drop of oil" could make all the difference for frontline operations then "charging toward the point between life and death."[40] With all signs pointing toward a drawn-out conflict waged on fronts as many as they were distant, it was clear that fuel conservation was to become an enduring requirement of the war.

Shifts in sylvan symbolism were also afoot. At a time when many were bracing themselves for a war to "liberate East Asia from white invasion and oppression," propagandists found in forests a powerful set of signifiers for Japan's soldierly spirit. And none more so than the cherry blossom, a tree whose multitudinous meanings were appropriated by wartime ideologues and turned into, in the words of Emiko Ohnuki-Tierney, "a symbol of soldiers' sacrifice for the emperor qua Japan."[41] What had once been for Koreans markers of cultural refinement now carried more sacrificial connotations.[42] With growing regularity, dispatches from the war front began to liken perished soldiers (and, especially, kamikaze pilots) to fallen cherry petals, the impermanence of which came to evince the fleeting nature of life itself. Went one popular wartime song from 1944:

> You and I, companion cherry blossoms,
> Flowered in the garden of the same military school.
> Just as the blossoms calmly scatter,
> We too are ready to fall for our country.[43]

That the cherry blossom had an outsized influence on the maturation of Japan's "way of the warrior" was a prominent leitmotif of wartime propaganda. To substantiate this claim, one senior forestry official turned to the following verse from Motoori Norinaga, one of the foremost Japanese philosophers of the eighteenth century, whose writings enjoyed a wartime revival owing in part to their nativist persuasion:

> Should someone ask,
> "What is the soul,
> Of Yamato, our ancient land?"
> It is the scent of mountain cherry blossoms
> In the morning sun[44]

In highlighting how forests had since time immemorial influenced the Japanese spirit, foresters found more than a stimulant for nationalist sentiment. They also found a way to position Japan shoulder to shoulder with its German ally. Just as the German *Volk* had supposedly emerged from the primordial forest, so had the Yamato race been raised in the cradle of the forest—an affinity that made both countries the two *pure* forest cultures of the world.[45]

Yet, while some Japanese were turning to their forest history to advance claims of ethnic purity and civilizational hierarchy, others were drawing from this same archive evidence of the fraternal bond between Japanese and Koreans. Among them was Suzuki Toyokazu, a veteran forestry official and prolific researcher, whose 1942 explication of the *Nihon shoki*, a chronicle of classical Japanese history, took pains to make room for Korea's place under the sun. Particularly salient to Suzuki was the following passage from Japan's creation myth that, in his reading, revealed the genesis of a shared regional forest history:

> By one version, Susanowo said, "In the islands of Korea, they have gold and silver. If I make my children's place this country, it will not have ships, and it will not be alright." Then he pulled out his beard and scattered it around. This became cedar. Then he pulled out the hair of his chest, and scattered it around. This became Japanese cypress. The hair from his butt became cedar, and the hair from his brow became camphor. Then he established their uses, saying "Sugi and Kusu, these trees both can be used for making ships. Hinoki can be used to build the villages' palaces. Maki can be used to make the coffins in the tombs of the people of the visible world. For food, plant and cultivate all the 80 kinds of fruit."[46]

Few legends more readily served the rhetorical needs of foresters in Korea than this narrative. It lent credence to the historical outlook that had colored the lenses of forestry experts from the very beginning of their tenure in Korea: that a peninsula once endowed with rich forests had been squandered by subsequent generations. It also underscored the utility of Korea's woodlands. As Suzuki was quick to point out, each of the sylvan gifts bestowed on Korea by the Shintō god of the sea and storms offered highly practical materials, from comestibles to coffins. Finally, the Japanese used this and similar passages to insinuate Korea into the full sweep of Japan's forest culture. Bound as they were by the same sylvan spirits, Suzuki averred, it was only natural that Japanese and Koreans toil side by side in defense of the sacerdotal throne.

TIGHTENED BELTS, PADDED CLOTHES

If one were to base an assessment of wartime forestry on the year-end reports of the Bureau of Agriculture and Forestry alone, it would seem as though little in the forestry world had changed. Apart from passing references to the "wartime situation" or updates on the output of war material, these reports for the most part suggest business as usual. The statistics compiled in their appendices, however, tell a different story. Two particular columns speak louder than the rest: those of projected fuel supply and demand. Set side by side, these figures reveal a harsh reality of life under total war conditions: the growing scarcity of domestic fuel. By one estimate from 1941, felling operations were consuming timber at a rate 150 percent greater than would allow for sustainable domestic supplies in timber and fuel. Arguably more alarming was the fact that, based on 1941 projections for firewood and charcoal demand, the timber stock accumulated on privately owned woodlands was on track to decrease by as much as 80 percent in only ten years.[47]

By the time Japan entered the Pacific War with its assault on Pearl Harbor, the delta between supply and demand in Korea was beginning to widen. Because so much of Korea's domestic fuel supply was bound for its rapidly growing urban areas, shortfalls varied considerably from province to province. Predictably, the greatest deficits were to be found in Kyŏnggi, where the capital city formed a major drain on surrounding hinterlands. According to one official estimate, by 1939 residents of Kyŏnggi required 4,711,000 *kan* more charcoal than they themselves were able to produce. In Kangwŏn, by contrast, where substantial charcoal production operations were in full swing, fuel markets actually ran a significant surplus of 2,927,000 *kan* of charcoal.[48] Access to fuel, in other words, was as much a matter of distribution as production and, given the clogged arteries of the wartime empire's military-industrial infrastructure, fuel transport was no easy obstacle.

But the root of concern was the specter of declining productivity—if woodlands were being drained, for how long could they reliably supply fuel? Interest in this question transcended the ethnic, class, and gender divisions of colonial society. Whether settler homemaker or Korean sharecropper, factory boss or migrant laborer, all needed fuel. In fact, Japanese households often carried comparatively larger fuel requirements, forcing many settlers to participate in black-market transactions.[49] Try as they might, however, not even Japanese residents of Seoul's wealthiest neighborhoods could fully circumvent the diminishing fuel supplies. The arrival of winter—heralded each year by the blustering "knife winds"—was met with no small measure of dread, as residents across the peninsula steeled themselves for a season as frigid as it was long.

In response, colonial officials, the KFA, and their provincial partners unveiled in 1940 yet another public outreach campaign, this one calling on residents of Korea to practice "a low-temperature lifestyle" (J: *teion seikatsu*; K: *chŏon saenghwal*) during winter months. The low-temperature lifestyle began in the fall, when schools and various civic groups organized preparation drives to stockpile proper fuel sources, insulate buildings, and ready winter garments.[50] The latter task involved lining clothes with cotton padding after they had been thoroughly washed—a last-chance effort to launder garments before streams and other clothes-washing sites froze over.

Although this campaign was predicated on the willing participation of all residents of Korea, its foot soldiers were women. As one editorial in the popular women's magazine *Yŏsŏng* put it, just as there was to be a new order of geopolitics in the Asia-Pacific, so was there to be "a new order in the kitchen."[51] To aid in this effort, an array of publications offered detailed action plans regarding domestic fuel rationing. They urged homemakers to, at minimum, purchase a thermometer, an instrument that became a marker of a calorically conscientious and thus dutiful wartime household.[52]

The low-temperature lifestyle entailed a different diet for humans and animals alike. Apart from hearty soups, hot foods were to be limited (to the degree that nutrient intake guidelines would allow), while the practice of feeding livestock hot slop was to be avoided altogether. Anyone at a loss for an energy efficient recipe need only consult one of the growing number of cookery columns published to support homemakers in their fuel economization efforts. The low-temperature lifestyle campaign urged Koreans to sleep with more bedding and, if possible, to consolidate the *ondol* to a single room. It called on households to creatively recycle heat sources, burn appropriately dried-out fuels, and remain cognizant at all times of potential sources of waste.[53] Austerity was paramount. Indulgences such as a warm bath were permitted only insofar as they maintained hygiene; travel by bus or car was to be limited only to essential business. Above all, Koreans were entreated to draw on their deep reserves of spiritual strength to endure the physical discomfort that kept close company with fuel shortages.[54]

According to numerous doctors and architects, the benefits of heeding these directives were manifold. Not only did the low-temperature lifestyle conserve precious fuel sources, but it also, they claimed, fostered a safer, healthier home. Simply by sealing the *ondol* mouth and carefully monitoring burning practices, families could significantly diminish the risk of home fires, then a serious problem in densely populated urban areas. Should they maintain appropriate indoor temperatures, they could also mitigate a number of health problems (such as headaches) and lethargic habits (such as pipe smoking) that had for decades been highlighted as pernicious by-products of Koreans' so-called "*ondol* lifestyle."[55]

As cheerleaders in Korea and Manchuria took to newspapers and radio broadcasts to drum up enthusiasm for this campaign, they turned to a rather unlikely exemplar of the low-temperature lifestyle: Nogi Maresuke, the Imperial Army general perhaps best known for committing ritual suicide on the day of the funeral of Emperor Meiji. For Japanese and even Koreans, Nogi was a household name: hero of the Russo-Japanese War, former governor-general of Taiwan, paragon of samurai loyalty. Late into the war, however, Nogi's name gained currency for a different reason: his supposedly superhuman resilience to the cold, a trait many attributed to the fact that his parents had routinely bathed him at a young age in ice-cold water in the depths of winter. Admired at once as a masculine warrior, a devoted servant of the emperor, and an outstanding physical specimen, Nogi was the perfect poster child of the low-temperature lifestyle. Imperial subjects across the continent were beseeched as winter set in to muster his mental and physical toughness.[56] Some parents took matters into their own hands by engaging in the practice of "cold water rubbing": bathing their children in ice water so as to gradually build up a resilience to the cold—a quality that many came to associate with Japan's warrior spirit.[57]

If the low-temperature lifestyle was realized through individual actions and daily decisions, its proponents also prevailed on Koreans to collectively tighten the social fabric of local society. Proactive communal vigilance was of utmost importance. In many cases, efforts to guard against waste were organized institutionally, as in the Charcoal Production Associations and Distribution Cooperatives. Important, too, were the "neighborhood patriotic units" (*aegukpan*)—the peninsular equivalent of Japan's own neighborhood associations (*tonarigumi*)—that mobilized units of ten to twenty households to carry out government directives, especially those related to rationing. Few sources capture the spirit of communal conservation better than a cartoon strip from a November 1942 edition of the *Maeil sinbo*, the only Korean-language newspaper in circulation in the closing years of the war (fig. 8.2). The sixty-second installment of the *Susume Hanchō-san* series, a comic meant to convey ideals of propriety to young readers, the strip depicts a confrontation between the elder Korean role model and a young (presumably) Korean cyclist over the latter's willingness to part ways with a small clump of charcoal. It highlights the obligation not only to appreciate every single joule of potential energy but also to speak up when confronted with profligacy.

The bonds of local society were further tested by the corruption that went hand in hand with fuel rationing. As the overseers of local fuel allowances, Neighborhood Patriotic Unit leaders wielded considerable power.

FIG. 8.2 A *Susume Hanchō-san* comic depicting a confrontation over wasted charcoal. (From *Maeil sinbo*, November 30, 1942.)

Their authority was not impervious to abuse. Malfeasance took various forms: turning a blind eye; forging documentation; doling out favors to friends and family members. Although a special taskforce was established in 1943 within the ranks of the Economic Police to thwart precisely these sorts of activities, illicit fuel economies persisted through the war, especially in the Greater Seoul area. As was also the case with the food rationing system, the processes underlying fuel allocations were clearly tilted in the favor of families and individuals that had cultivated connections with or gained positions of influence within local government bodies.[58]

Conspicuously absent in most wartime commentary on the low-temperature lifestyle were Japanese settlers. Despite the fact that the population of Japanese settlers and soldiers in Korea had by the 1940s swelled to more than nine hundred thousand, placing a major strain on already scant natural resources, Korea's fuel problem remained a definitively *Korean* problem. The role of Japanese settlers was, if anything, to lead the charge in the diffusion of economical heating practices and the tenets of forest-love thought. Endowed with a hardy Yamato spirit, Japanese settlers were to stand on the front lines of fuel rationing.

Yet, the words and deeds of Japanese settlers did not always square. According to Kageyama Nobukage, a longtime forestry bureaucrat, Japanese settlers were often less than paragons of efficiency. When, for instance, Japanese used *ondol* in their homes, field stations, and official residences, he remembered, they "would light it separately for each meal and light it again for their bathwater." Such behavior, he conceded, was "a terribly wasteful thing."[59] Although the war doubtless reined in these excesses, his testimony offers a reminder that those with the means and connections were able to operate to a certain degree outside the colonial state's conservationist agenda.

Korean reactions to these fuel conservation campaigns were mixed. Many worked with the state, however reluctantly, to police woodlands, boost charcoal production, and promote thermally efficient living conditions. Others resisted. For a good number of the three thousand or so merchants dealing in timber and firewood, the state's fuel control measures presented crippling commercial obstacles. Official proclamations calling on merchants to embrace a new "business ethic" and "economic morality" that placed imperial service before personal profit rang hollow.[60] Some of the more established dealers worked through Chambers of Commerce, the KFA, and other back channels to protest official policy; many more simply chose to skirt regulation altogether by turning to black markets.

These commercial pains, however, paled in comparison to the bodily privations endured by agriculturists, who felt the weight of these draconian regulatory measures most acutely. If, as Chǒn U-yǒn has written, some Korean farming communities had long been familiar with the expression "to starve to death or to freeze to death, both are death all the same," this notion surely found new salience in the wartime period.[61] Although the circumstances are far from clear in most cases, winter months saw their fair share of fatal instances of hypothermia, most of them involving infants, the elderly, and drunkards. Even if "the nighttime cold was the killer," as reports often charged, the fact that some of the deceased were discovered within their homes suggests that domestic fuel shortages were also at play.[62] The persistence of fuel-related criminal infractions—in the face of severe penalties, no less—further indicates that many Koreans could only withstand so much. Whatever the case, peninsular residents of every ilk took to describing the spring melt as an act of "liberation"—a term that, come August 1945, would gain an entirely new meaning for the Korean people.

CONCLUSION

Despite the multidimensional nature of wartime forest management, a single question about Japanese forestry in colonial Korea has monopolized scholarly attention: To what extent can we describe the colonial period as a "plundering" of Korea's natural resources? More than simply marginalizing the reforestation agenda of the colonial state, the myopic focus on this question has blinded scholars to other important facets of forest governance. The domestication of heat is one such lacuna. In their rush to gauge the severity of wartime denudation, forest historians in Korea have paid little heed to what resource centralization meant for individual households and the bodies residing therein. In placing macro-level data on declining stocks, increasing yields, and market transactions at the foreground of their damage assessment reports, scholars have left little room for consideration of a micro-level matter of grave concern to every corner of colonial society: fuel scarcity and its implications for domestic life. Framed more as a national trauma than a bodily experience, Korea's wartime deforestation has been narrated as a process largely removed from everyday life.

But it was not. The energy coursing through the metabolic pathways opened up by the war was directly linked to the daily schedules of civilian life. By war's end, households thirsted for calories no less than the military apparatus itself. In his account of the corporeal toll exacted by Japan's tenacious pursuit of industrial modernity, Brett Walker has suggested that "ecological food chains . . . are essentially about the transference of energy; and in some respects the politics of nations are, too."[63] One might add that these energy politics extended into the landscapes absorbed by Japan's expanding colonial empire. Resourcing the empire at war was not solely about fueling industry and supporting the military through the seizure of natural resources. It was also about regulating the home and the fuel consumption patterns that structured daily life.

In Korea, the escalation and protraction of hostilities prompted forestry officials and their local partners to probe ever more deeply into the materiality of the home as they worked to address the scarcity that only deepened under total war conditions. What came out of their efforts was a radical reconfiguration of energy pathways that, over the course of the long winter season, structured the corporeality of civilian life in the home front. It was indeed with good reason that residents of the peninsula turned to bodily metaphors to describe the hardship of winter, which variously "froze eyebrows,"[64] "penetrated bones,"[65] and "pierced flesh."[66]

Koreans were not alone in enduring the stiff winds of total war. The Nazi Occupation of the Netherlands brought far greater hardship upon the bodies of the Dutch people, who were by 1944 "creeping through parks and public gardens, past lanes and canals, judging everything on its burning qualities." In the ensuing "hunger winter"—a season of acute suffering in which more than fifteen thousand civilians succumbed to starvation and sickness—"tree-lined streets became bare in one night, while bridge-railings disappeared and little parks were razed to the ground."[67] Behind these desperation measures lay a Nazi blockade keeping fuel and food supplies from Dutch cities, a deprivation strategy that followed naturally from the logic of total war.

These fuel shortfalls seldom figure into histories of World War II, and understandably so. Given the systematic slaughter witnessed in both theaters, the day-to-day agonies of fuel famine seem almost trifling. It is no accident that, in the grand scheme of Nazi atrocities, the Dutch hunger winter has received only scant scholarly attention. Something similar might be said about Korean historiography. When compared to the forced relocation of hundreds of thousands of Korean laborers or the system of wartime sexual slavery, fuel shortages appear a daily inconvenience—a trial, to be sure, but nothing that approximates the cardinal sins of colonial rule.

Yet, life in Korea was sometimes "murderously cold."[68] For the civilian population of the peninsula, especially those residing in the northern provinces, fuel scarcity was central to the somatic experience of the war. Air raids and land invasions were for the most part a distant threat, at least until 1944. Of far more immediate concern were the energy requirements of each and every day. Fuel shortfalls were more than a seasonal tribulation. The simple act of searching for fuel taxed metabolisms already running on empty. Prolonged exposure to the cold weakened immune systems, opening the gates for illnesses that lingered well after winter had passed. Fuel insufficiency was perhaps not in and of itself a killer, but it did help create the structural conditions for increased morbidity.

Paying heed to these conditions enables us in turn to recognize, with Rob Nixon, "a different kind of violence, a violence that is neither spectacular nor instantaneous, but rather incremental and accretive, its calamitous repercussions playing out across a range of temporal scales."[69] What Nixon's notion of slow violence offers to the context of colonial Korea is, above all else, a broader appreciation of the slow-moving temporal dispersion of the economic and environmental consequences of state efforts to penetrate local society and control physical bodies. Although the physiological experience of fuel scarcity is but faintly suggested in the colonial archive, it was very much a material reality of life and survival under total war.

CONCLUSION

FLAGS WERE NOT THE ONLY THING KOREANS WERE SWINGING ON August 15, 1945, a day that brought Japanese surrender and national independence. Some swung batons at the window fronts of Japanese-owned businesses. Others swung hoes at the Shintō shrines that had come to symbolize Japan's assault on the Korean spirit. Anecdotal evidence suggests that still others swung hatchets at the trees ceremoniously planted by the colonial state, the cherry blossom chief among them. One former resident of Seoul vividly recalls how "immediately upon liberation from colonial rule, groups of local citizens spontaneously rose up and chopped down the cherry trees" that had been planted in front of his elementary school.[1] In Chinhae, a coastal town famous for its blossom-lined streets, these cathartic cuttings eventually gave way to a more systematic effort to swap out Japanese trees for varietals native to Cheju. Thus did Koreans embark on a project of land reclamation in the truest sense, a campaign to cleanse the landscape of the material vestiges of Japanese forestry.[2]

If such was the absolute goal of Koreans in 1945, they had their work cut out for them. Even with all the destruction the Asia-Pacific War had wrought, hillsides across the peninsula bore strong traces of the colonial forestry enterprise. In ways both monumental and minuscule, the colonial forestry project remained lodged in Korean soil—from the postharvest second-growth plantations in the northern provinces to the greenery at

Namsan Park. Changes in the forest were mirrored by changes in the urban built environment. Construction frames, railway lines, the electrical grid, and so many other materials central to colonial modernization had all been called forth from Korea's mountains. These materials were not conjured by bureaucrats. They were, rather, delivered to market through complex chains of extraction, processing, and circulation that fundamentally altered Koreans' relationship with their forests. They carried the sweat of laborers, the cut-marks of millers, the grading stamps of bureaucrats, and the product packaging of capitalists. Tracking these material transformations reveals the forest to be not so much a hinterland or afterthought as a space central to colonial authority and its developmental agenda.

Yet, forest management was more than an exercise in utilitarianism. Even before the Japanese annexed Korea, Japanese traditions of conservation became foundational to the logic and optics of colonial tutelage. In playing up the contrast between their own green hills and Korea's red soil, Japanese in Korea found a powerful rationale for colonial occupation. They won the support of elite Koreans by offering access to the silvicultural savvy of the Japanese and the scientific prowess of Europe. At the same time, they won recognition from the international community as a conservation leader in Asia, a tree-revering society capable of modernizing nature and modernizing nations. The authority of Japanese foresters derived from their ability not only to conserve nature but also to name it with scientific precision. If we are to fully understand forestry as a pillar of colonial authority, then we must also explain why so many Korean flora carry the surname of a single Japanese botanist—Nakai—in their taxonomic signature.[3]

In rearing trees, the Japanese colonial state also found new avenues to reorganize society. Simply by dictating who owned woodland on what terms, forestry officials enforced a code of land-use conduct that impinged on many different facets of rural life. Laws promulgated in the name of forest regeneration axed customary land-use arrangements, allowing the state to funnel woodland to Japanese corporations and settlers to a degree unseen with arable land. Through the creation of civic forestry associations, forestry officials found institutional pathways for resource discipline. Under the twin banners of "northern development" and "rural revitalization," they ushered in far-reaching programs of nomadic sedentization, fuel substitution, and labor coercion. If nothing else, the sowing of seeds became a powerful metaphor in colonial Korea for the benevolence of imperial rule. Amidst intensifying calls for the cultural and spiritual assimilation of

Koreans, forestry became a wellspring for the ideological undercurrents of imperial indoctrination.

We should be careful not to overstate the depth and breadth of these reforms. After all, if there were any corners of Korean society recalcitrant to colonial authority, it was precisely those placed under the jurisdiction of the Bureau of Forestry. Forests were spaces of stalwart resistance and active subversion. To this day, one can find carefully preserved monuments to this resistance on the slopes of Mount Paektu: "slogan trees" bearing the anti-Japanese messages supposedly carved by Kim Il-sŏng and his comrades in arms. A timberline perspective of colonial Korea demands that we reckon with the limits of state power. When viewed from the fire fields tucked away in the alpine recesses of the Kaema Plateau, forestry bureaucrats appear more a presence than a force. The growth of sprawling chemical complexes in northern Korea is a revealing metric of the changes wrought by colonial rule, but so is the stubborn persistence of swidden agriculture throughout the colonial period. When viewed from the farmhouses and fireboxes of Tanch'ŏn, the project of civic forestry appears less than the source of harmony and economy officials made it out to be. The pushback of farmers left its mark on forest governance, at least until the agrarian crisis and war gave the state surer footing for resource control.

Adaptation was a feature, not a bug, of environmental rule. At loggerheads with other colonial administrations, vulnerable to budgetary shortfalls, and helpless to do anything but bow their heads to market forces, foresters in Korea were far from almighty administrators. Woodland-tenure reform dragged on for twenty years not because the Government-General wanted to refine their maps but because of the shifting priorities of agrarian reform. Timber companies in Sinŭiju struggled to turn profits not because of the ineptitude of bureaucrats in Seoul but because of changing geopolitical realities and tumult in the global marketplace. Just when Korea seemed poised to achieve domestic sufficiency in timber production, the war in China upended this long-anticipated milestone.

Acknowledging that forestry bureaucrats pivoted, regrouped, caved, and deflected is not to detract from the coercive force of colonial rule. It is rather to give that force a touch of human complexity. For too long, the Government-General in Korea has operated anonymously, as some sort of featureless entity that executes the will of officialdom. Yet, much of what transpired in the forestry world was shaped by the experiences, visions, and prejudices of its individual practitioners. The architecture of forest policy would have looked quite different without the early influence of Saitō Otosaku, whose fingerprints are on every facet of its greenification framework. The ecological signature of colonial rule may well have involved significantly more nonnative species if not for the pioneering research of Ishidoya, Asakawa, and Chŏng.

Bringing these personalities to the fore is important, too, because it allows us to better understand the networks that tied the Japanese empire of forestry together. It is no trivial fact that Saitō Otosaku, Honda Seiroku, and so many other forestry professionals that populate this account spent much of their careers crisscrossing the Japanese empire and even the globe. If the composite nature of Japanese colonial forestry practices is best understood as a process of cross-pollination, then these career foresters were the bees. They took ideas, methods, and innovations in one territory and brought them to a new institutional and ecological context. In this way, methods of soil compaction in Austria informed erosion control projects in Aichi, innovations in land leasing in Hokkaido influenced forest laws in Korea, and outdoor-burial techniques pioneered in Korea shaped seed propagation methods back in Japan. Coordination between the Japan, Korea, and Taiwan Forestry Associations kept woodsmen abreast of what was happening elsewhere in the empire. Forest Experiment Stations channeled the flow of data and specimen from colony to colony, while instructional forests operated in each colony by the Imperial universities offered laboratories for woodsmen in training. These were the institutional anchor points of the Japanese empire of forestry.

The geography of the Japanese empire ensured that forestry developed distinctively in each administrative zone. For obvious reasons, what happened in Korea bore stronger similarities to forestry in Hokkaido, Karafuto, and Manchuria than it did Taiwan, the South Seas Mandate, or Indonesia. Customary land-use practices indigenous to Korea interfaced with German management principles and American timbering technologies differently than did those in Taiwan. The burial mounds that were so central to woodland-tenure reform in Korea scarcely registered in Karafuto. Forestry in Indonesia after 1942 was informed more by the practical experiences of bureaucrats in Taiwan than by the abstract principles of European foresters. Put simply, Japanese colonial forestry practices were many, various, and mutable.

The Japanese empire of forestry, in this sense, affords a new perspective on global forest history. Blending ideas of a national forest culture at home, claims to a command of forestry knowledge abroad, and messages of pan-Asian solidarity in the region, Japanese officials sharpened a distinctive ideology of imperial stewardship. The policy frameworks of forest management may have varied considerably from place to place, climate to climate, but the ideological inflection of forest love and emperor worship did not. What was international about the conservation movement to Koreans, Taiwanese, or Micronesians was not the hints of French legal doctrine or German managerial theory. It was how forestry bound them to a larger project of stocking Asia's forests for Asians.

That project impacted—indeed, devastated—lives and forests up and down the Pacific Rim. And yet, in the global history of forest conservation or the ample literature on green imperialism the Japanese Empire is almost nowhere to be seen. Historians readily turn to early modern Japan for insight into alternative traditions of sustainable forestry. That they would do well to track the evolution of those traditions into the era of high imperialism is a central proposition of this book. The transformation of the green archipelago into an empire of forestry matters not merely for what it tells us about the global diffusion of ideas about scientific forestry or resource conservation. It matters because it is entangled with the broader transition of Asia and its woodlands into the age of industrial capitalism. It matters, not least, because the Japanese empire of forestry outlived the colonial empire itself.

INDIGENIZING GREENIFICATION

When the American military arrived in southern Korea in the fall of 1945 they found a peninsula teetering on the brink of environmental crisis. In the view of Edgar Johnson, one of numerous forestry advisers to the United States Military Government in Korea, Korean timberland had been so "seriously overcut" that "every June people are in terror that more paddy lands will be silted over by quick flash floods."[4] To American eyes, this deforestation was not so much a result of Japanese colonialism as a by-product of the political vacuum created by the disintegration of the colonial state. "When the Japanese went home in 1945," went one dispatch from Seoul, "the Koreans got out their axes and cut wood to keep shivering millions warm."[5] Like their Japanese predecessors, Americans were quick to pile blame for any environmental problems onto the Korean people, whose credibility as capable conservators was questioned at every turn.

For Koreans and their forests, however, the worst was yet to come. With the sudden outbreak of the Korean War in June 1950, the peninsula was no longer a "forward operating base" but battle space itself. The ensuing scorched-earth campaign—waged to a large degree with incendiary and phosphorous bombs—laid waste to large swathes of Korea's landscape, etching into the pockmarked earth scars of war still visible today. By one estimate, over the course of just three years of hostilities, the peninsula's growing forest-stock decreased to somewhere between 36 and 40 percent of its antebellum level.[6] Carbonized by napalm, splintered by artillery fire, or hacked down by refugees, Korea's woodlands were casualties not only of combat but also of the desperate acts of survival it engendered.

Only in the late 1950s did the security situation on the peninsula stabilize enough to enable sustained reforestation. In North Korea, the ruling regime wasted no time in institutionalizing forest regeneration programs. Forestry experts were embedded within local agricultural cooperatives, nurseries were established throughout the country, and a Forest Planting Day was launched nationwide. At the center of it all stood Kim Il-sŏng, a steward-patriarch who came to embody the true forest-loving spirit of Korea, an ethos that stemmed in part from his years spent fighting for independence deep in the mountains. Yet, even as farmers, laborers, and soldiers sowed millions of seeds, each carrying "the love of Dear Leader," their efforts were directly undermined by the need to clear land for agriculture.[7] Faced with chronic food shortages, farming communities began to cultivate food wherever they could, and agricultural production quickly climbed up the hillsides. Although the paucity of historical documentation makes it difficult to assess the overall progress of this reforestation campaign, the catastrophic famine and flooding of the 1990s—the so-called "arduous march"—offers some indication of its limits.[8]

South Korea's reforestation plans were no less ambitious, but they faltered early on. This was not for lack of effort on the part of the Syngman Rhee administration. Working in tandem with the United Nations Korean Reconstruction Agency, the South Korean government initiated numerous reforestation programs geared toward erosion and flood control. The results were disappointing. A ballooning population, shoestring budget, and the lumber demands of urban reconstruction all conspired against these projects. By the late 1950s, as a result, bald mountains remained a defining feature of South Korea's landscape.

The scope of this deforestation was not lost on Park Chung-hee, the strongman leader who rose to power in 1961 through a military coup. With the military intensity that would define his developmental dictatorship, Park ushered in a period of high-speed reforestation. In the span of a decade, eleven different forestry laws were passed, each tackling a different arena of greenification—erosion control, swidden agriculture, land ownership, and so on. Alongside "smuggling, narcotics, gangs, and pseudo-journalists," illegal tree cutting was designated by Park as one of five "social evils" that needed to be urgently stamped out.[9]

By the early 1970s, a sprawling reforestation complex was growing in tandem with Park's New Village Movement (Saemaŭl Undong), a program of economic development and social mobilization that spread from the countryside to factories and cities across South Korea. The state provided seedlings, hatched village nurseries, and showered rewards on successful rural planting programs. As with Kim Il-sŏng in North Korea, this campaign revolved around Park himself, who never missed an opportunity to style himself a son of the soil. Broader socioeconomic forces also shifted in favor of forest regeneration: the importation of coal for domestic use and urban in-migration eased the strain placed on fledgling forests, while a strong state police apparatus provided for unprecedented levels of woodland protection.[10]

The results were astonishing, as anyone who has traveled to South Korea in recent years can attest. Park's first ten-year "Forest Rehabilitation Plan" saw 2.96 billion trees planted in 1.08 million hectares. A second ten-year plan reforested an additional 965,000 hectares.[11] To South Koreans, these thickened woodlands stood as a triumph of the statist developmentalism that defined Park's brand of authoritarian rule. To foreign observers, the greening of South Korea was eye-catching on another level: it offered an exportable model of "green-oriented development." The Food and Agriculture Organization of the United Nations spoke for many international aid groups when it recognized the Republic of Korea (ROK) in 2016 as an "exemplary case [in forest rehabilitation] that may provide lessons on overcoming extreme poverty for other developing countries facing a similar situation."[12] Some Korean scholars have gone so far as to dub this transformation a "Korean miracle"—a term typically reserved for descriptions of South Korea's broader economic takeoff under Park's rule.[13]

That Park's reforestation campaign unfolded against the backdrop of staggering industrial growth makes its accomplishments doubly impressive.

But miraculous it was not. It came as the hard-earned result of meticulous planning, extensive scientific research, and careful oversight. It was born of a coordinated campaign to redefine the parameters of forest use and reorient market behavior. It was the product of elaborate programs of surveillance and compulsion created by a modernization regime defined by its "strong disciplinary character."[14] Reforestation under Park, in other words, carried the same aims of resource regulation, social cohesion, and labor mobilization as the colonial state before it. Even if its outward-facing optics were framed as a Koreanization of forestry and a purification of the landscape, the mechanics of greenification were of a piece with colonial-era efforts.

Look no further than Park's war on swidden agriculture. Having had ample occasion to observe Korea's uplands from the military helicopters he preferred for his personal transport, Park was acutely aware of the persistence of "fire fields" in South Korea. To officials across agencies, these mountain dwellers posed a threat not just to the forest but also to national security—a fact driven home by the DMZ conflicts of 1967–68. Indeed, just as the Japanese feared that shifting cultivators might have shifting allegiances, so was the Park regime motivated by concerns with a communist insurgency in the highlands. Their response was to bring new military resources to bear on the problem of fire fields. Aerial surveillance of upland areas was increased as military units were detailed to forest patrols. In a prelude to the offensive to come, Park marshaled in 1964 a regiment of more than 1,500 security officers to sweep out timber bandits and swidden farmers from Mount Chiri, an important industrial logging site.

The centerpiece of Park's war on swidden, however, was an ambitious program of forced relocation and sedentization. Echoing colonial officials before them, Park and his forestry advisers likened the eradication of swidden to a civilizing mission, one that would wipe "human caterpillars" and their "primitive" way of existence from the mountains.[15] To do so, the Korean Forest Service began to move shifting cultivators into collective settlements, often at considerable cost to the state. In the span of a decade, no fewer than one million mountain dwellers were forcibly resettled through the 1966 Act on Swidden Removal (Hwajŏn Chŏngni Pŏp). The Park regime was willing to turn a blind eye to the grinding poverty endured by city dwellers, but mountain dwellers required the full force of state control. Like their Japanese predecessors, Korean foresters demanded a certain way of life and labor in the highlands and used the broader machinery of reforestation to assert it.[16]

A similar point may be made about domestic fuel economy, which came under renewed scrutiny during Park's rule. The largely untold story of South Korea's reforestation is an energy revolution—a shift in domestic fuel economies toward the combustion of coal. In only a few short years, the New Village Movement facilitated the installation or improvement of coal-burning furnaces in more than six million rural households.[17] Central to this campaign were *sanlimgye*, compulsory village forestry cooperatives that oversaw everything from the purchase of seedlings to labor mobilization. Government rhetoric to the contrary, *sanlimgye* were resurrections less of Chosŏn-era village customs than of colonial-era civic forestry associations. Under the motto "no barren land in my village," they led the charge in stocking fuel forests, policing consumption, and financing forestry works.[18] Here, too, we can observe parallels with colonial environmental rule. The interconnections between the forest and daily consumption patterns gave the Park regime an entry point into the home, and, like the Government-General, it did not hesitate to introduce its own forms of caloric control.

It is tempting, in hindsight, to attribute this environmental vision to Park himself. An extensive body of work, much of it bordering on hagiography, has done essentially that, locating the origins of South Korea's modern environmental conservation movement in the actions and words of Park.[19] One unfortunate by-product of this hyperfocus on Park is a marginalization of the forestry experts who surrounded him, and here we see still other entanglements with the colonial past.

Consider, for example, Hyŏn Sin-kyu, the trailblazing forest scientist who, in the face of persistent institutional discrimination, served as a prolific researcher in the Government-General's Forestry Experiment Station. His career, of course, did not stop there. After liberation he steadily rose through the ranks of Korea's forestry bureaucracy to become a central figure in Park's reforestation brain trust. To be sure, the course of Hyŏn's intellectual development had many tributaries, including a stint at the University of California, Berkeley (where he fine-tuned cross-breeding techniques) and time in Italy (where he became enamored with the Italian poplar).[20] But Hyŏn's training within Japanese scientific institutions immersed him early and deeply in research questions that would sustain his life's work. For example, his continued research on the hybridization of the pitch pine—a project he began as a master's student at Kyushu Imperial University—yielded in the 1970s a major breakthrough in forest genetics: the pitch-loblolly crossbred pine (*Pinus rigitaeda*). Later dubbed the "wonder tree of Korea," this fibrous, fast-growing hybrid was planted in large number during Park's reforestation project. Colonial institutions such as the Suwŏn School of Agriculture and Forestry, meanwhile, only expanded under Park's tenure. Absorbed by Seoul National University (where it remains today), this research and training facility stood squarely at the center of the scientific innovation that under-girded South Korea's high-speed green growth.[21]

My point here is not to suggest that South Korea's incredible gains in for-est accumulation are somehow *due* to the colonial experience. Park's refor-estation program was born of the particular circumstances of the ROK at the time—its Cold War context, its export-oriented growth, its authoritar-ian politics. Nationalist sentiments stirred Koreans to plant trees in their native soil with a degree of élan and efficiency unimaginable to colonial administrators. Advancements in timbering technology fundamentally altered the economics of the Korean lumber industry. For these reasons alone, one cannot simply draw a portrait of Korea's lush forests by connect-ing the dots between colonial rule and postwar campaigns.

But this portrait is also remarkably incomplete if it begins, as it so often does, in 1961, with Park's rise to power. Park's regime was not the first in the twentieth century to attempt to implant a new order on Korea's uplands. When Park declared that reforestation would be a national priority, he had at his disposal a model for forest governance that aligned neatly with his broader goals of capitalist development. It bears repeating that over 70 percent of the Korean peninsula is comprised of mountains and forest. Grand plans for industrial and agricultural development naturally extend into the woodlands, and this is what united foresters on either side of 1945. Both were tasked with reforestation in service of ambitious blueprints for state-building and economic growth. And both recognized that their limited resources required that they shift the burdens of that project onto the broader public and, especially, agrarian society.

How Korean woodsmen reconfigured Japanese programs of environ-mental rule is a question beyond the scope of this study. Suffice it to say that Park and his advisers shared with their predecessors a deep-seated faith in state forestry as a vehicle for delivering discipline, order, and rationality to the countryside. Taking the long view of forest governance across Korea's tumultuous twentieth century reveals not so much an uninterrupted framework of forest governance as a transcendent set of eco-anxieties and -aspirations. In a landmark study published more than two decades ago, Gi-Wook Shin and Michael Robinson enjoined scholars of colonial Korea to pursue "an ecological handling of historical traces," to eschew nationalist narratives in order to "better reclaim the land with a mind to restoring some of the density, richness, and complexity of the original ecosystem."[22] Placing Japanese and Korean woodsmen in the same field of analysis enables exactly that. It provides for not only new perspectives on the colonial experience but also a richer understanding of the place of the peninsula's woodlands in the developmental mentality of the modern state.

SHADOWS, OLD AND NEW

Concurrent with Park's "forest miracle" was the emergence of a new sphere of influence for the postwar Japanese empire of forestry: Southeast Asia. Cutting new trails through the hardwood tropical forests of the Philippines, Malaysia, and Indonesia were not Japanese settlers or soldiers but rather contractors and engineers, many of whom had first encountered the region decades earlier under the aegis of the Japanese military. They now returned as the eyes and ears of Japanese capital.[23] Moving like "spiders at the center of Japan's global economic web," Sumitomo, Mitsubishi, and other general trading companies (*sōgō shōsha*) used these proxies to discreetly position themselves as intermediaries in dense networks of timber extraction.[24]

The subsequent flow of Southeast Asian timbers into Japan was an unquestionable boon to Japanese millers and corporations, who processed sawlogs for domestic consumption and plywood for export abroad. It would be a mistake, however, to assume that the relief offered to Japanese woodlands was an unmitigated boost to Japan's forest health. To the contrary, these import schemes came with myriad problems of their own. As domestic timber prices fell, many woodland owners and corporate operators grew less interested in long-term forest management. Investors, entrepreneurs, and even local governments began to think twice about taking on costly forestry ventures on Japan's steep mountain slopes. And with the more recent turn to the importation of coniferous timber from the Pacific Northwest and Russia, domestic lumbering projects found themselves at a marked disadvantage in the international timber marketplace. The result: slower stand rotation, infrequent thinning, a reliance on monoculture plantation, and persistent erosion problems in upland communities. With good reason, economists have conceptualized the forest resource trade between Japan and Southeast Asia as a problem of "dual decay": that is, a case study of how "trade can negatively affect both importers' and exporters' environments."[25]

By the 1990s, Japan found itself at the center of a firestorm of criticism for the role it played in the tropical deforestation of Southeast Asia. Diminished biodiversity, the proliferation of palm-oil plantations, and the growing incidence of timber poaching were all identified as problems tied to Japanese-backed forestry projects in the region. Environmental activists were particularly alarmed by the tendency of these outfits to harvest and move on, paying little regard to the long-term sustainability of sites of extraction. For example, as harvesting sawlogs in the Philippines became prohibitively expensive in the mid-1960s, few general trading companies skipped a beat in shifting their investments and operations to Malaysia and Indonesia. Later incursions into the forests of Papua New Guinea and lagging reforestation efforts in Kalimantan raised further concerns about drifting capital in the region.[26]

Steps were eventually taken by Japanese enterprises to soften their ecological footprint abroad. The Japan Building Contractors Society, for example, issued guidelines on responsible timber procurements, while many corporations involved in the timber trade appreciably increased their investments in reforestation. Still, most of these more public relations–minded efforts treated the symptoms of dual decay, not its underlying causes.[27] Ultimately, they did little to address the structural trade imbalances and questionable business practices that undermined future-minded forest management. In fact, rather than curtail their involvement in the region, many Japanese corporations dug in their heels, working instead to style themselves as the torchbearers of sustainability. By holding up a mirror to Japan's own green hillsides, corporate Japan did their utmost to draw the public eye away from the ecological shadows they cast.

So it was that Japanese government agencies and corporate entities began to greenwash their ecological imprint in the region. In a manner not unlike Walmart, ExxonMobil, and other giant transnational corporations, Japanese corporations masterfully appropriated the idioms of "sustainable development" and "green growth" to reclaim the narrative. They did so in lockstep with the Japan Business Federation (Keidanren) and the Japanese government, which intensified its publicity efforts surrounding overseas reforestation programs. In 2002, for example, the Japanese government unveiled with much fanfare its "Asia Forest Partnership" initiative, a region-wide forum meant to connect government experts, civil society, and business leaders around issues of sustainability. A host of governmental agencies have also worked bilaterally with their counterparts in Indonesia and

Malaysia to coordinate reforestation pilot programs. To that end, special earmarks were made by the Ministry of Foreign Affairs for Official Development Assistance grants specifically concerned with "conservation and management of forest and the sustainable use of forest resources."[28]

As this book has shown, this agenda has a longer history than meets the eye. Japanese efforts to gain access to forest resources abroad have long rested on their conservationist credentials at home. For this reason, as John Knight has rightly noted, Japan's own postwar reforestation is best understood not simply as "a physical process" but also as "a powerful national discourse which obscures state accountability for the local environmental degradation the state has brought about."[29] This discourse did not emerge out of a vacuum after 1945. Baked into more recent Japanese claims to sustainable leadership are many of the same rhetorical devices, assumptions, and programs that buttressed the greenification framework erected in colonial Korea. In its sloganeering, its portrayal of the emperor as model conservator, and its invocation of an essentialized national forest culture, this discourse carries with it not-so-faint echoes from Japan's colonial past.

Today, Japan is not the only industrial giant casting shadows across the forests of Southeast Asia. Indeed, one of the more underappreciated developments in the region has been the growing role played by South Korean conglomerates and their concessionaires. As early as the 1960s, South Korean logging companies such as the Korean Development Company (Kodeco) began to make inroads into the forests of Indonesia.[30] Using strategies markedly similar to their Japanese counterparts, South Korean industrial combines such as the Sunkyong Group steered growing volumes of forest resources into South Korea and the global marketplace. For two straight decades, South Korea imported nearly US$1 billion of timber per year, with most of its raw timber coming from Malaysia and Indonesia. South Korean corporations also cornered a fair share of the market in the global plywood trade, eventually surpassing Japan as the principal exporter of plywood products to the United States. Meanwhile, the strain placed on South Korea's forests, like those across the Tsushima Strait, diminished as the material burdens of industrialization were shifted partly overseas.[31]

South Korea's growing presence in and reliance on Southeast Asian forests should prompt us to more carefully consider how the postwar recovery and economic ascendance of Asia's so-called "tiger economies" entailed contracting out deforestation abroad. Although scholars have long attended to the "export-oriented growth" strategies pursued by both Japan and South

Korea, they might also consider how "import-oriented" forest resource consumption figured into their industrial liftoff. In a remarkable redefinition of their colonial relationship, both countries now showcase their green credentials with equal fervor on the global stage as they attempt to transmit their reforestation expertise overseas. Such is perhaps a fitting convergence for a neighboring archipelago and peninsula whose roots have grown only more knotted with time.

NOTES

The following abbreviations are used for regularly referenced sources and archival collections:

CRI   Chōsen Sanrinkai, ed., *Chōsen ringyō isshi* (Keijō: Chōsen Sanrinkai, 1933).

DRSK   Doi Ringaku Shinkōkai, ed., *Chōsen hantō no sanrin: 20 seiki no zenhan no jyōkyō to bunken mokuroku* (Tokyo: Doi Ringaku Shinkōkai, 1974).

HYCTS   Han'guk Yŏksa Chŏngbo Tonghap Sisŭtem (Korean History Data Integration System), Kuksa P'yŏnch'an Wiwŏnhoe, Kyŏnggi-do, Kwach'on-si, South Korea.

JACAR   Kokuritsu Kōbunshokan, Ajia Rekishi Shiryō Sentā (National Archives of Japan, Japan Center for Asian Historical Records), Tokyo.

MRI   Dai Nippon Sanrinkai, ed., *Meiji ringyō isshi* (Tokyo: Dai Nippon Sanrinkai, 1931).

TYBK   Miyata Setsuko and Yi U-yŏn, eds., *Chōsen no sanrin seisaku* (Tokyo: Tōyō Bunka Kenkyūjo, Yūhō Bunko, 2009).

YB   Yūhō Bunko, Tōyō Bunka Kenkyūjo (Yūhō Collection, Research Institute for Oriental Cultures), Gakushūin University, Tokyo, Japan.

INTRODUCTION

1 A similar uprooting is related in Simon Estok and Kim Wŏn-jung, *East Asian Ecocriticisms: A Critical Reader* (New York: Palgrave Macmillan, 2013), 2–4.

2 On Korean public perceptions of *robinia pseudoacacia*, see, for example, Hong Sa-chong, "Akasia namu kwŏllyŏk kwa insaeng ŭl mutta," *Wŏlgan Chosŏn*, November 2010, https://monthly.chosun.com/client/news/viw.asp?ctcd=F&nNews Numb=201011100054.

3 On Japanese and Western perceptions of Korean deforestation, see Kwŏn Sŏg-yŏng, *Ondol ŭi kŭndaesa: Ondol ŭl tullŏssan Chosŏnin ŭi sam kwa yŏksa* (Seoul: Ilchogak, 2010).

4 C. S. Lee, H. J. Cho, and H. Yi, "Stand Dynamics of Introduced Black Locust under Different Disturbance Regimes in Korea," *Forest Ecology and Management* 189 (2004): 281–93.

5 Nancy Langston, *Forest Dreams, Forest Nightmares: The Paradox of Old Growth in the Inland West* (Seattle: University of Washington Press, 1995).

6 Kim Il-sŏng, *Works*, vol. 3 (P'yŏngyang: Foreign Languages Publishing House, 1980), 171.

7 Kim Chŏng-ŭn, "Let the Entire Party, the Whole Army and All the People Conduct a Vigorous Forest Restoration Campaign to Cover the Mountains of the Country with Green Woods," Korea Central News Agency, February 28, 2015.

8 "Forestry History," Korea Forest Service, accessed August 20, 2016, http://english.forest.go.kr/newkfsweb/html/EngHtmlPage.do?pg=/esh/koforest/UI_KFS_0101_020100.html&mn=ENG_01_02_01.

9 For recent reassessments of colonial land-tenure rights, see, for example, Yi U-yŏn, *Hanguk ŭi sallim soyujedo wa chŏngch'aek ŭi yŏksa, 1600–1987* (Seoul: Ilchogak, 2007); and Ch'oe P'yŏng-t'aek, *Ilcheha Chosŏn imya chosa saŏp kwa sallim chŏngch'aek* (Seoul: P'urŭn Yŏksa, 2009).

10 A lucid overview of debates on Korea's premodern forest history can be found in John S. Lee, "Protect the Pines, Punish the People: Forests and the State in Pre-industrial Korea, 918–1897" (PhD diss., Harvard University, 2017), 1–39. For a groundbreaking survey of Korea's premodern environmental history, see Kim Tong-jin, *Chosŏn ŭi saengt'ae hwan'gyŏngsa* (Seoul: P'urŭn Yŏksa, 2017).

11 K. Tak, Y. Chun, and P. M. Wood, "The South Korean Forest Dilemma," *International Forestry Review* 9, no. 1 (2007): 550.

12 Tak, Chun, and Wood, "The South Korean Forest Dilemma," 548.

13 Peter Duus, *The Abacus and the Sword: The Japanese Penetration of Korea, 1895–1910* (Berkeley: University of California Press, 1998).

14 For a discussion of this coinage, see, for example, TYBK, 271.

15 Two classic works are Ramachandra Guha, *The Unquiet Woods: Ecological Change and Peasant Resistance in the Himalaya* (Berkeley: University of California Press, 2000); and E. P. Thompson, *Whigs and Hunters: The Origins of the Black Act* (New York: Pantheon, 1975).

16 An exemplary case study is Nancy Lee Peluso, *Rich Forests, Poor People: Resource Control and Resistance in Java* (Berkeley: University of California Press, 1994).

17 Pamela McElwee, *Forests Are Gold: Trees, People, and Environmental Rule in Vietnam* (Seattle: University of Washington Press, 2017), 5.

18 See, for example, S. R. Rajan, *Modernizing Nature: Forestry and Imperial Economic Development, 1800–1950* (Oxford: Oxford University Press, 2006).

19 See, for example, Thaddeus Sunseri, *Wielding the Ax: Forestry and Social Conflict in Tanzania, 1820–2000* (Athens: Ohio University Press, 2009).

20 Diana Davis, *Resurrecting the Granary of Rome: Environmental History and French Colonial Expansion in North Africa* (Athens: Ohio University Press, 2007).

21 Gi-Wook Shin and Michael Robinson, *Colonial Modernity in Korea* (Cambridge: Harvard University Press, 1999), 17.

22 These include Gi-Wook Shin, *Peasant Protest and Social Change in Colonial Korea* (Seattle: University of Washington Press, 2014); Albert L. Park, *Building a Heaven on Earth: Religion, Activism, and Protest in Japanese Occupied Korea* (Honolulu: University of Hawai'i Press, 2014); and Holly Stephens, "Agriculture and Development in an Age of Empire" (PhD diss., University of Pennsylvania, 2017).

23 On the geospatial implications of Japanese railways on the Asian continent, see Kate McDonald, *Placing Empire: Travel and the Social Imagination in Imperial Japan* (Berkeley: University of California Press, 2017). On the place of railways in the commercial development of the region, see Tak Matsusaka, *The Making of Japanese Manchuria, 1904–1932* (Cambridge: Harvard University Asia Center, 2003).

24 See, for example, Soon-Won Park, *Colonial Industrialization and Labor: The Onoda Cement Factory* (Cambridge: Harvard University Press, 1999); and Carter Eckert, "Total War, Industrialization, and Social Change in Late Colonial Korea," in *The Japanese Wartime Empire, 1931–1945*, ed. Peter Duus, Ramon H. Myers, and Mark R. Peattie (Princeton: Princeton University Press, 1996), 3–40.

25 See, for example, Aaron S. Moore, *Constructing East Asia: Technology, Ideology, and Empire in Japan's Wartime Era, 1931–1945* (Stanford: Stanford University Press, 2013).

26 For a pioneering survey of natural resource politics in the Japanese empire, see Noda Kimio, ed., *Nihon Teikokuken no nōrin shigen kaihatsu: "Shigenka" to sōryokusen taisei no higashi Ajia* (Kyoto: Kyoto Daigaku Gakujutsu Shuppankai, 2013).

27 Joachim Radkau, *Wood: A History* (New York: Polity, 2011), 7.

28 Hugh Raup, "John Sanderson's Farm," *Forest History* 10, no. 1 (1966): 11.

29 James Scott, *Seeing Like a State: How Certain Schemes to Improve the Human Condition Have Failed* (New Haven: Yale University Press, 2001), 8.

30 Conrad Totman, *The Green Archipelago: Forestry in Pre-industrial Japan* (Athens: Ohio University Press, 1989), 1.

31 Radkau, *Wood: A History*, 296.

32 Michael Williams, *Deforesting the Earth: From Pre-history to Global Crisis* (Chicago: University of Chicago Press, 2003), 309.

33 Tessa Morris-Suzuki, "The Nature of Empire: Forest Ecology, Colonialism and Survival Politics in Japan's Imperial Order," *Japanese Studies* 33, no. 3 (2013): 228.

34 Jakobina Arch, *Bringing Whales Ashore: Oceans and the Environment of Early Modern Japan* (Seattle: University of Washington Press, 2017), 15.

35 The definitive treatment of these timbering operations is Peter Dauvergne, *Shadows in the Forest: Japan and the Politics of Timber in Southeast Asia* (Boston: MIT Press, 1997).

36 Anna Tsing, "Contingent Commodities: Mobilizing Labor in and beyond Southeast Asian Forests," in *Taking Southeast Asia to Market: Commodities, Nature, and People in the Neoliberal Age*, ed. Joseph Nevins and Nancy Lee Peluso, 27–43 (Ithaca, NY: Cornell University Press, 2008).

37 John Knight, "The Problem of Gaizai: The View from Japanese Forestry Villages," in *The Political Ecology of Tropical Forests in Southeast Asia*, ed. Lye Tuck-Po, Wil De Jong, and Abe Kenichi (Kyoto: Kyoto University Press, 2003), 273.

38 Totman, *The Green Archipelago*, 6.

39 Totman, *The Green Archipelago*, 1.

40 Richard Grove, *Green Imperialism: Colonial Expansion, Tropical Island Edens, and the Origins of Environmentalism* (Cambridge: Cambridge University Press, 1996).

41 K. Sivaramakrishnan, *Modern Forests: Statemaking and Environmental Change in Colonial Eastern India* (Stanford: Stanford University Press, 1999), 14.

42 Ian Tyrell, *Crisis of the Wasteful Nation: Empire and Conservation in Theodore Roosevelt's America* (Chicago: University of Chicago Press, 2015), 21.

43 Peter Vandergeest and Nancy Lee Peluso, "Empires of Forestry: Professional Forestry and State Power in Southeast Asia," *Environment and History* 12 (2006): 32.

CHAPTER ONE: IMPERIALIZING FORESTRY

1 Honda Seiroku, "Wagakuni jiriki no suijyaku to akamatsu," *Tōyō gakugei zasshi* 230 (1900): 468.

2 On Honda's broader ecological outlook, see Komeie Taisaku, "Kindai ringaku to kokudo no shokusei kanri: Honda Seiroku no 'Nihon shinrin shokubutsutai ron' o megutte," *Kūkan, shakai, chiri shisō* 17 (2014): 3–18.

3 Honda Seiroku, "Sekai ni okeru rinsō henka to kokuun no shōchō," *Ringakkai zasshi* 20 (1923): 59.

4 Honda Seiroku, "Rinsō no henka to kokuun no shōchō," *Chōsen nōkaihō* 11, no. 7 (1916): 4.

5 On the reception of his ideas, see Miyake Miyahisa, *Chōsen hantō no rinya kōhai no genin: Shizen kankyō hozen to shinrin no rekishi* (Tokyo: Nōrin Shuppan, 1976), 30.

6 For a closer look at Honda's career, see Chiba Tokuji, *Hageyama no bunka* (Tokyo: Gakuseisha, 1973).

7 Federico Marcon, *The Knowledge of Nature and the Nature of Knowledge in Early Modern Japan* (Chicago: University of Chicago Press, 2015), 291.

8 As qtd. in Totman, *The Green Archipelago*, 184.

9 Ian J. Miller, *The Nature of the Beasts: Empire and Exhibition at the Tokyo Imperial Zoo* (Berkeley: University of California Press, 2013), 5.

10 Julia Adeney Thomas, *Reconfiguring Modernity: Concepts of Nature in Japanese Political Ideology* (Berkeley: University of California Press, 2001), 10.

11 As qtd. in Tessa Morris-Suzuki, *The Technological Transformation of Japan: From the Seventeenth to the Twenty-First Century* (Cambridge: Cambridge University Press, 1994), 73.

12 Clancey, "Seeing the Timber for the Forest."

13 Conrad Totman, *Japan's Imperial Forest, Goryōrin, 1889–1946: With a Support-ing Study of the Kan/Min Division of Woodland in Early Meiji Japan, 1871–76* (Folkestone: Global Oriental, 2007), 11.

14 Margaret McKean, "Conflict over the Contemporary Fate of Common Lands in Meiji Japan," paper presented at the Annual Meeting of the Association for Asian Studies, March 1995.

15 Bureau of Forestry, ed., *Forestry of Japan* (Tokyo: Department of Agriculture and Commerce, 1910), 85.

16 MRI, 62.

17 Conrad Totman, *Japan: An Environmental History* (London: I. B. Tauris, 2014), 180.

18 On the geography of Meiji-era deforestation, see Chiba Tokuji, *Hageyama no kenkyū* (Tokyo: Nōrin Kyōkai, 1956).

19 MRI, 1–3.

20 Kume Kunitake, *The Iwakura Embassy 1871–73: A True Account of the Ambassa-dor Extraordinary and Plenipotentiary's Journey of Observation throughout the United States of America and Europe*, vol. 3: *Central Europe*, trans. A. Cobbing (Surrey: Curzon, 2002), 209.

21 Bureau of Forestry, ed., *Forestry of Japan*, 85.

22 Shimazaki Tōson, *Before the Dawn*, trans. William Naff (Honolulu: University of Hawai'i Press, 1987), 691.

23 MRI, iii.

24 Bureau of Forestry, ed., *Forestry of Japan*, 118.

25 Shiga Shigetaka, *Nihon fūkeiron*, in *Shiga Shigetaka Zenshū*, ed. Shiga Shigetaka Zenshū Kankōkai (Tokyo: Shiga Shigetaka Zenshū Kankōkai, 1928), 173–74.

26 The impact of these tours is taken up in Totman, *Japan's Imperial Forest*, 18–23.

27 For a critical assessment of Shintō environmentalism as ideology, see Aike P. Rots, *Shintō, Nature, and Ideology: Making Sacred Forests* (London: Bloomsbury, 2017).

28 Andō Tokio, *Tsūzoku kyōiku airin shisō* (Fukushima: Shōshiki Yōtatsu Shōkai, 1913), 1.

29 See, for example, Grant Birdsey Northrop, *Rural Improvement, 1880–* (1880; Ithaca, NY: Cornell University Press, 2009).

30 "Makino Nōshōmu daijin danwa," *Yomiuri shimbun*, July 20, 1892.

31 For a broader treatment of these ceremonial plantings, see Okamoto Kikuko, "Meijiki Nihon bunkashi ni okeru kinen shokuju no rinen to hōhō: Honda Seiroku 'Jusai zōrinhō' o chūshin ni," *Sōkadai bunka kagaku kenkyū* 10 (2014): 69–97.

32 For a pathbreaking study of school forests, see Takemoto Tarō, *Gakkōrin no kenkyū: Mori to kyōiku o meguru kyōdō kankei no kiseki* (Tokyo: Nōsangyoson Bunka Kyōkai, 2009).

33 On the origins of this institution, see MRI, 232–65.

34 Negishi Kenichiro, Tange Takeshi, Suzuki Makoto, and Yamamoto Hirokazu, "Chiba Enshūrin enkakushi shiryō," *Enshūrin* 46 (2007): 91.

35 Fukushima Yasunori, "Wagakuni ringaku sōsōki ni okeru rinseigaku ni tsuite," *Sanrin* 4 (2011): 13.

36 For a broader treatment of Takashima's career, see, for example, Shimazu Toshi-yuki, "Chirigakusha toshite no Takashima Hokkai," *Kūkan, shakai, chiri shisō* 15 (2012): 51–75.

37 Tyrell, *Crisis of the Wasteful Nation*, 34–35.

38 This project is examined in Chiba, *Hageyama no kenkyū*, 148–73.

39 MRI, vol. 2, 177.

40 Honda Seiroku, *Rinseigaku: Kokka to shinrin no kankei* (Tokyo, 1894), 5.

41 Totman, *The Green Archipelago*, 168.

42 On this point, see Satō Jin, *"Motazaru kuni" no shigen ron: Jisoku kanō na kokudo o meguru mō hitotsu no chi* (Tokyo: Tokyo Daigaku Shuppankai, 2011).

43 On Saitō's academic pedigree, see Takemoto, *Gakkōrin no kenkyū*, 160–91.

44 Takemoto Tarō, "Shokuminchi ni okeru ryōkka undō seisaku no igi: Saitō Oto-saku no ashi ato kara," paper presented at the Kankyō Seisakushi Kenkyūkai (The Environmental Policy History Research Group), 2012.

45 MRI, 232–36.

46 For a biography of Asakawa, see Takasaki Sōji, *Chōsen no tsuchi to natta Nihon-jin: Asakawa Takumi no shōgai* (Tokyo: Sōfūkan, 2002).

47 On these epidemiological factors, see Brett Walker, *The Conquest of Ainu Lands: Ecology and Culture in Japanese Expansion, 1590–1800* (Berkeley: University of California Press, 2006), 177–203.

48 Koseki Takayoshi, "Hokkaido ringyō to Hokudai," *Hokudai hyakunenshi, tsūsetsu* (1982): 789.

49 Koseki Takayoshi, "Hokkaidō ringyō no hatten katei," *Hokkaidō Daigaku Nōgakubu Enshūrin kenkyū hōkoku* 22, no. 1 (1962): 60.

50 Hokkaidō Ringyō Keiei Kyōgikai, ed., *Hokkaidō sanrin shi, senzen hen* (Sapporo: Hokkaidō Ringyō Kaikan, 1983), 89–91.

51 For a pioneering study of forestry in colonial Taiwan, see Kuang-chi Hung, "When the Green Archipelago Encountered Formosa: The Making of Modern Forestry in Taiwan under Japan's Colonial Rule," in *Environment and Society in the Japanese Islands: From Prehistory to the Present*, ed. Bruce Batten and Philip Brown (Corvallis: Oregon State University Press, 2015), 175.

52 On this and other survey efforts, see MRI, 458–77.

53 Hung, "When the Green Archipelago Encountered Formosa," 182–84.

54 These tactics are examined in Paul Barclay, *Outcastes of Empire: Japan's Rule on Taiwan's "Savage Border," 1874–1945* (Berkeley: University of California Press, 2017), 43–113.

55 MRI, 477.

56 On the early development of lumbering on the island, see, for example, Karafuto Ringyō-shi Hensankai, ed., *Karafuto ringyō shi* (1960; Tokyo: Ozorosha, 2005).

57 For the official account of these developments, see Ōji Seishi Kabushiki Kaisha, ed., *Ōji Seishi shashi* (Tokyo: Ōji Seishi Kabushiki Kaisha, 2001).

58 Ōji's forestry operations are examined in Ōji Seishi Kabushiki Kaisha, ed., *Ōji Seishi sanrin jigyōshi* (Tokyo: Ōji Seishi Kabushiki Kaisha, 1976).

59 Bank of Chosen, ed., *Economic History of Chosen* (Seoul: Bank of Chosen, 1920), 90–91.

CHAPTER TWO: KOREA, GREEN AND RED

1 This court dialogue is recorded in Kuksa P'yŏnch'an Wiwŏnhoe, ed., *Kojong Sillok* 11.3.5 (1874).

2 On the evolution of pine policies, see, for example, Pae Chae-su, Kim Sŏn-yŏng, Yi Ki-bong, and Chu Rin-wŏn, *Chosŏn hugi sallim chŏngch'aeksa* (Seoul: Imŏp Yŏn'guwŏn, 2002).

3 This argument is advanced in John S. Lee, "Postwar Pines: The Military and the Expansion of State Forests in Post-Imjin Korea, 1598–1684," *Journal of Asian Studies* 77, no. 2 (2018): 319–32.

4 On fuel demands, see Kwŏn, *Ondol ŭi kŭndaesa*, 33–67.

5 On systemic ecological problems, see Kim Hŭng-sun, "Chosŏn hugi sallim chŏngch'aek mit sallim hwangp'yehwa: Sijangjuŭijŏk koch'al kwa kŭ e taehan pip'an," *Han'guk Chiyŏk Kaebal Hakhoeji* 20, no. 2 (2008): 169–92.

6 On burial disputes, see Kim Kyŏng-suk, "Chosŏn hugi sansong kwa sahoe kaldŭng" (PhD diss., Seoul National University, 2008).

7 Davis, *Resurrecting the Granary of Rome*, 2.

8 See, for example, Owen Miller, "The Idea of Stagnation in Korean Historiography from Fukuda Tokuzo to the New Right," *Korean Histories* 2, no 1. (2010): 3–12.

9 On this topic, see, for example, Hyung Il Pai, *Heritage Management in Korea and Japan: The Politics of Antiquity and Identity* (Seattle: University of Washington Press, 2014); and E. Taylor Atkins, *Primitive Selves: Koreana in the Japanese Colonial Gaze, 1910–1945* (Berkeley: University of California Press, 2010).

10 See, for example, Mary Louise Pratt, *Imperial Eyes: Travel Writing and Transculturation* (London: Routledge, 1992).

11 E. W. Koons, "Afforestation in Korea," *Transactions of the Korea Branch, Royal Asiatic Society* 6 (1915): 36.

12 Horace Underwood, *The Call of Korea: Political—Social—Religious* (New York: Fleming Revell, 1909), 23.

13 Percival Lowell, *Chosön: Land of the Morning Calm, A Sketch of Korea* (Boston: Ticknor, 1886), 35.

14 Masanaga Yazu, *Chōsen Shiberia kikō* (Tokyo: Maruzen, 1894), 11.

15 Shiozaki Seigetsu, *Saishin no Kan hantō* (Osaka: Aoki Sūzandō, 1906), 9.

16 George Trumbull Ladd, *In Korea with Marquis Ito* (New York: Scribner's Sons, 1908), 19.

17 MRI, 505.

18 "Korean Letter from the Special Correspondent of Arboriculture," *Arboriculture: A Magazine of the International Society of Arboriculture* 4, no. 8 (1905): 182.

19 For a broad survey of these developments, see Lee Wooyoun (Yi U-yŏn), "Deforestation and Agricultural Productivity in Chosŏn Korea in the 18th and 19th Centuries," in *Community, Commons, and Natural Resource Management in Asia,* ed. Haruka Yanagisawa, 25–60 (Singapore: National University of Singapore, 2015).

20 On the disappearance of tigers, see Joseph Seeley and Aaron Skabelund, "Tigers—Real and Imagined—in Korea's Physical and Cultural Landscape," *Environmental History* 20 (2015): 475–503.

21 These exceptions include Yi U-yŏn, *Hanguk ŭi sallim soyujedo wa chŏngch'aek ŭi yŏksa, 1600–1987;* and Kim T., *Chosŏn ŭi saengt'ae hwan'gyŏngsa.*

22 As qtd. in W. Lee, "Deforestation and Agricultural Productivity in Chosŏn Korea," 36.

23 William Elliot Griffis, *A Modern Pioneer in Korea: The Life Story of Henry G. Appenzeller* (New York: Fleming Revell, 1912), 22.

24 Nitobe Inazō, *Thoughts and Essays* (Tokyo: Teibi, 1909), 324–25.

25 Ide Shōichi, *Chōsen no jitsujō* (Tokyo: Kōyūsha, 1910), 60.

26 Arakawa Gorō, *Saikin Chōsen jijō* (Tokyo: Shimizu Shoten, 1908), 32.

27 Arakawa, *Saikin Chōsen jijō*, 36.

28 "Notes and Scenes from Korea," *National Geographic Magazine* 19, no. 7 (1908): 499.

29 Homer Hulbert, *The Passing of Korea* (New York: Doubleday, 1906), 11.

30 For a pioneering study of these biogeographical differences, see Conrad Totman, *Pre-industrial Korea and Japan in Environmental Perspective* (Leiden: Brill, 2004).

31 Isabella Bird Bishop, *Korea and Her Neighbors: A Narrative of Travel, With an Account of the Recent Vicissitudes and Present Position of the Country* (New York: Fleming Revell, 1898), 41.

32 Ladd, *In Korea with Marquis Ito*, 306–7.

33 Mizuta Naomasa, ed., *Watanabe Toyohiko kōjyutsu, Chōsen Sōtokufu kaikodan* (Tokyo: Yūhō Kyōkai, 1984), 39.

34 Griffis, *A Modern Pioneer in Korea*, 22.

35 Angus Hamilton, *Korea: Its History, Its People, and Its Commerce* (Boston: J. B. Millet, 1910), 186.

36 William Richard Carles, *Life in Corea* (Boston: Macmillan, 1894), 110.

37 Taki Kumejirō Denki Hensankai, ed., *Taki Kumejirō* (Tokyo: Taki Kumejirō Denki Hensankai, 1958), 226–28.

38 Zenkoku Shinbun Rengōsha, ed., *Nihon shokuminchi yōran* (Tokyo: Nihon Keizai Shinshisha, 1922), 89.

39 Bird Bishop, *Korea and Her Neighbors*, 17.

40 These early disputes are examined in Pak Sŏng-jun, "1880-nyŏndae Chosŏn ŭi Ullŭngdo pŏlmok kyeyak ch'egyŏl kwa pŏlmokkwon ŭl tullŏssan kakkuk kwa ŭi kaltŭng," *Tongbug'a yŏksa nonch'ong* 43 (2014): 117–48.

41 On these negotiations, see, for example, Cho Jae-gon, "Pŭrinerŭ samlim ikwŏn kwa Ilbon ŭi taeŭng," *Yŏksa wa hyŏnsil* 88 (2013): 303–38.

42 A detailed account of this diplomatic posturing can be found in Kim Won-su, "Amnokkang wigi wa Ro-Il chŏnjaeng," *Sŏyang sahak yŏn'gu* 23 (2010): 115–41.

43 Cho J., "Pŭrinerŭ samlim ikwŏn kwa Ilbon ŭi taeŭng," 320–25.

44 Many of these cables are compiled in Kuksa P'yŏnch'an Wiwŏnhoe, ed., *Chuhan Ilbon Kongsagwan killok, 20* (Kwach'ŏn: Kuksa P'yŏnch'an Wiwŏnhoe, 1986).

45 This episode is related in Yumi Moon, *Populist Collaborators: The Ilchinhoe and the Japanese Colonization of Korea, 1896–1910* (Ithaca, NY: Cornell University Press, 2013), 83–85.

46 "Contention over Corea," *New York Tribune*, January 10, 1904.

47 Tanaka Kiyoji, *Kankoku shinrin shisatsu fukumeisho* (Tokyo: Nōshōmushō Sanrinkyoku, 1903), 5.

48 Tanaka, *Kankoku shinrin shisatsu fukumeisho*, 9–10.

49 Tanaka, *Kankoku shinrin shisatsu fukumeisho*, 22.

50 Tanaka, *Kankoku shinrin shisatsu fukumeisho*, 101.

51 Tanaka, *Kankoku shinrin shisatsu fukumeisho*, 40.

52 This critique is elaborated in Fujita Yoshihisa, "Kyū kankoku jidai no Chōsen ni okeru shinrin shigen to rinya riyō: 'Kankoku shinrin fukumeisho' kara no fukugen," *Aichi Daigaku Kokusai Mondai Kenkyūjo* 84 (1988): 1–33.

53 Tanaka, *Kankoku shinrin shisatsu fukumeisho*, 31.

54 Tanaka, *Kankoku shinrin shisatsu fukumeisho*, 31–32.

55 Tanaka, *Kankoku shinrin shisatsu fukumeisho*, 74.

56 A translation of this treatise can be found in John Lee, "Protect the Pines, Punish the People," 245–57.

57 Yi Chong-il, "Imŏp ŭi p'iryo," *Taehan Chaganghoe wŏlbo* 3 (1906): 13.

58 Yi, "Imŏp ŭi p'iryo," 15.

59 Ok Tong-gyu, "Imŏp ŭi p'iryo," *Sŏu* 1 (1908): 30.

60 Ok, "Imŏp ŭi p'iryo," 31.

61 Kim Chin-ch'o "Cholimhak ŭi p'iryo," *T'aegŭk hakpo* 1 (1909): 36–38.

62 Cho Hae-saeng, "Sam namu sikje cholimpŏp," *T'aegŭk hakpo* 13 (1907): 26–32.

63 One oft-referenced Chosŏn-era treatise on tree planting is Sŏ Yugu, *Imwŏn kyŏngjeji: Manhakchi*, trans. Pak Sunch'ŏl and Kim Yŏng (Seoul: Sowadang, 2010).

64 *Hwangsŏng sinmun*, November 10, 1908.

65 *Hwangsŏng sinmun*, December 1, 1908.

66 Ŭisinsa P'yŏnjippu, ed., *Ch'oesin samnimhak* (Seoul: Ŭisinsa P'yŏnjippu, 1909), 11.

67 This point is elaborated in Andre Schmid, *Korea between Empires, 1895–1919* (New York: Columbia University Press, 2002), 55–101.

68 Ŭisinsa P'yŏnjippu, *Ch'oesin samnimhak*, 12–13.

69 Chang Hyŏk-chu, "Boku no bungaku," in *Chō Kakuchū Nihongo sakuhinsen*, ed. Nam Pu-jin and Shirakawa Yutaka (Tokyo: Bensei Shuppan, 2003), 288.

CHAPTER THREE: RIGHTING THE WOODLANDS

1 TYBK, 305.

2 Chōsen Sōtokufu, ed., *Chōsen rinya chōsa hōkokusho* (Keijō: Chōsen Sōtokufu, 1924), 1–2.

3 See Edwin Gragert, *Landownership under Colonial Rule: Korea's Japanese Experience, 1900–1935* (Honolulu: University of Hawai'i Press, 1994).

4 Carter Eckert, *Offspring of Empire: The Koch'chang Kims and the Colonial Origins of Korea Capitalism* (Seattle: University of Washington Press, 1996), 1–65.

5 Takahashi Kishichirō, "Ondoru no kizukikata to nenryō (ichi)," *Chōsen* 94 (1922): 2.

6 Matsumoto Iori, "Chōsen no rinya seido," *Chōsen* 123 (1925): 45.

7 Matsumoto, "Chōsen no rinya seido," 44.

8 For the seminal essay on the tragedy of the commons, see Garrett Hardin, "The Tragedy of the Commons," *Science* 162 (1968): 1243–48.

9 On debates over population change in Chosŏn Korea, see Shin, *Peasant Protest and Social Change in Colonial Korea*, 24–27.

10 This outlook is examined in Hagino Toshio, *Chōsen, Manshū, Taiwan ringyō hattatsushi ron* (Tokyo: Rin'ya Kōsaikai, 1965), 64–65.

11 Yi Hang-jyun, "Chōsen no yama to funbo (san)," *Chōsen sanrinkaihō* 74 (1931): 13.

12 This viewpoint is expressed in, for example, Itagaki Yutaka, "Punsan ŭi soyuja e kohum," *Chōsen sanrinkaihō* 2 (1921): 9.

13 On the relationship between burial practices and colonial woodland-tenure reform, see Yi Sŏn-wŏk, "Shokuminchi Chōsen ni okeru rinya shoyūken kakutei kotei to bochi mondai," *Chōsenshi Kenkyūkai ronbunshū* 46 (2008): 155–84.

14 For an exhaustive treatment of these disputes, see Kim Kyŏng-suk, "Chosŏn hugi sansong kwa sahoe kaldŭng" (PhD diss., Seoul National University, 2008).

15 TYBK, 248–52.

16 CRI, 4–5.

17 CRI, 238–39.

18 Hagino, *Chōsen, Manshū, Taiwan ringyō hattatsu shiron*, 11.

19 See, for example, *Hwangsŏn sinmun*, June 16–25, 1908.

20 *Taehan maeil sinbo*, September 5, 1908.

21 As cited in Hagino, *Chōsen, Manshū, Taiwan no ringyō hattatsu shiron*, 5.

22 Pae Chae-su, "Samlimpŏp (1908) ŭi chijŏk sin'go chedo ka Ilche ŭi singminji imji chŏngch'aek e mich'in yŏnghyang e kwanhan yŏn'gu," *Han'guk Imhakhŏe chi* 90, no. 3 (2001): 403.

23 Hoon K. Lee, *Land Utilization and Rural Economy in Korea* (Chicago: University of Chicago Press, 1936), 183.

24 CRI, 20–21.

25 "Kantō mondai no shinsō," *Chōsen* 6 (1909): 3.

26 CRI, 24–25.

27 This account is derived from Yoshimura Tenchū to editor in chief of the Tokyo Nichinichi Shimbun: "Iwayuru Kantō mondai," handwritten letter, February 1, 1909, YB, 221.07/4.

28 CRI, 21.

29 See, for example, "Han'guk sallim ŭi tojŏk," *Taehan maeil sinbo*, December 22, 1908; and "Ilin ŭi kan'gye," *Taehan maeil sinbo*, December 23, 1908.

30 CRI, 28–29.

31 A detailed account of the volley of allegations between different press factions can be found in "Kantō mondai no shinsō," *Chōsen* 6 (1909): 3–5.

32 "Isshinkai no benbaku," *Asahi shimbun*, December 29, 1908.

33 "Korea," *Japan Weekly Mail*, December 23, 1908.

34 As qtd. in Komeie Taisaku, "Colonial Environmentalism and Shifting Cultivation in Korea: Japanese Mapping, Research, and Representation," *Geographical Review of Japan* 79, no. 12 (2006): 667.

35 This report is reprinted in CRI, 56–81.

36 On resonances with Hokkaido, see CRI, 436.

37 CRI, 78.

38 The Forest Ordinance is reprinted in DRSK, 20–22.

39 The criteria by which these distinctions were made were spelled out in the Standard for the Designation of Reserved National Forests (Yōsonchi yotei rinya sentei no hyōjun), which is reprinted in DRSK, 29.

40 See, for example, Saitō Otosaku, "Chōsen no sanrin ni tsuite," *Chōsen oyobi Manshū* 37 (1911): 14.

41 Hagino, *Chōsen, Manshū, Taiwan ringyō hattatsu shiron*, 63.

42 Tōyō Takushoku Kabushiki Kaisha, ed., *Tōtaku jū-nen shi* (1918; Tokyo: Tanseisha, 2001), 82–87.

43 These and other high-profile leaseholders are examined in Kang Chŏng-wŏn and Ch'oe Wŏn-gyu, "Ilche ŭi imya daebu chŏngch'aek kwa kŭ sŏngkyŏk: 1910, 1920-yŏndae daebu silt'ae wa kyŏngyŏng ŭl chungsim ŭro," *Han'guk minjok munhwa* 58 (2016): 299–347.

44 Kang and Ch'oe, "Ilche ŭi imya daebu chŏngch'aek kwa kŭ sŏngkyŏk," 307.

45 Chōsen Sōtokufu, Sanrinbu, ed., *Ringyō keieijō mohan to narubeki jiseki gaiyō* (Keijō: Chōsen Sōtokufu, 1926), 113–15.

46 Chōsen Sōtokufu, Sanrinbu, ed., *Ringyō keieijō mohan to narubeki jiseki gaiyō*, 28.

47 Yun Ch'iho, *Yun Ch'iho ilgi* (Seoul: National History Compilation Committee, 1974), entry for April 11, 1921.

48 Yuasa Katsuei, *Kannani and Document of Flames: Two Japanese Colonial Novels*, trans. Mark Driscoll (Durham, NC: Duke University Press, 2005), 129.

49 This translation is from Michael Seth, *A Concise History of Korea: Antiquity to the Present* (New York: Rowman and Littlefield, 2016), 321.

50 On the causes and consequences of the March First Movement in transnational perspective, see Erez Manela, *The Wilsonian Moment: Self-Determination and the International Origins of Anticolonial Nationalism* (Oxford: Oxford University Press, 2009).

51 A detailed, if one-sided, remembrance of the Pogil Island incident can be found in CRI, 369–76.

52 DRSK, 42.

53 TYBK, 269.

54 Chōsen Sōtokufu, ed., *Rinya Chōsa Iinkai jimu hōkoku* (Keijō: Rinya Chōsa Iinkai, 1936), 1–11.

55 Chōsen Sōtokufu, ed., *Chōsen no ringyō* (Keijō: Chōsen Sōtokufu, 1928), 16.

56 TYBK, 266.

57 His case file is reprinted in Chōsen Sōtokufu, ed., *Rinya Chōsa iinkai jimu hōkoku*, 112–15.

58 DRSK, 43.

59 Chōsen Sōtokufu, ed., *Chōsen no ringyō* (1928), 10.

60 Hagino, *Chōsen, Manshū, Taiwan ringyō hattatsushi ron*, 63.

61 Kwŏn Ok-yŏng, "Chōsen ni okeru Nihon teikokushugi no shokuminchiteki sanrin taisaku," *Rekishigaku kenkyū* 297 (1965): 5.

62 Caroline Ford, "Reforestation, Landscape Conservation, and the Anxieties of Empire in French Colonial Algeria," *American Historical Review* 113, no. 2 (2008): 362.

CHAPTER FOUR: ENGINEERING GROWTH

1 Chōsen Sōtokufu, ed., *Jubyō yōsei shishin, Dai ichi-gō* (Keijō: Chōsen Sōtokufu, 1919).

2 On the disparagement of Korean flora by Japanese commentators, see Emiko Ohnuki-Tierney, *Kamikaze, Cherry Blossoms, and Nationalism: The Militarization of Aesthetics in Japanese History* (Chicago: University of Chicago Press, 2002), 107.

3 See, for example, TYBK, 302–3.

4 Michael A. Osborne, "Acclimatizing the World: A History of the Paradigmatic Colonial Science," *Osiris* 15 (2000): 141.

5 As qtd. in Jun Uchida, *Brokers of Empire: Japanese Settler Colonialism in Korea, 1876–1945* (Cambridge: Harvard University Asia Center, 2011), 88.

6 For a groundbreaking examination of scientific collaboration in colonial Korea, to which my own account is greatly indebted, see Jung Lee, "Mutual Transformation of Colonial and Imperial Botanizing? The Intimate yet Remote Collaboration in Colonial Korea," *Science in Context* 29, no. 2 (2016): 179–211.

7 For a seminal treatment of the socially embedded nature of scientists, see Bruno Latour, *Science in Action: How to Follow Scientists and Engineers through Society* (Cambridge: Harvard University Press, 1988).

8 CRI, 8–9.

9 On early experimentation of this sort, see MRI, vol. 2, 450–54.

10 Chōsen Sōtokufu Ringyō Shikenjo, ed., *Gyōmu gaiyō* (Keijō: Chōsen Sōtokufu Ringyō Shikenjo, 1933), 1.

11 Bureau of Education, ed., *Manual of Education in Chosen* (Seoul: Government General of Chōsen, Bureau of Education, 1920), 83.

12 A list of course offerings can be found in Chōsen Sōtokufu, ed., *Suigen Kōtō Nōrin Gakkō ichiran* (Keijō: Chōsen Sōtokufu Suigen Kōtō Nōrin Gakkō, 1931), 52–53.

13 As qtd. in Jung Lee, "Mutual Transformation of Colonial and Imperial Botanizing?," 184.

14 On the origins of this facility, see Chōsen Sōtokufu Ringyō Shikenjo, ed., *Kōryō shikenrin no ippan* (Keijō: Chōsen Sōtokufu Ringyō Shikenjo, 1932).

15 On Asakawa's academic pedigree, see Takasaki, *Chōsen no tsuchi to natta Nihonjin*, 69–79.

16 Sallimch'ŏng Imŏp Sihŏmjang, ed., *Imŏp Sihŏmjang yuksimnyŏnsa* (Seoul: Sallimch'ŏng Imŏp Sihŏmjang, 1982), 1.

17 Jung Lee, "Mutual Transformation of Colonial and Imperial Botanizing?," 186.

18 Chōsen Sōtokufu, ed., *Jubyō yōsei shishin*, 1.

19 Takasaki, *Chōsen no tsuchi to natta Nihonjin*, 91.

20 Their findings were published as Chōsen Sōtokufu, ed., *Chōsen kyoju rōju meiboku shi* (Keijō: Chōsen Sōtokufu, 1919).

21 Jung Lee, "Mutual Transformation of Colonial and Imperial Botanizing?," 191.

22 Owing to a bestselling biography by Takasaki Sōji and a 2012 feature-length film adaptation under the title *Hakuji no hito*, Asakawa has been elevated in the public eye as a key contributor to the Japanese forestry project and an unusually open-minded colonist.

23 "Imŏp Sihŏmjang konhi saŏp kaesi," *Maeil sinbo*, June 7, 1922.

24 For contemporary coverage of this flood, see, for example, "Suhae wa kujekŭm mojip," *Tonga ilbo*, August 1, 1920; and "Suhae pinpin," *Tonga ilbo*, August 4, 1920.

25 A roster of FES personnel can be found in Chōsen Sōtokufu Ringyō Shikenjo, ed., *Chōsen Ringyō Shikenjo yōran* (Keijō: Chōsen Sōtokufu Ringyō Shikenjo, n.d.), 10–11.

26 Chōsen Sōtokufu Ringyō Shikenjo, ed., *Gyōmu gaiyō*, 1.

27 For a broad overview of FES research on afforestation, see Hayashi Yasuharu, "Chōsensan shuyō rinboku no hashu zōrin shiken," *Chōsen Ringyō Shikenjo hōkoku* 19 (1939): 1–111.

28 Hayashi, "Chōsensan shuyō rinboku no hashu zōrin shiken," 103.

29 See, for example, Shimada Teikichi, "Sabō ni kansuru shiken," *Chōsen Ringyō Shikenjo hōkoku* 3 (1926): 1–136.

30 Takasaki, *Chōsen no tsuchi to natta Nihonjin*, 95.

31 See, for example, Kamiya Kazuo, "Matsukemushi no keitai, seitai oyobi kiseibachi ni kansuru kenkyū," *Chōsen Ringyō Shikenjo hōkoku* 18 (1939): 1–110.

32 A digest of their recommendations for agroforestry can be found in Sawada Toshinobu, "Nōson ringyō buraku shidō shiken ni kansuru keika hōkoku," *Chōsen Ringyō Shikenjo tokuhō* (1943): 1–59.

33 See, for example, Kudō Ichirō, "Kakushu ondoru nenryō no zenryoku sokutei," *Chōsen Ringyō Shikenjo hōkoku* 16 (1934): 1–36.

34 Chōsen Sōtokufu Ringyō Shikenjo, ed., *Gyōmu gaiyō*, 24.

35 Kaburagi Tokuji, "Chōsen Ringyō Shikenjo jidai no kaiko," *Ringyō keizai* 22, no. 11 (1969): 43.

36 Son Yu-jŏng, "Ilche kangjŏmgi Hyŏn Sin-kyu ŭi imhakja urŏ ui sŏngjang kwa kŭ ŭimi," *Han'guk inmulsa yŏn'gu* 21 (2014): 540.

37 This biographical information is derived from Son Yu-jŏng, "Hyŏn Sin-kyu ŭi rigidedo sonamu yŏn'gu," *Han'guk Kwahaksa Hakhoeji* 27, no. 2 (2005): 27–60.

38 Hildi Kang, *Under the Black Umbrella: Voices from Colonial Korea, 1910–1945* (Ithaca, NY: Cornell University Press, 2001), 54.

39 On student-led political protest at Suwŏn, see Cho Sŏng-un, "Ilcheha Suwŏn Konong ŭi haksaeng undong kwa nulloksu undong," *Kyongju sahak* 14 (1995): 109–36.

40 Sallimch'ŏng Imop̆ Sihŏmjang, ed., *Imŏp Sihŏmjang yuksimnyŏnsa*, 5.

41 Son Y., "Ilche kangjŏmgi Hyŏn Sin-kyu ŭi imhakja ŭro ŭi sŏngjang kwa kŭ ŭimi," 526–29.

42 These developments are detailed in Yi Jung (Lee Jung), "Singminji kwahak hyŏmnyŏk ŭl wihan chungnipsŏng ŭi chŏngch'i: Ilche kangjŏmgi Chosŏn ŭi hyang'tojŏk singmul yŏn'gu," *Han'guk Kwahaksa Hakhoeji* 37, no. 1 (2015): 265–98.

43 Grove, *Green Imperialism*, 7.

44 This point is pressed home in Pae Chae-su, "Han'guk ŭi sallim pyŏnch'ŏn: Ch'ui, t'ŭkching, mit hamŭi," *Han'guk Imhakhoe chi* 98, no. 6 (2009): 659–68.

CHAPTER FIVE: THE TIMBER UNDERTAKING

1 "Ōryokkō Saiboku Kōshi no jigyō," *Keijō nippō*, December 21, 1915.

2 "Sallim ŭi wangguk," *Maeil sinbo*, February 13, 1934.

3 "Manchurian Timber," *Timber Trades Journal and Saw-mill Advertiser* 65 (1909): 894.

4 Sun Joo Kim, ed., *The Northern Region of Korea: History, Identity, and Culture* (Seattle: University of Washington Press, 2010), 8.

5 On elite Korean perceptions of this borderland, see Andre Schmid, "Rediscovering Manchuria: Sin Ch'aeho and the Politics of Territorial History in Korea," *Journal of Asian Studies* 56, no. 1 (1997): 26–46.

6 Resident-General of Korea, ed., *Annual Report on Reforms and Progress in Chosen (Korea)* (Seoul: Tōkanfu, 1908), 81.

7 See, for example, Manshū Kōhō Kyōkai, ed., *Ōryōkkō* (Shinkyō: Manshūkoku Tsūshinsha, 1937), i.

8 On the ambitions of Japanese technocrats in the Asian continent, see Moore, *Constructing East Asia,* 102–49.

9 Moore, *Constructing East Asia,* 15.

10 DRSK, 50.

11 Ōji Seishi Kabushiki Kaisha, ed., *Ōji Seishi sanrin jigyōshi*, 222.

12 A detailed analysis of the merits and demerits of each type of tree can be found in Chōsen Shokusan Ginkō Chōsaka, ed., *Chōsen no mokuzai* (Keijō: Chōsen Shokusan Ginkō Chōsaka, 1925).

13 Ernest H. Wilson, "The Vegetation of Korea," *Transactions of the Korea Branch of the Royal Asiatic Society* 9 (1918): 8.

14 These methods are described in Chōsen Sōtokufu Eirinshō, ed., *Chōsen Sōtokufu Eirinshō yōran* (Keijō: Chōsen Sōtokufu, 1912), 1–15.

15 Yi Sung-jun, *Ōryokkō jōryū shinrin shakubatsu jigyō annai* (Hu'chang: Ōryokkō Jōryū Shinrin Shakubatsu Jigyō Annai Hakkōjo, 1931), 5–10.

16 Mizuta, ed., *Watanabe Toyohiko kōjyutsu*, 34.

17 Ueda Gunji, *Kokkyo nihyaku ri* (Keijō: Kokkyo Nihyaku Ri Hakkōjo, 1929), 100–101.

18 These tensions are explored in Joseph Seeley, "Liquid Geography: The Yalu River and the Boundaries of Empire in East Asia, 1894–1945" (PhD diss., Stanford University, 2019), 84–96.

19 Watanabe Toyohiko, "Mokuzaikai no sūsei to Chōsenzai," *Chōsen sanrinkaihō* 71 (1931): 4.

20 Chōsen Shokusan Ginkō Chōsaka, ed., *Chōsen no mokuzai*, 31.

21 Ōryokkō Saiboku Kōshi, ed., *Ōryokkō no shinrin oyobi ringyō* (Antō: Ōryokkō Saiboku Kōshi, 1915), 199.

22 Chōsen Shokusan Ginkō Chōsaka, ed., *Chōsen no mokuzai*, 62.

23 DRSK, 51.

24 On the advent of aerial forest surveying on the Asian continent, see Nihon Ringyō Gijyutsu Kyōkai Shinrin Kōsoku Kenkyūkai, ed., "Manshū ni okeru kōkū shashin riyō no shinrin chōsa," *Shashin sokuryō* 8, no. 2 (1969): 96–101.

25 Ōryokkō Saiboku Kōshi, ed., *Ōryokkō no shinrin oyobi ringyō*, 192.

26 Abe Kaoru, *Chōsen toyū taikan* (Keijō: Minshū Jironsha, 1937), 100.

27 Wada Takashi, *Shingishū shi* (Shingishū: Shimada Sōbunkan, 1911), 3.

28 These administrative distinctions are parsed further in Aaron S. Moore, "'The Yalu River Era of Developing Asia': Japanese Expertise, Colonial Power, and the Construction of Sup'ung Dam," *Journal of Asian Studies* 72, no. 1 (2013): 115–39.

29 See, for example, "Yŏnglimch'ang ŭi pulsin," *Tonba ilbo*, December 1, 1923.

30 Chōsen Shokusan Ginkō Chōsaka, ed., *Chōsen no mokuzai*, 29.

31 "Kokkyō shōkai kōki," *Keijō nippō*, April 27, 1919.

32 "Tai mokuzaigyō kibō," *Keijō nippō*, August 11, 1919.

33 Ōji Seishi Kabushiki Kaisha, ed., *Ōji Seishi sanrin jigyōshi*, 223–25.

34 Abe, *Chōsen toyū taikan*, 100.

35 H. Lee, *Land Utilization in Korea*, 190.

36 For brief biographies of both men, see Shingishū Shōkō Kaigisho, ed., *Shingishū Shōkō Kaigisho jū-nen shi* (Shingishū: Shingishū Shōkō Kaigisho, 1937), 96.

37 Wada, *Shingishū shi*, 120.

38 On Tada's commercial leadership, see "Ima ya onozukara ninzuru kokkyō sōtoku-san," *Keijō nippō*, October 18, 1935.

39 Shingishū Shōkō Kaigisho, ed., *Shingishū Shōkō Kaigisho jū-nen shi*, 99–100.

40 A compilation of meeting proceedings can be found in Shingishū Shōkō Kaigisho, ed., *Shingishū Shōkō Kaigisho jū-nen shi*, 30–40.

41 See, for example, "Tae-Sinŭiiju nŭn ŏttonga," *Tonga ilbo*, March 3, 1926.

42 Williams, *Deforesting the Earth*, 371.

43 "Manshū ni okeru mokuzai jukyū to Ōryōkkōzai no shōrai," *Manshū nichinichi shimbun*, April 6, 1922.

44 On these tariff reforms, see Fukushima Yasunori, "Mokuzai keizai no kokusaika, shizen hogo: awasete Shōwa rinsei o furikaeru," *Sanrin* 1262 (1989): 70–75.

45 Pae Chae-su, "Ilcheha Chosŏn ŭi mokchae sukŭp chŏngch'aek e kwanhan yŏn'gu," *Sallim kyŏngje yŏn'gu* 6, no. 1 (1998): 30.

46 On post-earthquake timber provisions, see Nōshōmushō Sanrinkyoku, ed., *Kantō Daishinsai to mokuzai oyobi shintan* (Tokyo: Teikoku Shinrinkai, 1924).

47 Shingishū Shōkō Kaigisho, ed., *Shingishū Shōkō Kaigisho jū-nen shi*, 3.

48 "Waga tairiku seisaku to Chōsen no tōchi o ayamaru Chōsen mokuzai kanzei tokurei haishi hantai iken," JACAR, A08072545200.

49 "Mokukanzei mondai tokurei teppai ikan Kantōgawa to Chōsen no kōsō iyoiyo shinken o kuwaekuru," *Manshū nichinichi shimbun*, October 23, 1928.

50 *Teikoku Gikai Shūgiin giji sokkiroku*, vol. 18 (52nd sess., February 1927), 354.

51 *Teikoku Gikai Shūgiin giji sokkiroku*, vol. 23 (56th sess., March 1929), 465–66.

52 On Manchukuo in the Japanese imaginary, see Louise Young, *Japan's Total Empire: Manchuria and the Culture of Wartime Imperialism* (Berkeley: University of California Press, 1999). On the urban construction boom in Manchukuo, see Emer O'Dwyer, *Significant Soil: Settler Colonialism and Japan's Urban Empire in Manchuria* (Cambridge: Harvard Asia Center, 2015).

53 "Shakai mondaika sen to suru Shingishū no seizai jigyō," *Ōkkō nippō*, June 14, 1933.

54 "Shizainan kanwa sarezu zaikai no kunō shinkoku," *Ōkkō nippō*, August 24, 1934.

55 "Sennai no shizaikan ni Karafutozai ga shinshutsu su," *Ōkkō nippō*, August 27, 1933.

56 These marching orders are spelled out in Chōsen Sōtokufu, Sanrinbu, ed., "Hokusen shinrin kaitaku jigyō keikakusho, shinrin kankei no bun" (Keijō: Chōsen Sōtokufu, Sanrinbu, 1932), YB: reel B318.

57 As qtd. in Komeie, "Colonial Environmentalism and Shifting Cultivation in Korea," 672.

58 "Kadenmin kaihatsu wa kin'yū shisetsu ga kyumu," *Ōkkō nippō*, December 25, 1932.

59 On the relationship between swidden and border security, see Chōsen Sōtokufu, Nōrinkyoku, ed., *Hokusen kaitaku jigyō keikaku ni yoru kadenmin shidō oyobi shinrin hogo shisetsu gaiyō* (Keijō: Nōrinkyoku, 1934).

60 See, for example, Odauchi Michitoshi, "Chōsen kandenmin no shakaiteki kōsatsu," *Tōyō* 27, no. 11 (1924): 5–21.

61 "Hwajŏnmin ŭi pangch'uk indosang chungdae munje," *Tonga ilbo*, July 10, 1929.

62 For rhetoric of this sort, see, for example, "Kaden no hanashi," *Keijō nippō*, June 15, 1928.

63 See, for example, "Nong'chon ŭi mollak," *Tonga ilbo*, May 29, 1931; and "Sallimpŏp kwa hwajŏnmin" *Tonga ilbo*, December 16, 1933.

64 As qtd. in Komeie, "Colonial Environmentalism and Shifting Cultivation in Korea," 675.

65 For Hashimoto's assessment of the "fire-field problem" in Korea, see Chōsen Sōtokufu, ed., *Kaden chōsa hōkokusho* (Keijō: Chōsen Sōtokufu, 1928).

66 On the creation of these guidance zones, see Ch'oe P'yŏng-t'aek, "Chosŏn Ch'ongdokpu ŭi hwajŏn chŏngni saŏp," *Han'guk munhwa* 58 (2012): 167–74.

67 DRSK, 138–39.

68 These hired guns are described in Shirai Yomo, "Hokusen seishi no tanjyō to hisoku kyōika no sanrin jigyō," *Kamipa gikyōshi* 26, no. 9 (1972): 420–33.

69 Sin Min-jŏng, "Shokuminchiki Chōsen, Kōgendō chiiki ni okeru kaden, kadenmin ni kan suru kenkyū: Tōa nippō kiji no bunseki o chūshin ni," *Ringyō keizai* 62, no. 6 (2009): 3–8.

70 Ch'oe In-hwa, "Kankoku ni okeru kokuyūrin no keiei keikaku to shigyō no tenkai katei ni kansuru kenkyū," *Hokkaidō Daigaku Nōgakubu Enshūrin kenkyū hōkoku* 48, no. 1 (1991): 34.

71 "Manpōsen no kōji wa keizai bunya ni henkaku," *Ōkō nippō*, March 16, 1934.

72 Kang Chŏng-wŏn, "1930-yŏndae Ilche ŭi Chosŏn kongŏphwa wa sallim chŏngch'aek," *Han'guk kŭn-hyŏndaesa yŏn'gu* 79 (2016): 208.

73 Kang C., "1930-yŏndae Ilche ŭi Chosŏn kongŏphwa wa sallim chŏngch'aek," 208.

74 Shingishū Shōkō Kaigisho, ed., *Shingishū Shōkō annai* (Shingishū: Shingishū Shōkō Kaigisho, 1938), 76.

75 On these negotiations, see Moore, "'The Yalu River Era of Developing Asia,'" 124–26.

76 On this new spatial order, see Hirose Teizō, "Shokuminki Chōsen ni okeru Suihō hatsudenjo kensetsu to ryūbatsu mondai," *Niigata Kokusai Jōhō Daigaku, Jōhō Bunka Gakubu kiyō* 1 (1998): 54.

77 Pae, "Ilcheha Chosŏn ui mokchae sukŭp chŏngch'aek e kwanhan yŏn'gu," 25.

78 For language of this sort, see, for example, Paek Ŭl-sun, "Kankoku kokuyūrin ni okeru basshutsu, ikurin jigyō no tenkai katei ni kansuru shiteki kenkyū," *Hokkaidō Daigaku Nōgakubu Enshūrin kenkyū hōkoku* 47, no. 1 (1990): 44.

CHAPTER SIX: CIVIC FORESTRY

1 Shioda Masahiro, *Chōsen sanrin shiryō* (Keijō: Chōsen Sanrinkai, 1934).

2 Tokumitsu Nobuyuki, *Chōsen no rinsō* (Keijō: Chōsen Sōtokufu Ringyō Shikenjo, 1938).

3 For criticisms of this sort, see, for example, DRSK, 84.

4 Watanabe Toyohiko, "Rinsei no hongi," *Chōsen* 176 (1930): 82.

5 Gi-Wook Shin and Do-Hyun Han, "Colonial Corporatism: The Rural Revitalization Campaign, 1932–1940," in *Colonial Modernity in Korea*, ed. Shin and Robinson, 76. See Sheldon Garon, *Molding Japanese Minds: The State in Everyday Life* (Princeton: Princeton University Press, 1997).

6 Stephens, "Agriculture and Development in an Age of Empire," 2.

7 One important exception is Matsumoto Takenori and Chung Seung-Jin, "Water Management Projects and Floods/Droughts in Colonial Korea: The Case of the Man'gyŏng River in the Honam Plain," *Acta Koreana* 20, no. 1 (2017): 173–93.

8 CRI, 362.

9 See Yun Hae-dong, *Singminji ŭi hoaesaek chidae: Han'guk ŭi Kundaesŏng kwa singminjuŭi pip'an* (Seoul: Yŏksa Pip'yŏngsa, 2003).

10 Peluso, *Rich Forests, Poor People*, 4.

11 CRI, 464–65.

12 Yun, *Yun Ch'iho ilgi*, entry for June 11, 1921.

13 A compilation of speeches from this event can be found in "Ch'uksa wa ch'ukchŏn," *Chōsen sanrinkaihō* 1 (1921): 16–25.

14 Chōsen Sōtokufu, ed., *Chōsen no ringyō* (1925), 66.

15 This biographical information was reconstructed from HYCTS, accessed March 10, 2018, http://db.history.go.kr/item/level.do?levelId=im_101_10746.

16 HYCTS, accessed March 22, 2019, http://db.history.go.kr/item/level.do?itemId =im&setId=339556&position=5.

17 Uchida, *Brokers of Empire*, 5.

18 Uchida, *Brokers of Empire*, 5.

19 Stephens, "Agriculture and Development in an Age of Empire," 131–202.

20 On these charcoal promotion efforts, see Kakeba Sadakichi, "Mokutan zōsan taisaku," *Chōsen sanrinkaihō* 105 (1933): 3–12.

21 CRI, 360.

22 Kwang-Ok Kim, "Colonial Body and Indigenous Soul," in *Colonial Rule and Social Change in Korea, 1910–1945*, ed. Hong Yung Lee, Yong Chool Ha, and Clark W. Sorenson (Seattle: University of Washington Press, 2013), 278.

23 On *myŏn*-level conflicts, see Kang Chŏng-wŏn, "1910-yŏndae Ilche ŭi Chosŏn sallim soyu wa iyong e kwanhan insik: kongdongch'ejŏk soyu wa ip'oegwŏn ŭl chungsim ŭro," *Han'guk minjok munhwa* 56 (2015): 83–120.

24 DRSK, 77–78.

25 "Rinyazei no fuka ni tsuite," *Keijō nippō*, February 15–17, 1933.

26 Ch'oe Pyŏng-t'aek, "1930-yŏndae chŏnban Ilche ŭi minyulim chŏngch'aek 'chŏnhwan' kwa imya seje toip ŭi paegyŏng mit ŭimi," *Han'guksa yŏn'gu* 138 (2007): 200–201.

27 Ch'oe P., "1930-yŏndae chŏnban Ilche ŭi minyulim chŏngch'aek 'chŏnhwan' kwa imya seje toip ŭi paegyŏng mit ŭimi," 200.

28 James Scott, *Weapons of the Weak: Everyday Forms of Peasant Resistance* (New Haven: Yale University Press, 1987), xvi.

29 Shin, *Peasant Protest and Social Change in Colonial Korea*, 30.

30 Shin, *Peasant Protest and Social Change in Colonial Korea*, 54.

31 For a comprehensive survey of these conflicts, see Kim Yong-dal, *Nongmin undong* (Ch'ŏnan: Tongnip Kinyŏmgwan Han'guk Tongnip Undongsa Yŏn'guso, 2009).

32 On this "crowded field" of rural movements, see A. Park, *Building a Heaven on Earth*, 117–50.

33 As qtd. in Shin, *Peasant Protest and Social Change in Colonial Korea*, 89.

34 As qtd. in Bruce Cumings, *North Korea: Another Country* (New York: New Press, 2004), 116.

35 "Tanchŏn ch'ŏngnyŏn ch'angnip," *Tonga ilbo*, November 25, 1926.

36 Shin, *Peasant Protest and Social Change in Colonial Korea*, 101.

37 Yi Chun-sik, "Tanch'ŏn sallim chohap pandae undong ŭi chŏn'gae kwajŏn kwa sŏngkyŏk," *Sahoe wa yŏksa* 28 (1991): 114.

38 "Tanch'ŏn chungmaeng kinyŏmil manse sakon ŭi chŏnmal," *Chungoe ilbo*, January 31, 1930.

39 Tanch'ŏn Kunji P'yŏnch'an Wiwŏnhoe, ed., *Tanch'ŏn kunji* (Seoul: Tanch'ŏn Kunji P'yŏnch'an Wiwŏnhoe, 1971), 140–42.

40 Yi C., "Tanch'ŏn sallim chohap pandae undong ŭi chŏn'gae kwajŏn kwa sŏngkyŏk." 121.

41 A police report of this and related incidents is reproduced in "Tansen shinrin kumiai ni kansuru bumin no bōjō ni kansuru ken," in *Gendaishi shiryō,* ed. Kajimura Hideki and Kang Tŏk-sang (Tokyo: Misuzu Shobō, 1982), 395–96.

42 "Tansen shinrin kumiai ni kansuru bumin no bōjō ni kansuru ken," 395.

43 See, for example, "Tanch'ŏn sakon rŭl kihwa ro kyŏngmun salp'o rŭl kido," *Maeil sinbo,* July 30, 1930.

44 Guha, *The Unquiet Woods,* 185.

45 Guha, *The Unquiet Woods,* 7.

46 Ch'oe P., "1930-yŏndae chŏnban Ilche ŭi minyulim chŏngch'aek 'chŏnhwan' kwa imya seje toip ŭi paegyŏng mit ŭimi," 188.

47 "Rinyazei no fuka ni tsuite," *Keijō nippō,* February 15, 1933.

48 Shin and Han, "Colonial Corporatism," 71.

49 Watanabe Shinobu, *Minyūrin shidō hōshin taikō seitei ni tsuite* (Keijō: Chōsen Sōtokufu Nōrinkyoku, 1933), 117.

50 See, for example, Kakeba Sadakichi, "Minyūrin kaizensaku no ichi, shokuju henchō yori kiri oshimi no kyōsei" (self-published, 1931), YB: M4–122.

51 Chōsen Sōtokufu, ed., *Shokurin no hiketsu* (Keijō: Chōsen Sōtokufu, 1933), 6.

52 Suzukawa Tokio, "Nōyōrinchi no setsuei," *Chōsen nōkaihō* 1 (1936): 56.

53 Suzukawa, "Nōyōrinchi no setsuei," 55.

54 Chōsen Sanrinkai, ed., *Minyūringyō jisekishū* (Keijō: Chōsen Sanrinkai, 1934), 73–75.

55 Ueno Naoaki, *Chōsen, Manshū no omoide: Kyū Ōji Seishi jidai no kiroku* (Fujisawa: Shinbisha Seisaku, 1975), 6.

56 Kermit Roosevelt, "After Tigers in Korea: An Elusive Hunt for the Finest in Their Race, in the Cold 'Land of the Morning Calm,'" *Asia: Journal of the American Asiatic Association* 24, no. 4 (1924): 257.

57 Government-General of Chosen, ed., *Annual Report of Administration of Chosen, 1937–1938* (Seoul: Government-General of Chosen, 1938), 132.

58 Hermann Lautensach, *Korea: A Geography Based on the Author's Travels and Literature,* trans. Eckart Dege and Katherine Dege (Berlin: Springer, 1988), 57.

59 Lautensach, *Korea,* 433.

60 Harada Toshio, "Sanrin hōkoku to shiteki kansatsu," *Chōsen sanrinkaihō* 164 (1938): 49.

CHAPTER SEVEN: FOREST-LOVE THOUGHT

1 Yajima Sugizō, "Kinen shokuju ni tsuite," *Chōsen sanrinkaihō* 133 (1936): 8.

2 Yajima, "Kinen shokuju ni tsuite," 9.

3 Yajima, "Kinen shokuju ni tsuite," 10.

4 Yajima, "Kinen shokuju ni tsuite," 7–8.

5 Kada Naoji, "Airin undō no shakaika," *Chōsen sanrinkaihō* 75 (1931): 29.

6 For a lucid overview of the historiography of Japanese nature-myths, see Rots, *Shinto, Nature and Ideology in Contemporary Japan*, 47–65.

7 On Japanese racial theories undergirding assimilation policy, see Oguma Eiji, *A Genealogy of "Japanese" Self-Images*, trans. David Askew (Melbourne: Transpacific, 2002).

8 For Korean coverage of this procession, see, for example, "Ch'ingyŏngsik chŏlch'a," *Taehan maeil sinbo*, May 6, 1910.

9 CRI, 37–38.

10 On these plowing rituals, see James Palais, *Confucian Statecraft and Korean Institutions: Yu Hyŏngwŏn and the Late Chosŏn Dynasty* (Seattle: University of Washington Press, 1996), 592.

11 CRI, 40.

12 Dōke Atsuyuki, "Shinrin to dōka," *Chōsen oyobi Manshū* 45 (1911): 17.

13 Yi Kwang-su, *Yi Kwang-su chŏnjip* (Seoul: Nuri Midiŏ, 2011), 493.

14 This policy memo is reproduced in Takemoto, *Gakkōrin no kenkyū*, 166–67.

15 CRI, 44.

16 Kada, "Airin undō no shakaika," 28.

17 Suzukawa Toshio, "Hantō no rinsei to kinen shokuju," *Chōsen sanrinkaihō* 120 (1935): 6.

18 Itō Jūjirō, "Mori no megumi to airin," *Chōsen sanrinkaihō* 120 (1935): 7.

19 Keishō-Hokudō, ed., *Sabō o kataru* (Keishō-Hokudō, n.d.).

20 "Airin shisō no yōkō to shokurin jigyō no shinchoku o hakare," *Keijō nippō*, April 26, 1935.

21 On this empire-wide celebration, see Kenneth Ruoff, *Imperial Japan at Its Zenith: The Wartime Celebration of the Empire's 2,600th Anniversary* (Ithaca, NY: Cornell University Press, 2010).

22 "Kigen 2,600-nen kinen jigyō no susume," *Chōsen sanrinkaihō* 161 (1938): 58.

23 DRSK, 73.

24 "Aelim sasang ŭi hamyang ŭn kukka ŭi bu rŭl tŏmnun kŏt," *Maeil sinbo*, April 3, 1935.

25 "Chōsen ringyō kongo no ikikata oyobi airin shisō fukyū hōsaku ni tsuite no kaitō," *Chōsen sanrinkaihō* 140 (1936): 70.

26 See Takemoto, *Gakkōrin no kenkyū*, 168–69.

27 Todd Henry, *Assimilating Seoul: Japanese Rule and the Politics of Space in Colonial Korea, 1910–1945* (Berkeley: University of California Press, 2014), 134.

28 "Chōsen ringyō kongo no ikikata oyobi airin shisō fukyū hōsaku ni tsuite no kaitō," 90.

29 On the relationship between national identity and theories of climate, see, for example, Oguma, *A Genealogy of "Japanese" Self-Images*, 260–85.

30 Maruyama Jōzō, "Shinrin no bisei to fukei shisetsu," *Chōsen* 179 (1930): 20.

31 Maruyama, "Shinrin no bisei to fukei shisetsu," 36.

32 "Chōsen ringyō kongo no ikikata oyobi airin shisō fukyū hōsaku ni tsuite no kaitō," 90.

33　On radio broadcasting in colonial Korea, see Michael Robinson, "Broadcasting, Cultural Hegemony, and Colonial Modernity, 1924–1945," in *Colonial Modernity in Korea*, ed. Shin and Robinson, 52–69.

34　CRI, 498.

35　"Kongo no nōgyō gakkō ni okeru ringyō kyōiku ni tsuite," *Chōsen sanrinkaihō* 140 (1936): 88.

36　Nansen-sei [pseud.], "Ikuju to ikuji," *Chōsen sanrinkaihō* 74 (1931): 11.

37　Takemoto, *Gakkōrin no kenkyū*, 173.

38　Okazaki, "Kinen shokuju ni tsuite," 6.

39　On tree planting in the colonial capital, see Henry, *Assimilating Seoul*, 22–64.

40　On the growth of public green spaces in metropolitan Japan, see Thomas Havens, *Parkscapes: Green Spaces in Modern Japan* (Honolulu: University of Hawai'i Press, 2011).

41　See, for example, Honda Seiroku, "Kōdōju no shokusai o susume," *Chōsen nōkaihō* 8 (1922): 10–14.

42　As qtd. in Jung-Hwa Kim and Kyung-Jin Zoh, "Inventing Modern Taste at the Changgyeongwon Botanical Garden," *Landscape Research* 42, no. 5 (2017): 582.

43　As qtd. in Kim and Zoh, "Inventing Modern Taste at the Changgyeongwon Botanical Garden," 585.

44　Yajima, "Kinen shokuju ni tsuite," 7–8.

45　On the development of alpinism in Korea, see Son Kyŏng-sŏk, *Han'guk tŭngsansa oe Han'guk sanak chonansa, Han'guk sŭk'i paltalsa* (Seoul: Imaunt'in, 2010).

46　For an account of Western interest in this "Oriental Alpine summer resort," see "Many Visit the Diamond Hills," *New York Times*, November 11, 1928.

47　As qtd. in Kyung-Joon Lee, *Successful Reforestation in South Korea: Strong Leadership of Ex-President Park Chung-Hee* (self-published, 2013), 43.

48　A list of these products can be found in Chōsen Sōtokufu Nōrinkyoku, ed., *Chōsen sanrin bunka tenrankai shi* (Keijō: Chōsen Sōtokufu Nōrinkoyku, 1935), 53–57.

49　On the cultural cachet of department stores in colonial Korea, see Katarzyna Cwiertka, *Cuisine, Colonialism and Cold War: Food in Twentieth-Century Korea* (London: Reaktion, 2012), 47–57.

50　"Chōsen sanrin bunka tenrankai no jōkyō," *Chōsen sanrinkaihō* 121 (1935): 54.

51　Chōsen Sōtokufu Nōrinkyoku, ed., *Chōsen sanrin bunka tenrankai shi*, 3.

52　Kada, "Airin undō no shakaika," 27.

53　On changing perceptions of domesticity in colonial Korea, see, for example, Theodore Jun Yoo, *The Politics of Gender in Colonial Korea: Education, Labor, and Health, 1910–1945* (Berkeley: University of California Press, 2008).

54　"Chōsen sanrin bunka tenrankai no jōkyō," 66.

55　"Chōsen sanrin bunka tenrankai no jōkyō," 55.

56　"Chōsen Sōtokufu Nōrinkyoku, ed., *Chōsen sanrin bunka tenrankai shi*, 51–52.

57　On wartime tree-planting campaigns in Japan, see Nakashima Kōji, "Jūgo-nen sensōki no ryokka undō: sōdōin taiseika no shizen no hyōshō," *Hokuriku Shigaku* 49 (2000): 1–22.

58 Okazaki, "Kinen shokuju no jisaika o teishō," 3.

59 Saitō Otosaku, "Chōsen no ryokka undō ni tsuite," *Chōsen* 179 (1930): 61.

CHAPTER EIGHT: A STIFF WIND BLOWS

1 "Ringyō jijō," *Chōsen sanrinkaihō* 156 (1938): 51.

2 CRI, i–ii.

3 See, for example, Kang Yŏng-sim, "Ilche sigi (1937–1945) chŏnsi imjŏng ha esŏ ŭi sallim sut'al," *Han'guksa yŏn'gu* 102 (1998): 261–90.

4 Micah Muscolino, *The Ecology of War in China: Henan Province, the Yellow River, and Beyond, 1938–1950* (Cambridge: Cambridge University Press, 2014), 5.

5 Ozaki Shinji, *Mō boku ha Keijōkko ni wa modorenai: Chōsen hantō ni nokoshita ai to nasake no monogatari* (Tokyo: Sekai Nippō, 1995), 32.

6 Rob Nixon, *Slow Violence and the Environmentalism of the Poor* (Cambridge: Harvard University Press, 2013), 2.

7 Nixon, *Slow Violence*, 19.

8 On the ecological implications of the war for the Japanese archipelago, see William Tsutsui, "Landscapes in the Dark Valley: Toward an Environmental History of Wartime Japan," *Environmental History* 8, no. 2 (2003): 294–311.

9 Ch'oe I., "Kankoku ni okeru kokuyūrin no keiei keikaku to shigyō no tenkai katei ni kansuru kenkyū," 39–41.

10 DRSK, 148.

11 Hagino, *Chōsen, Manshū, Taiwan ringyō hattatsu shiron*, 141.

12 Paek, "Kankoku kokuyūrin ni okeru basshutsu, ikurin jigyō no tenkai katei ni kansuru shiteki kenkyū," 39.

13 Ch'oe Pyŏng-t'aek, "Ilcheha chŏnsi ch'ejegi (1937–1945) imŏp tongwŏnch'aek kwa sallim chawŏn kongch'ul," *Han'guksa hakpo* 32 (2008): 279.

14 Hagino, *Chōsen, Manshū, Taiwan ringyō hattatsu shiron*, 122.

15 The mandate of KFDC is laid out in Chōsen Sōtokufu, ed., *Chōsen Ringyō Kaihatsu Kabushiki Kaisha seturitsu yōkō* (Keijō: Chōsen Sōtokufu, 1937).

16 Ch'oe P., "Ilche ha chŏnsi ch'ejegi imŏp tongwŏnch'aek kwa sallim chawŏn kongch'ul," 280.

17 Kang Y., "Ilche sigi chŏnsi imjŏng ha esŏ ŭi sallim sut'al," 273–74.

18 Kang Y., "Ilche sigi chŏnsi imjŏng ha esŏ ŭi sallim sut'al," 270.

19 Ch'oe Pyŏng-t'aek, "Chŏnsi ch'eje ha Ilche ŭi mulcha sugŭp mit t'ongje chŏngch'aek: Kyŏngsŏng ŭi sint'an sugŭp t'ongje rŭl chungsim ŭro," *Yŏksa wa hyŏnsil* 53 (2004): 261.

20 "Mokchae nŭn kyŏlchŏn ŭi mugi," *Maeil sinbo*, August 20, 1943.

21 Ōji Seishi Kabushiki Kaisha, ed., *Ōji Seishi sanrin jigyōshi*, 408–20.

22 On the wartime circulation of fossil fuels, see Victor Seow, "Carbon Technocracy: East Asian Energy Regimes and the Industrial Modern, 1900–1957" (PhD diss., Harvard University, 2014), 157–88.

23 Kaburagi Tokuji, "Tōa no keizai kensetsu to mokuzai shigen," *Chōsen sanrinkaihō* 167 (1939): 5–7.

24 Hagino, *Chōsen, Manshū, Taiwan ringyō hattatsu shiron*, 143.

25 Pae Chae-su, "Ilche ŭi Chosŏn sallim chŏngch'aek e kwanhan yŏn'gu: Kugyurim chŏngch'aek rŭl chungsim ŭro" (PhD diss., Seoul National University, 1997), 264.

26 Kang Y., "Ilche sigi chŏnsi imjŏng ha esŏ ŭi sallim sut'al," 279.

27 This boatbuilding campaign merits comparison with that described in John Lee, "Postwar Pines," 321–24.

28 On fighting with fire during World War II, see Stephen Pyne, *Fire in America: A Cultural History of Wildland and Rural Fire* (Seattle: University of Washington Press, 1997).

29 See Jameson Karns, "A Fire Management Assessment of Operation FuGo," *Fire Management Today* 75, no. 1 (2017): 53–58.

30 Tsutsui, "Landscapes in the Dark Valley," 300.

31 Ch'oe P., "Ilche ha chŏnsi ch'ejegi imŏp tongwŏnch'aek kwa sallim chawŏn kongch'ul," 291.

32 As qtd. in Park Kyoung-hee, "State and Food in South Korea: Moulding the National Diet in Wartime and Beyond" (PhD diss., University of Leiden 2013), 53, 202.

33 Kang Y., "Ilche sigi chŏnsi imjŏng ha esŏ ŭi sallim sut'al," 278.

34 Kōtō Torao, "Shintanrin jigyō kaizen no hitsuyō to sono jikkō hōhō ni tsuite," *Chōsen sanrinkaihō* 161 (1938): 24.

35 Kang Y., "Ilche sigi chŏnsi imjŏng ha esŏ ŭi sallim sut'al," 284.

36 "Aelim cho palmyŏng sogam," *Tonga ilbo*, December 1, 1935.

37 See, for example, Chōsen Sanrinkai, ed., *Minyū ringyō jisekishū*, 51.

38 "Ondol ŭro in han pŏmjoe," *Maeil sinbo*, April 21, 1938

39 On the wartime Shintōization of the home and Korean responses thereto, see Henry, *Assimilating Seoul*, 168–204.

40 Fukushima Eisaku, "Nenryō sestuyaku to jyūgo no mori," *Chōsen sanrinkaihō* 159 (1938): 29.

41 Ohnuki-Tierney, *Kamikaze, Cherry Blossoms, and Nationalism*, 10.

42 Ike Kiyoshi, "Kokudo bōei to shinrin shigen no aigo," 6.

43 As qtd. in John Dower, *War without Mercy: Race and Power in the Pacific War* (New York: Pantheon, 1987), 214.

44 Ueki Homiki, "Nihon seishin to jyumoku no aigo," *Chōsen sanrinkaihō* 161 (1938): 10–13.

45 For rhetoric of this sort, see, for example, Ike Kiyoshi, "Shinrin shigen no jūyōsei to shinrin seisaku," *Chōsen sanrinkaihō* 196 (1941): 1–5. On the conservation measures of the Third Reich, see Frank Uekotter, *The Green and the Brown: A History of Conservation in Nazi Germany* (Cambridge: Cambridge University Press, 2006).

46 Suzuki Toyokazu, "Aiju, airin to waga kokuminsei," *Chōsen sanrinkaihō* 200 (1942): 6.

47 Both projections are examined in Ch'oe P., "Ilche ha chŏnsi ch'ejegi imŏp tongwŏnch'aek kwa sallim chawŏn kongch'ul," 292.

48 DRSK, 160.

49 On black market activities in wartime Korea, see Yi Ŭn-hŭi, "1940-yŏndae chŏnban Singminji Chosŏn ŭi amsijang: saenghwal mulcha rŭl chungsim ŭro," *Tongbang hakchi* 166 (2014): 255–91.

50 "Hagwŏn edo chŏon saenghwal," *Maeil sinbo*, October 31, 1941.

51 Kim Hong-jin, "Puŏk ŭi sinch'eje," *Yŏsŏng* 5, no. 10 (1940): 34.

52 See, for example, "Chŏnsi kajŏng kwa saenghwal ŭi hamnihwa," *Sin sidae* 3, no. 7 (1943): 40–49.

53 Pak Tong-jin, "Chŏnsi ha chut'aek kwa yŏllyo munje," *Chogwang* 9, no. 1 (1943): 114–18.

54 For a fuller treatment of this campaign, see David Fedman, "Wartime Forestry and the 'Low Temperature Lifestyle' in Late Colonial Korea, 1937–45," *Journal of Asian Studies* 77, no. 2 (2018): 333–50.

55 On discourses regarding Koreans' *ondol* lifestyle, see David Fedman, "The Ondol Problem and the Politics of Forest Conservation in Colonial Korea," *Journal of Korean Studies* 23, no. 1 (2018): 25–64.

56 On popular perceptions of Nogi's physical toughness, see Sasaki Hideaki, *Nogi Maresuke: Yo wa shokun no shitei o koroshitari* (Tokyo: Minerba Shobō, 2005), 45–46.

57 On settler colonialism in the frigid Manchurian frontier, see Norman Smith, "'Hibernate No More!': Winter, Health, and the Great Outdoors," in *Empire and Environment in the Making of Manchuria*, ed. Smith (Vancouver: University of British Columbia Press, 2017), 130–51.

58 On the politics of food scarcity in wartime Korea, see Park, "State and Food in South Korea," 25–181.

59 TYBK, 433.

60 See, for example, Eguchi Miyokichi, "Atarashii shōnin seishin," *Sōdōin* 2, no. 8 (1940): 79–81.

61 Chŏn U-yŏn, *Mori to Kankoku no bunka*, trans. Kim San-yun (Tokyo: Kokusho Kankōkai, 2004), 137.

62 See, for example, "Tongsa sammyŏng," *Maeil sinbo*, January 30, 1940.

63 Brett Walker, *Toxic Archipelago: A History of Industrial Disease in Japan* (Seattle: University of Washington Press, 2010), 177.

64 Ozaki, *Mō boku ha Keijōkko ni wa modorenai*, 170.

65 Kajiyama Toshiyuki, *Clan Records: Five Stories of Korea*, trans. Yoshiko Dykstra (Honolulu: University of Hawai'i Press, 1995), 161.

66 "Sarinjŏk hokhan," *Maeil sinbo*, January 11, 1940.

67 Henri Van Der Zee, *The Hunger Winter: Occupied Holland, 1944–1945* (Omaha: University of Nebraska Press, 1988), 77.

68 "Sarinjŏk hokhan," *Maeil sinbo*, January 11, 1940.

69 Nixon, *Slow Violence*, 2.

CONCLUSION

1 Iksop Lee and S. Robert Ramsey, *The Korean Language* (New York: SUNY Press, 2000), 132.

2 On the postcolonial politics of floral extirpation, see Todd Henry, "Ch'anggyŏng Garden as Neocolonial Space: Spectacles of Militarism and Industrial Development in Early South(ern) Korea," *Journal of Korean Studies* 21, no. 1 (2016): 7–43.

3 On Nakai Takenoshin and plant classification in the Japanese Empire, see Jung Lee, "Between Universalism and Regionalism: Universal Systematics from Imperial Japan," *British Journal for the History of Science* 48, no. 4 (2015): 661–84.

4 "Korean Aid," in *Hearings before the Committee on Foreign Affairs, Eighty-First Congress, First Session* (Washington, DC: Government Publishing Office, 1949), 79.

5 "Yanks Saving Korean Farms by Forestry," *Chicago Daily Tribune*, November 8, 1948.

6 Jae Soo Bae, Rin Won Joo, and Yeon-Su Kim, "Forest Transition in South Korea: Reality, Path and Drivers," *Land Use Policy* 29 (2012): 202.

7 Michael Seth, *North Korea* (London: Macmillan, 2018), 198.

8 On the ideological underpinnings of environmental thought in North Korea, see Robert Winstanley-Chesters, *Environment, Politics, and Ideology in North Korea: Landscape as Political Project* (London: Rowman and Littlefield, 2014).

9 For a broad overview of this policy framework, see, for example, Yi Kyŏng-jun, *Han'guk ŭi sallim nokhwa 70-yŏn* (Kyŏnggi: Han'gukhak Chungang Yŏn'guwŏn Ch'ulp'anbu, 2015).

10 These factors are examined in Kim Chong-ch'ŏl, *Sallim nokhwa sŏnggong kijŏk ŭi nara Han'guk: Han'guk ŭi sallim nokhwa sŏnggong yŏksa sillok: saji* (Seoul: Han'guk Imŏp Sinmun, 2011).

11 Tak, Chun, and Wood, "The South Korean Forest Dilemma," 551.

12 Food and Agriculture Organization, ed., *Integrated Policy for Forests, Food Security, and Sustainable Livelihoods: Lessons from the Republic of Korea* (Rome: Food and Agriculture Organization, 2016), 1.

13 See, for example, Yi Kye-min, *K'orian mirŏk'ŭl: Sumŭn kijŏktŭl, Sup ŭi yŏksa, saero ssŭda: sallim nokhwa ŏje wa onŭl* (Kyŏnggi: Nanam, 2015).

14 Carter Eckert, *Park Chung Hee and Modern Korea: The Roots of Militarism, 1866–1945* (Cambridge: Belknap Press of Harvard University Press, 2016), 3.

15 See Jaeyoung Ha, "Diligence by Design: Resettlement and Rehabilitation of 'Mountain Dwellers' during the Pak Chŏng Hŭi regime, 1965–1978," paper delivered at the "UCLA-UCSD Graduate Student Workshop," UC San Diego, December 2018.

16 On Park's crackdown against swidden, see Sin Min-jung, "Han'guk chŏngbu ŭi hwajŏn chŏngni saŏp chŏn'gae kwajŏng kwa hwajŏnmin ŭi silt'ae (1965–1970-nyŏn)," *Kyŏngje sahak* 50 (2011): 69–103.

17 Kim Chung-yum, *From Despair to Hope: Economic Policymaking in Korea, 1945–1979* (Seoul: Korea Development Institute, 2011), 255–56.

18 Don Koo Lee, Ki Cheol Kwon, and Yohan Lee, "The Role and Contribution of Sanlim-kyes during Saemaul Undong of the Republic of Korea in the 1970s," *Forest Science and Technology* 14, no. 2 (2018): 47–54.

19 See, for example, C. Kim, *From Despair to Hope*.

20 On Hyŏn and his central role in the greening of Korea, see Yi Kyŏng-jun, *San e mirae rŭl simta* (Seoul: Sŏul Taehakkyo Ch'ulp'anbu, 2006).

21 For the official account of this institutional growth, see Sŏul Taehakkyo, ed., *Suwŏn Nonghak chilsimnyŏn* (Seoul: Sŏul Taehakkyo Ch'ulp'anbu, 1976).

22 Shin and Robinson, *Colonial Modernity in Korea*, 5.

23 On the role of Japanese expertise in developing Southeast Asia, see Hiromi Mizuno, Aaron S. Moore, and John DiMoia, eds., *Engineering Asia: Technology, Colonial Development, and the Cold War Order* (London: Bloomsbury, 2018).

24 Dauvergne, *Shadows in the Forest*, 33.

25 Kami Seo and Jonathan Taylor, "Forest Resource Trade between Japan and Southeast Asia: The Structure of Dual Decay," *Ecological Economics* 45 (2003): 92.

26 Dauvergne, *Shadows in the Forest*, 3.

27 The controversy surrounding the sourcing of tropical timber for the construction of a new stadium for the 2020 Tokyo Olympics speaks to the ongoing nature of these issues. See, for example, "Tokyo's Wooden Olympic Stadium Using Timber Linked to Rights Abuses, Charities Say," *Reuters*, April 21, 2017.

28 Dauvergne, *Shadows in the Forests*, 26.

29 John Knight, "A Tale of Two Forests: Reforestation Discourse in Japan and Beyond," *Journal of the Royal Anthropological Institute* 3, no. 4 (1997): 725.

30 Tsing, "Contingent Commodities," in *Taking Southeast Asia to Market,* ed. Nevins and Peluso, 27–43.

31 Nigel Dudley, Jean-Paul Jeanrenaud, and Francis Sullivan, *Bad Harvest? The Timber Trade and the Degradation of Global Forests* (New York: Routledge, 2014), 30–31.

BIBLIOGRAPHY

PRIMARY SOURCES

Periodicals and Newspapers

Arboriculture
Asahi shimbun
Chicago Daily Tribune
Chogwang
Chōsen
Chōsen nōkaihō
Chōsen oyobi Manshū
Chōsen Ringyō Shikenjo hōkoku
Chōsen Ringyō Shikenjo tokuhō
Chōsen sanrinkaihō
Chungoe ilbo
Hwangsŏng sinmun
Japan Weekly Mail
Keijō nippō
Maeil sinbo
Manshū nichinichi shimbun
National Geographic Magazine
New York Times
New York Tribune
Ōkkō nippō
Ringakkai zasshi
Sōdōin
Sŏu
T'aegŭk hakpo
Taehan Chaganghoe wŏlbo

Taehan maeil sinbo
Timber Trades Journal and Saw-mill Advertiser
Tonga ilbo
Tōyō gakugei zasshi
Wŏlgan Chosŏn
Yomiuri shimbun
Yŏsŏng

Other Primary Sources

Abe Kaoru. *Chōsen toyū taikan.* Keijō: Minshū Jironsha, 1937.

Andō Tokio. *Tsūzoku kyōiku airin shisō.* Fukushima: Shōshiki Yōtatsu Shōkai, 1913.

Arakawa Gorō. *Saikin Chōsen jijō.* Tokyo: Shimizu Shoten, 1908.

Bank of Chosen, ed. *Economic History of Chosen.* Seoul: Bank of Chosen, 1920.

Bird Bishop, Isabella. *Korea and Her Neighbors: A Narrative of Travel, With an Account of the Recent Vicissitudes and Present Position of the Country.* New York: Fleming Revell, 1898.

Bureau of Education, ed. *Manual of Education in Chosen.* Seoul: Government-General of Chōsen, Bureau of Education, 1920.

Bureau of Forestry, ed. *Forestry of Japan.* Tokyo: Department of Agriculture and Commerce, 1910.

Carles, William Richard. *Life in Corea.* Boston: Macmillan, 1894.

Chang Hyŏk-chu. "Boku no bungaku." In *Chō Kakuchū Nihongo sakuhinsen,* edited by Nam Pu-jin and Shirakawa Yutaka. Tokyo: Bensei Shuppan, 2003.

Chōsen Sanrinkai, ed. *Minyū ringyō jisekishū.* Keijō: Chōsen Sanrinkai, 1934.

Chōsen Shokusan Ginkō Chōsaka, ed. *Chōsen no mokuzai.* Keijō: Chōsen Shokusan Ginkō Chōsaka, 1925.

Chōsen Sōtokufu, ed. *Chōsen kyoju rōju meiboku shi.* Keijō: Chōsen Sōtokufu, 1919.

———, ed. *Chōsen no ringyō.* Keijō: Chōsen Sōtokufu, 1925.

———, ed. *Chōsen no ringyō.* Keijō: Chōsen Sōtokufu, 1928.

———, ed. *Chōsen Ringyō Kaihatsu Kabushiki Kaisha seturitsu yōkō.* Keijō: Chōsen Sōtokufu, 1937.

———, ed. *Chōsen rinya chōsa hōkokusho.* Keijō: Chōsen Sōtokufu, 1924.

———, ed. *Jubyō yōsei shishin, Dai ichi-gō.* Keijō: Chōsen Sōtokufu, 1919. https://doi.org/10.11501/929712.

———, ed. *Kaden chōsa hōkokusho.* Keijō: Chōsen Sōtokufu, 1928.

———, ed. *Rinya Chōsa Iinkai jimu hōkoku.* Keijō: Rinya Chōsa Iinkai, 1936.

———, ed. *Shokurin no hiketsu.* Keijō: Chōsen Sōtokufu, 1933.

———, ed. *Suigen Kōtō Nōrin Gakkō ichiran.* Keijō: Chōsen Sōtokufu Suigen Kōtō Nōrin Gakkō, 1931.

Chōsen Sōtokufu, Nōrinkyoku, ed. *Chōsen sanrin bunka tenrankai shi.* Keijō: Chōsen Sōtokufu, Nōrinkyoku, 1935.

———, ed. *Hokusen kaitaku jigyō keikaku ni yoru kadenmin shidō oyobi shinrin hogo shisetsu gaiyō.* Keijō: Chōsen Sōtokufu, Nōrinkyoku, 1934.

Chōsen Sōtokufu Eirinshō, ed. *Chōsen Sōtokufu Eirinshō yōran*. Keijō: Chōsen
Sōtokufu Eirinshō, 1912

Chōsen Sōtokufu, Sanrinbu, ed. "Hokusen shinrin kaitaku jigyō keikakusho, shinrin
kankei no bun." Keijō: Chōsen Sōtokufu, Sanrinbu, 1932. YB: reel B318.

———, ed. *Ringyō keieijō mohan to narubeki jiseki gaiyō*. Keijō: Chōsen Sōtokufu,
1926.

Chōsen Sōtokufu Ringyō Shikenjo, ed. *Chōsen Ringyō Shikenjo yōran*. Keijō: Chōsen
Sōtokufu Ringyō Shikenjo, n.d.

———, ed. *Gyōmu gaiyō*. Keijō: Chōsen Sōtokufu Ringyō Shikenjo, 1933.

———, ed. *Kōryō shikenrin no ippan*. Keijō: Chōsen Sōtokufu Ringyō Shikenjo,
1932.

Government-General of Chosen, ed. *Annual Report of Administration of Chosen,
1937–1938*. Seoul: Government-General of Chosen, 1938.

Griffis, Willian Elliot. *A Modern Pioneer in Korea: The Life Story of Henry G.
Appenzeller*. New York: Fleming Revell, 1912.

Hamilton, Angus. *Korea: Its History, Its People, and Its Commerce*. Boston: J. B.
Millet, 1910.

Honda Seiroku. *Rinseigaku: Kokka to shinrin no kankei*. Tokyo, 1894.

Hulbert, Homer. *The Passing of Korea*. New York: Doubleday, 1906.

Ide Shōichi. *Chōsen no jitsujō*. Tokyo: Kōyūsha, 1910.

Kajiyama Toshiyuki. *Clan Records: Five Stories of Korea*. Translated by Yoshiko
Dykstra. Honolulu: University of Hawai'i Press, 1995.

Kakeba Sadakichi. "Minyūrin kaizensaku no ichi, shokuju henchō yori kiri oshimi
no kyōsei." Self-published, 1931. YB: M4–122.

Karafuto Ringyō shi Hensankai, ed. *Karafuto ringyō shi*. 1960. Tokyo: Ozorosha,
2005.

Keishō-Hokudō, ed. *Sabō o kataru*. Keishō-Hokudō: n.p., 1938. https://doi.
org/10.11501/1092374.

Kim Il-sŏng. *Works*. Vol. 3. Pyongyang: Foreign Languages Publishing House, 1980.

Koons, E. W. "Afforestation in Korea." *Transactions of the Korea Branch, Royal
Asiatic Society* 6 (1915): 35–42.

Kuksa P'yŏnch'an Wiwŏnhoe, ed. *Kojong Sillok*. Seoul: Kuksa P'yŏnch'an Wiwŏnhoe,
1968.

Kume, Kunitake. *The Iwakura Embassy 1871–73: A True Account of the Ambassador
Extraordinary and Plenipotentiary's Journey of Observation throughout the United
States of America and Europe*. Vol. 3: *Central Europe*, translated by A. Cobbing.
Surrey: Curzon, 2002.

Ladd, George Trumbull. *In Korea with Marquis Ito*. New York: Scribner's Sons, 1908.

Lautensach, Hermann. *Korea: A Geography Based on the Author's Travels and
Literature*. 1945. Translated by Eckart Dege and Katherine Dege. Berlin: Springer,
1988.

Lowell, Percival. *Chosön: Land of the Morning Calm, A Sketch of Korea*. Boston:
Ticknor, 1886.

Manshū Kōhō Kyōkai, ed. *Ōryōkkō*. Shinkyō: Manshūkoku Tsūshinsha, 1937.

Masanaga Yazu. *Chōsen Shiberia kikō*. Tokyo: Maruzen, 1894.

Nakama Teruhisa, ed. *Nihon chiri fūzoku taikei*. Vol. 16. Tokyo: Shinkōsha, 1930.

Nitobe, Inazō. *Thoughts and Essays*. Tokyo: Teibi, 1909.

Northrop, Grant Birdsey. *Rural Improvement, 1880-*. 1880. Ithaca, NY: Cornell University Press, 2009.

Nōshōmushō Sanrinkyoku, ed. *Kantō Daishinsai to mokuzai oyobi shintan*. Tokyo: Teikoku Shinrinkai, 1924.

Odauchi Michitoshi. "Chōsen kandenmin no shakaiteki kōsatsu." *Tōyō* 27, no. 11 (1924): 5–21.

Ōryokkō Saiboku Kōshi, ed. *Ōryokkō no shinrin oyobi ringyō*. Antō: Ōryokkō Saiboku Kōshi, 1915.

Ozaki Shinji. *Mō boku ha Keijōkko ni wa modorenai: Chōsen hantō ni nokoshita ai to nasake no monogatari*. Tokyo: Sekai Nippō, 1995.

Resident-General of Korea, ed. *Annual Report on Reforms and Progress in Chosen (Korea)*. Seoul: Tōkanfu, 1908.

Roosevelt, Kermit. "After Tigers in Korea: An Elusive Hunt for the Finest in Their Race, in the Cold 'Land of the Morning Calm.'" *Asia: Journal of the American Asiatic Association* 24, no. 4 (1924): 257–60.

Shiga Shigetaka Zenshū Kankōkai, ed. *Shiga Shigetaka Zenshū*. Tokyo: Shiga Shigetaka Zenshū Kankōkai, 1928.

Shimazaki, Tōson. *Before the Dawn*. Translated by William Naff. Honolulu: University of Hawai'i Press, 1987.

Shingishū Shōkō Kaigisho, ed. *Shingishū Shōkō annai*. Shingishū: Shingishū Shōkō Kaigisho, 1938.

———, ed. *Shingishū Shōkō Kaigisho jū-nen shi*. Shingishū: Shingishū Shōkō Kaigisho, 1937.

Shioda, Masahiro. *Chōsen sanrin shiryō*. Keijō: Chōsen Sanrinkai, 1934.

Shiozaki, Seigetsu. *Saishin no Kan hantō*. Osaka: Aoki Sūzandō, 1906.

Sŏ Yugu. *Imwŏn kyŏngjeji: Manhakchi*. Translated by Pak Sunch'ŏl and Kim Yŏng. Seoul: Sowadang, 2010.

Taki Kumejirō Denki Hensankai, ed. *Taki Kumejirō*. Tokyo: Taki Kumejirō Denki Hensankai, 1958.

Tanaka Kiyoji. *Kankoku shinrin shisatsu fukumeisho*. Tokyo: Nōshōmushō Sanrin-kyoku, 1903.

Tokumitsu Nobuyuki. *Chōsen no rinsō*. Keijō: Chōsen Sōtokufu Ringyō Shikenjo, 1938.

Tokyo Daigaku Shuppankai, ed. *Teikoku Gikai Shūgiin giji sokkiroku*. Tokyo: Tokyo Daigaku Shuppankai, 1984.

Tōyō Takushoku Kabushiki Kaisha, ed. *Tōtaku jū-nen shi*. 1918. Tokyo: Tanseisha, 2001.

Ueda Gunji. *Kokkyo nihyaku ri*. Keijō: Kokkyo Nihyaku Ri Hakkōjo, 1929.

Ueno, Naoaki. *Chōsen, Manshū no omoide: Kyū Ōji Seishi jidai no kiroku*. Fujisawa: Shinbisha Seisaku, 1975.

Ŭisinsa P'yŏnjippu, ed. *Ch'oesin samnimhak*. Seoul: Ŭisinsa P'yŏnjippu, 1909.

Underwood, Horace. *The Call of Korea: Political—Social—Religious*. New York: Fleming H. Revell, 1909.

United States Government Publishing Office, ed. *Hearings before the Committee on Foreign Affairs, Eighty-First Congress, First Session*. Washington, DC: Government Publishing Office, 1949.

Wada Takashi. *Shingishū shi*. Shingishū: Shimada Sōbunkan, 1911.

Watanabe Shinobu. *Minyūrin shidō hōshin taikō seitei ni tsuite*. Keijō: Chōsen Sōtokufu Nōrinkyoku, 1933.

Wilson, Ernest H. "The Vegetation of Korea." *Transactions of the Korea Branch of the Royal Asiatic Society* 9 (1918): 8.

Yi Kwang-su. *Yi Kwang-su chŏnjip*. Seoul: Nuri midiŏ, 2011.

Yi Sung-jun. *Ōryokkō jōryū shinrin shakubatsu jigyō annai*. Hu'chang: Ōryokkō Jōryū Shinrin Shakubatsu Jigyō Annai Hakkōjo, 1931.

Yuasa Katsuei. *Kannani and Document of Flames: Two Japanese Colonial Novels*. Translated by Mark Driscoll. Durham, NC: Duke University Press, 2005.

Yun Ch'iho. *Yun Ch'iho ilgi*. Seoul: National History Compilation Committee, 1974.

Zenkoku Shinbun Rengōsha, ed. *Nihon shokuminchi yōran*. Tokyo: Nihon Keizai Shinshisha, 1922.

SECONDARY SOURCES

Arch, Jakobina. *Bringing Whales Ashore: Oceans and the Environment of Early Modern Japan*. Seattle: University of Washington Press, 2017.

Atkins, E. Taylor. *Primitive Selves: Koreana in the Japanese Colonial Gaze, 1910-1945*. Berkeley: University of California Press, 2010.

Bae, Jae Soo, Rin Won Joo, and Yeon-Su Kim. "Forest Transition in South Korea: Reality, Path and Drivers." *Land Use Policy* 29 (2012): 198-207.

Barclay, Paul. *Outcastes of Empire: Japan's Rule on Taiwan's "Savage Border," 1874-1945*. Berkeley: University of California Press, 2017.

Batten, Bruce, and Philip Brown, eds. *Environment and Society in the Japanese Islands: From Prehistory to the Present*. Corvallis: Oregon State University Press, 2015.

Chiba Tokuji. *Hageyama no bunka*. Tokyo: Gakuseisha, 1973.

———. *Hageyama no kenkyū*. Tokyo: Nōrin Kyōkai, 1956.

Cho Jae-gon, "Pŭrinerŭ samlim ikwŏn kwa Ilbon ŭi taeŭng." *Yŏksa wa hyŏnsil* 88 (2013): 303-38.

Cho Sŏng-un. "Ilcheha Suwŏn Konong ŭi haksaeng undong kwa nulloksu undong." *Kyongju sahak* 14 (1995): 109-36.

Ch'oe In-hwa. "Kankoku ni okeru kokuyūrin no keiei keikaku to shigyō no tenkai katei ni kansuru kenkyū." *Hokkaidō Daigaku Nōgakubu Enshūrin kenkyū hōkoku* 48, no. 1 (1991): 1-79.

Ch'oe P'yŏng-t'aek. "Chŏnsi ch'eje ha Ilche ŭi mulcha sugŭp mit t'ongje chŏngch'aek: Kyŏngsŏng ŭi sint'an sugŭp t'ongje rŭl chungsim ŭro." *Yŏksa wa hyŏnsil* 53 (2004): 255-82.

———. "Chosŏn Ch'ongdokpu ŭi hwajŏn chŏngni saŏp." *Han'guk munhwa* 58 (2012): 167–74.

———. "Ilcheha chŏnsi ch'ejegi (1937–1945) imŏp tongwŏnch'aek kwa sallim chawŏn kongch'ul." *Han'guksa hakpo* 32 (2008): 267–305.

———. *Ilcheha Chosŏn imya chosa saŏp kwa sallim chŏngch'aek.* Seoul: P'urŭn Yŏksa, 2009.

———. "1930-yŏndae chŏnban ilche ŭi minyulim chŏngch'aek 'chŏnhwan' kwa imya seje toip ŭi paegyŏng mit ŭimi." *Han'guksa yŏn'gu* 138 (2007): 177–215.

Chŏn U-yŏn. *Mori to Kankoku no bunka.* Translated by Kim San-yun. Tokyo: Kokusho Kankōkai, 2004.

Clancey, Gregory. "Seeing the Timber for the Forest." In *A History of Natural Resources in Asia: The Wealth of Nature,* edited by Greg Bankoff and Peter Boomgaard, 123–41. Basingstoke: Palgrave Macmillan, 2007.

Cumings, Bruce. *North Korea: Another Country.* New York: New Press, 2004.

Cwiertka, Katarzyna. *Cuisine, Colonialism and Cold War: Food in Twentieth-Century Korea.* London: Reaktion, 2012.

Dauvergne, Peter. *Shadows in the Forest: Japan and the Politics of Timber in Southeast Asia.* Boston: MIT Press, 1997.

Davis, Diana. *Resurrecting the Granary of Rome: Environmental History and French Colonial Expansion in North Africa.* Athens: Ohio University Press, 2007.

Dower, John. *War without Mercy: Race and Power in the Pacific War.* New York: Pantheon, 1987.

Dudley, Nigel, Jean-Paul Jeanrenaud, and Francis Sullivan. *Bad Harvest? The Timber Trade and the Degradation of Global Forests.* New York: Routledge, 2014.

Duus, Peter. *The Abacus and the Sword: The Japanese Penetration of Korea, 1895–1910.* Berkeley: University of California Press, 1998.

Duus, Peter, Ramon H. Myers, and Mark R. Peattie, eds. *The Japanese Wartime Empire, 1931–1945.* Princeton: Princeton University Press, 1996.

Eckert, Carter. *Offspring of Empire: The Koch'ang Kims and the Colonial Origins of Korea Capitalism.* Seattle: University of Washington Press, 1996.

———. *Park Chung Hee and Modern Korea: The Roots of Militarism, 1866–1945.* Cambridge: Belknap Press of Harvard University Press, 2016.

Estok, Simon, and Kim Wŏn-jung, eds. *East Asian Ecocriticisms: A Critical Reader.* New York: Palgrave Macmillan, 2013.

Fedman, David. "The Ondol Problem and the Politics of Forest Conservation in Colonial Korea." *Journal of Korean Studies* 23, no. 1 (2018): 25–64.

———. "Wartime Forestry and the 'Low Temperature Lifestyle' in Late Colonial Korea, 1937–45." *Journal of Asian Studies* 77, no. 2 (2018): 333–50.

Food and Agriculture Organization, ed. *Integrated Policy for Forests, Food Security, and Sustainable Livelihoods: Lessons from the Republic of Korea.* Rome: Food and Agriculture Organization, 2016.

Ford, Caroline. "Reforestation, Landscape Conservation, and the Anxieties of Empire in French Colonial Algeria." *American Historical Review* 113, no. 2 (2008): 341–62.

Fujita, Yoshihisa. "Kyū kankoku jidai no Chōsen ni okeru shinrin shigen to rinya riyō: 'Kankoku shinrin fukumeisho' kara no fukugen." *Aichi Daigaku Kokusai Mondai Kenkyūjo* 84 (1988): 1–33.

Fukushima Yasunori. "Mokuzai keizai no kokusaika, shizen hogo: Awasete Shōwa rinsei o furikaeru." *Sanrin* 1262 (1989): 70–75.

———. "Wagakuni ringaku sōsōki ni okeru rinseigaku ni tsuite." *Sanrin* 4 (2011): 12–20.

Garon, Sheldon. *Molding Japanese Minds: The State in Everyday Life*. Princeton: Princeton University Press, 1997.

Gragert, Edwin. *Landownership under Colonial Rule: Korea's Japanese Experience, 1900–1935*. Honolulu: University of Hawai'i Press, 1994.

Grove, Richard. *Green Imperialism: Colonial Expansion, Tropical Island Edens, and the Origins of Environmentalism*. Cambridge: Cambridge University Press, 1996.

Guha, Ramachandra. *The Unquiet Woods: Ecological Change and Peasant Resistance in the Himalaya*. Berkeley: University of California Press, 2000.

Ha, Jaeyoung. "Diligence by Design: Resettlement and Rehabilitation of 'Mountain Dwellers' during the Pak Chŏng Hŭi Regime, 1965–1978." Paper presented at the "UCSD-UCLA Graduate Student Workshop," UC San Diego, December 2018.

Hagino Toshio. *Chōsen, Manshū, Taiwan ringyō hattatsushi ron*. Tokyo: Rin'ya Kōsaikai, 1965.

Hardin, Garrett. "The Tragedy of the Commons." *Science* 162 (1968): 1243–48.

Havens, Thomas. *Parkscapes: Green Spaces in Modern Japan*. Honolulu: University of Hawai'i Press, 2011.

Henry, Todd. *Assimilating Seoul: Japanese Rule and the Politics of Space in Colonial Korea, 1910–1945*. Berkeley: University of California Press, 2014.

———. "Ch'anggyŏng Garden as Neocolonial Space: Spectacles of Militarism and Industrial Development in Early South(ern) Korea." *Journal of Korean Studies* 21, no 1 (2016): 7–43.

Hirose Teizō. "Shokuminki Chōsen ni okeru Suihō hatsudenjo kensetsu to ryūbatsu mondai." *Niigata Kokusai Jōhō Daigaku, Jōhō Bunka Gakubu kiyō* 1 (1998): 39–58.

Hokkaidō Ringyō Keiei Kyōgikai, ed. *Hokkaidō sanrin shi, senzen hen*. Sapporo: Hokkaidō Ringyō Kaikan, 1983.

Kaburagi Tokuji. "Chōsen Ringyō Shikenjo jidai no kaiko." *Ringyō keizai* 22, no. 11 (1969): 43–46.

Kajimura Hideki and Kang Tŏk-sang, eds. *Gendaishi shiryo*. Tokyo: Misuzu Shobō, 1982.

Kang, Hildi. *Under the Black Umbrella: Voices from Colonial Korea, 1910–1945*. Ithaca, NY: Cornell University Press, 2001.

Kang Chŏng-wŏn. "1910-yŏndae Ilche ŭi Chosŏn sallim soyu wa iyong e kwanhan insik: Kongdongch'ejŏk soyu wa ip'oegwŏn ŭl chungsim ŭro." *Han'guk minjok munhwa* 56 (2015): 83–120.

———. "1930-yŏndae Ilche ŭi Chosŏn kongŏphwa wa sallim chŏngch'aek." *Han'guk kŭn-hyŏndaesa yŏn'gu* 79 (2016): 185–224.

Kang Chŏng-wŏn and Ch'oe Wŏn-gyu. "Ilche ŭi imya daebu chŏngch'aek kwa kŭ sŏngkyŏk: 1910, 1920-yŏndae daebu silt'ae wa kyŏngyŏng ŭl chungsim ŭro." *Han'guk minjok munhwa* 58 (2016): 299–347.

Kang Yŏng-sim. "Ilche sigi (1937–1945) chŏnsi imjŏng ha esŏ ŭi sallim sut'al."
Han'guksa yŏn'gu 102 (1998): 261–90.

Karns, Jameson. "A Fire Management Assessment of Operation FuGo." *Fire Management Today* 75, no. 1 (2017): 53–58.

Kim, Chung-yum. *From Despair to Hope: Economic Policymaking in Korea, 1945–1979.* Seoul: Korea Development Institute, 2011.

Kim, Jung-Hwa, and Kyung-Jin Zoh. "Inventing Modern Taste at the Changgyeongwon Botanical Garden." *Landscape Research* 42, no. 5 (2017): 574–91.

Kim, Kwang-Ok. "Colonial Body and Indigenous Soul." In *Colonial Rule and Social Change in Korea, 1910–1945,* edited by Hong Yung Lee, Yong Chool Ha, and Clark W. Sorenson, 264–313. Seattle: University of Washington Press, 2013.

Kim, Sun Joo, ed. *The Northern Region of Korea: History, Identity, and Culture.* Seattle: University of Washington Press, 2010.

Kim Chong-ch'ŏl. *Sallim nokhwa sŏnggong kijŏk ŭi nara Han'guk: Han'guk ŭi sallim nokhwa sŏnggong yŏksa sillok: saji.* Seoul: Han'guk Imŏp Sinmun, 2011.

Kim Hŭng-sun. "Chosŏn hugi sallim chŏngch'aek mit sallim hwangp'yehwa: Sijangjuŭijŏk koch'al kwa kŭ e taehan pip'an." *Han'guk Chiyŏk Kaebal Hakhoeji* 20, no. 2 (2008): 169–92.

Kim Kyŏng-suk. "Chosŏn hugi sansong kwa sahoe kaldŭng." PhD diss., Seoul National University, 2008.

Kim Tong-jin. *Chosŏn ŭi saengt'ae hwan'gyŏngsa.* Seoul: P'urŭn Yŏksa, 2017.

Kim Won-su, "Amnokkang wigi wa Ro-Il chŏnjaeng." *Sŏyang sahak yŏn'gu* 23 (2010): 115–41.

Kim Yong-dal. *Nongmin undong.* Ch'ŏnan: Tongnip Kinyŏmgwan Han'guk Tongnip Undongsa Yŏn'guso, 2009.

Komeie, Taisaku. "Colonial Environmentalism and Shifting Cultivation in Korea: Japanese Mapping, Research, and Representation." *Geographical Review of Japan* 79, no. 12 (2006): 664–79.

———. "Kindai ringaku to kokudo no shokusei kanri: Honda Seiroku no 'Nihon shinrin shokubutsutai ron' o megutte." *Kūkan, shakai, chiri shisō* 17 (2014): 3–18.

Knight, John. "The Problem of Gaizai: The View from Japanese Forestry Villages." In *The Political Ecology of Tropical Forests in Southeast Asia,* edited by Lye Tuck-Po, Wil De Jong, and Abe Kenichi, 265–82. Kyoto: Kyoto University Press, 2003.

———. "A Tale of Two Forests: Reforestation Discourse in Japan and Beyond." *Journal of the Royal Anthropological Institute* 3, no. 4 (1997): 711–30.

Koseki Takayoshi. "Hokkaidō ringyō no hatten katei." *Hokkaidō Daigaku Nōgakubu Enshūrin kenkyū hōkoku* 22, no. 1 (1962): 26–94.

———. "Hokkaido ringyō to Hokudai." *Hokudai hyakunenshi, tsūsetsu* (1982): 789–800.

Kuksa P'yŏnch'an Wiwŏnhoe, ed. *Chuhan Ilbon Kongsagwan killok, 20.* Kwach'ŏn: Kuksa P'yŏnch'an Wiwŏnhoe, 1986.

Kwŏn Ok-yŏng. "Chōsen ni okeru Nihon teikokushugi no shokuminchiteki sanrin taisaku." *Rekishigaku kenkyū* 297 (1965): 1–18.

Kwŏn Sŏg-yŏng. *Ondol ŭi kŭndaesa: Ondol ŭl tullŏssan Chosŏnin ŭi sam kwa yŏksa.* Seoul: Ilchogak, 2010.

Langston, Nancy. *Forest Dreams, Forest Nightmares: The Paradox of Old Growth in the Inland West.* Seattle: University of Washington Press, 1995.

Latour, Bruno. *Science in Action: How to Follow Scientists and Engineers through Society.* Cambridge: Harvard University Press, 1988.

Lee, C. S., H. J. Cho, and H. Yi. "Stand Dynamics of Introduced Black Locust under Different Disturbance Regimes in Korea." *Forest Ecology and Management* 189 (2004): 281–93.

Lee, Don Koo, Ki Cheol Kwon, and Yohan Lee. "The Role and Contribution of Sanlim-kyes during Saemaul Undong of the Republic of Korea in the 1970s." *Forest Science and Technology* 14, no. 2 (2018): 47–54.

Lee, Hoon K. *Land Utilization and Rural Economy in Korea.* Chicago: University of Chicago Press, 1936.

Lee, Iksop, and S. Robert Ramsey. *The Korean Language.* New York: SUNY Press, 2000.

Lee, John S. "Postwar Pines: The Military and the Expansion of State Forests in Post-Imjin Korea, 1598–1684." *Journal of Asian Studies* 77, no. 2 (2018): 319–32.

———. "Protect the Pines, Punish the People: Forests and the State in Pre-industrial Korea, 918–1897." PhD diss., Harvard University, 2017.

Lee, Jung. "Between Universalism and Regionalism: Universal Systematics from Imperial Japan." *British Journal for the History of Science* 48, no. 4 (2015): 661–84.

———. "Mutual Transformation of Colonial and Imperial Botanizing? The Intimate Yet Remote Collaboration in Colonial Korea." *Science in Context* 29, no. 2 (2016): 179–211.

———. "Singminji kwahak hyŏmnyŏk ŭl wihan chungnipsŏng ŭi chŏngch'i: Ilche kangjŏmgi Chosŏn ŭi hyang'tojŏk singmul yŏn'gu." *Han'guk Kwahaksa Hakhoeji* 37, no. 1 (2015): 265–98.

Lee, Kyung-Joon. *Successful Reforestation in South Korea: Strong Leadership of Ex-President Park Chung-Hee.* Self-published, 2013.

Lee, Wooyoun (Yi U-yŏn). "Deforestation and Agricultural Productivity in Chosŏn Korea in the 18th and 19th Centuries." In *Community, Commons, and Natural Resource Management in Asia,* edited by Haruka Yanagisawa, 25–60. Singapore: National University of Singapore, 2015.

Manela, Erez. *The Wilsonian Moment: Self-Determination and the International Origins of Anticolonial Nationalism.* Oxford: Oxford University Press, 2009.

Marcon, Federico. *The Knowledge of Nature and the Nature of Knowledge in Early Modern Japan.* Chicago: University of Chicago Press, 2015.

Matsumoto, Takenori, and Chung Seung-Jin. "Water Management Projects and Floods/Droughts in Colonial Korea: The Case of the Man'gyŏng River in the Honam Plain." *Acta Koreana* 20, no. 1 (2017): 173–93.

Matsusaka, Tak. *The Making of Japanese Manchuria, 1904–1932.* Cambridge: Harvard University Asia Center, 2003.

McDonald, Kate. *Placing Empire: Travel and the Social Imagination in Imperial Japan*. Berkeley: University of California Press, 2017.

McElwee, Pamela. *Forests Are Gold: Trees, People, and Environmental Rule in Vietnam*. Seattle: University of Washington Press, 2017.

McKean, Margaret. "Conflict over the Contemporary Fate of Common Lands in Meiji Japan." Paper presented at the Annual Meeting of the Association for Asian Studies, March 1995.

Miller, Ian J. *The Nature of the Beasts: Empire and Exhibition at the Tokyo Imperial Zoo*. Berkeley: University of California Press, 2013.

Miller, Owen. "The Idea of Stagnation in Korean Historiography from Fukuda Tokuzo to the New Right." *Korean Histories* 2, no 1. (2010): 3–12.

Miyake Miyahisa. *Chōsen hantō no rinya kōhai no genin: Shizen kankyō hozen to shinrin no rekishi*. Tokyo: Nōrin Shuppan, 1976.

Mizuno, Hiromi, Aaron S. Moore, and John DiMoia, eds. *Engineering Asia: Technology, Colonial Development, and the Cold War Order*. London: Bloomsbury, 2018.

Mizuta, Naomasa, ed. *Watanabe Toyohiko kōjyutsu, Chōsen Sōtokufu kaikodan*. Tokyo: Yūhō Kyōkai, 1984.

Moon, Yumi. *Populist Collaborators: The Ilchinhoe and the Japanese Colonization of Korea, 1896–1910*. Ithaca, NY: Cornell University Press, 2013.

Moore, Aaron S. *Constructing East Asia: Technology, Ideology, and Empire in Japan's Wartime Era, 1931–1945*. Stanford: Stanford University Press, 2013.

———. "'The Yalu River Era of Developing Asia': Japanese Expertise, Colonial Power, and the Construction of Sup'ung Dam." *Journal of Asian Studies* 72, no. 1 (2013): 115–39.

Morris-Suzuki, Tessa. "The Nature of Empire: Forest Ecology, Colonialism and Survival Politics in Japan's Imperial Order." *Japanese Studies* 33, no. 3 (2013): 225–42.

———. *The Technological Transformation of Japan: From the Seventeenth to the Twenty-First Century*. Cambridge: Cambridge University Press, 1994.

Muscolino, Micah. *The Ecology of War in China: Henan Province, the Yellow River, and Beyond, 1938–1950*. Cambridge: Cambridge University Press, 2014.

Nakashima Kōji. "Jūgo-nen sensōki no ryōkka undō: sōdōin taiseika no shizen no hyōshō." *Hokuriku shigaku* 49 (2000): 1–22.

Negishi Kenichiro, Tange Takeshi, Suzuki Makoto, and Yamamoto Hirokazu. "Chiba Enshūrin enkakushi shiryō." *Enshūrin* 46 (2007): 57–121.

Nevins, Joseph, and Nancy Lee Peluso, *Taking Southeast Asia to Market: Commodities, Nature, and People in the Neoliberal Age*. Ithaca, NY: Cornell University Press, 2008.

Nihon Ringyō Gijyutsu Kyōkai Shinrin Kōsoku Kenkyūkai, ed. "Manshū ni okeru kōkū shashin riyō no shinrin chōsa." *Shashin sokuryō* 8, no. 2 (1969): 96–101.

Nixon, Rob. *Slow Violence and the Environmentalism of the Poor* (Cambridge: Harvard University Press, 2013

Noda Kimio, ed. *Nihon Teikokuken no nōrin shigen kaihatsu: "Shigenka" to sōryokusen taisei no higashi Ajia.* Kyoto: Kyoto Daigaku Gakujutsu Shuppankai, 2013.

O'Dwyer, Emer. *Significant Soil: Settler Colonialism and Japan's Urban Empire in Manchuria.* Cambridge: Harvard University Asia Center, 2015.

Oguma, Eiji. *A Genealogy of "Japanese" Self-Images.* Translated by David Askew. Melbourne: Transpacific, 2002.

Ohnuki-Tierney, Emiko. *Kamikaze, Cherry Blossoms, and Nationalism: The Militarization of Aesthetics in Japanese History.* Chicago: University of Chicago Press, 2002.

Ōji Seishi Kabushiki Kaisha, ed. *Ōji Seishi sanrin jigyōshi.* Tokyo: Ōji Seishi Kabushiki Kaisha, 1976.

———, ed. *Ōji Seishi shashi.* Tokyo: Ōji Seishi Kabushiki Kaisha, 2001.

Okamoto Kikuko. "Meijiki Nihon bunkashi ni okeru kinen shokuju no rinen to hōhō: Honda Seiroku 'Jusai zōrinhō' o chūshin ni." *Sōkadai bunka kagaku kenkyū* 10 (2014): 69–97.

Osborne, Michael A. "Acclimatizing the World: A History of the Paradigmatic Colonial Science." *Osiris* 15 (2000): 135–51.

Pae Chae-su. "Han'guk ŭi sallim pyŏnch'ŏn: ch'ui, t'ŭkching, mit hamŭi." *Han'guk Imhakhoe chi* 98, no. 6 (2009): 659–68.

———. "Ilche ŭi Chosŏn sallim chŏngch'aek e kwanhan yŏn'gu: Kugyurim chŏngch'aek rŭl chungsim ŭro." PhD diss., Seoul National University, 1997.

———. "Ilcheha Chosŏn ŭi mokchae sukŭp chŏngch'aek e kwanhan yŏn'gu." *Sallim kyŏngje yŏn'gu* 6, no. 1 (1998): 20–39.

———. "Samlimpŏp (1908) ŭi chijŏk sin'go chedo ka Ilche ŭi singminji imji chŏngch'aek e mich'in yŏnghyang e kwanhan yŏn'gu." *Han'guk Imhakhoe chi* 90, no. 3 (2001): 398–412.

Pae Chae-su, Kim Sŏn-yŏng, Yi Ki-bong, and Chu Rin-wŏn. *Chosŏn hugi sallim chŏngch'aeksa.* Seoul: Imŏp Yŏn'guwŏn, 2002.

Paek Ŭl-sun. "Kankoku kokuyūrin ni okeru basshutsu, ikurin jigyō no tenkai katei ni kansuru shiteki kenkyū." *Hokkaidō Daigaku Nōgakubu Enshūrin kenkyū hōkoku* 47, no. 1 (1990): 1–70.

Pai, Hyung Il. *Heritage Management in Korea and Japan: The Politics of Antiquity and Identity.* Seattle: University of Washington Press, 2014.

Pak Sŏng-jun. "1880-nyŏndae Chosŏn ŭi Ullŭngdo pŏlmok kyeyak ch'egyŏl kwa pŏlmokkwon ŭl tullŏssan kakkuk kwa ŭi kaltŭng." *Tongbug'a yŏksa nonch'ong* 43 (2014): 117–48.

Palais, James B. *Confucian Statecraft and Korean Institutions: Yu Hyŏngwŏn and the Late Chosŏn Dynasty.* Seattle: University of Washington Press, 1996.

Park, Albert L. *Building a Heaven on Earth: Religion, Activism, and Protest in Japanese Occupied Korea.* Honolulu: University of Hawai'i Press, 2014.

Park, Kyoung-hee. "State and Food in South Korea: Moulding the National Diet in Wartime and Beyond." PhD diss., University of Leiden, 2013.

Park, Soon-Won. *Colonial Industrialization and Labor: The Onoda Cement Factory.* Cambridge: Harvard University Press, 1999.

Peluso, Nancy Lee. *Rich Forests, Poor People: Resource Control and Resistance in Java.* Berkeley: University of California Press, 1994.

Pratt, Mary Louise. *Imperial Eyes: Travel Writing and Transculturation.* London: Routledge, 1992.

Pyne, Stephen. *Fire in America: A Cultural History of Wildland and Rural Fire.* Seattle: University of Washington Press, 1997.

Radkau, Joachim. *Wood: A History.* New York: Polity, 2011.

Rajan, S. R. *Modernizing Nature: Forestry and Imperial Economic Development, 1800–1950.* Oxford: Oxford University Press, 2006.

Raup, Hugh. "John Sanderson's Farm: A Perspective for the Use of the Land." *Forest History* 10, no. 1 (1966): 3–11.

Rots, Aike P. *Shintō, Nature, and Ideology in Contemporary Japan: Making Sacred Forests.* London: Bloomsbury, 2017.

Ruoff, Kenneth. *Imperial Japan at Its Zenith: The Wartime Celebration of the Empire's 2,600th Anniversary.* Ithaca, NY: Cornell University Press, 2010.

Sallimch'ŏng Imoṗ Sihŏmjang, ed. *Imŏp Sihŏmjang yuksimnyŏnsa.* Seoul: Sallimch'ŏng Imoṗ Sihŏmjang, 1982.

Sasaki Hideaki. *Nogi Maresuke: Yo wa shokun no shitei o koroshitari.* Tokyo: Minerba Shobō, 2005.

Satō Jin. *"Motazaru kuni" no shigen ron: Jisoku kanō na kokudo o meguru mō hitotsu no chi.* Tokyo: Tokyo Daigaku Shuppankai, 2011.

Schmid, Andre. *Korea between Empires, 1895–1919.* New York: Columbia University Press, 2002.

———. "Rediscovering Manchuria: Sin Ch'aeho and the Politics of Territorial History in Korea." *Journal of Asian Studies* 56, no. 1 (1997): 26–46.

Scott, James. *Seeing Like a State: How Certain Schemes to Improve the Human Condition Have Failed.* New Haven: Yale University Press, 2001.

———. *Weapons of the Weak: Everyday Forms of Peasant Resistance.* New Haven: Yale University Press, 1987.

Seeley, Joseph. "Liquid Geography: The Yalu River and the Boundaries of Empire in East Asia, 1894–1945." PhD diss., Stanford University, 2019.

Seeley, Joseph, and Aaron Skabelund. "Tigers—Real and Imagined—in Korea's Physical and Cultural Landscape." *Environmental History* 20 (2015): 475–503.

Seo, Kami, and Jonathan Taylor. "Forest Resource Trade between Japan and Southeast Asia: The Structure of Dual Decay." *Ecological Economics* 45 (2003): 91–104.

Seow, Victor. "Carbon Technocracy: East Asian Energy Regimes and the Industrial Modern, 1900–1957." PhD diss., Harvard University, 2014.

Seth, Michael. *North Korea.* London: Macmillan, 2018.

Shimazu Toshiyuki. "Chirigakusha toshite no Takashima Hokkai." *Kūkan, shakai, chiri shisō* 15 (2012): 51–75.

Shin, Gi-Wook. *Peasant Protest and Social Change in Colonial Korea*. Seattle: University of Washington Press, 2014.

Shin, Gi-Wook, and Michael Robinson. *Colonial Modernity in Korea*. Cambridge: Harvard University Press, 1999.

Shirai Yomo. "Hokusen seishi no tanjyō to hisoku kyōika no sanrin jigyō." *Kamipa gikyōshi* 26, no. 9 (1972): 420–33.

Sin Min-jŏng. "Han'guk chŏngbu ŭi hwajŏn chŏngni saŏp chŏn'gae kwajŏng kwa hwajŏnmin ŭi silt'ae (1965–1970-nyŏn)." *Kyŏngje sahak* 50 (2011): 69–103.

———. "Shokuminchiki Chōsen, Kōgendō chiiki ni okeru kaden, kadenmin ni kan suru kenkyū: Tōa nippō kiji no bunseki o chūshin ni." *Ringyō keizai* 62, no. 6 (2009): 1–15.

Sivaramakrishnan, K. *Modern Forests: Statemaking and Environmental Change in Colonial Eastern India*. Stanford: Stanford University Press, 1999.

Smith, Norman. "'Hibernate No More!' Winter, Health, and the Great Outdoors." In *Empire and Environment in the Making of Manchuria*, edited by Smith, 130–51. Vancouver: University of British Columbia Press, 2017.

Son Kyŏng-sŏk. *Han'guk tŭngsansa oe Han'guk sanak chonansa, Han'guk sŭk'i paltalsa*. Seoul: Imaunt'in, 2010.

Son Yu-jŏng. "Hyŏn Sin-kyu ŭi rigidedo sonamu yŏn'gu." *Han'guk Kwahaksa Hakhoeji* 27, no. 2 (2005): 27–60.

———. "Ilche kangjŏmgi Hyŏn Sin-kyu ŭi imhakja urŏ ui sŏngjang kwa kŭ ŭimi." *Han'guk inmulsa yŏn'gu* 21 (2014): 505–44.

Sŏul Taehakkyo, ed. *Suwŏn Nonghak chilsimnyŏn*. Seoul: Sŏul Taehakkyo Ch'ulp'anbu, 1976.

Stephens, Holly. "Agriculture and Development in an Age of Empire: Institutions, Associations, and Market Networks in Korea, 1876–1945." PhD diss., University of Pennsylvania, 2017.

Sunseri, Thaddeus. *Wielding the Ax: Forestry and Social Conflict in Tanzania, 1820–2000*. Athens: Ohio University Press, 2009.

Tak, K, Y. Chun, and P. M. Wood. "The South Korean Forest Dilemma." *International Forestry Review* 9, no. 1 (2007): 548–57.

Takasaki Sōji. *Chōsen no tsuchi to natta Nihonjin: Asakawa Takumi no shōgai*. Tokyo: Sōfūkan, 2002.

Takemoto Tarō. *Gakkōrin no kenkyū: Mori to kyōiku o meguru kyōdō kankei no kiseki*. Tokyo: Nōsangyoson Bunka Kyōkai, 2009.

———. "Shokuminchi ni okeru ryōka undō seisaku no igi: Saitō Otosaku no ashi ato kara." Paper presented at the Kankyō Seisakushi Kenkyūkai (Environmental Policy History Research Group), 2012.

Tanch'ŏn Kunji P'yŏnch'an Wiwŏnhoe, ed. *Tanch'ŏn kunji*. Seoul: Tanch'ŏn Kunji P'yŏnch'an Wiwŏnhoe, 1971.

Thomas, Julia Adeney. *Reconfiguring Modernity: Concepts of Nature in Japanese Political Ideology*. Berkeley: University of California Press, 2001.

Thompson, E. P. *Whigs and Hunters: The Origins of the Black Act*. New York: Pantheon, 1975.

Totman, Conrad. *The Green Archipelago: Forestry in Pre-industrial Japan*. Athens: Ohio University Press, 1989.

———. *Japan: An Environmental History*. London: I. B. Tauris, 2014.

———. *Japan's Imperial Forest, Goryōrin, 1889–1946: With a Supporting Study of the Kan/Min Division of Woodland in Early Meiji Japan, 1871–76*. Folkestone: Global Oriental, 2007.

———. *Pre-industrial Korea and Japan in Environmental Perspective*. Leiden: Brill, 2004.

Tsing, Anna. "Contingent Commodities: Mobilizing Labor in and beyond Southeast Asian Forests." In *Taking Southeast Asia to Market: Commodities, Nature, and People in the Neoliberal Age*, edited by Joseph Nevins and Nancy Lee Peluso, 27–43. Ithaca, NY: Cornell University Press, 2008.

Tsutsui, William. "Landscapes in the Dark Valley: Toward an Environmental History of Wartime Japan." *Environmental History* 8, no. 2 (2003): 294–311.

Tyrell, Ian. *Crisis of the Wasteful Nation: Empire and Conservation in Theodore Roosevelt's America*. Chicago: University of Chicago Press, 2015.

Uchida, Jun. *Brokers of Empire: Japanese Settler Colonialism in Korea, 1876–1945*. Cambridge: Harvard University Asia Center, 2011.

Uekotter, Frank. *The Green and the Brown: A History of Conservation in Nazi Germany*. Cambridge: Cambridge University Press, 2006.

van der Zee, Henri. *The Hunger Winter: Occupied Holland, 1944–1945*. Omaha: University of Nebraska Press, 1988.

Vandergeest, Peter, and Nancy Lee Peluso. "Empires of Forestry: Professional Forestry and State Power in Southeast Asia." *Environment and History* 12 (2006): 31–64.

Walker, Brett. *The Conquest of Ainu Lands: Ecology and Culture in Japanese Expansion, 1590–1800*. Berkeley: University of California Press, 2006.

———. *Toxic Archipelago: A History of Industrial Disease in Japan*. Seattle: University of Washington Press, 2010.

Williams, Michael. *Deforesting the Earth: From Pre-history to Global Crisis*. Chicago: University of Chicago Press, 2003.

Winstanley-Chesters, Robert. *Environment, Politics, and Ideology in North Korea: Landscape as Political Project*. London: Rowman and Littlefield, 2014.

Yi Chun-sik. "Tanch'ŏn sallim chohap pandae undong ŭi chŏn'gae kwajŏn kwa sŏngkyŏk." *Sahoe wa yŏksa* 28 (1991): 108–40.

Yi Kye-min. *K'orian mirŏk'ŭl. 3, sumŭn kijŏktŭl, sup ŭi yŏksa, saero ssŭda: sallim nokhwa ŏje wa onŭl*. Kyŏnggi: Nanam, 2015.

Yi Kyŏng-jun. *Han'guk ŭi sallim nokhwa 70-yŏn*. Kyŏnggi: Han'gukhak Chungang Yŏn'guwŏn Ch'ulp'anbu, 2015.

———. *San e mirae rŭl simta*. Seoul: Sŏul Taehakkyo Ch'ulp'anbu, 2006.

Yi Sŏn-wŏk. "Shokuminchi Chōsen ni okeru rinya shoyūken kakutei kotei to bochi mondai." *Chōsenshi Kenkyūkai ronbunshū* 46 (2008): 155–84.

Yi Ŭn-hŭi. "1940-yŏndae chŏnban Singminji Chosŏn ŭi amsijang: Saenghwal mulcha rŭl chungsim ŭro." *Tongbang hakchi* 166 (2014): 255–91.

Yi U-yŏn. *Hanguk ŭi sallim soyujedo wa chŏngch'aek ŭi yŏksa, 1600–1987.* Seoul: Ilchogak, 2007.

Yoo, Theodore Jun. *The Politics of Gender in Colonial Korea: Education, Labor, and Health, 1910–1945.* Berkeley: University of California Press, 2008.

Young, Louise. *Japan's Total Empire: Manchuria and the Culture of Wartime Imperialism.* Berkeley: University of California Press, 1999.

Yun Hae-dong. *Singminji ŭi hoaesaek chidae: Han'guk ŭi Kundaesŏng kwa singminjuŭi pip'an.* Seoul: Yŏksa Pip'yŏngsa, 2003.

INDEX

French colonialism, 8, 49–50, 97
Friends of the West Academic Society
journal, 66
fruit trees, 210
fuel collection, 69, 78, 96, 111, 161, 167–68, 211,
212. *See also* fuel consumption
fuel combustion patterns, 111–12
fuel conservation campaigns, 211–13, 216–19;
women as target of, 167, 195, 216
fuel consumption: and deforestation, 56, 62;
by Japanese settlers, 215–16, 219; rationing,
218–19; state control of, 12, 151; wartime,
201–2, 211, 212–13, 215–20, 221. *See also* fuel
conservation campaigns; fuel substitution;
ondol
fuel forests, 112, 155, 231
fuel substitution, 155, 167–68, 197, 211–12; fuel
replacement campaigns, 97–98, 206
fuel supplies, 4, 18, 101, 112, 167, 215–16,
220–22
Fujiwara Ginjirō, 197, 198
Fukunaga Kosuke, 114–15
Fukushima Eisaku, 213
Fukushima Yasunori, 35
Fundamentals of Our National Polity
(Kokutai no hongi), 183–84

gaizai (timber from the outside), 14
Garon, Sheldon, 150
German forestry, 8, 13, 214
Gilpin, William, 186
ginseng, 10, 53
global timber market, 132
Gotō Hisaaki, 81
Gotō Soichi, 162
Government-General of Korea (Chōsen
Sōtokufu), 8, 89, 152, 225–26; redistricting
efforts, 93, 157. *See also* Forest Experiment
Stations; Forest Owners Associations;
Korean Forestry Association; Northern
Development Plan; Rural Revitalization
Campaign; Ugaki Kazushige
Gragert, Edwin, 75
Great Code of National Governance
(Gyongguk Daejon), 48
Great Kantō Earthquake, 133–34
Great Korea Association (Taehan Hyŏphoe),
65
Great Korean Forest Society (Taehan Sallim
Hyŏphoe), 67
Greater East Asia Co-prosperity Sphere, 178
"green archipelago" (Totman), 12–18, 36, 55

"green imperialism" (Grove), 15–16, 96–97
"greenificationism" (Yi U-yŏn), 7, 20
Griffis, William Elliot, 54, 57
ground cover, 166–67
Grove, Richard, 15, 116
Guanzi, 66
Guha, Ramachandra, 8, 163
Guide to Seedling Development (Jubyō yōsei
shishin), 106
Gwangmu emperor (King Kojong), 47, 53, 59,
65

hageyama. See bald mountains
Hakuji no hito (film), 249n22
Hamilton, Angus, 57
Han, Do-Hyun, 150, 165
Han Sang-nyŏng, 153
Handbook to the Colonies, 58
handicrafts, 194–95
Hansŏng Bank, 153
Hartig, Robert, 35
Hashimoto Denzaemon, 141
Hayashi Yasuharu, 110–11
Hazama Fusatarō, 80
Henry, Todd, 212
Hibiya Park, 189
Hideyoshi, 48, 76, 208
Hino Tsutomu, 60
Hŏ Tal-kyu, 162
Hoffman, Amerigo, 36
Hokkaido, 15, 39–41, 45, 87, 134, 226
Hokkaido Development Agency (Kaita-
kushi), 41
Hokkaido Uncultivated Land Disposal Act
(1897), 41
Home Ministry (Japan), 35, 37
homemakers, 167, 182, 195, 216
Honda Seiroku, 38, 39, 66, 226; digest of
Japan's "old and famous trees," 107; as
father of parks, 24, 189; "red pine ruination
theory" (*akamatsu bōkokuron*), 23–24, 46;
textbook on *rinseigaku*, 37
Hong Chong-hwa, 185
Hulbert, Homer, 55
Hung, Kuang-chi, 42
Hwanghae: protests over irrigation
association labor requirements, 160;
woodland leases, 88, 89
hyangyak (village contracts), 165
hydropower, 144, 146
Hyŏn Sin-kyu (Kayama Nobuo), 113–15, 117, 231
hypothermia, 220

WEYERHAEUSER ENVIRONMENTAL BOOKS

A Storied Wilderness: Rewilding the Apostle Islands, by James W. Feldman

Iceland Imagined: Nature, Culture, and Storytelling in the North Atlantic, by Karen Oslund

Quagmire: Nation-Building and Nature in the Mekong Delta, by David Biggs

Seeking Refuge: Birds and Landscapes of the Pacific Flyway, by Robert M. Wilson

Toxic Archipelago: A History of Industrial Disease in Japan, by Brett L. Walker

Dreaming of Sheep in Navajo Country, by Marsha L. Weisiger

Shaping the Shoreline: Fisheries and Tourism on the Monterey Coast, by Connie Y. Chiang

The Fishermen's Frontier: People and Salmon in Southeast Alaska, by David F. Arnold

Making Mountains: New York City and the Catskills, by David Stradling

Plowed Under: Agriculture and Environment in the Palouse, by Andrew P. Duffin

The Country in the City: The Greening of the San Francisco Bay Area, by Richard A. Walker

Native Seattle: Histories from the Crossing-Over Place, by Coll Thrush

Drawing Lines in the Forest: Creating Wilderness Areas in the Pacific Northwest, by Kevin R. Marsh

Public Power, Private Dams: The Hells Canyon High Dam Controversy, by Karl Boyd Brooks

Windshield Wilderness: Cars, Roads, and Nature in Washington's National Parks, by David Louter

On the Road Again: Montana's Changing Landscape, by William Wyckoff

Wilderness Forever: Howard Zahniser and the Path to the Wilderness Act, by Mark Harvey

The Lost Wolves of Japan, by Brett L. Walker

Landscapes of Conflict: The Oregon Story, 1940-2000, by William G. Robbins

Faith in Nature: Environmentalism as Religious Quest, by Thomas R. Dunlap

The Nature of Gold: An Environmental History of the Klondike Gold Rush, by Kathryn Morse

Where Land and Water Meet: A Western Landscape Transformed, by Nancy Langston

The Rhine: An Eco-Biography, 1815-2000, by Mark Cioc

Driven Wild: How the Fight against Automobiles Launched the Modern Wilderness Movement, by Paul S. Sutter

George Perkins Marsh: Prophet of Conservation, by David Lowenthal

Making Salmon: An Environmental History of the Northwest Fisheries Crisis, by Joseph E. Taylor III

Irrigated Eden: The Making of an Agricultural Landscape in the American West, by Mark Fiege

The Dawn of Conservation Diplomacy: U.S.-Canadian Wildlife Protection Treaties in the Progressive Era, by Kirkpatrick Dorsey

Landscapes of Promise: The Oregon Story, 1800-1940, by William G. Robbins

Forest Dreams, Forest Nightmares: The Paradox of Old Growth in the Inland West, by Nancy Langston

The Natural History of Puget Sound Country, by Arthur R. Kruckeberg

WEYERHAEUSER ENVIRONMENTAL CLASSICS

Environmental Justice in Postwar America: A Documentary Reader, edited by Christopher W. Wells

Making Climate Change History: Documents from Global Warming's Past, edited by Joshua P. Howe

Nuclear Reactions: Documenting American Encounters with Nuclear Energy, edited by James W. Feldman

The Wilderness Writings of Howard Zahniser, edited by Mark Harvey

The Environmental Moment: 1968–1972, edited by David Stradling

Reel Nature: America's Romance with Wildlife on Film, by Gregg Mitman

DDT, Silent Spring, and the Rise of Environmentalism, edited by Thomas R. Dunlap

Conservation in the Progressive Era: Classic Texts, edited by David Stradling

Man and Nature: Or, Physical Geography as Modified by Human Action, by George Perkins Marsh

A Symbol of Wilderness: Echo Park and the American Conservation Movement, by Mark W. T. Harvey

Tutira: The Story of a New Zealand Sheep Station, by Herbert Guthrie-Smith

Mountain Gloom and Mountain Glory: The Development of the Aesthetics of the Infinite, by Marjorie Hope Nicolson

The Great Columbia Plain: A Historical Geography, 1805–1910, by Donald W. Meinig

CYCLE OF FIRE

Fire: A Brief History, second edition, by Stephen J. Pyne

The Ice: A Journey to Antarctica, by Stephen J. Pyne

Burning Bush: A Fire History of Australia, by Stephen J. Pyne

Fire in America: A Cultural History of Wildland and Rural Fire, by Stephen J. Pyne

Vestal Fire: An Environmental History, Told through Fire, of Europe and Europe's Encounter with the World, by Stephen J. Pyne

World Fire: The Culture of Fire on Earth, by Stephen J. Pyne

ALSO AVAILABLE:

Awful Splendour: A Fire History of Canada, by Stephen J. Pyne